THE KEY OF LIFE

ASTROLOGY OF THE "LUNAR NODES"

A Comprehensive Guide for All Astrologers

PRASH TRIVEDI

2nd Edition 2008

Distributed by:

Lotus Brands, Inc.
P.O. Box 325
Twin Lakes, WI 53181 USA
Tel: 262-889-8501 or 1-800-824-6396
Fax: 262-889-2461
E-mail: lotuspress@lotuspress.com
Website: www.lotuspress.com

Illustrated by Vela

ISBN 0-940985-33-0

Printed for Prash Trivedi by
Sagar Printers & Publishers
New Delhi - 110 001

Om Shri Ganeshaye Namah

We pay our obeisance to Lord Ganesha,
The remover of obstacles, the Patron of the Scribes,
And the Lord of Astrology

Om Shri Durgaye Namah

We pay our obeisance to Goddess Durga,
The destroyer of darkness, the Protector of the Righteous,
And the Bestower of all knowledge and wisdom.

Om RahuveNamah

Om Ketave Namah

"Dedicated to all the students of the Divine Science of Jyotish"

ACKNOWLEDGEMENT

Would like to thank all of those who have been a help in this
journey - you know who you are ...

FOREWORD

Rahu and *Ketu*, the North and South Nodes of the Moon respectively, are probably the most interesting, profound and mysterious of all planetary influences in Vedic astrology. As the dragon's head and the dragon's tail of western astrological thought the two nodes represent powerful psychic forces beyond our personal control or understanding. They deal with the secret, hidden, eccentric, spiritual or perverse sides of life - the higher and lower ranges of human activity beyond the normal scope covered by the seven major planets.

The nodes are closely connected to world events and global trends-the broader streams of destiny and the collective influences that can overwhelm our personal karma, including destructive occurrences like wars or plagues. They are also key indicators of future social developments. For example, the mass media relates to Rahu, which represents new, popular and expansive trends, while much of the cutting edge of science and technology, like computers, relates to Ketu, which represents insight, precision and unlocking the secrets of nature. In this regard Rahu and Ketu have a place in Jyotish (Vedic or Indian astrology) similar to that of the outer planets of Uranus, Neptune and Pluto in western astrology which are also used for collective phenomenon.

Rahu comes from the Sanskrit root 'rah' meaning to hide and refers to what is secret, mysterious and profound or a cave. Rahu obscures or protects and indicates Maya, which is not only illusion but also any magical power or captivating knowledge. Ketu comes from the root 'ci' meaning to highlight, appear or become consciousness or a flag.

Prash Trivedi offers what is probably the longest, most researched and most original book on Rahu and Ketu published in modern times. He has studied the classics thoroughly and understands the ancient symbolism of the nodes, which he explains with great lucidity. But he is no mere repeater of old information. Like a research scientist who carefully examines all the data before drawing any new conclusions, he adds important new insights based upon his own experience which expands the range of traditional meanings in order to cover modern conditions today. He has examined the role of the nodes in numerous charts, several of which are highlighted as important examples in the book, and is not simply indulging in unfounded speculation when he introduces his opinion into the text.

In this book, Trivedi reveals himself as one of the most promising young writers on Vedic astrology coming out of India today. He is also easily one of the best Indian writers on Vedic astrology in an English idiom. Though there are many good new books on Vedic astrology coming out of India recently, unfortunately most are poorly written and hard to understand for westerners. Though born and raised in India, Trivedi's style is not traditionally Indian, but quite clear and contemporary almost as if written by an American. His mind reflects a global perspective not bound to any limited cultural sphere. Most notably, Trivedi combines a deep spiritual view along with practical methods of chart interpretation in a remarkably balanced approach that will be of interest both to nuts and bolts predictive astrologers and those for whom the spiritual and mystical side is most important. The Rahu-Ketu Experience is worthy of serious examination by all students of Vedic astrology and all those interested in the great mysteries of life, death, karma and transformation. We look forward to many more such books from the author in the coming years.

Dr. David Frawley (Pandit Vamadeva Shastri)
Author, Astrology of the Seers, Yoga and Ayurveda etc.
President, American Council of Vedic Astrology

LIST OF ILLUSTRATIONS

IMAGES

TABLES

YANTRAS (Numerological Totems)

LIST OF CHARTS

All the charts have been made using the Birth Data sources unless otherwise indicated. Birth Time Rectification has been done for the charts, where accurate birth time is unavailable. All charts are constructed using *Lahiri Ayanamsa*.

INTRODUCTION

A global vision of astrology is dawning upon us as we stand on the brink of entering a New Age. This new astrology, which has the potential of becoming the universal religion of the future instead of just being an art of peeping into the future, is being birthed out of the synthesis and integration of all the existing systems. There is in truth nothing 'new' about this 'new astrology' as it is just a rediscovering of the knowledge, which has existed since the beginning of time and was known in its pristine purity to the ancients.

The present day astrology can basically be divided into two main systems – Vedic and Western. Both are in a sense complimentary to each other as one takes care of the weaknesses of the other. The Vedic System known as *Jyotish* or Vedic Astrology however is much more precise and advanced than the Western System, and is thus likely to form the core of the New Astrology. Western astrology on the other hand has some basic anomalies like operating with the astronomically inaccurate Tropical Zodiac, but a detailed discussion on that is not relevant to this book. However there is an area in which both seem to be lacking; though 'ignoring' would be a better term to use.

This area relates to the astrology of the _Lunar Nodes_. What comes as a greater surprise is that the neglect is continuing and precious little is being done to restore the balance! The extent of the neglect can be gauged by the fact that not a single definitive book dealing specifically with the lunar nodes has come out as yet in either Vedic or Western astrology. Though some of the Western astrologers have penned down some of their thoughts and observations on the lunar nodes, their works are in no way comprehensive as they totally neglect the knowledge from other systems. In India, the home of Vedic astrology, only a few preliminary works have been published till date.

One of the reasons given by the critics who completely ignore the nodes is that they are mere mathematical points. The Ascendant and Midheaven are also mathematical points but their influence is never under any question. The Ascendant as we know is one of the ways Earth is symbolically represented in a chart. It is basically a representation of the rotational motion of earth around its axis.

The other being the position of the Sun in a chart, which is nothing but a representation of the position of the earth in its annual orbit around the Sun. Another reason given is that they have no mass and therefore cannot give results like the other planets with mass. This is based upon the theory quite popular among alot of astrologers with scientific inclinations, that the planets impart their influence through some sort of waves, the nature of which depends upon the physical constitution of the planets. These yet unknown waves are supposed to be a part of the material universe and thus the hope is that they are sure to be detected some time in the near future.

It is true that the waves from the planets reach us but these waves originate and affect us on the *astral* & *causal* planes. Searching for them in the physical plane and relating them to mass or other such properties will obviously yield no results. Planets can thus be said to be physically dead but astrally & causally alive. Astrology, is to a large extent an astral science and our forefathers had recognized this fact. This is the reason why they did not look upon planets as balls of gas and matter but as individuals in the image of human beings operating from the astral realm. The energies they relayed were positively and negatively used by the astral beings known as Gods and Demons respectively. The mythologies of all ancient civilizations are full of these astral battles between Gods and the Demons. Since the nodes were also present on the astral plane they have also found place in these mythologies. This is the reason why we will begin this book with a chapter dealing with how the various ancient civilizations perceived them.

The ancients also took Astrology into the causal realm, the plane of pure consciousness, which has been touched upon in the chapter relating to the esoteric significance of the nodes. All the ancient seers were of the opinion that great cosmic forces coming from distant regions in the universe, of which the planets were decoders and transmitters for our solar system, govern life on earth. Part of this knowledge of these distant star systems was stored in form of the use of the 27 *Nakshatras* (lunar mansions or asterisms) widely used in Vedic astrology. The relationship of the nodes with these asterisms, which establishes their place in the real cosmic astrology, is discussed in a chapter dedicated to the asterisms ruled by the nodes. The ancient Vedic seers also envisioned some methods to gain mastery over these forces, which involved the use of gems, herbs, *mantra*, *yantra*, and *yogic* techniques that have been touched upon in the concluding chapter dealing with the propitiation of the nodes.

If the ancients did invent these imaginary planets there must have been some need for them. They would have encountered some cosmic forces influencing affairs on Earth that they could not represent or understand through the existing planets. They must have also felt the enormous influence the eclipses have on human affairs on Earth. There is no doubt that the relationship between the Earth, the Moon and the Sun holds the key to the life on our planet. It is no coincidence that Moon is just about the right size and right distance from the Earth to cover the Sun exactly during an Eclipse. Moon symbolizes, as is common knowledge, the Mother principle, which balances the Father principle that Sun is seen to represent. Again it is well known that the interplay between these two principles is the causative force behind all creation.

The nodes are in fact the only planets, which are a direct result of this interplay and thus an important part of the forces representing creation. Thus ignoring them is like denying a part of our very existence. All creation is a result of imbalance as no activity in nature can take place if everything is in a perfectly balanced state. This statement finds support in all the creation mythologies as well as the dictums of modern physics. The lunar nodes are therefore the symbolic representations of this very imbalance between the Yin and Yang principles of nature, as they are sort of energy vortexes formed by the interplay of solar and lunar energies. In a way they sustain life with all its dualities and thus it comes as no surprise that the ancient Vedic seers referred to them as planets representing *Maya*, the illusionary power sustaining the myth of creation.

Since duality is everywhere nodes are present everywhere, from a smallest atom to the largest galaxies and from the physical plane to the causal plane. Even every planet in our solar system transmits its influence through its nodes, which are represented by its latitude. Here we are dealing only with the Lunar Nodes because these planetary nodes don't have a distinct individuality like the lunar nodes, as the planets don't revolve around the Earth like the Moon does.

There have been a lot of theories put forward regarding the true conception of the lunar nodes. Some say they are invisible black discs that lie within the plane of the ecliptic. Some say the geographical North Pole is the north node and its counterpart the South Pole is the south node. Some say that they are the bright and dark sides of the Moon. In short everything 'north' has been attributed to the north node and everything 'south' to the south node. All these definitions make sense to a degree but in this work we would go with a widely recognized conception, which in a way is the original conception devised by the ancient Vedic seers and has stood the test of time.

According to this conception, in pure astronomical terms the nodes are the points of intersection of the Moon's orbit around the Earth with the ecliptic, which is nothing, but an ellipse formed by the path of Earth's orbit around the Sun. In other words they are the intersection points of the two planes formed by the orbits of the Earth and the Moon. The planes of these two orbits intersect each other at 5 degrees, 8 minutes and 40 seconds. The line of intersection is known as the <u>Nodal Axis</u>.

The point where Moon crosses the ecliptic while traveling from south to north is known as *Rahu*, the 'North' or the 'Ascending' node. The point where Moon crosses the ecliptic while traveling from north to south is known as *Ketu*, the 'South' or the 'Descending' node. All the mathematical calculations to ascertain the latitude of the nodes are done using this conception. The nodes are thus two points 180° apart, which is why the Nodes are always placed opposite to each other in an astrological chart.

Being placed opposite to each other does not mean that they counteract each other. They in fact act in a complimentary fashion. Since the opposition aspect, which is a seventh house aspect as per Vedic astrology, is very similar in its nature and functioning to the seventh sign Libra, balance is the key idea underlying the functioning of the nodal axis. What this balance means and how it manifests in astrological charts has been dealt with in detail in the sections dealing with the placement of the nodal axis in different signs and houses.

After the problem of definition is solved the next one to come up is that of interpretation. As expected different astrologers and systems interpret the influence of the nodes differently. The present day perspective of the nodes in the two main systems, Western and Vedic, is dealt with in a separate chapter.

Among the various systems, Vedic astrology gives the maximum importance to the influence of nodes in governing human affairs on Earth. Thus in tribute to the Vedic seers of the past who recognized their true importance, the North Node would be referred to by its Sanskrit equivalent _Rahu_ and the South Node would be referred to as _Ketu_ throughout this book. Another simple reason for using this nomenclature is that it is more convenient.

The question, which is very much tangled with that of interpretation, is of weightage. Some astrologers use the nodes sparingly, as they don't think that they cover any new areas other than those already covered by the other planets. This is why emphasis has been laid on those areas in human affairs that cannot be dealt with by the use of other planets. For example no other planet can be used to unravel the genetic heritage or the past lives of an individual, even though Vedic astrology provides for some degree of interpretation through various harmonic charts. A chapter dealing with the involvement of the nodes in areas like genetics and reincarnation, which has always been a part of Vedic Astrology has been included.

Others are of the view that they don't act independently and just reflect the energies of the planets they are associated with by placement or aspects. A lot of example horoscopes of well-known personalities have been included to show that the nodes do not only act independently but also give results with a suddenness and intensity, which other planets cannot emulate. Though in Western astrology the outer planets are known to give sudden and transforming results, they can't do so with the regularity of the nodes and have their limitations because of their slow moving nature. For instance, Pluto and Neptune do not get to transit even half of a chart in one lifetime. Moreover they are generational planets, which only work powerfully in certain individual charts.

Astrology in my view is incomplete without involving the science of numbers or Numerology. The universe is in a sense a game of numbers where numbers can be seen as symbols with certain qualities attached with and manifesting through each one of them - every sign has a number attached with it; every planet has a number associated with it. It follows that the nodes are also associated with certain numbers. How these associations are derived and what they signify is discussed in a separate chapter devoted to the numerological significance of the nodes. These derivations are just my personal opinions and thus may or may not agree with existing astro-numerological standards. If numbers can allow space for certain planetary energies known as the nodes then there seems to be no reason why astrology cannot.

At present the humanity is living in times where everything including time is in an accelerated state. This may be due to the fact that we are living at the cusp of two astrological World Ages as the equinox shifts from Pisces to Aquarius. There is no clear consensus

as yet as to the cycle of time the change of the Ages is taking place.
There is also a possibility that this change is taking place simultaneously on various lesser and greater cycles, but a detailed discussion on this is beyond the scope of this work. Whatever the case
may be the inclusion of the nodes in mundane astrology dealing
with the present times becomes very important as they represent
the cycles of time. The role of the lunar nodes in shaping the twen-
tieth century and the role they might play in the future is discussed
in a separate chapter.

The main aim of this work is to spark an interest in the astrology
of the lunar nodes among astrologers belonging to every school of
thought. Since the astronomically correct Sidereal Zodiac, which
takes the precession of the earth's axis into account, has been preferred throughout this work, the Western astrologers familiar with
the Tropical Zodiac might face some inconvenience. I sincerely regret this but in my view the astrology of the future will be based
solely upon the Sidereal Zodiac.

As always nothing in this work can be said to be the final word
and everything is open to interpretation. If more astrologers start
using the nodes in their analysis than many more secrets relating to
their nature, significations and functioning are sure to be revealed.
We may yet choose to ignore them or completely deny their existence, but we must remember that this is the case with astrology as a
whole too when its influence and validity is constantly put to question by its critics.

It is my earnest hope that the principles and observations included
in this work would be at least scrutinized and tested by the students
of astrology before being rejected as invalid. It would be a step in
the right direction in the development of the 'new astrology' if the
lunar nodes were restored to their rightful place.

Prash Trivedi
June' 2001
Email: astrology@karmablueprint.com
Website: www.osfa.org.uk

The Gods and Demons churning the Celestial Ocean

CONTENTS

1. THROUGH THE EYES OF THE ANCIENTS

If there is one symbolism that is found in all the ancient cultures known to us then it is the symbolism relating to the serpent forces. Since most of the astrological knowledge of the various ancient civilizations has been lost through time, we cannot find any direct mention of the lunar nodes anywhere except the Vedic scriptures, even though some recent findings show that they were well known in Europe, Africa, the Americas and China. One thing, which can be said with certainty, is that all the ancient civilizations have had some sort of representation for the serpent power that the lunar nodes are identified with.

This serpent power was an object of veneration in most of these cultures as it represented some powerful cosmic force at play in the human life on Earth. Most of the ancients realized that this force was directly related with the all-powerful sustainer of the Universe, Time. Snakes were the most obvious outward symbols for this force and thus this veneration usually took the form of the Snake worship. The snake with its tail in its mouth became the most widespread symbol for representing the cyclic nature of time. This symbol now widely known by the Greek term *Ouroborous* was in fact found in all the known ancient civilizations.

Various other images like the snake encircling the world egg became symbols depicting the influence and hold that time had on human lives on earth. These different cultures either viewed the snake or the serpent power as the greatest evil or the source of highest wisdom depending upon their evolutionary status at that point of time in history. Some cultures like the Vedic were aware of the fact that this force could display both extremes and thus did not inculcate lop-sided views.

Most of the ancient cultures knew about the tremendous influence eclipses had on human affairs on earth as they were seen to precede wars, famines, natural disasters and other such events. Since the deduction of the lunar nodes is only one step away from the phenomenon of an eclipse, it is highly improbable that they were not aware of the existence of the lunar nodes. This too when the serpent force signified by the lunar nodes was tightly interwoven in their respective religions and cultures. Let us take a look at how some prominent civilizations accommodated this cosmic force within their culture.

Egyptian Civilization

Egyptian civilization is supposed to have its roots in the surviving knowledge of the ancient civilization presently known as *Atlantis*, which was supposed to be devastateded by a great flood around 12,000 years ago. Though on the first look the ancient Egyptian civilization comes across as a predominantly solar culture, a closer look reveals that the serpent power was an integral part of their religion and society. It can be seen in the symbolism of snakes in the Pharaoh's crown and other ornaments.

Snakes, especially cobras were a symbol of royalty as they seemed to represent certain celestial forces guiding human affairs on earth, and thus it was important for the Pharaohs who were treated like representatives of God on earth to be in touch with them. How important the snake imagery or the serpent power was in Egyptian society can be gauged from the fact that even *Cleopatra* chose to die by a method preferred by all royalty - snakebite!

Some of their inscriptions like the image of the snake of time contorting into a series of individual spirals within a greater spiral, clearly show that they were aware of the cyclic nature of time and had an understanding of the greater and lesser cycles of time. The earliest images of the well-known symbol of the snake biting its own tail are also found in the Egyptian civilization. More importantly, it shows that they deliberately used the snake as a symbol of time, which tells us they had a fair idea of what cosmic forces did lie behind the snake imagery. This is probably the reason why they did not use snake as a symbol of fear but as that of power and wisdom.

The fact that Egyptians were good astronomers and had affinity with constellations like *Orion* is no longer a secret. They regularly related heavenly events like the annual appearance of *Sirius* with the earthly events like the flooding of Nile. Since they also observed Sun's movement throughout the year they must surely have studied the phenomenon of the eclipses. In order to predict the future eclipses correctly they would have had to develop an ephemeris, which involved the lunar nodes.

They also had a legend about a snake called *Delphi*, which used to pursue the Sun everyday only to be cut down to pieces in the night by Sun's helpers. In the morning this snake reassembled itself and pursued the Sun again.

A one eyed serpent known as *Uraeus* is the most important of Egyptian symbols outside of the main archetypes like *Osiris* (the supreme male deity), *Isis* (the feminine counterpart of Osiris), *Horus* (the son of Osiris and Isis) etc. He is said to be the right or solar eye of *Ra* (the Sun God). It was considered a highly spiritual and occult force in much the same way as the nodes.

In one of their legends there is the mention of a serpent named *Apep* who was the enemy of *Ra* (the Sun God). He was supposed to represent all darkness and evil as well as complete wisdom and enlightenment. It is very clear that *Apep* represents the same cosmic force, which the nodes represent in Astrology.

Combining all these thoughts together, one cannot help but assume that the lunar nodes were a part of the highly developed ancient Egyptian astrology, of which only a small fraction is available for interpretation at present.

Greek Civilization

Most of Greek Mythology and culture has roots in the Egyptian

Civilization. The serpent power finds mention in the ancient Greek culture through many a celestial battle between the serpents and the Gods. The most famous of these battles is the killing of *Hydra*, the sea serpent with nine heads by *Hercules*, the son of Jupiter. *Hydra* is the longest constellation in the sky and also covers the largest area. The astrological signs of Cancer, Leo, Virgo and Libra can be seen placed along its northern side. *Hercules*, the great warrior, is also a constellation in the sky placed close to the star *Vega*.

According to Greek mythology, Hercules also slew the constellation *Draco* (the Dragon), which is placed by its side in the sky, as one of his twelve labours. The Greeks were well aware of the cosmic serpent forces emanating through various constellations and they saw *Hydra* and *Draco* as their main celestial transmitters. Since they also knew about the other inner planets in the solar system, it is quite probable that they knew about the presence of the lunar nodes that relayed these celestial energies for our solar system. Since very little of the astrology of the ancient Greeks survives today we do not find any mention of the lunar nodes.

Somehow they felt that subduing or winning over these forces was an important part of the lessons to be learnt before one could attain immortality. This is what in my view killing of the serpentine constellations by *Hercules* symbolized. In another story, *Apollo* the Sun God slays a huge serpent near *Delphi*. This is an indication that the Greeks knew about the constant struggle between Sun and the serpent forces. This monster serpent that Apollo subdued can very well be seen to symbolize the lunar nodes.

The Greeks also knew how the serpent power was related to cycles of creation and destruction through the knowledge they gained from the Egyptians. They were the ones who came up with the term *Ouroboros*, meaning 'devouring its tail' for the famous symbol of the snake biting its own tail.

Biblical View

The only completely negative view of the serpent power was the one propagated in Europe through Christianity. The famous story of *Adam* and *Eve* in which Eve is tempted and convinced by a serpent to take a bite at the forbidden fruit in the Garden of *Eden*, is what is given as the reason behind the mistrust of the serpent power. This story in fact is symbolic of the role serpent power played during creation. It showed that the serpent power was responsible for introducing time into a timeless state.

As discussed earlier, life in our Universe cannot exist without some imbalance within nature that causes 'time' to be born. This story seems to have been derived from some other ancient cultures like the Babylonian or the Sumerian that all have similar legends involving a symbolic Garden of Eden, but the meaning was obviously twisted by the church in a typical display of dark and confused Middle Age mentality.

The 'snake' thus became the symbol of all that was considered evil. The mindless propagation of this lop-sided view is the reason behind the fear and contempt for this cosmic force that took root in the psyche of the collective, especially in the West. The early Western astrology could not deal with the lunar nodes properly just because of this inherent negative bias. Since the renaissance and after that the coming of Theosophy, things have been rectified to an extent, but somehow the modern civilization is yet to see these forces in the same light as the ancients did.

Chinese Civilization

Since the Chinese civilization is one of the oldest and most distinct civilizations, its culture has undergone many changes in time but it has been able to preserve its knowledge of the serpent power through the *Dragon* symbolism.

Chinese mythology and folk tales are full of stories involving Dragons of various kinds. The Dragon is in fact the representative symbol of the Chinese culture for the outside world. The fact that the Dragon symbolism in a way represented the same cosmic forces, which the lunar nodes signify in astrology, has now been proved beyond doubt. It thus comes as no surprise that a lot of astrologers prefer to refer to the north node (Rahu) as the *Dragon's head* and south node (Ketu) as the *Dragon's tail*.

In Chinese astrology the year of the Dragon was considered very auspicious. It may be just a coincidence but it is interesting to note that the person with a Chinese origin who made the greatest worldwide impact in the 20th century, Bruce Lee, was born in the year of the Dragon (1940). As we will see later he had a prominent nodal axis influence in his chart (chart no. 22). The fact that they associated the Dragon with astrology is a pointer to the possibility that the ancient Chinese astrology may have had a detailed understanding of the lunar nodes in much the same way as Vedic astrology.

In Chinese culture the Dragon was associated with the height of wisdom and the vision of a highly refined and sophisticated civilization. Chinese still associate the Dragon with the phenomenon of rain and propitiated it through elaborate dance ceremonies and rituals. It was one of the cultures that saw this force in a positive way but they were aware of its negative side as well. This can be seen in its folktales where both the good and evil Dragons are involved.

Mayan Civilization

According to one reliable view, the ancient Maya called themselves *chanes*, which literally means 'serpents'. A particular rattlesnake specie *Crotalus durissus durissus,* which they called *Ahau Can* meaning 'great lordly serpent', was very important to them as their whole culture was based upon it. This subspecies of rattlesnake has a particular design on its skin comprising of interlocking crosses and squares. This pattern was reflected in most of their art and architecture.

They were supposed to be taught the laws of space, mathematics, astronomy, calendrics and astrology by this great lordly serpent. *Ahau Can* sloughs off its skin around mid-July when the Sun reaches the highest point of the sky for the second time in a year. Thus a correlation between the Sun and the serpent is established, both renewing themselves together. *Ahau Can* replaces its fangs every 20 days, which in turn forms the basic unit of the Mayan calendar.

Mayans were well aware of the planets and their movements as is clear from their accurate calendar based upon the movement of Venus. They were also aware of the Milky Way and the star clusters like the *Pleiades* that held special importance for them. It is not a far-fetched possibility that they knew about the existence of lunar nodes as well and used them in their astrological calculations.

Their main God was known as *Quetzalcoatl*, a term which means 'feathered serpent'. It is interesting to note that it represented a band of bearded foreigners that had landed amongst them and gave them knowledge to build a new culture. Since they were good numerologists and astronomers they were pointing towards some cosmic force in the heavens through this 'feathered serpent' imagery. Again it is quite possible that this cosmic force is the same force that is represented by Rahu and Ketu in today's astrology.

They had developed a precise calendar, which can accurately predict solar eclipses over Mexico City even today. Overall the Mayans seem to have a culture completely based upon the serpent power but they perceived it as a wise, friendly force rather than an evil, destructive force. Since there is a lot still to be unearthed about the Maya one might in the future get access to their secrets, which in turn might reveal a lot more about the forces represented by the lunar nodes.

Native American Indian Cultures

Most of the Native Indian tribes in both North and South America have maintained a deep relationship with the serpent power for as long as they have existed. Its influence can be felt in every aspect of their society - religion, art, architecture, healing etc. Most of the religious ceremonies involved collective smoking by the whole of the tribe, to induce a feeling of togetherness and experiencing a collective trance. Smoking as we will discuss later is one of the significations of Rahu.

The healing of the tribe was the job of a *Shaman*, a spiritual guide who put himself in a trance through the use of hallucinogenic herbs. This is very typical of the involvement of nodal energy in the healing process. The wise man or elder in the native Indian legends was always ,referred to as the 'grandfather'. Grandfather again as we will find out later is a signification of the nodes.

The deep reverence for the serpent power, which they perceived as a powerful and constructive force in the long run, can be gauged from the fact that the *Hopi* tribe of Northern Arizona has a special 'snake dance' ceremony, with the specific aim of propitiating the serpent power. They are very connected to mother earth both emotionally and spiritually and feel that a great serpent lies within the earth whose turning would cause great earthquakes and natural disasters whenever the time is ripe for the ending of the present age. This clearly shows that like every other ancient culture they relate serpent power with cycles of time.

Much wisdom about how the serpent power (lunar nodes) causes the expansion and subsequent fall of a civilization can be gained from their prophecies and teachings. The native Indian tribes still continue to use the imagery of the serpents to describe any contemporary event. Even the ruthless and bloody taking over of North American continent by the Europeans which led to complete extinction of many of the native Indian tribes is described in an absorbing story, involving the white serpent (the Europeans) and the red serpent (the native Indians). It is interesting to note that they even termed the roads and railway lines the Europeans built as 'snakes'!

Vedic Civilization

If there is one source in the present day and age where one can find most information relating to the lunar nodes and the forces they represent, then it has to be the surviving remains of the ancient Vedic civilization.

All the areas relating to the lunar nodes like origin, astrological interpretation, esoteric significance etc. are covered in the ancient Vedic scriptures. The Vedic civilization predates all the ancient civilizations discussed as yet. As the Vedas themselves declare, they came into being along with the birth of the universe. The *Puranic* legend relating to the origin of Rahu and Ketu goes something like this -

A celestial demon known as *Swarbhanu* undertook a severe penance invoking Lord *Brahma,* the creator among the trinity. When finally Brahma did appear before him he asked for a boon, which involved conferring on him the status of a planet. *Brahma* granted the boon as a fruit of his penance and disappeared.

In a later time, the gods and demons were involved in a collective churning of the *Kshirsagar* or the celestial ocean. *Vasuki,* the serpent king was used as a cord to churn the mountain known as *Mandara,* which in turn was resting upon the *Kurma Vatara* (tortoise incarnation) of Lord *Vishnu.*

As a result of churning, all the impurities of the ocean manifested themselves as a deadly poison called *Halahala.* At the request of the

Lord Shiva drinking the deadly poison which came out of the churning

gods, *Shiva*, the destroyer among the trinity, drank the poison. After this plants, animals and other useful things came out. *Shree*, the goddess of prosperity, also emerged and chose Vishnu, the preserver among the trinity, as her husband.

Finally *Dhanvantari*, the celestial physician, came out with a pot containing *Amrita* or the divine nectar. Since there was a pact that everything will be distributed equally among the gods and demons, the demons wanted their share of the nectar known to confer immortality. They immediately grabbed the pot and because of their demonic nature soon forgot about the pact.

The gods requested Lord Vishnu for help. Vishnu himself did not want the demons to partake the divine nectar, as that would mean that evil forces would gain permanence, leaving little chance for goodness to thrive in the world. To achieve his end, Vishnu took the form of an enchantress who took the responsibility of distributing the nectar to the gods and demons. She made them sit in two different lines and started distributing the nectar to the line of gods.

The plan was to finish the nectar before the turn of the demons came. The demons captivated by the beauty of the celestial maiden were not able to notice the trick, but one of them *Swarbhanu*, saw through the trick and stealthily infiltrating the ranks of the gods, managed to drink the nectar. Vishnu knowingly overlooked his presence, as he was aware of the boon given by Brahma to him.

Two of the gods, Sun and Moon discovered his presence and asked Vishnu to destroy him. Vishnu severed Swarbhanu's head with his *sudarshan chakra* (celestial disc), but this did not kill him as he had already partaken the nectar. The severed head was joined with a serpent's tail and conferred by Brahma the status of a planet known as *Rahu*, while the remaining body was attached to the head of a serpent and given planetary status with the name *Ketu*.

Due to this incident Swarbhanu, now divided in two, became a bitter enemy of the Sun and the Moon. He took upon himself to afflict the Sun and Moon eternally through his newfound planetary status. This is when the eclipses started to happen according to this

The various treasures coming out of the churning

puranic legend. Thus also began the trend of perceiving the eclipses as the swallowing of the Sun and the Moon by Rahu and Ketu.

Since this is a story relating to the astral/causal plane, I feel that it relates to the material plane at a point of time in the evolution of our solar system, when the Moon's orbit and distance from earth became exactly such that the phenomenon now known as the total eclipse could take place. In another sense it represents the churning of the ocean of existence, which lies within each one of us. From this churning many precious things and many poisonous things come out which manifest as the so-called good and bad qualities.

Amrita or the nectar of immortality, signifying true and supreme knowledge, helps one overcome the slavery of time. The involvement of the serpent Vasuki in this churning shows the involvement of the lunar nodes (serpent forces) with the continuous churning going on within our selves. It also shows we cannot achieve the nectar of immortality without the help of the cosmic forces symbolized by the lunar nodes.

The next important thing the ancient Vedic seers developed was a method for accurately timing these eclipses. This required true astronomical conception of the lunar nodes, which involved an accurate knowledge of the earth's orbit and Moon's orbit and the relationship between these two ecliptics. The fact that they were successful in doing so can be seen from the fact that the ephemeris developed by them can still determine the precise latitude of the nodes and predict present day eclipses with a high degree of accuracy. It is interesting to note that all this happened much before the birth of modern astronomy in the West!

Vedic Astrology then included the nodes in its sphere and gave Rahu and Ketu a distinct individuality by assigning them with a separate nature and significations. The main astrological work on Vedic Astrology compiled by sage *Parashara*, who was the grandson of sage *Vasishtha*, known as *Brihat Parashara Hora Shastra*, gives more than adequate space to throw light on the lunar nodes and their influence in human affairs. Rahu and Ketu were given prominence in other astrological works as well like *Jaimini Sutras*, authored by sage *Jaimini*. Vedic astrology also granted the nodes rulership of the twenty-seven asterisms, lending them a cosmic perspective way beyond the solar system astrology.

The serpent power in its cosmic and esoteric aspects can also be seen manifesting in most of the *puranic* mythologies and through the major deities governing the functionings of our universe – *Ganesha* wears a serpent around his waist; Shiva wears a serpent around his neck; Vishnu reclines on a serpent bed formed by king of the serpents known as *Sheshanag*; and goddess *Durga* holds a serpent in one of her hands.

Krishna, an incarnation of Vishnu, kills a several-headed serpent called *Kaliya* in a story very reminiscent of the Greek legend of Apollo slaying the serpent monster near Delphi. The esoteric significance of the nodes derived from these Vedic legends is discussed in detail in Chapter 6.

The ancient Vedic view of the nodes is quite different from the interpretations of present day Vedic astrologers. The ancient seers saw the nodes as forces, which had to be properly understood and utilized so that true knowledge was gained leading to liberation from the bondage of cycles of time.

Somewhere in the Middle Ages unnecessary fear and contempt for these forces crept in due to a variety of reasons, all having roots in the overall darkness prevailing in those times. Slowly but surely the light, however dim, is now beginning to shine again, and with it the real truth behind these forces known to our forefathers is starting to be revealed.

Dhanvantari, the Celestial Physician coming out with the pot containing Amrita, the Divine Nectar

2. THE PRESENT DAY PERSPECTIVE

There are basically two main astrological systems in use at present - Western and Vedic. There are a lot of differences as well as similarities between these systems, but a discussion on that is beyond the scope of this book. However as mentioned earlier, the Vedic System is astronomically in tune with the actual position of the planets and constellations in the sky. Let's have a quick summarized look at how these two systems view the nodes.

In Western System

The names Dragon's Head (north node) and Dragon's Tail (south node), used by western astrologers are derived from 'Cauda Draconis' and 'Caput Draconis' respectively. Lately, astrologers using the western system usually relate the nodes to the past life karmic patterns. The good karma from the past life is supposed to manifest through the north node while the south node is supposed to carry the bad karma from the past life. The general attitude towards the nodes in western astrology can be well summarized in these words by a 17th century English astrologer, W.Lily -" The Head of the Dragon (north node) is of the nature of Jupiter and Venus and of himself a fortune. The Tail of the Dragon (south node) is quite contrary to the Head, for he is evil." Although these words possess a Middle Age tinge, the way the nodes are viewed in Western astrology hasn't changed much since then.

The north node (Rahu) is seen as a benefic, which has a nature similar to that of Jupiter and Venus combined. It is considered closer to Jupiter in its significations as it is seen as a point of easy expansion. It is supposed to bring good luck to the area of life signified by wherever it is placed in a chart. It is also supposed to boost up the power of the planets it is placed in conjunction with. The planet conjunct the north node is often considered the defining planet of the chart. It is considered really fortunate for the native when it is placed close to vital points like the Ascendant and the Midheaven. It is also considered to give excellent results in transits and synastry as well.

The south node (Ketu) on the other hand is seen as a malefic, which has nature similar to that of Mars and Saturn combined. It is identified more closely with Saturn as it is seen to signify adversities and limitation. It is seen as a highly internalising influence and is considered bad for outer worldly success. It is also supposed to hinder the progress in the area of the chart where it is posited. When it is placed in conjunction with a planet, then the flow of energies from that planet are supposed to be obstructed. It is considered to be a separative influence in synastry and is supposed to carry bad luck in its transits.

The nodes are not assigned rulership of any sign and thus cannot own any houses in a chart. This limits their role to just being inlet and outlet points of karmic energy. Some western astrologers have lately rediscovered that the south node signifies completion of some karma that one has been working on in the previous lives. It thus becomes the significator of what we have already learnt and perfected in our past lives. The north node on the other hand is seen to open up new karmic spheres in one life. It is thus considered the point where work is required in the present incarnation.

In Vedic System

The majority of the present day Vedic astrologers regard both the nodes as malefic forces in a chart. Rahu is considered a greater malefic than Ketu and thus is seen as the most malefic influence in a chart. There is a sort of fear psychosis attached to the interpretation of the nodes especially among the orthodox Vedic astrologers.

One of the reasons for this is that nodes were seen to represent influences, which were not considered proper in the Middle Age's society and culture. For example they are supposed to bring foreign influences into one's life, which was seen as a sort of corruption of one's soul, as all foreigners were looked down upon as *Mlechhas* (outcastes). This was in all probability done to maintain racial genetic purity. Nowadays, since things like foreign travel and foreign influences have become an accepted norm in urban India at least, the more progressive Vedic astrologers are beginning to see the nodes in a different light. This shift in mentality as we will discover in chapter 13. is basically a shift from a Ketu way of thinking to a more Rahu one.

Let us first discuss the view of the orthodox astrologers who see Rahu as a natural malefic with a nature similar to that of Saturn. One important rule in Vedic astrology is that a natural malefic can function as a temporary benefic in a chart depending upon its placement and house ownership. Rahu should, like Saturn be seen to work in a benefic way in some cases. The fact that the orthodox astrologers apply this principle rarely in the case of Rahu is another case. He is supposed to pervert or distort the energy of the planet he is associated with by aspect or conjunction. The major period and transits of Rahu are all seen to be troublesome in one way or the other.

Ketu is seen as a natural malefic with a nature similar to that of Mars. He is thus considered a lesser malefic and is seen as a more spiritual planet than Rahu, but he is often considered a bigger hurdle as far as material success is concerned. Rahu is supposed to give material success in some cases but often without inner contentment. Together they are seen to be the cause behind most of the psychological disorders, attraction towards the lower dark side of life, incurable diseases, possession by negative entities, sudden negative events etc.

The original understanding about Rahu and Ketu as expounded by the ancient seers like *Parashara* and *Jaimini* is quite vast and also different in the sense that the positive sides to the nodes are also included. According to them, Rahu represents knowledge and Ketu liberation thus making the nodes the most influential forces in human life. In their works the nodes are not always the villains they are made out to be by present day orthodox astrologers and can give good or bad results depending upon their placement. The progressive Vedic astrologers are all slowly coming around to this balanced view of the nodes, though there are still a lot of misconceptions floating around.

Since the Vedic system does not usually incorporate the outer planets in its analysis, most of the influences pertaining to Uranus, Neptune and Pluto are assigned to the nodes. Rahu is seen as a sort of Uranus and Neptune combined. It is supposed to carry the illusionary, imaginative, hallucinogenic, dissolving, and disintegrating influence of Neptune as it is the planet representing *Maya* (illusory quality of nature). It is also seen as an eccentric, creative, disruptive, individualizing and revolutionary force that Uranus embodies in the Western system.

Ketu is regarded as a psychic, wilful, detaching, penetrating, manipulative, and catastrophic force much in the same way as Pluto is seen in the Western system. The sign rulership of Rahu and Ketu in the Vedic system, which we will discuss in the next chapter, confirms this identification.

Besides assigning them co-rulership of signs, the Vedic system of astrology or *Jyotish* assigns rulership of *Nakshatras* to the nodes. The use of the 27 celestial asterisms spanning the same 360° as the constellations is a speciality of Jyotish, as they are not used in Western astrology. As we will discover in Chapter 14., this assigning is very important. Besides giving the nodes a cosmological perspective, it is helpful in determining their rulership, exaltation and debilitation, and deciphering their esoteric and numerological significance.

Synthesis

Any rigidity or strict adherence to any one particular system in the interpretation of the nodes is bound to create problems as every system has its pluses and minuses. A more balanced view is required when one is dealing with sensitive points like the nodes. This balance involves leaving out the idiosyncrasies associated with a system and an integration of whatever is worth retaining in any system. For example Rahu does not always act like a good boy as perceived in Western astrology. It functions in a positive Jupiterian manner under only certain conditions that are well delineated in the Vedic system.

On the other hand assigning a permanent bad boy image to Rahu as is the case with present day Vedic astrology is also wrong because Rahu can act in a positive manner, which even the greatest supposed to be benefics like Jupiter and Venus are not capable of emulating.

However it is the Vedic system that brings out the true negatives of Rahu as it is seen to cause problems through excess, over expansion or unnecessary dissipation of energies. It is also supposed to cause one to blindly follow mass trends or collective influences.

The Western view of seeing Ketu as a negative, contracting, restrictive, limiting influence holds true to an extent, but it should not be forgotten that it also represents the area where one's greatest talent lies. It is a highly internalising force and thus should be regarded as the most spiritual among the planets, being the significator of liberation. Ketu's positive role in helping one develop strong concentration and providing a penetrating insight along with a philosophical disposition is highlighted by the Vedic system.

The way Rahu and Ketu are perceived as karmic outlet and inlet points respectively in the Western system, is of much use in understanding what a soul has set out to achieve in its present incarnation. The transit results of the nodes as per the Western system also tabulate quite well with the observations. The area represented by the house transited by Rahu does receive the greatest attention and that by Ketu does require the greatest care. Applying the Western astrology principles in synastry also yields accurate results.

The Vedic conception of the nodes causing unpleasant incidents, negative psychic phenomenon, strange and incurable diseases, and deep-rooted psychological disorders does hold true in experience. However such intense events require the presence of a badly afflicted nodal axis supplemented by other weaknesses in the chart. The nodes on a whole can be seen as constructive forces in the long run even though they may force an individual or the collective to go through hard times. The suffering the nodes cause is usually to neutralize the bad karma from past lives. It is true that a lot of the shortcomings of the present human civilization arise from concentration on the lower aspects of the energy of the nodes but this is also the case with all the other planets as well.

It is important to note that India, the home of Vedic astrology, is a poor country. The negative material significations of the nodes like poverty, hunger, epidemics etc. are much more widespread than in say, U.S.A or Europe. This is probably one of the reasons why Vedic astrologers highlight the negative aspect of the nodes much more than Western astrologers who don't have to deal much with such significations. In fact they have to deal more with material success, which they attribute to Rahu. We will see in Chapter 14. how the materially prosperous countries are more under the influence of Rahu, while ancient civilizations like India and Egypt are more under the influence of Ketu.

The nodes are also seen to relay the energies of the outer planets as assumed in Vedic astrology, but this effect is more prominent only if they are in association with the outer planets. Rahu will function in a truly Uranian manner only if it is conjunct Uranus and a Neptunian manner if it is conjunct Neptune. Ketu will also relay Uranian energies when it is conjunct Uranus even though it will retain its inherent Plutonian nature.

As far as the nature and significations of the lunar nodes are concerned, the bulk of the understanding comes from the works of ancient Vedic seers like Parashara and Jaimini and other comparatively recent seers like *Varahamihira, Kalidasa* and *Matreshwara*. The major period indications and the results of placement of the nodes in the harmonic ninth chart are also based upon the works of these seers. The special planetary *Yogas* or combinations, involving the nodes have also been taken straight from these ancient texts, though the interpretations have been modified to an extent to maintain their relevance in the present day and age.

Wherever there are differences among various systems evolved by these seers on issues like sign ownership, the point of view that could be arrived at with using common astro-sense, has been included. Some points of view from alternative astrological works like the *Lal Kitab* along with some personal intuitions/opinions have also been included after they were seen to work well in practical applications.

✳ ✳ ✳

Vishnu, in the form of Mohini, distributing the nectar to the Gods while the Demons look on captivated by her charm

3. LET'S GET TO KNOW THEM

This is the most important section in my view because once we understand what the nodes are all about it is very easy to incorporate them in actual prediction and analysis. As mentioned earlier we would be analysing Rahu and Ketu in much the same way as a psychologist analyses the personality of any individual. This personal approach used by ancient Vedic seers helps in establishing their characteristics in such a way that we get a fair idea of how they will function in a particular chart, without having to remember all the rules and results.

As discussed in the introduction, all planets are live beings on astral/causal planes which relay their energy on the physical plane through the physical planets in our solar system, in much the same way as our astral/causal body finds its material expression through the physical body. The better an astrologer relates to any planet as an individual the easier astrology becomes.

Both the nodes are taken to be as a male planet by a lot of astrologers, but the view of the ancient sages is that they are neutral planets and thus cannot be classified as either male or female. They will be referred to as 'it' rather than he/she throughout this book.

RAHU

APPEARANCE

Rahu's appearance is being discussed because it is seen to affect a person's appearance when it is in a position to do so in a nativity.

Rahu has a body of a serpent connected to a human head, and thus is fearful to behold.

The various names assigned to Rahu in Vedic texts - the fierce, the terrible, the appalling, the serpent, the head, the blue, the black, the fanged, half-bodied, the smoky headed, having blood red eyes, having death like looks, having big whiskers - give a clue to its appearance.

Rahu is supposed to be the second eldest among the planets but the face shows no such elderly characteristics. In fact it has a strange, hypnotic touch to its face, which it imparts to the natives when placed close to the cuspal degrees of the first or the second house in a chart. Its face is said to be black with a smokish tinge. There is no equal of ..ahu in imparting out of the ordinary faces and appearances.

In my view the face of Jazz legend *Miles Davis* is a good example of what Rahu can do to one's appearance. It is experienced that a lot of the present day beauty queens who get sudden fame through winning international beauty pageants have either Rahu in the second house or connected in some way to the Ascendant or second house.

Rahu is seen to represent tall persons. Any connection of Rahu with the Ascendant in a chart adds to the height of the native. Rahu also has a predominantly airy constitution, which is usually associated with a wiry or lean physique.

Among the five senses Rahu is especially connected with the sense of hearing. A highly developed sense of hearing or complete deafness helps identify a Rahu personality.

According to one view it is supposed to be uncouth in appearance and shabbily dressed in black pauper's clothing, but there are other views that show Rahu to be having the appearance of a fierce warrior dressed immaculately in bright-multicoloured clothing.

In a way these two types of appearances represent the dual nature of Rahu – one that can give material prosperity and the other which gives material adversity. Usually the material adversity side has

May Divine Rahu bestow its Grace upon us

more spiritual benefits attached with it, which is not to say that there is no spiritual growth when Rahu gives material prosperity.

The colours associated with Rahu are — flame red and bright yellow; sea green; all shades and variations of blue like sky blue; purple and violet; all shades of brown; all the pastel shades and sunset colours. Electric blue is a colour which is strongly connected with Rahu. In the spectrum of electromagnetic waves or different types of light, Rahu represents ultraviolet light, which as we know is invisible to the human eyes as it falls out of the visible spectrum of light represented by *VIBGYOR*.

There is also a certain sort of lordliness attached to its appearance and manners in much the same way as Sun. However there is a subtle difference as the lordliness that Sun displays has a certain benevolence attached to it. The charisma and magnetism attached with Rahu is also quite different from the Sun in much the same way a light emitted by an electric bulb is different from the sunlight.

Despite its lordliness its glance is downwards. This can be used to trace the people with strong influence of Rahu on the Ascendant. It can also be used to judge the state of mind of a person at any given point in time. A downward glance relates to a predominantly Rahu or Saturn state of mind. It must be remembered that Saturn also has a downward glance.

In Vedic traditions its image is made in a variety of ways. One image has four arms holding a trident, a sword and a discus. The remaining hand is making a gesture, which grants boons. Its head is facing south and is decorated with a hessonite crest jewel. It is shown riding a lion. Another image has it with only two hands, one holding a blanket and the other a palm leaf. It is seen as riding on a chariot driven by eight horses. Another image has Rahu holding a spear and scimitar. As we will discover in the next few sections, all these images reveal Rahu's functionings and attributes.

ATTRIBUTES

Rahu is supposed to be a mighty and naughty child of *Maya* (illusory power of nature), and thus has a lot of dualities attached to its *Mayavi* (illusory) nature. It relates more to the Seventh Ray energy of esoteric astrology as it represents a force displaying all the possibilities within the realm of existence.

'Rahu' translates into 'the seizer'. It is interesting to note that the

Sanskrit term for a planet, *'graha'* also translates into 'seizer'. The planets definitely are seizers in the sense that they seize human beings and make them act or behave in a certain way. Another interesting fact to note is that an eclipse is called a *'grahan'* in Sanskrit, meaning 'seized'. It is appropriate, as in a way Rahu seizes the Sun during an eclipse.

The various names assigned to Rahu in Vedic texts - the chief; the advisor of the demons; the minister of the demons; ever-angry; the tormentor; bitter enemy of the luminaries; lord of illusions; one who frightens the Sun; the one who makes the Moon lustreless; the peacemaker; the immortal (having drunk the divine nectar); bestower of prosperity, wealth and ultimate knowledge - give a clue to its basic energy and attributes.

Rahu can thus be said to be associated with the dualities of nature and their subsequent fusion. It can be the deceitful, shady, untrustworthy sort of character when working through its lower aspect. Its energy is supposed to be behind all sorts of criminal tendencies, unlawful activities, and perversions.

It is discontent incarnate and is never satisfied in much the same vein as the famous 'rolling stone' lines - " I can't get no satisfaction...". It can lie, cheat, betray trust or go to any extreme to achieve its ends. Its nature in these lower aspects covers all the bad points of the dark side of the human psyche. Thus it comes as no surprise that it is the originator of many types of morbid fears, suspicions, sadistic, and self-destructive tendencies.

All this negativity of Rahu can be equated with a sort of negative Saturn, Mercury and Venus combined. The point to note out here is that the greater degree of intensity that Rahu possesses makes the situation more dangerous than is the case with other planets. The saving grace is that it only occasionally manifests the extremes of these negative qualities.

However all these negative tendencies have a positive side to them. For example the revolutionary nature of Rahu stems from its innate dislike for authority (Sun). When the authority is corrupt and mindless, as is generally the case in present times, this revolutionary spirit becomes very important. Without a revolt both on an internal and external level no meaningful change can take place.

Rahu is the force that creates a *Robin Hood*. Despite being an outlaw he utilized his tendencies for the greater good. This is usually the case when Rahu functions through its higher principle. It retains some of its dual nature even when it is functioning through its highest aspect. The main difference when it works through this principle is that its aims become much more unselfish and humanitarian. It will still lie or cheat to achieve its ends but the goal would usually be in harmony with the cosmic plan.

It is seen that it retains a quarter of its illusory nature even when functioning in its most spiritual mode. A very good example of this can be seen in the life of *Krishna* (Chart no.4), the eighth incarnation of Vishnu in the present round of Ages. He is supposed to have taken birth in the ending phase of the *Dwapara Yuga* (Silver Age) around 5000 years ago.

He was a revolutionary for his times in every sense of the word as he broke all the existing social and religious taboos, and was the main architect of *MahaBharata*, a highly destructive World War. His chart is discussed in a later chapter that deals with the nodal axis influence in various houses. He did not mind using any method whatsoever including lying to fulfil his work on Earth, but everything he did was to manifest the cosmic plan, which is exactly how Rahu functions when working through its higher principle.

Since Vishnu is the deity governing the planet Mercury and has a definite connection with the serpent power as discussed earlier, it is inferred that Rahu is closely related to Mercury. It shares qualities like wit, versatility, quickness of thought, and communication ability with Mercury.

Rahu being an illusory planet, possesses a basic Mercurial nature with some spice added to it. Some wise men postulate that Mercury has a quarter influence of the nodes attached to it even when it has no relation with them in a chart. This can be seen from its rulership of Gemini and Virgo, the signs that Rahu is most comfortable in. This topic is dealt with in further detail when Rahu's sign rulership, exaltation and debilitation are discussed.

It has been experienced that in a nativity, only Mercury and Jupiter can control Rahu's energy. Rahu is also a significator of intellect in much the same way Mercury is, but the difference is that Rahu has to do more with the intuitive part of the intellect instead of the calculative, informational, discriminating part. This is why Rahu when working through its higher principle can be seen as the higher aspect of Mercury, which relates to real knowledge and the ability to look through illusions.

Rahu also gets influenced to a large extent by the planets it is associated with in a chart. Like Mercury it relays their energies without losing its inherent nature in the process. This mutable quality of Rahu is what makes it behave sometimes like Mars, Jupiter or even the Sun and the Moon.

Rahu, when relaying the energy of Mars, appears more aggressive even though a certain degree of aggression is inherent in its nature. It can boost the Martian energy in a chart but can also cause its perversion in many a case. Most of the unnecessary violence perpetuated on this planet has its roots in this perversion.

It has been noticed in observations that most of the charts of criminals of all types have Rahu influencing the energy of Mars in some way or the other. The famous criminal *John Dillinger* has Mars-Rahu conjunction in eighth house. Even *Saddam Hussein* has Mars-Rahu conjunction in his fifth house!

However this combination is also found in the charts of revolutionaries, who are fighting for a just cause, as it provides the vitality to go ahead with one's thinking. The celebrated Indian revolutionary warrior, *Shivaji*, who fought against the Moghul rule in India, has a Mars-Rahu conjunction in his chart.

Rahu also functions in a Jupiterian manner as advocated by Western astrology, only when it is associated with Jupiter in some way. Rahu has an airy disposition and thus possesses an inherently expansive nature that is similar to Jupiter's expansive nature, but there are a lot of differences, as Jupiter is the planet of law while

Rahu is lawlessness incarnate. The merging of these two energies can sometimes create a good balance and at other times cause disaster through over-expansion especially on the material plane.

This over expansive nature of Rahu causes unnecessary scattering or wasting away of energies in a lot of cases, but there is a lesson to be learnt in the events that follow as a result. The disintegrating influence of Rahu through ungrounded optimism and expansion is in fact one of its most dangerous traits.

Although Rahu is an airy planet it is quite fixed in its approach. The perfect example of how the air element can be unrelenting and powerful is a tornado, which blows everything that comes in its way.

There is a creative side to Rahu's nature and disposition, which resembles that of Sun. Rahu is a force which can either nourish a personality like Sun nourishes all life on earth, or just consume it like the harsh desert Sun which is not conducive to life. Rahu is also related to the egoic self-consciousness in much the same way as Sun, the only difference being the fact that Rahu is not the real thing but only a mirage.

It can be said that while Sun represents our true personality, and relates directly with the spark of the Godhead within us, Rahu represents the outer personality we have formed through our experiences in our numerous lives. This is why Rahu is sometimes known as the 'Artificial Sun'.

Rahu's presence in the sign Leo or the Ascendant or any association with Sun assists in easy expression of the soul personality. This expression manifests in the outer world as self-confidence, self-assurance and creativity. In a negative sense it can manifest as selfishness, pride, self-aggrandizement or megalomania.

Rahu has an innate reverence for the Universal Mother principle, which in our solar system manifests through Moon. Even though Rahu is said to have enmity with Moon, the major scope of its activity is lunar in a lot of ways. This is because Rahu is born out of the causative force sustaining this Universe, which is supposed to be feminine in its attributes.

It is termed as the 'Negative Moon' by some astrologers as it seems to represent the dark side of the lunar nature. Though true to an extent, as Rahu does further hallucination, illusion, paranoia and other such mental states, this is still a lopsided view, because certain very spiritual *yogas* (combinations) involving the Rahu-Moon combination find mention in the works of ancient Vedic seers.

Another reason for this identification is that it has the power to strengthen, weaken or completely neutralize the lunar forces. The presence of Rahu in the sign Cancer or fourth house or its association with Moon in a chart is a sure indicator of importance of a mother figure in the life of a native in some form or the other.

Again a lot depends upon the aspect, lower or higher, through which Rahu is functioning in a chart. For example, there is a difference between a negative trance induced by use of drugs or other negative methods, and a spiritual trance induced by dissolving the mind and the ego in the divine consciousness. In both cases Rahu has a significant part to play, and the catch lies in the difference in degree of evolution. Since in the present day and age Rahu functions through its higher principle in relatively few individuals, the 'Negative Moon' theory holds true for the majority.

The planet, which Rahu most closely resembles, is Saturn, and as we will discover later it even shares the rulership of a sign with Saturn. Besides sharing an airy temperament, another thing they have in common are the colours Blue and Black.

Rahu's close relationship with Saturn can be seen from the fact that it represents Ultra Violet light, which falls just before the Violet light of the visible spectrum, represented by Saturn. In this way Rahu can be seen as a higher octave of Saturn. The fact that Ultra Violet light is not visible to human eyes highlights the more mysterious functioning's of Rahu as compared to Saturn.

Just like Saturn, Rahu is supposed to have a lazy disposition and is a long-term planner. It can thus give a constantly worrying nature. The human follies like greed, avarice and selfishness resulting from an excess of Saturnine energy are also attributed to the lower aspects of Rahu.

Most of the devilish (to use a Christian term) aspects of human nature attributed by astrologers to Saturn are in fact related to Rahu. Rahu and not Saturn is the Devil (or *Satan*), which all the puritans and pseudo-religionists fear, but they don't realize that in their own extreme way they are falling prey to the same force that they term as devilish. As the wise know, there is no such thing as evil or pure in nature - everything that exists is sacred!

Rahu can be considered to be the expert among the planets when it comes to scheming and plotting. It is the master of manipulation. This is why it can be said to be a better politician than Saturn. It comes as no surprise that the polity of Rahu is not always orthodox or bound by prevailing social standards. Insensitivity is a term that can be ascribed to Rahu in much the same way as Saturn.

The adversities that both these planets seem to inflict are just lessons that always turn out to be rewarding in the long run. Success when it comes through Rahu or Saturn arrives only after some sort of a struggle. The only difference is that Rahu gives it with a certain degree of suddenness while Saturn grinds slowly. Rahu like Saturn is quite an expert at raising people up and then bringing them down, but gives lasting success as well, if one does not completely lose one's head.

Rahu however acts in a predominantly Saturnine fashion only when it is associated with Saturn in a nativity, or is placed in the tenth/eleventh houses, or is placed in the signs Capricorn/Aquarius.

There is a strong Venusian tinge to Rahu's nature, which usually shows itself in a love of show and pomp when Rahu is functioning through its lower aspect. Rahu is capable of manifesting highest Venusian energies like universal love, compassion and harmony as well when working through its higher principle.

The Venusian tendencies of Rahu are highlighted when it is placed in the sign Taurus or the second house, or is in association with Venus. There is a strong urge for comfort and luxury when Rahu is manifesting these energies on an earthy plane. In my view earth is the secondary element of Rahu.

This is where the materialistic side of Rahu comes out, and

probably this is the reason why it is seen as a planet giving great material prosperity in the Western system. The problem is that this materialistic side of Rahu usually knows no boundaries and can be said to be responsible for the terrible phenomenon known as greed, which is the core reason behind all the present day mess in which humanity finds itself.

Rahu also has a diplomatic nature, which is very similar to that of Venus. Rahu like Venus is by nature a social planet and enjoys company. Rahu is supposed to give an artistic temperament in much the same way as Venus, but as always there is a touch of unorthodoxy involved. Rahu's Venusian side is highlighted when it is either associated with Venus in a nativity, or is placed in the second/ seventh l ʝuses, or is posited in the signs Taurus/Libra.

Rahu has a peculiar heavy, hypnotic and sarcastic tone to its voice, which it usually imparts to a native when it is related in some way with the second or third house. The voice of the famous songwriter/ singer *Bob Dylan* who has Rahu placed in his second house in his chart is a very good example of a 'Rahu-voice'.

Sarcasm is one of the main aspects of the nature and disposition of Rahu and it is second only to Ketu when it comes to giving a sarcastic and hurting tongue. There is often a wonderful sense of humour attached to Rahu's sarcastic nature. This is why Rahu along with Mercury can be regarded as the king of satire among planets.

Rahu shares some of its nature with two of the outer planets as well. Rahu is a revolutionary, creative, shocking, individualistic force in much the same vein as Uranus. As we would discover later, it is assigned co-rulership of a sign in the Vedic system that has Uranus as its co-ruler in the Western system.

Rahu knows no national boundaries and thus has a very international and all-inclusive perspective on things, a quality very similar to that of Uranus. This international perspective of Rahu also causes major problems when it is working through a lower principle, in much the same way the negative use of Uranian energies can be quite destructive.

There is a special relationship between Rahu and Neptune as

both are the planets representing the ocean of illusion, which forms a backdrop for the play of existence. Rahu when working through its higher principle displays positive Neptunian qualities like heightened awareness of higher realms, true compassion for all existence and a need for rising above the illusion of the material realm.

When working through its lower principle it drowns one in illusions and fantasies usually relating to the lower dark sides of existence. Rahu is the planet of intuition, extra sensory perception and other such phenomenon related with the astral body. Rahu, like a negative Neptune, can make one lose one's self in chasing after mirages or hallucinations, which can either be induced by drugs or other techniques.

Cloudiness is a term common to both these planets when functioning through their lower aspect. Rahu is the force or emotion behind such things as suicide and homicide, where it totally clouds the capacity for clear thinking. This vagueness, cloudiness and confusion, usually related with Neptune, is attributed to Rahu in the Vedic system. Rahu is the planet of delusions and psychosis.

If Rahu is working through its higher aspect, then this confusion usually leads to wisdom and enlightenment. Rahu has a Dionysian way of thinking very similar to that exemplified by *Aldous Huxley*-

" road to excess leads to the palace of wisdom ".

In Vedic astrology Rahu is supposed to maintain friendly relations with Mercury, Venus and Saturn. It is neutral towards Jupiter and Mars and maintains enmity with Sun and Moon. Rahu is also said to have a predominantly *tamasic* disposition.

According to the ancient Vedic wisdom, nature has three major *gunas* (attributes) - *rajasic* (active), *sattwic* (balanced) and *tamasic* (passive) - the interplay which creates, sustains and finally ends the Universe. One must remember that Rahu can function in all the above mentioned modes - Rahu functions in a *Rajasic* mode when giving prosperity, in a *Sattvic* mode when giving knowledge and wisdom. It can also function in a state beyond the three attributes - the eternal state beyond time, space where the source of everything manifest and unmanifest lies.

Tamasic attribute is the one relating to the dark destructive side of nature. It is basically a retarding attribute that relates to rest, inertia, inactivity, demoniac tendencies and destruction of forms. It is important too in the sense that it would not be able to work if we did not sleep! It then comes as no surprise that Rahu likes the night time and functions most strongly in the couple of hours following midnight. This is probably the reason why most criminals choose this time for their activities.

Rahu when working through its lower nature, gives a superficial nature and a tendency to be swayed by mass trends. This attribute of Rahu envelops the majority of humanity in the present times.

Since Rahu is the Dragon's head, it is always looking ahead which means that it signifies the future. It is the force that detaches us from the past and in the process attaches us to the future. The fact that everybody is living on hope, which of course relates to the future, just exemplifies the significance of Rahu in our lives.

Sometimes it can make people so futuristic that the ability to exist in the present is lost. It is the force that made *Charles Darwin* come up with a theory of linear evolution in time. Rahu's illusionary power can make us believe that time is linear and not cyclic, and that the future is always better than the past. It must be added that Darwin was not a closed minded individual and it is the Neo-Darwinists who have distorted and established Darwin's theory as the ultimate truth.

In a chart Rahu's placement defines the area where new growth will take place in this incarnation. It is an area where one is initially a bit reluctant to step into, like entering a pool of cold water. If one gets over the initial hesitation, this is the most productive area of one's life, and one is sure to be rewarded proportional to the effort one puts in.

Rahu represents the path we are trotting in the present life and the lessons we will learn along the way. How smooth one's progress along this path would be depends upon the actions in the present life, one's previous lives i.e. karma, and one's evolutionary level.

Rahu causes most trouble to those individuals who like holding onto the past and are opposed to any sort of change. Rahu's maxim is that the only thing permanent is change, so it sometimes uses harsher methods in dealing with such people. This is the reason behind the sudden misfortune one might encounter due to the influence of Rahu – most of the times it is to facilitate change and with it help in the evolutionary journey of the soul. Thus in a way Rahu is basically our capacity to learn.

When one is involved in activities, which are retarding as far as one's evolution is concerned, under the influence of lower aspects of Rahu, there is a lesson to be learnt. This lesson manifests as the same treatment being meted out to the native through Ketu's influence, sometime in the future. It is a simple case of − " reap as you shall sow".

The ruler of the sign Rahu is posited in, for a nativity, can be termed as the **karmic distribution control planet**. The placement of this planet represents the area where the native will distribute his/ her energies in the present incarnation. Whether these energies are positive or negative, refined or base, constructive or destructive, depends upon the previous life karma and evolutionary level of the native involved. This can be judged from the overall energies represented by the main chart along with the other harmonic charts.

The two signs and the two houses occupied by Rahu and its dispositor define the path the soul has chosen for the present life. In a way the karmic distribution control planet is one of the keys to deciphering a chart. It is generally seen that the house where this planet is placed gets highlighted and the native usually experiences a certain degree of luck as far as its significations are concerned.

Lal Kitab makes an interesting point that if Jupiter and Venus are conjunct in a chart, they can together be treated as Rahu. This relates to the fact that Rahu acts as a bridge between Jupiter who is the preceptor of the Gods, and Venus, who is the preceptor of the Demons. Rahu is the only planet which can unify these apparently opposing energies. This also relates with the fact that Rahu can be seen as a benefic force akin to the combination of two main benefic planets, Jupiter and Venus. The house where Rahu is placed in a chart usually provides oppurtunities for growth as if both Jupiter and Venus are placed there.

SIGNIFICATIONS

The significations of Rahu follow directly from its nature and disposition. For example, the criminal nature of Rahu manifests itself in thefts, looting, blackmail, murder and other criminal activities. All type of law breaking activities can be said to be significations of Rahu.

Since law breaking usually leads to imprisonment, Rahu is considered to be the significator of all types of imprisonment and confinement as well. In some cases it is also responsible for the death penalty, torture or any other misfortune a native has to deal with. It is thus the significator of all the gangsters, criminals and other persons involved in the so-called underworld. Extortion and blackmailing are typical Rahu significations.

Rahu when working through its lower principle is also responsible for most of the perversions that afflict humanity at the moment. It has the power to pervert and distort the energy of all the other planets.

Sexual deviations and offences are the result when Rahu affects the Venusian energy.

Brutality, sadism, insensitivity and ruthlessness are the consequences of the distortion of Martian energy.

Asceticism, unnecessary tortures inflicted upon self and others, excessive rigidity and orthodoxy, and repressive father figures are usually the results of Rahu exaggerating Saturnine influences.

Excessive materialism, misuse of position and authority, religious bigotry etc. are the symptoms of perversion of Jupiterian energy by Rahu.

Self–aggrandizement, power and control games are the result of the clouding of the Solar energy by Rahu.

Emotional and psychological disturbances, fears and phobias, isolation, lunacy manifest themselves when Rahu distorts the Lunar energy.

Unnecessary lying, deceit, trickery, harmful intent are some of the results of Mercurial energy coming in touch with a base Rahu.

However Rahu when working through its higher principle, elevates the energy of the planets it is associated with and gives them a spiritual intent. Further discussion on these lines is carried out in the chapter dealing with association of Rahu with other planets.

Rahu is the significator of 'smoke' in all its forms and thus can be said to be responsible for the air-pollution, a major concern in today's world. In fact it is the significator of all types of pollution along with Saturn, Mars, Ketu and the outer planets.

Smoking in all its forms also comes under the significations of Rahu. A lot of research has gone into the psychology behind smoking but no accurate theory has come up as yet - another Rahu mystery.

Smoke is in fact one of the main symbols used to represent the illusory nature of *Maya*. Smoke as a symbol also connects Rahu with other planets as well. The old adage – 'there is no smoke without a fire' - connects Rahu with Mars, the planet governing fire. Rahu connects with Jupiter in much the same way as smoke connects with air. If the deep underlying significance of the relationship between 'smoke' and Rahu is understood, a lot is revealed regarding the force Rahu represents.

The illusions that Rahu creates in our minds disappear in time and space in the same way smoke does in the air. Still the smoker keeps on smoking for the momentary pleasure he/she derives from it while we keep on chasing one mirage after another, for within these illusions lies the joy of our existence.

Clouds are also sometimes related to Rahu as they have the power to temporarily hide the Sun. The cloudiness of thoughts, vision can also be attributed to Rahu. 'Confusion' that results from this cloudiness is one of the keywords associated with the functioning of Rahu. Clouds have always been related to the Gods and the subtle realms, and some cultures saw the cloud designs as signs in the sky forecasting the future. The God of rain, who was propitiated by almost all the agriculture-based cultures, was also related to clouds.

Rahu is the key that opens the doors to the subtle planes. 'Surreal' is another word intimately associated with Rahu. This is why it can be regarded as the significator of all the occult practices. African *Voodoo* is a very good example of such an art that can be used for positive as well as negative purposes.

Rahu is the indicator of the level of awareness we have of our astral body. Sometimes this awareness is so high that the hold on the physical body is completely lost, which leads to a situation where a person experiences difficulty even in just staying alive for working out his/her karma. This astral plane sensitivity gives mediumship capacity; the level of which again depends upon the plane, which Rahu is functioning from.

In evolved souls this capacity is used to establish contact with higher cosmic deities governing the functionings of the Universe, while in lower category mediums it is just used to establish contact with the spirit world.

All sorts of trance states and phenomenon like extra sensory perception and near death experiences can be attributed to the nodes. Since Rahu provides the urge to drown one's sense of self through various methods including the use of intoxicants, it is said to be the significator of all types of drugs and alcohol.

This in turn means that Rahu represents the pushers and all the other people associated with the drug, alcohol and cigarette industry. When working through its lower aspect it makes a native either indulge in these vices or make a profession out of their production and distribution. When one thinks how much these vices affect the present day society all across the world one gets some inkling of the immense influence Rahu has on human affairs!

Geographically Rahu represents the areas like forests,

uncultivable lands, high mountains, deserts, and other extreme landscapes that are termed exotic in present day terminology.

Among these extreme places it generally prefers an area with a sizeable serpent population. For example among forests it prefers sandalwood forests.

Being a cold, dry plane it also prefers places with cold and dry climates. Extreme weathe phenomenon related to the atmosphere like high-speed winds, tornadoes, and cyclones are related to Rahu.

It is supposed to be the ruler of the <u>Southwest</u> direction. This means that Rahu will govern the south-western part of everything, from a house to a country. It is useful to note that in a chart, the 8th and 9th houses correspond to this direction.

The American south–west especially *Arizona* is a very good example of an area totally under the influence of Rahu. The way this applies in chart interpretation is that a native under prominent influence of Rahu, is seen to either permanently live in such areas, or go on expeditions to strange, exotic and sometimes extreme places. Thus Rahu can be said to be the planet influencing explorers.

In modern times though, Rahu is more of a big city dweller completely immersed in all the illusions it has to offer. The so-called cosmopolitan cities of today like *New York* have a lot to owe to Rahu's energy for their emergence. Therefore it is either forests or big cities – just another one of the dualities of Rahu.

Mining is one of the activities governed by Rahu. Rahu in a general way can be said to be the significator of all types of underground activities like exploring caves etc. Among the metals extracted from the mining process Rahu has a special liking for iron and lead. It can thus be associated with the historical Iron Age.

Rahu is also associated with iron alloys like steel. In India a special alloy made of 5 different metals called *panchdhatu* (five metals) is associated especially with Rahu. The rings, amulets and other totems made for propitiating Rahu are supposed to be made of this special alloy. Mica and asbestos are also considered Rahu significations.

Among the gems it has special affinity for hessonite quartz. Brown agate and brown tourmaline are also Rahu gems. These find use in rings, amulets and other totems made for propitiating Rahu.

It can be seen that people associated with mining of different metals and industries like iron and steel usually have some connection of Rahu with Saturn with the 10th house in their charts.

Mining of petroleum also falls under the significations of Rahu. Petroleum or as it is appropriately called 'Black Gold', is one of Rahu's main gifts to the industrial age. The Middle East nations can be thankful to Rahu for their economic prosperity, while the environmentalists have no choice but to consider it as their number one enemy when it is working through its lower material aspect. It is interesting to note that *Islam*, the dominating religion of this region is a very Saturn-Rahu sort of religion.

One of the most obvious significations of Rahu is its relationship with the reptilian kingdom. It governs all types of snakes living on land or under water. Snakes as we know depend upon their sense of hearing as they have very poor eyesight. In fact all the animals that have a highly developed sense of hearing, and communicate using sounds with frequencies above and below the human audible range such as whales, sharks, dolphins etc. can be seen to be related to Rahu.

The snake charmers and all other people whose lives are very much entwined with that of the reptiles and the above mentioned animals could be said to be under a heavy influence of Rahu.

From this relationship with snakes, directly follows Rahu's association with all sorts of poisons. It is interesting to note that since most of the drugs and medicines used in the Western systems of medicine like Allopathy and Homeopathy are poisons, Rahu has a deep relationship with these modern day systems of healing.

This gives Rahu a hold over the pharmaceutical industry, which as of today is the second largest industry in the world! Rahu in general has a strong relationship with all sorts of healing, which in modern times relates to the medical profession. It thus relates to anaesthetists and all those involved in administering poisons for curing diseases.

The diseases mainly associated with Rahu are those involving an imbalance of the biological air humour in the body – arthritis, eczema, ulcers, paralysis, digestion problems and nervous disorders. Other diseases include skin diseases like itches, boils, lycoderma, small pox, chickenpox etc

Different types of the di: :ase cancer can also be attributed to Rahu as they involve uncontrol d growth of cells in a certain tissue.

Polio is one of the pa· ilytic diseases, which is a signification of Rahu. Breathing disorders like asthma and lung disorders like tuberculosis involve Rahu along with Saturn. All the present day diseases, which have their origin in air, water, or any other type of pollution, can be attributed to Rahu.

In today's industrial age a lot of people have to work in poisonous environments, which has led to the birth of a number of new diseases, most of which fall under Rahu's domain. Strange disorders like Elephantiasis are also Rahu significations.

Rahu is also connected with most of the sexually transmitted diseases. If a statistical research were carried out Rahu would be found to be one of the main indicators of the modern day nemesis known as AIDS. Rahu also governs strange unrecognised diseases, which in some cultures are supposed to be a result of possession by negative entities or energies.

Accidents, which result in death or loss of a limb or a body organ, are considered to be a signification of the nodes. Those relating to the loss of the eyes or limbs are especially connected with Rahu. Deafness and other disorders related with the sense of hearing are related with Rahu. This is especially the case when Rahu is placed in the third or eleventh houses.

Lunacy, insanity, suicidal tendencies and other such mental states all come under significations of Rahu. Rahu is also responsible for most of the psychological disorders. The 'asylum' can be considered to be a place very much owned by the nodes.

Rahu governs all sorts of poisonous chemicals like fertilizers, pesticides, and disinfectants that are in use in the present times. It also governs all the substances with a strong pungent smell like the sulphur-dioxide gas. In other words Rahu has a role to play whenever a poisonous substance is involved. This includes all the vocations involving poisonous substances like making of toiletries, plastics etc.

Along with Uranus Rahu can thus be said to be the originator of the 'Plastic Age'. This association can be seen from 'Kekule's dream episode' discussed later in this section. Organic chemistry is directly related to plastic technology. This is another of Rahu's significations that environmentalists would not like to hear about too much, as the non-biodegradable waste piles all across the world get bigger with each passing day.

Among other living creatures Rahu also represents all the multi-legged creatures, which covers most of the insect kingdom. It has special affinity for Wasps and Scorpions. It automatically follows that the bites received from these creatures are considered to be an indication of Rahu in action.

All the people associated in research or any other activity involving insects like beekeeping etc. can be said to be under the influence of Rahu.

Ants are also one of the favoured species of Rahu. In some parts of India feeding ants is considered one of the ways of propitiating Rahu.

In the plant kingdom Rahu represents the insect eating plants like the pitcher plant. It also represents all the flowering plants like jasmine, *henna* (myrtle), *raat-ki-raani* etc. whose scent attracts snakes. Rahu is connected to all plants having blue flowers. Bush is supposed to be the favourite plant of Rahu. Rahu is said to have a special affinity with *durva*, a type of grass.

Among the edible plants and foods Rahu especially represents *urad dal* (split black gram), *masoor dal* (yellow lentil), *saunf* (aniseed), *illaichi* (cardamom), *paan* (betel leaves) and ginger. A special mixture of seven cereals made in rural India called *Satnaja* (seven cereals) is considered a special signification of both Rahu and Ketu.

Rahu is also a significator of all types of oils - edible or inedible. It has a special liking for *sarson* (mustard oil). The hemp plant is a special favourite of Rahu. In fact Rahu relates to all plants having intoxicating effects on human beings.

Rahu also signifies all foods and drinks that have an astringent, peculiar, extremely spicy or biting taste. Thus Rahu signifies preparations and sauces like vinegar. It is also seen to represent all the non-vegetarian and other *tamasic* (base, unwholesome) foods.

Garlic is one of the spices, which Rahu is most associated with. There is in fact a whole legend about how Garlic is connected with Rahu, which will be covered in the chapter dealing with the Esoteric Significance of Rahu. It follows that it is associated with all types of alcoholic beverages and narcotics.

Among clothes Rahu connects most with trousers, socks or anything worn below the waist. It generally relates to all type of clothes, which have its colours, as described in the section dealing with its appearance. Rahu when working through its materialistic principle relates more to synthetic and flashy fabrics than natural fabrics. Black coloured blankets are a special Rahu signification.

The use of animal skins in making various products also comes under the influence of Rahu. It especially signifies items made from elephant tusks. Rahu even governs all the vocations, which in any way involve elephants.

Rahu as you must have guessed by now governs hunting and poaching. This is another one of the significations of Rahu that has wreaked ecological havoc in recent times. All industries like the leather industry and people involved in them come under the influence of Rahu.

Gambling and all other forms of speculation is also one of the activities governed by Rahu. It thus rules over casinos and also the stock markets which are nothing but casinos wearing the mask of economics and industrial growth. Las Vegas, which interestingly lies in south-western part of United States, is a perfect example of a Rahu-city.

The people connected with lottery businesses, stock exchanges, horse racing and other such activities can be said to be under the influence of Rahu. It is noticed that the money when made through such activities is never ever utilized properly, and in the long run ends up causing much suffering to the person involved. It must be getting clear to the readers that Rahu is the luck factor behind instant success and failure in the modern times.

There is no equal to Rahu when it comes to giving fame, fortune, prestige and authority, which is probably the reason why Western astrologers regard it as the greatest benefic force. The area in which this success is attained usually relates to the significations of the house Rahu is placed in, in a nativity.

Rahu imparts sensitivity to the mass trends and the collective psyche, which an individual can utilize either to further personal ends or serve humanity. Along with the outer planets it signifies the force that makes one blindly follow mass trends. Rahu is a political planet in the sense that it can put a person in tune with the collective longings. As discussed earlier, it also possesses a nature that very much defines present day politicians. All types of political and military coups are an area of Rahu expertise.

All significant political, social or economic revolutions like the French or American Revolution, can be attributed to Rahu functioning in tandem with the outer planets. Whether a person acquiring fame and fortune through its influence would use it for the benefit of the collective again depends upon the evolutionary level of the soul involved.

All vocations that require an understanding of the pulse of the collective are connected with Rahu. Along with Mercury, Uranus and Neptune, Rahu governs the mass media and all the persons involved in it. Television personalities and movie stars all owe a lot to Rahu for their success. Today, even well known personalities in every vocation like politics, sports etc. require help from media (Rahu) for their fame and success. Negative media can be a difficult force to deal with at an individual level as it can lead to instant infamy.

Rahu is also the co-significator of all types of photography along with Neptune. Photography is one of the major tools utilized by the television and cinema influences of the modern times. It is interesting to note that the two largest movie-making enterprises of the world, Hollywood and *Bollywood* (Indian Film Industry), are located in the southwestern part of their respective countries, America and India.

The recent phenomenon of entertainment through video and computer games is very much associated with Rahu. Virtual reality, which is now getting very close to mimicking reality in real-life simulators, is another of Rahu's effort to play God, by creating another illusionary world within the existing illusionary Universe.

Psychologists differ on where these developments are leading humanity, but one thing for sure, these are all activities of Rahu working through its lower materialistic aspect. This is not to say there are no positive uses of this technology, but as of now the negative side is dominant.

As mentioned before, Rahu governs the fashion experts in various fields Rahu is the planet governing creativity and inspiration. It thus represents artists involved in different arts with unorthodoxy being the only meeting point.

Manic depression, which is usually associated with creative individuals, is also a Rahu signification. In painting, Rahu can be related to all the different strands of so-called 'modern art'.

In the musical realm, Rahu along with the outer planets is the main force behind the emergence of rock, jazz, new age, fusion and other contemporary musical trends like techno, all of which represent a major shift from the classical genre of music. However, what is now known as 'Rock music' has a lot to do with Jupiter's energy just like the 'Blues' have a lot to do with Saturn's energy.

Rahu represents people involved in bizarre vocations like magicians, sorcerers, wizards, shamans, hypnotists, fairy tale and science fiction writers, or any other vocation dealing with illusion and imagination. Juggling is a special Rahu signification, as Rahu is seen to represent the arms by some astrological schools of thought.

As we will see later it has special relationship with Gemini, the sign representing the arms and hands.

In general, Rahu deals with occupations which are more materially profitable. The pirates of the olden times were also under heavy influence of Rahu. The one-eyed pirate leader is a very typical Rahu character. In fact Rahu relates one with sea faring vocations, especially when it is placed in one of the water signs or associated with planets like Moon or Neptune in a nativity.

Comedians and satirists, especially the well-known media savvy ones, utilize the humour aspect of Rahu's nature for their success.

Psychologists, psychotherapists and other such people dealing with the human psyche and collective influences also require help from Rahu's insight.

Prophets, seers and other such people who can visualize the future by being in tune with the collective influences, or understanding the functionings of the universal mind, need the services of a well placed and strong Rahu in their charts as well.

Rahu is a shadow planet in a literal sense as it loves all types of shadowy activities. Its secretive and deceptive nature associates it with all the secret service institutions all around the world. Spies, detectives, mystery writers and all other such people usually have a prominent Rahu influence in their chart.

As mentioned earlier, Rahu has an international perspective on everything. It can be said to be the force behind transforming the world into a 'global village'; a 'global market' might be the right term to use, considering the dominance economics has over everything else in the present times.

Rahu along with Uranus is responsible for the information technology boom over the past decade, which has brought people all across the world closer to each other primarily through Internet and the World Wide Web.

Rahu is also connected to all international social, political, religious and economic institutions like Red Cross, United Nations, The World Bank etc. Thus in a way Rahu can be seen as a peacemaker which was the view of many ancient Vedic seers who thought it had a diplomatic nature.

Though the bodies like U.N that are co-ruled by Jupiter may prove to be ineffective in the long run, at least they act like a vent through which the grievances of various nations find temporary release. The present day events like the evolution of a common European currency are all triggered by the force Rahu represents. If it had its way we would have a one world government, as Rahu shares all the utopian ideas of Neptune as exemplified by John Lennon's famous lines – "Imagine there is no country... and the world would live as one". Well, he and other dreamers like him may be proved right the way things are unfolding!

In personal affairs things like foreign travels, fluency in foreign languages, contact with foreigners, and just about everything foreign is signified by Rahu. It should be remembered that Saturn also has a role to play in foreign things and affairs. Foreign connection is usually established in whatever area is signified by the house or planet Rahu is associating with in a chart. Whether the foreign connection will help or hinder the fortunes of the native involved depends upon the forces affecting Rahu in his/her chart.

Rahu represents an energy that tries to establish harmony among the various races and allows for their free intermingling. This side of Rahu is easily noticed in the modern times. The famous and controversial *Bennetton Ad campaign* puts this into perspective!

Rahu is a special significator of the family of languages, which have a script where all the writing is done from right to left like Persian, Arabic, Urdu etc. Since these languages are all predominantly part of the Islamic culture, Rahu can be said to have a strong connection with Islamic thought, religion and countries. It is thus no wonder then that most of the international terrorism in today's world stems from these countries. It is also interesting to note that most of the finances of these countries come, as mentioned earlier, from another Rahu signification, petroleum.

Rahu has also a special liking for English, as it is the accepted international language. It can be said to be the force behind the sorcery of English language that makes it so popular all across the world.

Rahu's influence is considered heavy on widows, people of lower caste (which in present day world translates into lower economic stature) and people belonging to other faiths etc. In general Rahu is considered the significator of all bad company.

People having one arm, one eye or one leg are also considered as those under heavy malefic influence of Rahu. This is because Rahu is supposed to be the cause behind things like divorce, death of partner, conversion to another religion, accidents involving losing an organ or a limb. In the Middle-Ages, people who suffered from any of these misfortunes were always looked at with an eye of suspicion as they were said to have a mean and selfish disposition. This is obviously an unhealthy attitude but as mentioned before, Rahu was seen as the outcaste among planets in the Middle-Age's interpretation of Vedic astrology. Anything that was even vaguely related with its energy was treated with contempt.

Vedic Astrology also relates Rahu to hard manual labour, hunger, poverty, death of close friends or relatives and other unfortunate events and circumstances. These significations are very similar to those of Saturn and can be seen at work on a massive scale in the so-called third world countries.

Rahu is also associated with obesity and physical strength. Japanese Sumo wrestlers are perfect examples of the Rahu's expansive principle working on the physical body. Wrestlers, athletes and all other people involved in intense physical activity are supposed to be under the influence of Rahu. Rahu's association with the third house or Mars gives a lot of energy and stamina, producing a lot of athletes.

Among family relations, Rahu is related with paternal grandfather and maternal grandmother. This signification of Rahu has a lot of implications in the field of genetics. These implications are dealt with in detail in a later section devoted to the role of the nodes in genetics and reincarnation.

Rahu is the planet of intuition and inspiration. It can be said to be the originator of all the ideas that strike in our minds like lightning. Incidentally, the ancients considered Rahu the planet signifying the phenomenon of lightning in nature.

This in turn means that Rahu is a planet connected with electricity. Rahu along with Uranus is responsible for all the developments in electronics that have taken place since the beginning of the industrial age. Michael Faraday must surely be under a tremendous influence of Rahu to have attempted his famous kite experiment!

All the electric lights that illuminate our world in the nighttime can be said to be associated with Rahu. As mentioned earlier Rahu is known as the 'Artificial Sun', a definition that goes well, considering the neon god it has introduced, adding to the illusion and glamour of the modern times. Rahu has in a way created its own artificial Sun for its favoured time, the nighttime.

Even though typing is considered a Mercury signification, it is intimately connected with Rahu. Rahu is directly connected with the invention of the typewriter, which sparked off a revolution now known as the media. Rahu as discussed earlier is intimately connected with Mercury, and facilitates distribution of knowledge and information.

Coming back to the inspiration part, it is seen that the fields requiring such intuitional flashes like astrology, philosophy and modern science require the presence of a strong Rahu in the chart. The chart of *Edison* who was a prolific inventor, has been discussed in a later chapter to highlight this point. Rahu thus represents deep research, invention or discovery in every field. It is no wonder then that Edison discovered the electric bulb - the artifical sun of the modern times.

A major scientifc and technological breakthrough occurred through a dream. The German chemist, *Kekulé von Stradonitz,* had a dream of serpents chasing each other's tails in a circle, which led him to the discovery of the circular structure of a chemical compound called Benzene. We can easily see that only Rahu can be behind a dream which involved snakes chasing their own tails. In Kekule's chart one finds an exact Rahu-Mercury conjunction !

Kekulé was apparently neither a particularly good practical chemist nor an inspiring teacher. His main contributions to chemistry were theoretical and speculative. At the time that he began his research most chemists thought that the structure of molecules was unknowable, since reactions would disturb the structure unpredictably.

The significance of this discovery can be seen from the fact that all the modern organic chemistry is based upon the discovery of the structure of Benzene. Without it there would be almost no pharmaceutical products, plastics, polymers, synthetic dyes, fibre glass materials etc. In fact much of the chemicals we use in our everyday lives are based on principles of organic chemisty.

Albert Einstein (Chart no.6) said in his autobiography that he was given the theory of relativity in a dream. To give another example, the inventor of the sewing machine was stymied, and was given a dream breakthrough as he saw Native Americans carrying spears through the forest - spears with holes in them. The composer Schumann told others he had a series of a violent explosions in his ears, after which he began to hear the music of angels. He said he was not the composer but the secretary of what he had heard.

The 'Sky' was also seen as a signification of Rahu by ancient Vedic seers. The shade of blue, which the sky has after sunset, was considered the colour most favoured by Rahu. In the Western system Uranus is seen to represent sky and the sky blue colour.

Rahu along with Mercury and Saturn thus signifies birds, the creatures that have ruled the skies for long. Rahu has a special connection with the Owl, which is dwelt upon in the section dealing with the esoteric significance of the nodes. In fact Rahu has a connection with all the creatures that are active in the night.

In the modern era, Rahu was one of the driving forces behind man's urge to fly and thus represents all types of flying machines. All type of accidents in the air involving flying machines such as collisions, crashes and hijackings have a connection with Rahu. It also governs people involved in vocations involving almost continuous flying, such as airline crews.

Rahu's expansive nature extends from our atmosphere to the deep space as well. Along with Pluto and Uranus, Rahu is responsible for the recent developments in space research and astronomy as well. The events related to sky and space, including the phenomenon involving sightings of U.F.O's (Unidentified Flying Objects) all across the world, are again the result of the energy of Rahu. They are basically representations of the longing of the collective to re-establish contact with the stars and other worlds that Rahu is privy to. A lot of scholars are of the opinion that the connection has already begun. This is quite plausible considering the increasing influence of Rahu on humanity in the last few hundred years.

Rahu is thus one of the main forces behind the so-called new-age movement, which also represents an underlying longing of the collective. Though this movement has a lot of potential for the evolution of humanity, as an entity it also has a lot of illusions and personal interests clouding its manifestations. The negative energy associated with some of the cults and their leaders involved in this movement, conveys a wrong impression to the masses, making the task of reaching out to their instinctual awareness even harder. This is due to the different levels of Rahu energy associated with this movement. This movement is still in its infancy but at least it is a step in the right direction as far as the future is concerned.

An important duality attached to Rahu that must be understood, is that when working through its higher principles it stands against the very things that it perpetuates, while working through its lower aspects. Rahu is the force acting through a healer who cures the diseases, which Rahu itself signifies. One might see it as the golden rule of poison neutralizing poison manifesting itself, but it is more than that.

Rahu can be compared with a coin having two sides with opposing natures. Rahu represents the criminal and at the same time represents the detective who pursues the criminal. If there weren't any law- breakers there wouldn't be a need for law enforcers!

Despite all the pollution it is responsible for creating through its lower significations, Rahu in its more benign aspect is also the force behind an environmentalist who is trying his best to stop the plundering of earth's environment and ecology. Therefore it is important that one is not overawed by the negative significations of Rahu, for there are positive sides to each one of them. After all there is a cosmic law which simply states that good always triumphs in the end.

Ancient Vedic seers saw Rahu as the significator of all knowledge as it was the planet representing *maya* (illusory quality of nature) itself, and thus was privy to her secrets. It was seen that it revealed the secrets of nature in the material realm when working through its lower aspects, which it has been doing in the past 500 years through the modern branches of science.

When working through its higher principle it was supposed to reveal the knowledge of the subtle planes like the astral and causal.

To conclude it must be said that Rahu is a representation of a cosmic force, which is necessary for the sustenance of the drama of life. We are free to term it demoniac or evil or whatever we wish, but the fact remains that this force is nothing but a display of all possibilities and extremes within the realm of existence.

The fact that it is here to stay with us is relayed through the *puranic* legend of Rahu becoming immortal after having drunk the divine nectar. The force that binds us to the play of life can also relieve us of the bondage of time, if we only learn to see and respect it for what it is without any prejudices.

RULERSHIP, EXALTATION, DEBILITATION & MOOLATRIKONA

This is the most controversial territory as many views abound as to the sign rulership of Rahu. The Western system refuses to assign Rahu the rulership of any sign. In Vedic Astrology different systems assign Rahu different signs as regards to rulership, exaltation and debilitation.

Before we delve into establishing the rulership, exaltation and debilitation signs of Rahu let's consider the relationship Rahu has with other planets-

It is friends with Saturn, Mercury and Venus.

It is neutral towards Mars, Jupiter.

It is the enemy of Sun and Moon.

It is important to note that Rahu is more inimical to Sun as compared to Moon.

Ancient Vedic seers see Rahu as very similar in nature to Saturn. The fact that it represents ultraviolet light, which follows violet light represented by Saturn, shows that it is a sort of higher octave of Saturn. If Rahu had to be a co-ruler of any sign it had to be one of the Saturnine signs, Capricorn or Aquarius. Since the air element dominates Rahu, Aquarius, an air sign, is the automatic choice.

This is also the view of Sage *Parashara,* whose works pretty much define present day Vedic Astrology. In my view this is the right choice as there are a lot of factors to back it up.

Even Western Astrologers realized that there was more to Aquarius than just Saturn. To account for that gap they assigned Uranus co-rulership of Aquarius. We have already discussed the similarities between the nature and significations of Rahu and Uranus. The nature of the sign Aquarius also aligns perfectly with these planets.

The shades of blue colour that are related with Aquarius are very similar to those attached with Rahu. According to *Puranic* scriptures, *Shiva,* the deity governing Aquarius is supposed to have a blue colour and has a serpent wrapped around his neck. These two characteristics establish his relationship with the serpent power and Rahu, even though there are many other similarities in the realm of inner nature and disposition.

Rahu as we have discussed earlier, is the planet governing electricity, and there is no doubt as to Aquarius being an electric sign. Rahu also represents the subtle electric forces of the etheric or heavenly realm, which the sign Aquarius is seen to represent. Aquarius is a positive, futuristic sign representing forward movement, while Rahu is also a futuristic force that is always looking ahead.

The humanitarian, all inclusive, philosophical disposition of

Aquarius when it is functioning through its higher aspect, is also very in tune with Rahu's disposition in its higher aspect. Rahu as we may recall is the force that attempts to break down all boundaries of race, age, status, nationality and religion to usher in a feeling of oneness of humanity, which in a sense embodies the spirit of Aquarius.

Because of its co-rulership of Aquarius, Rahu is supposed to be a *Yogakaraka* (a favourable and important planet) for Taurus, Gemini, Libra and Aquarius Ascendants. This is due to the fact that for these Ascendants the sign Aquarius falls in important houses like the first, fifth, ninth and tenth.

Within Aquarius Rahu is stronger when placed in the following degrees; 3°20' - 6°40', 16°40' - 20° and 26°40' - 30°. It is strongest at 16°40' - 20°. The reasons behind this assigning of degrees will be explained in the next chapter dealing with *Nakshatras* and the *Navamsha* chart.

The physical characteristics of Rahu also find their true expression through the natives born with Aquarius rising on the Ascendant. The famous American President Abraham Lincoln is a very good example for understanding the physical characteristics of Rahu vis-à-vis Aquarius Ascendant.

Aquarius is a fixed air sign and thus can be compared with solid air. The fact that air can be quite a strong force, can be experienced when one tries to walk against a high-speed wind. As discussed earlier, Rahu though being an airy planet is fixed in its character.

Virgo is another sign where something seems to be missing, as the rulership of Mercury does not cover all the subtleties involved in this sign. Some Western astrologers have also realized this and are planning to introduce Chiron, an asteroid supposed to be functioning as a planet, as the co-ruler of Virgo. It makes sense to a degree as Chiron is supposed to be a healer, but there is still a lot of work to be done to establish Chiron as a planet affecting human affairs.

What some ancient Vedic seers did, was to assign to Rahu the co-rulership of Virgo as well. Sage *Parashara* also agrees with this by stating that some wise men give Rahu, the co-rulership of Virgo.

There are again some indications that help us understand why some wise men think that Rahu should be the co-ruler of Virgo. As mentioned earlier Rahu has earth as its secondary element, which goes well with the earthy nature of Virgo.

My personal theory is that Rahu connects to humanity through Aquarius and to earth through Virgo. However, the most important indication comes through the similarity in nature and disposition between Mercury and Rahu.

As discussed earlier Rahu shares colours, qualities and other attributes with Mercury. Some significations of Virgo like diseases, service, healing, enmity, power, material expression etc. seem to strike a chord with Rahu. As we will discover later Rahu is deeply related to the number '6' and Virgo is the 6th sign.

Within Virgo, Rahu is stronger when placed in the following degrees; 0° - 3°20', 16°40' - 20°, 26°40' - 30°. It is strongest at 16° 40' - 20°.

As far as exaltation/debilitation of Rahu is concerned, Sage *Parashara* has suggested Scorpio to be the exaltation sign of Rahu, through which it naturally follows that Rahu is in its fall in Taurus. Scorpio being the intense, secretive, mysterious, occult sign, it is no surprise that Rahu with its mysterious nature should like being posited there. Scorpio also has a lot of serpent symbolism attached to it.

Some astrologers consider Rahu exalted in Taurus and consider Scorpio as its fall. It is the classic case of making a choice between Rahu's material and occult side. Taurus is no doubt a more stable sign positioning for Rahu, but the fixed Taurus is no way suited to Rahu's mutability. Moreover it is the sign of exaltation of Rahu's enemy, Moon.

In my view, the opinion that assumes Gemini as the exaltation sign of Rahu is the most appropriate. Gemini is an airy, mutable sign very much in tune with the nature of Rahu. Another important reason relates to the constellations or asterisms Rahu presides over.

In Vedic astrology the twelve signs are divided into twenty-seven equal parts known as *Nakshatras* (asterisms). These asterisms are basically different constellations that lie close to the belt of the Zodiac. Each of the nine planets (including Rahu and Ketu) has been assigned rulership over three of these asterisms.

Among them the ones governed by Rahu are known as *Ardra* (Betelgeuse), *Swati* (Arcturus) and *Shatabhisha* (lambda-Aquarius). They fall in the signs of Gemini, Libra and Aquarius respectively. This is why Rahu has added affinity with these three signs. This is also the reason why Rahu shares a lot of its qualities with the ruler of these signs - Mercury, Venus and Saturn. The asterisms ruled by both the nodes will be discussed in detail in the next chapter.

It can be seen that most of the planets are exalted only in signs, which contain at least a part of the asterism ruled by them. For example Sun is exalted in Aries, a sign that contains *Krittika* (Pleiades), an asterism represented by Sun himself. Now since Rahu is the co-ruler of Aquarius we are left with only two options - Libra and Gemini.

It is experienced that the duality associated with the sign Gemini is more in tune with the dual nature of Rahu. Also Rahu is closer in nature to Mercury than it is to Venus. In my view Gemini is the exaltation sign of Rahu. Sage *Parashara* partly agrees with this in the sense that he assigns Gemini as the *moolatrikona* sign of Rahu.

Within Gemini Rahu is stronger when placed in the following degrees; 3°20' - 6°40', 13°20' - 16°40', 26°40' - 30°. It is strongest at 13°20' - 16°40'.

This automatically means that Sagittarius is the debilitation sign for Rahu but this does not mean that Rahu cannot function well in Sagittarius.

It is seen that Rahu's ability to create havoc is reduced when placed in any of Jupiter's signs. In fact Rahu in Gemini can be more troublesome if it is functioning through its lower aspect even though it might give material prosperity. Rahu in Gemini however helps the native resolve the dualities of life when working through its higher aspect.

Besides exaltation, debilitation and sign-rulership Vedic astrology has a concept of *moolatrikona*, which basically means the next best placement after exaltation. It is given more weight than own house placement.

In my view <u>Scorpio is the *moolatrikona* sign of Rahu</u>. Scorpio as we have seen was a strong contender for the exaltation sign of Rahu. Within Scorpio, Rahu is stronger when placed in the following degrees; 6°40' - 10°, 16°40' - 20°, 26°40' - 30°. It is strongest at 6°40' - 10°.

As a final note we can say that Rahu is strong in the signs of Gemini, Virgo, Scorpio and Aquarius. The dictum of sage *Parashara* that Rahu functions well in the signs of Cancer, Virgo, Scorpio and Sagittarius is also worth applying as a general rule.

ASPECTS

In the Western system the aspects commonly used are conjunction, vigintile, quindecile, semi-sextile, decile, semi-square, sextile, quintile, square, tredecile, trine, sesqui-square, biquintile, inconjunct, opposition and parallel, so they are applied in case of Rahu as well.

In Vedic astrology besides conjunction (same sign) and the seventh house aspect (opposition), Rahu is assigned a fifth house and ninth house aspect which is similar to the trine aspect in Western astrology, operating both forward and backward in the Zodiac.

The opposition aspect doesn't hold much significance in case of the nodes, because if one planet is opposing a node it is bound to be conjunct the other node. For example Rahu opposing Sun automatically means that Ketu is conjunct Sun and thus does not need to be dealt with separately.

It is seen that the conjunction and trine aspects are the ones that are most important for Rahu when one is dealing with the associations of Rahu with other planets. The aspects are applicable no matter what degrees the planets are occupying in the respective signs and thus no particular orb needs to be defined.

This means that if in a nativity, Rahu is in Scorpio and Jupiter is in Pisces, then Rahu will be considered to be in trinal relationship with Jupiter, no matter at what degrees they are placed in their respective signs. However it is helpful to remember that the aspects usually have more significance if they have smaller orbs. A 5° orb usually gives the full results of the aspect or conjunction.

When relating Rahu with the houses it is experienced that only the conjunction and the trine aspects retain significance. For example if Rahu were placed in the tenth house, it would basically influence the affairs of second, sixth and tenth houses only.

As is the case with all other planets, Rahu's influence is enhanced when it is placed very close to the midpoints of the houses especially the important points like the Midheaven and the Ascendant. Rahu's influence is also increased when it is placed very close to any planet, especially the luminaries.

MOTION & MODE OF FUNCTIONING

The nodes have a permanent retrograde motion and so Rahu is always moving backwards through the zodiac i.e. from Taurus to Aries to Pisces and so on. Rahu is one of the slow moving planets and completes one round of the zodiac in around 18 months. The speed varies from 3' to 11' per solar day.

It must be noted that some astrologers and astrological systems say that the nodes have a forward motion as well for short periods of time. In my view the permanent retrogression theory works well for ascertaining transit as well as natal chart results.

One interesting facet of Vedic astrology is the assigning of a vehicle to every planet. The speed and the nature of the motion of this vehicle, which usually is an animal, signify the way the planet involved will impart its results. The speed of the manifestation of results of different planets varies and can be interpreted through the speed of its vehicle.

Rahu is assigned the Lion, the king of the jungle as its vehicle. There are esoteric reasons behind this assigning, which will be dealt with in a later section. As is common knowledge, lion just lazes around for a better part of the day especially when he is not hungry. Rahu also behaves lazily and in most cases delays manifestation of its results in a nativity.

The lion when he is hunting uses the technique of stealthily coming up from behind and pouncing on its prey with a sudden quick burst of speed. This is also exactly the way Rahu imparts its results whenever it decides to. Its results both good and bad manifest in such an unexpected and sudden manner that the native involved hardly has any time to react to the situation. Among the planets, Rahu is only second to Ketu in giving quick and sudden results.

Coming up from behind signifies that the native is usually caught unawares by an event or a chain of events, when Rahu perpetuates them. Sometimes even the lion cannot catch the prey in one attempt. Similarly Rahu also achieves his goal for a particular chart through a series of events rather than just a single event. The point to note is that individual events among these series of events still retain their surprise element.

Another interesting key to the secrets of Rahu's functioning is provided by an alternative astrological work known as *Lal Kitab*, which translates into -'The Red Book'. It relates Rahu with the elephant, which in my view reveals a lot as to the way Rahu functions.

The elephant is a slow but persistent walker and is always on the move, which tallies well with the slow but continuous walk towards the future that Rahu represents. It also corresponds well with its long major period of 18 years (discussed in the next section).

The elephant can also run at quite high speeds if the need arises. This is an aspect that Rahu manifests through its quick results. The elephant needs and loves expansive areas to roam about it in much the same vein as Rahu, who likes to be expansive in its motives and plans. Some other aspects of its nature — a very good long-term memory, need for being in a group, peaceful disposition if left alone — are also fairly similar to Rahu's disposition.

Sometimes the elephant is known to lose its head out of extreme anger and its behaviour then becomes very unpredictable. The same is the case with Rahu, which when severely afflicted or working through its lower aspects, can either create havoc in one's personal life or adversely affect the life of others around one in much the same way a mad elephant wreaks havoc in its surroundings.

Another interesting facet of Vedic astrology is assigning distances to every planet. Rahu represents a distance of 20 *Yojanas*. *Yojana* is a very flexible unit and one *yojana* can be anything between 5 to 9 miles. This was considered a long distance in the medieval times and thus Rahu was significator of long distance travel.

TIMING

Every planet needs a certain window in time to manifest its energies. A planet is only free to influence events on certain times when its energy is dominant. Again Vedic Astrology comes into the picture as it has a lot of methods for isolating and assigning different time periods to different planets when they would be able to bestow their results freely. The most important of these methods for event timing is the system of planetary periods.

Every planet including Rahu and Ketu is assigned a major period, the values of which range from 6 to 20 years. What planet's major period is operating at birth and what part of its total period is remaining is calculated using the Moon's longitude.

The general characteristics of the major period of Rahu, which lasts 18 years and involves minor periods of other planets, are discussed in detail in the "Periods and transits" section. Since it takes 120 years to cover all the major periods of all the planets and very few of us live that long, it is seen that many of us never experience Rahu's major period. However Rahu gets the opportunity to have minor and sub minor periods within the major and minor periods of other planets.

Within a year, every planet relates with a season. Rahu along with Saturn is associated with the peak winter season, which generally falls in the months of December, January or February in the northern hemisphere.

Vedic astrology divides the year into two halves - *Uttarayana* (North residence of the Sun) and *Dakshinayana* (South residence of the Sun). 21st June to 22nd December is the period when Sun tropically transits the signs from Cancer to Sagittarius and is known as *Dakshinayana*. 22nd December to 21st June is the period when Sun tropically transits the signs from Capricorn to Gemini, and is known as *Uttarayana*. It is said that the Gods and godly qualities are stronger during the northern residence of the Sun and Demons and demoniac tendencies are stronger during the southern residence of the Sun. It follows that all malefics including Rahu are supposed to be stronger during *Dakshinayana*.

Within a month Rahu is supposed to be strong on days when Moon is transiting the constellations governed by Rahu i.e. *Ardra* (Betelgeuse), *Swati* (Arcturus) and *Shatabhisha* (lambda-Aquarius). This day should not be taken literally as one day in a solar month. This transit though usually around 24 hours in duration, can be stretched over two solar days. For example if Moon enters the asterism of *Swati* at 14.00 hrs on say Thursday it will stay there till around 14.00 hrs on Friday.

In the Vedic calendar, a lunar month or the period between two Full Moons, is divided into 30 lunar days. These 30 days are further divided into 15 lunar days each, of the waning and waxing phase. Each one of these 15 lunar days is called a '*tithi*'. A tithi repeats itself twice in one lunar month. For example *Ekadasi*, the eleventh tithi, would correspond with the eleventh lunar day of both the waxing and waning phases. Rahu relates to *Ashtami* or the eighth tithi, which corresponds to the eighth lunar day in the waxing and waning cycle. Some scholars relate Rahu with *Panchami* as well, because snakes are supposed to be worshipped then.

Within a week, as is common knowledge, every day is associated with a planet. There is again some confusion among Vedic astrologers relating to assigning Rahu co-rulership of the weekdays.

In my view, <u>Wednesday and Saturday</u> can be assigned to Rahu as its days. It can be seen that this is not arbitrary as Rahu is very closely related to Mercury and Saturn, and as discussed earlier shares the rulership of signs with them.

In my view Rahu is more strongly connected to Wednesday. This is because in the sequence of major periods, Rahu's major period is placed between those of Mars and Jupiter, so it is not very surprising that it should be connected with a day between Tuesday (Mar's day) and Thursday (Jupiter's day), which happens to be Wednesday.

Within a day, Rahu's energies are seen to be strongest during sunset and the couple of hours following sunset. This is why the sunset time is considered to have strong vibrations, which as always can be either negative or positive. No wonder then that Arizona, which as mentioned earlier, has a strong connection with Rahu and is known to have the most scenic and surreal sunsets in the world.

As mentioned earlier Rahu is also strong throughout the night time. It is seen that birth at any of these times often highlights the significance of Rahu in the life of a native.

In my experience I have seen that the results of Rahu, like flashes of intuition etc. occur mainly during the hours assigned to it. Those who are under a strong influence of Rahu prefer to stay up and work in the night time.

An important aspect of timing events in Vedic astrology is the assigning of a certain period of time in human life to every planet. This works on the theory that every planet matures at a certain age after which it can fully manifest its results.

Rahu is supposed to mature in the 42nd year. The period from 42 to 47 years is considered the time when Rahu manifests its complete results in a nativity. For convenience's sake this period will be referred to as Rahu-time throughout this work.

It is seen that some natives have a sudden rise, fall or transformation when they reach this age. Even though not drastic in some cases, but a change surely takes place in everybody's life in the 42nd year. What exactly will happen depends upon the position of Rahu and the overall inclination of the nativity.

Forty-two is the age when one begins one's journey on the downward spiral as health declines and mental processes weaken. Another way of looking at this is that a person is at the peak of his powers at this age. It is the halfway point if we consider 84 to be the normal life span. In an ideal case it should represent the summit, where upon reaching, one must start the descent. Nature as always plays its games and for some it is just the start of the ascent!

This time is in a way related to the eighth house and represents the time when after the midlife crisis (36-42y) one starts to slowly separate oneself from the material world (seventh house activities), and begins to confront realities like death. An increased dependence upon others and an interest in otherworldly subjects is also supposed to start from this age.

In Vedic astrology the age from 40-45 is assigned to the fourth house. It is considered a time when a person is in full control of his family affairs and is trying to find the peace within. It is a time for internal reflection. However it would mean different things for different people depending upon the influences their fourth house carries.

It is also beneficial to remember that the period ranging from 42nd to the 56th year is assigned to Mars. In the same vein the period from 69th to 108th year is ascribed to Saturn, Rahu and Ketu, the three planets associated with old age. Rahu's influence will be felt strongly in this age span.

Other important years when Rahu is more active relate to the transit of Rahu. Rahu returns to its original position as mentioned before in 18 and 2/3 years, so the 19th, 38th, 57th, 76th years are also seen as Rahu's years.

Among these the 19th year is the most important as it is what we can term as the first Rahu-Return. This is the year when the adolescent grappling with finding his/her way in the big bad world usually gets a break. Sometimes the direction chosen at this time holds throughout life and in some cases it is just a temporary relief. This is discussed in further detail in the chapter dealing with the transits of the nodes.

All the above rules are useful in both Predictive as well as Electional astrology. As part of Electional astrology, the Vedic system has special rules for finding out the best time for travel. One of these rules relates directly to Rahu. According to this rule, on particular weekdays Rahu's face is supposed to lie in a particular direction. Travelling in that direction means travelling right into the mouth of Rahu. One is advised not to travel in that direction on that particular day for having a beneficial journey.

The direction of the location of Rahu's head on different weekdays are - North for Sunday, North West for Monday, West for Tuesday, South West for Wednesday, South for Thursday, South East for Friday and East for Saturday.

SYMBOLS

The main symbols associated with Rahu are the trident and the magnet. The trident, a powerful symbol revered by many ancient cultures is esoterically connected with the three-pronged functionings of nature. It is thus a symbol of fusion, which Rahu is seen to represent. Rahu's ability to bring forth order out of chaos through fusion, integration, blending and coordination of the three attributes of nature is also related with this symbol.

The magnet with a horseshoe shape is the main symbol of Rahu representing its powerful but illusory magnetic quality. Magnetism is in a sense one of the phenomenon, which helps keep the illusion of the perceptible Universe alive. It is directly related to the main illusory force within nature, which as discussed earlier is directly related to Rahu.

Rahu acts like a magnet in the sense that it can attract fortune or misfortune, worldly riches or real knowledge depending upon the quality and attributes of the soul involved. Rahu's magnetic force attracts people towards materialism in much the same way a light source attracts the insects. The eventual fate of the insects is no secret! Rahu as discussed earlier is also the planet behind a peculiar type of captivating personal magnetism attached with certain people.

The symbol ' Ω ' which is widely used these days to represent

Rahu is a sort of half *Ouroborous* (the circular symbol where two snakes are biting each other's tail). It is the upper or northern half of the complete circle of time. As mentioned earlier Rahu is associated with the North of everything. It can also be seen as the head part of the circle and thus connects with Rahu, the head.

Rahu is classified as a *dhatu* (metal) planet and is thus connected with non-live things in general. This classification is of use in *Prashna* or Horary Astrology. For example if someone is asking a question when Rahu is placed in the Ascendant of the chart of the moment, than one can conclude that it has to do with some material non live issue.

A simple straight line is an occult symbol related to Rahu. It was usually put to use in making amulets and other totems connected for propitiating Rahu.

Rahu as we know holds a sword in his hand for the purpose of attack and defence. Thus Sword is another symbol related to Rahu. It can be said to represent the cutting, merciless side of Rahu which can either cut the ties of materialism through knowledge, or punish those who fall victim to their lower natures. On an esoteric level it relates to its presiding deity Durga who also holds a sword in her hand. As we would discuss later in the concluding chapter, swords in general are donated to ward off the bad effects of Rahu.

These symbols are of much use in palmistry, which in my view is an integral part of astrology. A magnet, a trident or a sword sign in the hand or the feet or any other part of the body is an indicator of the dominant role Rahu will play in the life of the native involved.

KETU

APPEARANCE

Ketu, the oldest among the planets, has a serpent hood attached to a human body. It is a bit scary to even visualize and thus it is no surprise that it is fearful to behold.

Snakes are supposed to have hypnotic and penetrating eyes,

May Divine Ketu bestow its Grace upon us

which Ketu bestows to a native when it has anything to do with the first or second houses in a nativity. The stronger the connection the more apparent the effect.

The various names assigned to Ketu in Vedic texts - the fierce; the terrible; the appalling; the serpent; the tail; the earth coloured; the fanged; half-bodied; the smoky bodied; having eyes like glowing gemstones; having fierce death inflicting looks - give a clue to its appearance.

Ketu is seen to represent short people. Any relationship of Ketu with the Ascendant reduces the height as shown by other factors in a nativity. All the psychological theories about short people having a certain nature and tall people having a different nature stem from the involvement of the nodes. Nodes always complicate things and these tall-short complexes are no exception.

Just as Rahu is seen to represent lean people, Ketu is seen to represent fat people. It just loves putting fat on people and inflating the tummy especially in old age. In fact Ketu can be said to represent all the short and stocky types.

Ketu's serpent face is of the colour of smoke, the type that comes out from the burning of wood.

Being a fiery planet, it also imparts a predominantly fiery constitution to a native when affecting the Ascendant in any way.

Ketu like Rahu adds a certain strange and hypnotic quality, something that is very hard to put one's finger on, to a person's appearance when it is placed quite close to the Ascendant degrees. How it exactly affects a native's appearance is difficult to describe in words. To get a better mental picture one might like to have a look at the late *Nusrat Fateh Ali Khan*, a renowned Pakistani musician, who to a large extent typifies what Ketu does to one's appearance. *Janis Joplin*, who has Ketu exactly conjunct her Ascendant, is another example of a distinctive Ketu personality.

A very strong Ketu personality is one, which just by its presence, somehow shakes other people up and makes them feel either extremely uncomfortable or mesmerizes them to the extent that they cannot help but feel strongly attracted.

Big earlobes or ears are one of the indicators of a Ketu personality. Ketu's glance is upwards and this can be used to single out a Ketu personality. However it is useful to remember that Sun and Mars also have upward glances.

Among the senses Ketu relates more to the sense of smell. A developed sense of smell or the complete absence of it also helps in the identification of a Ketu-type.

According to one view it has an uncouth appearance and is dressed in torn clothes very much like a beggar or an ascetic. The other view shows it dressed immaculately in clothes, involving a variety of bright and fiery colours.

This difference in perception, as is the case with Rahu, portrays the two sides of Ketu; one, which bestows material prosperity and the other that makes one go through material adversity.

The colours associated with Ketu are - the muddy earth colour and all other earthy shades; all shades of grey; bright and fiery shades of yellow, red and orange; all the colours seen in the sky during sunrise. Turquoise and a dark muddy sort of green which can be seen in the gemstone generally known as *cat's eye*, are also Ketu colours. In the spectrum of electromagnetic waves or different types of light, Ketu represents Infra Red light, which as we know is invisible to the human eye as it falls out of the visible spectrum (VIBGYOR).

In Vedic traditions Ketu's image is made in a variety of ways. One image has four arms holding a mace, an arrow and a flag. The remaining hand is making a gesture, which grants boons. Its head is facing south and is decorated with a cat's eye crest jewel. It is supposed to ride a vulture and a snake. Another image has two arms with one holding a mace and the other is making a gesture, which grants boons. In some images its snakehead is seen to be decorated with a luminous star, which shines in darkness emphasising the enlightenment potential of Ketu as a planet. Just like Rahu these images reveal a lot relating to Ketu's functionings and attributes, as we will find out in the next few sections.

ATTRIBUTES

In Vedic traditions Ketu is directly linked with *Ganesha*, the first-born child of the universe, and consequently the ancient seers saw it as the <u>Eldest among the planets</u>. It is also said to be the <u>head of all the stars</u> <u>and planets</u>. It is the beginning and the end of all things. It is the unpredictability factor inherent in the Universe.

The word Ketu translates into 'the banner' or 'the sign'. This word is also associated with the comets and asteroids and other such objects in the sky that served as 'signs'. As we will discover later comets and asteroids have a deep connection with Ketu. After the assigning of the two nodes the planetary status in the creation legend described earlier, Brahma assigned them the names Rahu and Ketu. Ketu as we will discover later has a flag or banner as its main symbol.

Sage *Parashara* says Ketu is akin to Rahu and so most of the names and qualities attached with Rahu apply to Ketu as well. However ancient seers also gave it separate names like *shikhi* (one having a tail), *dhwajah* (Flag) and *tamas* (darkness). Flag as we will see later is the main symbol of Ketu. Calling it *tamas* is justified in the sense that it is a planet that as we would discover in this section is strongly related to the dark, inert, illusory and retarding aspect of nature.

In the language of the esoterists it can be said to represent the First Ray energy, as it relates to the original primordial force behind universal creation and dissolution.

Ketu represents the extremes – creation and destruction, matter and spirit, the primitive and the most refined, the children and the very old and so forth. These extremes meet, as is seen by the fact that very old people develop a nature very similar to that of children.

Ketu is childlike in the sense that its desire and will is not very conscious. Just like children, Ketu can be cruel and will do anything including steal, lie and throw tantrums to get what it wants. Ketu when working through its material aspect confers this childish materialism. Just as kids want toys to play with, the elders also require their own toys in the material world to play around with.

Ketu can cause people to act in a perverted, unreasonable manner in much the same way as Rahu does, but the motives of Ketu are always different. Ketu is fanaticism incarnate and thus can be the most dangerous force among the planets to deal with, as it is not open to reason.

One can at least sit down and talk things out with a Rahu personality, but such a thing is not usually possible with the pure Ketu types. Irrationality is the word, which in my view sums up Ketu's nature in its lower aspects. This irrationality turns into the highest knowledge, when one discovers that everything in nature is not very rational, as the physicists find in the world of quantum physics.

There are always terms like unpredictability and probability associated with the functionings of the Universe and it is in this window of possibilities that Ketu seems to revel! Ketu relays an extremely impressionable and eccentric energy, which is difficult for most of us to handle. 'Erratic' and 'Sublime' are two words which relate most to the two main modes of Ketu's nature and functioning.

Ketu thus can be equated with chaos and disorder within the universal system. Ketu is thus a force connected with surprises, exceptions, strangeness and any other bizarre phenomenon. Ketu is thus also the planet of intuitive awareness and all other states beyond the realms of rational perception.

Most of the problems Ketu causes arise from a lack of sense of limits. Balance and diplomacy are not its strong points as it is more interested in the extremes. In the words of *Jim Morrison*, a poet with a prominent Ketu influence in his chart - " I am only interested in the extremes. All the other things are, well, just in between."

Ketu's irrationality often turns into a lack of mercy and can produce personalities like *Hitler*. Ketu is the military man who inflicts extreme torture on an enemy soldier in the name of war and patriotism. In its other aspect it also produces individuals like *Mother Teresa* who highlight the other extreme, selfless service. It is interesting to note that Hitler has Ketu in his third house while Mother Teresa has Ketu in her twelfth house.

Ketu thus holds within itself the possibilities of the exploiter and the exploited, the sinner and the redeemer, the tyrant and the saviour. Ketu represents the strength that can stand up against all odds and at the same time also the weakness or vulnerability that can give in to the slightest pressure.

The unconsciousness attached with Ketu can breed morbid fears, suspicion, superstition, sadism, amorality and other undesirable traits. Ketu's functioning in these dark realms can be summarized in a quote by *Antonin Artaud*, poet-actor - "eroticism, a thirst for violence, bloodlust, an obsession with horror, collapse of moral values, social hypocrisy, sadism, perjury, depravity etc."

Even these dark horrors when perpetuated by Ketu have a certain innocence attached with them as they have their roots in the instinctual awareness of the collective.

All the fears that Ketu seems to represent are related to the idea of death one-way or the other. Ketu as mentioned earlier represents all types of endings. The end of anything, especially those things we cherish, is never a comforting idea for anyone. The only comfort one can derive from Ketu is by holding onto the past. In some cases it manifests as attachment with past places, relationships and achievements. In others it manifests as an attachment with thought forms, ideas and faculties which one has worked on and developed in previous lives.

Ketu represents the inertia, which resists change because of its strong attachment to the past. Sometimes this attachment is so strong that a person can lose one's ability to live in the present or face the future.

The phenomenon of ghosts, which are nothing but souls with astral/etheric bodies hovering around the places that they were attached to in their human incarnation, is one of the examples of Ketu's functioning.

Ketu is the planet, which gives us our worldly identity in the present incarnation. It is not be confused with the Sun, which represents our connection with the divine source. Ketu is the force that attaches us to our roots in the form of our family, ancestors, race, region, religion etc.

Rahu is the force that tries to make us outgrow our roots while Ketu tries to make us hold on to them. The balance is struck when one imbibes all the positives from one's roots and utilizes them for the betterment of the whole. The emergence of the message - "Think globally, act locally", is a sort of reflection on this fusion.

The lesson of letting go and moving on is the biggest lesson attached with Ketu. It is also the force, which when approached without fear and prejudice can dissolve the past and in the process set one free from the bondage of time.

A Rahu person is more likely to say 'forget about the past' while an evolved Ketu person is more likely to say 'let's learn from the past'. Herein lies the main difference in the approach of Rahu and Ketu - Rahu is always concerned about the future and Ketu is always concerned about the past. The nodes are thus the linking forces between the past and the future and somewhere in the middle lies 'the present' of our existence.

Ketu is most closely associated with the planets Sun, Mars and Jupiter and shares many of their qualities. Ketu can give the independence of spirit and the ability to transcend external influences in much the same way as Sun.

Ketu is a wilful planet that can give powers of intense concentration, deep perception and penetrating insight in equal measure to the Sun.

It also resembles Sun in the sense that it is a hot, dry and fiery planet. The cruelty associated with the Sun, which can be felt on a hot summer day in the equatorial region, or through the insensitive behaviour of father figures resonates with the cruelty inherent in Ketu.

The dictum - "force which gives life can also take life,"- applies to both Sun and Ketu equally. The solar part of Ketu's nature is highlighted if it is somehow connected with Sun in a chart or is placed in the sign Leo or in the fifth house.

Ketu is referred to as 'the Negative Sun' because it is seen to obstruct, negate or darken the Sun. Ketu has the power to completely dissolve the Sun, which as we know represents our sense of self. This is the reason why it was considered the most powerful among the planetary forces by Vedic seers of the past.

This dissolution aspect is not at all negative in the sense that we can realize our unity with the whole only after this sense of self that separates us from others is dissolved.

The problem is that Ketu does not always dissolve the Sun completely but afflicts it partially. This can in some cases manifest as a lack of self-confidence and at other times as self-aggrandizement.

Ketu can distribute Sun's energy in a destructive or a constructive way depending upon which aspect it is functioning through. Since Ketu usually internalizes the energy of any planet it is associated with, it can internalize the energy of the Sun giving clear and deep insight. It either leads to clarity or confusion, again depending upon the evolutionary level of the soul involved.

It can be said that Ketu's domain starts where the domain of Mars ends. In a way it represents the extremes of Martian energy, which as with everything can be either positive or negative. Ketu is a hot, dry, fiery, quick and sharp planet and so is Mars.

Vedic astrology always considered Ketu as similar to Mars and so all the Martian significations – enmity, accidents, violence, domination, arguments, misunderstanding, litigation, anger, energy, will, courage, self-confidence etc. – apply to Ketu as well. As we will discover later Ketu is the co-ruler of a Martian sign.

Ketu shows its Martian side to a greater degree if it is either associated with Mars in a chart or placed in the first/eighth house or posited in the signs Aries/Scorpio.

Ketu's close relationship with Mars can be seen from the fact that it represents Infra Red light, which falls just after the Red light of the visible spectrum, represented by Mars. Thus Ketu can be seen as a higher octave of Mars. The fact that Infra Red light is not visible to human eyes highlights the more mysterious functionings of Ketu as compared to Mars.

Ketu is at moments even more impulsive than Mars. It is hard to imagine because Mars is quite an impulsive planet in itself. Both planets represent instinctual awareness with the only difference lying in the fact that Ketu represents something much deeper.

Ketu like Mars usually does not have a great interest in social decorum or formalities, and thus a native under a strong influence of Ketu is seen to, intentionally or unintentionally, ignore the rules of idealized social behaviour.

Ketu is a planet of strong likes and dislikes. This is mainly the reason for its characteristics like intolerance, aggression, rudeness and impetuosity. With Ketu these obviously find much stronger expression than they do through Mars.

Like Mars, Ketu is the planet of revenge and vengeance but the difference is that unlike Mars, whose anger is temporary, Ketu never forgives or forgets and its grudge can sometimes last for several lifetimes. This makes Ketu the most revengeful among planets.

Both are planets of 'war'. Ketu represents both the aggressor and defender just as there are aggressive and defensive sides to Mars. Ketu when working through its lower principle is responsible for all sorts of atrocities, tortures and other abnormalities in the physical and mental realms in much the same way as Mars. It can't be stressed too much that Ketu represents the extremes in these realms, which are in my view incorrectly associated with Mars.

Ketu is more of a collective force denoting large-scale events while the influence of Mars is more personal. Ketu can in fact be seen as the collective force from which the personal planet Mars is born. Ketu on an individual level can pervert the Mars energy and produce psychosis, but also cause it to internalise where one fights with the enemy within instead of hurting others.

Ketu has a very deep connection with Jupiter. It is about the only planet that Ketu respects and pays heed to. A connection of Ketu with Jupiter in a nativity usually goes a long way in tempering the negative qualities of Ketu. Such a placement is a significator of some good karma from previous lives.

Ketu shares the desire to teach in much the same way as Jupiter. It goes without saying that Ketu is much more intense with his teachings and has a tendency to cram one's ideas down other's throat.

It can be said that while Rahu denotes our capacity to learn Ketu represents our desire to teach. If Rahu is the planet of knowledge then Ketu is the planet of wisdom.

Just like Jupiter, Ketu is also a planet representing auspiciousness and well being on all levels. Ketu can act like a benefic in much the same way as Jupiter especially when it is giving the results of good karma from past lives.

A well placed Ketu has the power to relay all the Jupiterian significations – luck, grace, fortune, material and spiritual beneficence, inner fulfilment, creativity, harmony, ethics, idealism, love of rituals, inner knowledge, joy of existence etc., but it should be remembered that Ketu has a tendency to go to extremes even when manifesting these positive qualities. For example, Ketu can take Jupiter's love for outer rituals and get too iconoclastic.

There is always some sort of struggle involved and good fortune does not flow as smoothly as it does in case of Jupiter.

Ketu usually functions in a Jupiterian manner only when it is in some way associated with Jupiter by aspects or placed in the ninth/ twelfth house or posited in Jupiter's signs, Sagittarius/Pisces.

In Western astrology Ketu is equated with Saturn, a view that holds true when Ketu is neutralizing the bad karma from previous lives. Ketu can be a very limiting, constrictive influence in much the same vein as Saturn.

Ketu is the master of tragedy and it has no equal among planets as far as manufacturing tragic situations is concerned. It can make one reach the depths of despair through a series of unfortunate events. Ketu reflects all the negative Saturnine effects – depression, melancholy, miserliness, gloominess, selfishness etc. It is quite merciless when it is working in this mode.

It can make paupers out of kings in the blink of an eye. In such cases it is very difficult to maintain optimism for the future because in extreme cases Ketu leaves one with not even a single ray of hope to cling onto. This is where the weak souls resort to methods like suicide while the stronger ones brave their share of destiny with determination.

Suicide as we know is no solution, as the soul has to confront its karmic destiny in one life or the other. Moreover like Saturn, Ketu's lessons are always for the long-term benefit of the soul involved. It is the case of 'reap as you shall sow' all over again. Ketu usually acts in a true Saturnine fashion only when it is somehow connected with Saturn.

Like Saturn, Ketu is a separative, detaching force. It can lead one to the state of *Vairagya* i.e. disillusionment and detachment from the game of life. This is good in the sense that it can help one grow spiritually, but it might also make one neglect one's worldly duties or stop one from fulfilling one's karma on earth. This is what *Krishna* tries to make *Arjuna* understand through his teachings in *Gita* – fulfilling one's karma in life without forming any new attachments is the key to liberation.

Ketu is very much an introvert by nature as opposed to the extroverted energy of Rahu. Ketu however can be more aggressive than Rahu when it opens up. Ketu is also a more straightforward conversationalist as compared to Rahu even though Ketu's expression may lack clarity.

Ketu is very much a contracting force as compared to the expansive nature of Rahu. Rahu is thus concerned with attaining knowledge by an externalised use of attention while Ketu is more interested in attaining wisdom through an internalising of the power of our attention. Attention as we know is one of the most precious possessions we have, and we are all different only because we use our attention in different ways.

Ketu like Rahu has to relay the energies of the planets it is associated with in a nativity. Thus it relates to the other planets as well.

When related with the Moon by aspect or being placed in the

fourth house or the fourth sign (Cancer), it adds a psychic touch to the mind of the native involved. A strong psychic connection with the mother or a mother figure is seen with this configuration.

Ketu is the most psychic among planets and sometimes its energies are difficult to handle for highly impressionable planets like the Moon. When working through its lower aspect Ketu can give rise to all sorts of fears, phobias, idiosyncrasies and other morbid and unnatural mental states.

It is interesting to note that for most of us these fears are usually more pronounced in the childhood stage, which is supposed to be governed by the Moon. It can also give an attachment to the lower dark side of life and an interest in black magic and other such unwholesome occult practices.

When strong and working through its higher principle, Ketu can also elevate the mind to a degree that the native has access to the secrets relating to the functionings of the Universe. It can also take the mind beyond the material world thus opening a window of opportunity for liberation.

Ketu governs the spirit world and can thus connect one's mind with that realm. This is often a retarding influence from an evolutionary perspective because it complicates matters as if our attachments with those who are alive are not enough.

In many cases Ketu's relationship with the Moon gives a strange sense of being pursued or stalked. There is a constant awareness of some sort of danger lurking around which in extreme cases manifests as the phenomenon known as paranoia. Such people usually cannot get over the death of near and dear ones and find themselves haunted by the spirit of the dead.

All that is attributed to the sixth sense relates one way or the other to Ketu. When Ketu is connected with the Moon in a nativity, some sixth sense faculty is easily noticeable. Generally speaking, there is always some degree of psychic touch attached with the significations of the house/sign/planet Ketu is associated with.

As we discussed earlier, Mercury always has some part of the nodes associated with it. Ketu can either pervert the Mercurial significations in much the same way as Rahu or add depth to them. How exactly Ketu will function again depends upon the evolutionary level of the soul involved!

No matter from which aspect, higher or lower, Ketu is functioning it is seen to add a degree of seriousness to the usually jovial Mercury nature. Ketu does have a comic side to its nature but it is a different type of sense of humour than that of Rahu.

Ketu's sense of humour is usually related to some individual going through a series of unfortunate events that make them look silly. Ketu can be thus considered the instinct within each of us that makes us laugh, and in doing so humiliate others when they are caught up in a silly or unfortunate situation. The works of Charlie Chaplin exemplify this Ketu-humour almost perfectly.

Ketu's critical nature combined with Mercury's discriminatory power can either produce a genius when these energies are directed inwards, or the irritating neighbourhood critic whose energies are scattered outside without attaining a proper understanding.

Ketu is a planet of deep insight, which when combining with Mercury's adaptability and dexterity, can give great intellectual and philosophical acumen.

Ketu behaves in a Mercurial fashion only when it is related with Mercury in some way or is posited in the third/sixth houses in a nativity.

As is the case with other planets Ketu can refine Venusian energy or pervert in the same way as Mars does when it afflicts Venus. Ketu can confer artistic talents, which are basically the fruits of past life exertions, in a particular area of art.

Ketu is thus the planet of prodigies, who, very early in life start exhibiting their skills, artistic or otherwise. Ketu on the one hand has a liking for luxury and comforts in a very Venusian fashion, but on the other hand has a tendency to completely shun them.

Even its love is restricted to a few when it is working through its lower aspects and is all-inclusive when it is expressing its highest energies. It often manifests the extremes of Venusian energies, sometimes within a single lifetime. Ketu usually chooses platonic love over other forms of love.

Ketu affects the Venusian significations only when it is somehow related to Venus by being placed in its signs, constellations or second/seventh houses.

Ketu shares a lot of the qualities that are attributed to Pluto in Western astrology. Ketu like Pluto relates with the primordial forces present at the beginning of creation. Ketu is a wilful, psychic planet in much the same way as Pluto. Ketu and Pluto together encompass the realm covered by the terms enigma and enigmatic.

It is a planet denoting depth in every aspect of existence and is more concerned with the underlying forces than the surface superficialities in much the same way as Pluto. These two planets lie at the core of everything that exists.

Ketu also relates to the dark, destructive, manipulative side of nature as exemplified by Pluto. It follows that Ketu and Pluto also share attributes like chaos, disorder on a universal level and idiosyncrasies, unpredictability, paranoia etc. on a personal level. Ketu as we will discover later is also assigned co-rulership of a sign co-ruled by Pluto as per the Western system.

In my view Ketu is also related to the other planet Neptune in the sense that it represents dissolution on all levels. Also 'water' is the secondary element of Ketu. In fact Ketu can be said to be hiding its emotional nature under a fiery exterior in much the same way Rahu hides its material (earthy) nature under an intellectual (airy) exterior.

Ketu is a very emotional planet and represents extreme, complex and intense emotional states. In other words it is a psychologist's nightmare. These emotional states are more Neptunian in their quality than the normal emotions represented by inner planets like Moon and Venus. The emotional side of Ketu is highlighted when it is placed in one of the watery signs Cancer, Scorpio, Pisces or the watery houses like fourth/eighth/twelfth.

As expected the nodes among themselves cover all the four elements as Rahu holds sway over the earth and air elements and Ketu relates to the fire and water elements.

Ketu is the planet that makes people define their identities. Some people identify themselves with their country through patriotic emotions. Some use race or religion as their yardstick. Most of the religious and racial fanaticism and orthodoxy stems from the influence of Ketu.

Ketu makes individuals define smaller boundaries as well - neighbourhood, social and economic status, sex, caste, creed, family and finally the personal boundary.

Ketu is the planet representing isolation and alienation, and produces most of the introverted types who would rather remain within their shell than interact with others. The positive aspect to be had from this is that such natives don't shy away from loneliness, but utilize that period of isolation in some positive activities like self-introspection.

In some cases Ketu types do interact but within the well defined boundary of family, community, race, religion, country etc. Only when Ketu is strong and working through its higher principle does it allow people to dissolve these boundaries.

Ketu also represents part of the genetic baggage everyone is carrying. There is usually a strong sense of attachment with one's roots in natives under a strong influence of Ketu. It is important to understand one's roots, as that understanding is required for fulfilling one's karma in the present life.

Developing attachments or a false sense of vanity in relation to one's roots is just another type of fanaticism, which is quite widespread in the present day humanity. Only a strong Ketu working through its higher principle can give the independence of spirit to grow above these roots and look at everything with an open mind and heart.

Ketu is the planet that deals with the past on an individual as well as collective level. The sign and house placement of Ketu in a chart shows the area, which we have been working on, in our previous incarnations. It is the place where our true talent lies.

Ketu represents the faculty that we have perfected over a series of incarnations and thus comes naturally to us in the present life. This is the reason why there is always a sort of ambition and obsessive streak attached with the area Ketu is placed in a nativity. Thus it is the area where a lot of our frustration lies and also where we are most vulnerable.

The key to achieving one's goals in the Ketu-area is to understand Ketu as a force similar to Mars and Saturn combined. It is interesting to recall that Vedic astrology relates Ketu with Mars and Western astrologers with Saturn. Mars represents energy and Saturn timing, and so a balance has to be established between these aspects.

It is seen that in some cases a native is overaggressive in the Ketu-area, or in other cases there is a complete lack of effort with everything being left to chance. This is an area in one's life where patience is required until the opportunity comes along, but effort is required to ensure that it does not slip away.

No wonder it is the most difficult area to deal with in any incarnation and is usually the root cause of most of our unhappiness. Too much emphasis on this area is also not good as it retards the new growth that the Rahu area represents.

The way Rahu and Ketu harmonize with each other can be best seen through an example. Suppose Ketu is placed in the ninth house in the sign Taurus. This means Ketu is working through the fire (ninth house element) and earth (Taurus) elements, which in turn means that our talents lie in the practical (earth) and intuitional (fire) understanding of ninth house significations – religion, philosophy etc.

This position of Ketu would require Rahu to be placed in the third house in the sign Scorpio. This means that this understanding has to be distributed in a sensitive (water – Scorpio) and all-inclusive (air – third house) way through the third house significations – writing, communication, travelling etc.

The houses that are in trine with Rahu's positioning which in this case are the seventh (partners) and the eleventh (friends) also form a part of the backdrop for the distribution of these energies. It is needless to add that the more evolved the soul the more harmonious is this exchange between Rahu and Ketu.

The dispositor of Ketu in a nativity can be called the karmic suction control planet or the karmic inlet control planet. One's talent in the present incarnation can usually be deciphered through this planet and its placement. In most of the cases the talents are directly related with the significations of this planet.

If Venus happens to be this planet then the emphasis is on the artistic side, and if this planet is Saturn than organizational acumen is seen and so forth. The two signs and houses occupied by Ketu and its dispositor in a nativity are the key to unravelling the talents, aptitudes and basic nature of the individual involved.

Also the relationship (through aspect or sign positioning) between the two karmic control planets usually defines the way the native will progress in the present life. If a strong relationship between these two planets exists in a nativity than a sort of extreme fatedness is associated with the life of the native involved.

Just like *Lal Kitab* relates Rahu with the combination of Venus and Jupiter, it relates Ketu with the conjunction of Mars and Saturn. This relates to the fact that Ketu acts as a bridge between the seemingly conflicting energies of Mars and Saturn. This is why balancing the signification relating to where Ketu is placed in a chart is akin to balancing the energies of Mars conjunct Saturn. One has to mix aggression with caution, action with patience, impulse with restraint for good results in the areas under Ketu's influence

SIGNIFICATIONS

To begin with, I must say, the majority of Rahu's significations that were discussed earlier can be applied to Ketu as well. Ketu shares most of the base significations of Rahu when it is working through its lower principle including criminal activities, distortion of other planet's energies and so on.

As far as criminal activities are concerned, Ketu represents most of those attributed to Rahu. In addition, it also represents the cases when an innocent is accused or pronounced guilty of a crime he/she had no involvement in. All sorts of tragedies where innocents suffer due to machinations of others or plain injustices involve Ketu at some level.

Most of the drastic and sometimes criminal actions one indulges in due to either an extreme burst of anger or just plain simple circumstance can be attributed to Ketu. Ketu thus represents all the "victims of circumstance". Rahu as we know is much more calculative and conscious when involved in such things.

Geographically Ketu represents all the extreme and inhospitable environments, but being a hot dry planet it prefers equatorial deserts like the Sahara. All the explorations and adventures, which involve such regions, can be considered to be significations of Ketu.

Ketu signifies all the uncultivable land. It also represents all the land occupied by cemeteries, sanctuaries, prisons etc.

Among the directions Ketu represents the Northwest along with the Moon. This means that the northwest part of almost everything from a house to a country relates to Ketu on some level. It is interesting to note that the north-western part of India is a desert known as the *Thar* Desert. The north-western part of the North American continent is Alaska, an inhospitable icy desert! It is useful to note that in a chart the 5th and 6th houses correspond to this direction.

Ketu is also seen to have an influence on the southwestern direction along with Rahu. Some seers are of the opinion that Ketu exerts influence in all the directions.

I have found this to be true to some extent, but for all practical purposes Ketu can be seen to represent the South of everything (along with Mars). For example, the geographical South Pole will come under the influence of Ketu. Similarly Rahu can be seen to represent the North of everything (along with Mercury). Consequently, the geographical North Pole will come under the influence of Rahu.

Ketu represents the ascetic energy, which makes one retreat into the forest and wilderness. It is also a big city dweller when working through its materialistic aspect. Sometimes it also makes the philosophically oriented live in a big city just to fulfil their karma or witness the chaos that pervades there.

Ketu is even more closely related to the reptilian kingdom than Rahu. Its favourite creatures are all types of lizards, spiders, scorpions and snakes. Some seers are of the opinion that only Ketu and not Rahu represents snakes. There is also a theory that those under prominent influence of Rahu are in fact afraid of snakes.

In my view both Rahu and Ketu represent snakes but Ketu has a slight edge as it represents the hood part of snakes. This means that it is a stronger significator of snakebite and poisons than Rahu. So along with Rahu it is related to all the modern day industries involving poisonous substances.

Ketu has a snake hood as its head and represents the act of biting, which has injecting of poison as its purpose. Thus it represents all activities like vaccination or giving shots where poison is injected into the body.

Ketu is especially related to the vocations involving the use of animal skin. This is especially true when the skins are those of reptiles and sea/aquatic creatures. The leather and fur industry and all the people involved in them can be said to be utilizing Ketu's energy.

Among the land mammals Ketu is most closely connected with dogs. This can be seen from the fact that Ketu rules over the sense of smell and dogs have the strongest sense of smell. According to recent research dogs can discern and locate diseases in human beings using their sense of smell. Dogs were even used by NASA to find out whether the rocks brought from Mars contained foreign life forms or not. According to one theory dogs recognize the smell of every living creature on our planet.

All the ancient cultures are unanimous about the fact that dogs had the power to see spirits and other creatures of the astral realm. As we know this astral sensitivity is a Ketu attribute. We'll discuss Ketu's relationship with dogs in detail in Chapter 6.

Ketu also rules over the strange fishes and creatures residing in the oceans like the octopus, sea horses, starfishes, electric eels, and all the light emanating creatures. Among insects Ketu relates specifically to the firefly even though Ketu connects with the entire insect kingdom. Cockroaches, which are supposed to be the creatures that can survive any sort of cataclysm can be categorised as a Ketu creature.

Among flying creatures Ketu has a special affinity with bats. As we know birds fall under Rahu's domain but bats are not exactly birds. Bats have a lot of mystery attached to them and any creature with mystery attached to it will fall under Ketu's domain.

The Eagle which is an esoteric symbol for the higher functionings of the sign Scorpio has a strong connection with Ketu. The eagle is symbolic of Ketu working through its higher principle. It can kill snakes, which in a way represent Ketu's lower functioning. The legendary bird *Phoenix*, which is known by different names in different cultures, is another symbol of Ketu. In legend it is the bird, which tried to reach the sun and got burnt, like the story of *Icarus* in Greek mythology. Phoenix is the bird, which rises from the ashes of Icarus. It thus signifies the regeneration principle inherent in Ketu, which tells us that there is always a new beginning after an end.

Ketu represents all the scavengers and parasites in the animal kingdom. As such it relates to hyenas, vultures, fleas, ticks, tapeworms and all such creatures. As mentioned earlier Ketu has a strong connection with vultures, as the vulture is supposed to be its vehicle. Ketu also signifies all the desert creatures like camels, rodents and reptiles.

In Vedic astrology a male goat is considered a special significator of Ketu. Vedic wisdom also relates Ketu with *Kasturi*, a very strongly scented external organ that some deers possess. It is supposed to have the sweetest smell among the natural fragrances. On the other hand Ketu represents creatures with a very strong noxious smell like skunks.

Among the foods Ketu is a special significator of horse gram. Among the cereals it has a strong connection with rye and barley. A special mixture of seven cereals made in rural India called *Satnaja* (seven cereals) is considered a special signification of Ketu. It also signifies groundnuts and other such foods that grow below the surface - all the root foods including potatoes, yams, radishes, carrots etc.

It is the significator of all types of oils, natural and synthetic. Among the oils it has a special affinity with castor oil. Vedic astrology assigns sesame seeds as a special significator of Ketu. Ketu along with Sun, Mars and Jupiter rules over the foods which produce heat in the body like almonds, cashew nuts, walnuts, ginger and saffron etc.

Ketu is the significator of the coconut tree and all the products made from it. Many of the people living in small islands and coastal areas are completely dependent upon the coconut tree for their survival, thus revealing Ketu's hold over them. Ketu being the desert planet rules over all the desert foods like dates. All the tasteless and bland foods, herbs and drinks fall under Ketu's domain.

Among the plant kingdom Ketu signifies all the desert plants like cactus, deep-sea plants like seaweed and plants with earth tones/ light brownish coloured flowers. It rules over all the parasitic plants like ivy. Ketu has an influence over all hallucinogenic plants like hemp, peyote, poppies, mushrooms etc. All types of fungus fall under Ketu's domain. Ketu rules over all strange and exotic plants like the *Pandanus* Tree. Ketu is said to have a special affinity with *kusha*, a type of grass.

Among clothes Ketu represents all dirty and worn out clothes. Ketu is a special significator of clothes with holes in them. These days such clothes are intentionally made as a fashion statement. Ketu also represents clothing with its colours, which are described in the earlier section dealing with Ketu's appearance. Ketu is more strongly related to clothes worn above the waist as opposed to Rahu, which governs clothes worn below the waist. Ketu relates to all types of waistbands.

Ketu represents all types of ascetic robes and saffron coloured clothing, which is symbolic of renunciation. On the other hand Ketu represents all types of eccentric and multi- coloured clothing. Clothes with stripes or checks are special Ketu significations. In fact they are said to allow Ketu to see. Ketu as we know is just a tail with a serpent's head and can thus be considered blind. Ketu being the planet ruling over animal skins represents all types of leather and fur clothing.

Among ornaments Ketu rules nose rings and earrings. Piercing of ears and nose is a process closely related to Ketu. Ketu's functioning in a chart can be judged by seeing if the above-mentioned processes are smooth or give rise to complications like infections. We shall discuss this further in Chapter 15.

Ketu relates to all ornaments made from the metals and gemstones it rules over. It primarily rules óver Iron and all the alloys made from it. It is a special significator of a special type of alloy made by combining eight different types of metals known as *Ashtudhatu* (eight metals). According to Vedic astrology all rings and totems made for propitiating Ketu are supposed to be made from this alloy.

Among the gemstones *Cat's-Eye* or chrysoberyl is most closely related to Ketu. Turquoise, lapis lazuli and tiger's eye are also categorized as Ketu's gemstones. Turquoise is a gemstone that was extensively used by all the ancient cultures, which strongly related it with the occult. Lapis Lazuli is known to keep one free from influence of negative astral entities like spirits etc.

Ketu is a tribal planet and thus represents all the surviving indigenous tribal cultures and peoples including the Native American Indians and Australian Aborigines. In fact Ketu represents all the so-called primitive cultures and people. This is a classic case, which brings out the conflicting sides of the nodes. Rahu represents the modern culture and civilizations with materialistic expansion as their main motive, while Ketu represents ancient and primitive cultures focused on spiritualistic living in harmony with nature.

Ketu is the planet symbolising innocence and thus rules over children, only up till the age they lose their innocence, which varies from individual to individual. Ketu represents old people usually above the age of sixty-nine.

Among family relations Ketu represents the maternal grandfather and paternal grandmother. It is also the significator of the mother's ancestral family. As we can see Ketu completes the ancestral picture along with Rahu. The implications of this are discussed in the Genetics and Reincarnation Chapter.

According to the dictums of *Lal Kitab* Ketu also represents male progeny. I have seen this dictum to work perfectly in a number of charts. A strong Ketu is a precondition for having worthwhile male progeny which one can derive pleasure from.

Ketu represents all homeless, destitute, dispossessed, down and out members of society. Just like Rahu, Vedic Astrology assigns the *mlechha* (outcaste) status to Ketu. In the snobbishly puritanical medieval times it represented foreigners and outcastes. The term outcast in modern times can be translated into one having no money, an outlaw or a misfit in society. It also represents amputees and especially relates to people with one or both hands missing. As per Vedic Astrology Ketu along with Rahu is the significator of all types of bad company.

Ketu is the planet representing sudden gain or loss. All the extreme events like paupers becoming kings and kings becoming paupers can be ascribed to Ketu. One must remember that Saturn also can give the same result but with Ketu such events happen very quickly, while with Saturn they happen slowly over a period of time.

Just as Rahu signifies our exploration of the deep space Ketu signifies our exploration of the sub-atomic realm. Ketu is thus the significator of the quantum physics with all its probabilities and uncertainties. It is no surprise that all the known physical laws are dissolved when dealing with the realm of the infinitely small.

Ketu also has a deep relationship with Biology especially in the area of genetics. Ketu can be seen as the carbon atom, which is the basic building block of all organic life. Thus it is related to organic chemistry and all its offshoots like the carbon fibre, fibreglass and plastic industry.

Among the planets Ketu is the sole significator of the world of micro-organisms. Micro-organisms are the most primitive forms of life - in fact they are the first in the evolutionary chain of the emergence of life. Ketu as we know is a planet of beginnings. Ketu rules over all the oceanic micro-organisms like blue green algae etc. Ketu as we will find out later is the co ruler of the sign representing the ocean, Pisces.

Recently there has been a lot of research on how the sea algae's are an excellent food for humans and could solve the world's food problem. One can say that Ketu's energies are involved in propagating these studies.

We can see that Ketu represents all the small creatures in tune with its contracting nature while Rahu represents big creatures like elephants (the biggest land animal in the present) in tune with its expansive nature.

In the micro-organisms category we find the organisms responsible for most of the present day diseases - viruses and bacteria. Viruses as we know have baffled biologists for long, as they show both living and non-living characteristics. In fact they can be said to be on the borderline between living and non-living. This doesn't surprise us astrologers, as anything to do with Ketu has to have a bit of mystery! It follows that Ketu represents most of the viral and bacterial infections. Such diseases are so numerous that it is not possible to list them here. We can say that most of the diseases, which are infectious, are related to either Rahu or Ketu.

Ketu is usually the cause behind mass epidemics like Cholera, which was appropriately named Black Death after it decimated a quarter of Europe's population in the 15th century. Any disease, which assumes epidemic proportions, has Ketu working behind the scenes. AIDS is one such present day disease, which is very much a Ketu signification.

Ketu is also the cause behind many of the disorders arising from an imbalance of the *pitta* (heat element) in the body. Wounds, fevers, cuts, rashes, boils, indigestion, and other inflammatory conditions can be attributed to Ketu along with Sun and Mars. Since Ketu is the significator of worms the conditions like intestinal worms are also Ketu significations.

Ketu as discussed earlier is the significator of fungii and so all types of fungal infections and diseases caused by fungus poisoning are related to Ketu. *Ergot*, a fungus which mainly affects Ketu cereals, rye and barley, is full of poisonous and hallucinogenic chemicals. The famous drug of the sixties, LSD, is derived from this fungus. Recent research has shown that it was the cause behind the sudden epidemics, which involved hallucinatory states followed by death, recorded in certain regions of Europe and America over the last 500 years. The famous Salem witch hunt in the small township of Salem in America in which hundreds of innocent women were executed on the charges of practising witchcraft was a direct result of one such epidemic. Obviously the residents didn't know that it was the fungus and not witchcraft which was causing the epidemic. It is interesting to note that both of them are Ketu significations and so is slaughter of innocent people.

Ketu being the significator of the sense of smell directly relates to a highly developed or completely absent sense of smell. Since Dog is a special signification of Ketu, it follows that dog-bite is also an event falling in Ketu's domain. Rabies, an incurable disease that can result through dog bite also becomes a Ketu signification.

The ancients saw Ketu as the planet signifying all hidden treasures. It is generally seen that snakes accompany any treasure buried in the earth. Ketu thus represents all the treasure hunters of past and present. In the present times Ketu also signifies the search for petroleum, minerals, metals and other such modern day treasures.

Ketu also represents the persons involved in searching for underground water in dry landscapes. Ketu being related with the core of everything, relates to the sciences trying to understand the core of earth. It signifies all the people involved in sciences like geology and anthropology.

To sum it all up Ketu is related with all types of underground research and exploration. Rahu on the other hand is more involved with atmospheric, space studies and exploration.

Ketu is the planet representing the past and thus it represents all the people and vocations involved with the past in some way. Historians, antique dealers, archaeologists, art restorers etc. can be said to be under strong Ketu influence. Institutions dealing with the past such as museums are also a Ketu signification.

Ketu has a strong connection with the law and lawyers if it is sharing its influence with the sixth house or Mars. It has a strong fascination for getting to the truth of any matter. It is also the planet which Vedic Astrology describes as the one causing harm to enemies, which is what litigation is all about in the majority of cases.

Ketu as we know likes to deal with events that have already happened i.e. the past events. Thus it has a strong influence over people involved in crime solving professions like detectives, forensic experts etc.

Rahu as mentioned earlier rules over Secret Service Institutions. Ketu is the planet, which is more interested in uncovering the secrets of these institutions. Ketu is thus more of a spy planet. Consequently it represents all the institutions and persons involved in such activities.

Ketu is related to all types of institutions and people involved in the insurance business. We know insurance is an eighth house affair and involves Saturn. Ketu's association with either involves a native with insurance in one form or other. Ketu along with Saturn and the twelfth house also signifies all types of taxes. It represents those working in the income tax departments and also those who get caught in tax frauds.

All types of deep sea and underwater diving can be said to be a Ketu signification even though the energies of the planets Moon and Neptune are also involved. Ketu as we will find out later is the coruler of Pisces, the sign of the oceans. Any type of marine research especially the kind carried out at extreme depths involves Ketu's energies. As we discussed earlier, Ketu represents the creatures, which can survive in these extreme conditions. Pearl diving is another such profession where Ketu is involved along with the Moon.

Just like Rahu, Ketu represents both sides of the coin. For example it represents poachers and on the other hand represents the forest guards. Similarly it also represents the people having psychological problems and the psychologist who deals with them. In ancient times, psychology was a part of astrology, which as we will find later is intimately connected with Ketu. Which side of the coin Ketu will function from can usually be judged from its placement and the overall inclination of the chart.

We can see that Ketu shares some of its vocational significations with Rahu. In an individual chart the best way to see which among them is giving the particular vocation common to both, is that Rahu's energy would be behind it if it is very gainful in material terms. Ketu on the other hand just about gives enough for subsistence through its occupations.

Since Ketu is a fiery planet it has a lot to do with all types of fire accidents along with Sun and Mars. Again it is related with the negligent or intentional fire starter, and also the fire fighters. Ketu is connected with the fire departments all around the world.

Ketu is also related with all the fiery activities of nature like volcanic eruptions. As we know volcanic eruptions spew out a lot of ash, which is another of Ketu's significations. In India the ascetics spew ash around their body as a symbol of renunciation, which as we discussed earlier falls under Ketu's domain.

Ketu is a planet signifying all types of catastrophes. It is the planet of retribution and thus represents nature's destructive aspect. All major catastrophes like an asteroid hitting earth and eliminating the dinosaurs within a very short space of time can be called Ketu events. Earthquakes, volcanic eruptions, tidal waves, meteor/asteroid/comet impacts are all examples of Ketu's energy at work.

Vedic wisdom reveals a deep connection between Ketu and comets. Comets are considered to be the children of Ketu and are referred to as *Dhumketu's* (Explosive sons of Ketu). The fact that the appearance of the comets is very Ketu-like with their large tail gives weight to this theory. Comets have been considered as omens of approaching catastrophes or cataclysms - both Ketu significations, in most of the ancient cultures.

Ketu rules all types of geological disturbances in general as it is the planet signifying the activities beneath the earth's surface. One must remember though that Pluto's energy is involved in all the above-mentioned phenomena. Ketu and Pluto as we would find later in this chapter are the corulers of the sign governing destruction and regeneration, Scorpio.

Keeping on with the retribution theme, we find that if Rahu represents indulgent behaviour like taking drugs, then Ketu represents the rehabilitation time. Ketu is thus connected with all types of rehabilitation institutions.

Ketu is a restrictive confining planet, when it is making one pay for one's actions and consequently rules over prisons along with Saturn. Orphanages, penitentiaries and other such institutions for helping the unfortunate among us, paying for their previous life karmas, are also related with Ketu. Ketu being the planet most closely associated with the term 'madness' has a strong connection with asylums.

As we discussed earlier Ketu has a religious side to it in much the same way as Jupiter and Sun, and so it signifies all places of religious or occult significance. This aspect of Ketu is discussed further in the chapter dealin ᵞ with the esoteric significations of the nodes.

Ketu being the planet d aling with the phenomenon of death on the material plane, has a strong influence on places like cemeteries, graveyards, and burial grounds. As we know it is the planet signifying the past and so all the ancient or historic monuments, structures and places, like the Pyramids, Stonehenge, and Easter Island etc. are Ketu significations. In fact Ketu is the significator of any place, thing or structure with some sort of mystery attached to it.

Continuing with this theme Ketu is the repository of the secrets and mysteries concealed in the Universal Mind. As we know it is the planet of beginnings and is directly related to the beginning of Creation. It thus deals with subjects like Astrology, which come into being along with the creation of the manifested universe. Among all the planets, inner and outer, Ketu is most intimately connected

LET'S GET TO KNOW THEM

with Astrology - the most universal among the sciences. Its presiding deity as per Vedic traditions *Ganesha* (the elephant headed first born son of nature), is considered the foremost among seers and astrologers. He is in fact custodian of all astrological knowledge. I would deal with the relationship between Ketu and its deity in the chapter dealing with the esoteric significance of the nodes.

Being a planet signifying all types of esoteric knowledge, Ketu governs all the arcane subjects like occult, magic and alchemy etc. Since it is also the significator of our psychic faculties it is the significator of phenomena like telepathy, hypnotism etc. Ketu pretty much embodies all the areas covered by the phrase "sixth sense". It represents psychics, tarot card readers, hypnotists and all other people involved in similar professions. Being the planet representing the past it is a special significator of 'past life regression' and all the people who explore this realm.

Ketu is especially related to an Indian sect known as the '*Aghoras*'. They usually stay in cemeteries and in some cases are known to eat the human flesh out of the unburnt remains of the funeral pyres as part of their rituals. *Robert Svoboba* has made this sect quite famous through his books like '*Aghora* - The Left Hand Path of God'. Ketu is a strong significator of all the paths that lead to attaining transcendental knowledge, but it seems to have a slight bias towards the '*tantric*' or the left hand path.

Ketu can be said to be the significator of all such strange sects all over the world. All the modern sects like *Heaven's Gate*, where the members finally end up doing a mass suicide, are usually under a strong influence of Ketu.

Along with the Sun, Ketu is the planet directly related to our attention, the greatest gift we possess. It is thus the planet representing the level of our insight, discernment and awareness. A strong Ketu in a chart gives all these qualities in good measure, and thus is the main energy behind the visionary power of the prophets and seers of past and present.

Ketu is an intuitive, psychic force, which can connect us with both the lower and higher realms of existence, beyond the material plane. It is not without reason that Ketu is considered the strongest amongst planets including the Sun. It is the most penetrative force, which can connect us with the divine spark present in each one of us. Ketu symbolises the root of everything - the Creation - Universal Mind - Existence and last but not least Ourselves.

Vedic Astrology thus related the practice of *Yoga* with Ketu. Yoga is nothing but a way to speed up one's evolutionary process. Yoga can be said to be a short cut on the evolutionary path. The final aim of yoga is liberation from the cycles of birth and death, which as we know is a Ketu signification. Saturn is the planet, which can cut bonds and attachments, but Ketu is the only planet that can cut them completely so that liberation becomes possible.

In a way Ketu is a bestower of liberation to everyone when the manifest universe is dissolved and all the souls merge with the Eternal and Absolute. Only Ketu is privy to the wisdom that there is nothing like final liberation. Even those souls who attain liberation in one cycle may have to take birth in the next creation.

Ketu is a representation of a cosmic force, which represents the beginning and ending of the drama of existence. We are free to term it demoniac, malefic or evil or whatever we wish, but the fact remains that this force is nothing but a display of all possibilities and extremes within the realm of existence. It is in fact a very benefic force without which it is impossible for us to go beyond space and time and the cycle of birth and death.

RULERSHIP, EXALTATION, DEBILITATION & MOOLATRIKONA

This is again a controversial territory as many views abound as to the sign rulership of Ketu. The Western system refuses to assign Ketu the rulership of any sign. In Vedic Astrology different systems assign Ketu different signs as regards to rulership, exaltation and debilitation.

Before we delve into establishing the rulership, exaltation and debilitation signs of Ketu let's consider the relationship Ketu has with the other planets -

It is friends with Mars and Jupiter.
It is neutral towards Saturn, Mercury and Venus.
It is the enemy of Sun and Moon.

It is important to note that Ketu is more inimical to Moon as compared to Sun.

Ancient Vedic seers see Ketu as very similar in nature to Mars. If Ketu had to be a co-ruler of any sign it had to be one of the Martian signs, Aries or Scorpio. The choice between them is difficult to make as Ketu relates to both fire and water elements.

It can be seen that Ketu shares a lot of characteristics with the sign Aries like beginnings, fieriness, eccentricity, childishness, single-minded approach etc., but the sage *Parashara*, whose works pretty much define present day Vedic Astrology, assigns Ketu the co-rulership of Scorpio. In my view this is the right choice as there are a lot of factors to back it up.

Even Western astrologers realized that there was more to Scorpio than just Mars. To account for that gap they assigned Pluto the co-rulership of Aquarius. We have already discussed the similarities between the nature and significations of Ketu and Pluto. The nature of the sign Scorpio aligns perfectly with these planets.

The smoky colour related with Ketu is very similar to smoky/black colour attached with the sign Scorpio. According to *Puranic* scriptures, *Rudra* (the terrible form of Shiva), the deity governing Scorpio is supposed to have a smoky/black colour and has a serpent wrapped around his neck. These two characteristics establish his relationship with the serpent power associated with Ketu even though there are many other similarities in the realm of inner nature and disposition.

Ketu as we have discussed earlier is the planet governing endings. There is no doubt as to Scorpio being the sign of destruction and regeneration. Ketu like Scorpio is privy to the secrets and mysteries of nature's functionings. Scorpio is a negating sign representing wisdom inherent in the past, in the same sense that the 8th house represents past in a chart.

The philosophical, intensely penetrative and liberating influence of Scorpio when it is functioning through its higher aspect is also very in tune with Ketu's disposition in its higher aspect. Ketu as we may recall is the force that attempts to break down all types of conditioning to usher in a feeling of oneness with the universe, which in a sense embodies the spirit of the sign Scorpio.

Because of its co-rulership of Scorpio, Ketu is supposed to be a Yogakaraka (a favourable and important planet) for Cancer, Scorpio, Aquarius and Pisces Ascendants. This is due to the fact that for these Ascendants the sign Scorpio falls in important houses like the first, fifth, ninth and tenth.

Within Scorpio, Ketu is stronger when placed in the following degrees; 16°40' - 20°, 20° - 23°20'. It is strongest at 16°40' - 20°. The reasons behind this assigning of degrees will be explained in the next chapter dealing with Nakshatras and the Navamsha chart.

The physical characteristics of Ketu also find their true expression through the natives born with Scorpio rising on the Ascendant. The famous American poet and singer Jim Morrison, whose chart is discussed in detail in the next chapter, is a very good example for understanding the physical characteristics of the Ketu vis-à-vis Scorpio Ascendant.

Scorpio is a fixed water sign and thus can be compared with solid water. Ice is a good example of solidified water and Ketu definitely has ice-like crystallization qualities and a fixidity of approach similar to Scorpio.

Pisces is another sign where something seems to be missing, as the rulership of Jupiter does not cover all the subtleties involved in this sign. Western astrologers having realized this, assigned Neptune the co-rulership of Pisces.

What some ancient Vedic seers did was assign to Ketu the co-rulership of Pisces. In my view this holds true as well. Sage Parashara also agrees with this by stating that some wise men give Ketu, the co-rulership of Pisces.

Within Pisces, Ketu is stronger when placed in the following degrees; 13°20' - 16°40', 16°40' - 20°, 26°40' - 30°. It is strongest at 16°40' - 20°.

There are again some indications that help us understand why some wise men think that Ketu should be the co-ruler of Pisces. As mentioned earlier Ketu has water as its secondary element, which goes well with the watery nature of Pisces.

My personal theory is that Ketu connects to humanity through Pisces and to the earth through Scorpio. However, the most important indication comes through the similarity in nature and disposition between Jupiter and Ketu.

As discussed earlier Ketu shares colours, qualities and other attributes with Jupiter. Significations of Pisces like endings, intuition, receptivity, negation, seclusion, destiny, past lives, karmic retribution, escapism, losses, expenses, charity, limitation, imprisonment, connectivity with subtle planes, fantasy, paranoia, subconscious mind, dreams, visions, sorrow, renunciation, liberation etc. seem to strike a chord with Ketu.

Ketu's rulership of Pisces completes a full circle as Rahu rules Aquarius the sign preceding Pisces. As we know the signs Aquarius and Pisces represent the highest aspirations of humanity. They are the signs representing knowledge, enlightenment and liberation. It is appropriate that the nodes, which symbolize the same, should be intimately connected with the last two signs of the zodiac.

As far as exaltation/debilitation of Ketu is concerned, many views abound which give Ketu exaltation in Aries, Gemini, Virgo, Scorpio, Sagittarius and Pisces. Among these I prefer the view, which takes Sagittarius to be Ketu's exaltation sign.

There are several reasons for this. First and foremost is that Ketu likes being in Jupiter's signs as Jupiter is the only planet, which Ketu respects. As discussed earlier Ketu's bad influence is only mitigated by aspect from Jupiter. As we have seen it is co-ruler of Pisces, one of Jupiter's signs. That leaves us with Sagittarius, a fiery sign in tune with Ketu's fiery nature.

The operating field of Sagittarius - pilgrimages, philosophy, religion, inner life, ethical disposition, higher mind, initiation, self realization - is perfectly suited to Ketu's higher functionings. Moreover the optimistic disposition of Sagittarius helps tone down the negative, pessimistic and constricting side of Ketu.

Another important reason relates to the constellations or asterisms Ketu presides over. As discussed earlier, in Vedic astrology the twelve signs are divided into twenty-seven equal parts known as *Nakshatras* (asterisms). These asterisms are basically different constellations that lie close to the belt of the Zodiac. Each of the nine planets (including Rahu and Ketu) has been assigned rulership over three of these asterisms.

Among them the ones governed by Ketu are known as *Ashwini* (a-Arietes), *Magha* (Regulus) and *Mula* (á-Sagittari). They fall in the signs of Aries, Leo and Sagittarius respectively. This is why Ketu has added affinity with these three signs. This is also the reason why Ketu shares a lot of its qualities with the ruler of these signs - Mars, Sun and Jupiter. These asterisms would be discussed in detail in the next chapter.

It can be seen that most of the planets are exalted only in signs, which contain at least a part of the asterism ruled by them. For example Sun is exalted in Aries, a sign that contains *Krittika* (Pleiades), an asterism represented by Sun himself. Now since Ketu can not be exalted in the sign of its enemy Sun we are left with only two options - Aries and Sagittarius.

Ketu functions well in Aries but considering that it is more benevolent in Jupiterian signs I would give Sagittarius as the exaltation sign of Ketu. Sage *Parashara* partly agrees with this in the sense that he assigns Sagittarius as the *moolatrikona* sign of Ketu.

Within Sagittarius, Ketu is stronger when placed in the following degrees; 0° - 3°20', 23°20' - 26°40', 26°40' - 30°. It is strongest at 0° - 3°20'.

This automatically means that Gemini is the debilitation sign for Ketu. Barring childishness, Ketu has very little in common with the airy, dual, playful, communicative, exploring nature of Gemini.

However Ketu when placed in Gemini helps the native resolve the dualities of life when working through its higher aspect. It is seen that Ketu usually doesn't create too much havoc when placed in Mercury's signs.

In my view <u>Aries is the *moolatrikona*</u> (next best to exaltation) sign of Ketu. Aries as we know just about loses the race to Sagittarius for becoming the exaltation sign of Ketu. Some scholars even take Ketu to be the co-ruler of Aries.

Within Aries, Ketu is stronger when placed in the following degrees; 0° - 3°20', 23°20' - 26°40', 26°40' - 30°. It is strongest at 0° - 3°20'.

As a final note we can say that Ketu is strong in the signs of Aries, Scorpio, Sagittarius and Pisces. In some cases Ketu is seen to be strong when placed in Leo, especially when aspected by Jupiter. One mustn't forget that like all other planets the nodes can work through their higher aspect through all the signs. The above-mentioned indications are only for ascertaining the strength of their influence in a particular nativity.

ASPECTS

The aspects of Ketu are similar to Rahu. We will however go through them again for your convenience.

For reasons discussed in the section dealing with Rahu's aspects, it is generally seen that the conjunction (same sign) and trine (fifth/ninth) aspects are the ones that are most important for Ketu when one is dealing with the associations of Ketu with other planets. The aspects are applicable no matter what degrees the planets are occupying in the respective signs and thus no particular orb needs to be defined.

This means that if in a nativity, Ketu is in Aries and Mars is in Sagittarius, then Ketu will be considered to be in trinal relationship with Mars no matter at what degrees they are placed in their respective signs. However it is helpful to remember that the aspects usually have more significance if they have smaller orbs. A 5° orb usually gives the full results of the aspect or conjunction.

When relating Ketu with the houses it is again experienced that only the conjunction and the trine aspects retain significance. For example, if Ketu were placed in the fourth house it would basically influence the affairs of the fourth, eighth and twelfth houses only.

As is the case with all other planets Ketu's influence is enhanced when it is placed very close to the midpoints of the houses especially the important points like the Midheavan and the Ascendant. Ketu's influence is also increased when it is placed very close to any planet, especially the luminaries.

MOTION & MODE OF FUNCTIONING

The nodes have a permanent retrograde motion and so Ketu always moving backwards through the zodiac from Aries to Pisces and so on. Ketu like Rahu is one of the slow moving planets and completes one round of the zodiac in around 18 months. The speed is the same as that for Rahu - around 3' per solar day.

One interesting facet of Vedic astrology is the assigning of a vehicle to every planet. The speed and the nature of the motion of this vehicle, which usually is an animal, signify the way the planet involved will impart its results. The speed of the manifestation of results of different planets varies and can be interpreted through the speed of its vehicle.

Ketu is assigned the Vulture, the king of the scavengers as its vehicle. There are esoteric reasons behind this assigning, which will be dealt with in a later section. As is common knowledge, vultures just laze around sitting on top of trees for better part of the day. Ketu also behaves lazily and in most cases delays manifestation of its results in a nativity. It can give lethargy and idleness when strongly influencing a native.

Vultures use their strong sense of smell to locate their food. Sense of smell as we know is a Ketu signification. The way vultures actually descend on a carcass in a group and go about eating their prey is representative of the way Ketu acts when given the opportunity to do so in a native's life.

In some mythological texts Ketu is said to ride a snake. Snake is again a very lazy creature that can hibernate for months on end. Snake, when he is hunting, uses the technique of stealthily coming up from behind and pouncing on its prey with a sudden quick burst of speed. Since Ketu has a snake hood as its head, this is exactly the way Ketu imparts its results whenever it decides to.

Its results both good and bad manifest in such an unexpected and sudden manner that the native involved hardly has any time to react to the situation. There is no equal of Ketu among the planets for giving quick and sudden results. Coming up from behind signifies that the native is usually caught unawares by an event, when Ketu perpetuates it. Unlike Rahu, Ketu usually achieves his goal for a particular chart through a single event rather than a series of events just like a snake bites its prey only a single time.

Another interesting key to the secrets of Ketu's functioning is provided by an alternative astrological work known as *Lal Kitab*, which translates into -'The Red Book'. As discussed earlier it relates Ketu with dogs, which in my view reveals a lot as to the way Ketu functions when it is in its *rajasic* (materially active) mode.

The dog is a hyperactive animal with a short life span. It corresponds well with Ketu's short major period of 7 years (discussed in the next section). Even though it may sound offensive natives with a strong Ketu functioning in its worldly mode have many doglike qualities. They are loyal, restless, caring, affectionate and last but not the least, ever ready to bite. Ketu's tendency to give sharp quick results can be compared with a dog-bite.

The Red Book likens such a Ketu to being a loyal servant to its master (represented by Jupiter). In the third world countries most of the dogs are roaming around the street instead of living in houses as pets, so natives with such a Ketu are seen to have a habit of aimlessly roaming around. The roaming mystics and ascetics who are signified by Ketu functioning in its non-worldly mode are also roaming around, but their roaming has an underlying spiritual sensibility.

As discussed earlier the planets are assigned distances in Vedic astrology. Ketu represents a distance of 7 *Yojanas* (1 yojana- 5 to 9 miles). Ketu thus becomes the automatic significator of the journeys, which involve the above-mentioned distance.

TIMING

Vedic astrology assigns Ketu its own major period in which to show its results. The general characteristics of the major period of Ketu, which lasts 7 years and involve minor periods of other planets, are discussed in detail in the "Periods and Transits" section. Since it takes 120 years to cover all the major periods of all the planets and very few of us live that long, it is seen that many of us never experience Ketu's Major Period. One must remember that just like Rahu, Ketu has minor and sub-minor periods within the major and n_nor periods of other planets to show its results.

Within a year, every planet relates to a season. Ketu along with Sun and Mars is associated with the peak <u>summer season</u>, which generally falls in the months of May and June in the northern hemisphere.

As discussed in the section on Rahu, like all malefics, Ketu is stronger during *Dakshinayana* (northern residence of the Sun - 21st June to 22nd December).

Within a month Ketu is supposed to be strong on days when Moon is transiting the constellations governed by Ketu i.e. *Ashwini* (á-Arietes), *Magha* (Regulus) and *Mula* (á-Sagittari). This day should not be taken literally as one day in a solar month. This transit though usually around 24 hours in duration can be stretched over two solar days. For example if Moon enters the asterism of *Magha* at 14.00 hrs on say Thursday it will stay there till around 14.00 hrs on Friday.

Within a lunar month Ketu relates to *Chaturthi* or the fourth tithi, which corresponds to the forth lunar day in the waxing and waning cycle. Within a lunar fortnight Ketu is seen to be strong in *Krishna paksha*, the dark fortnight when Moon is waning.

Within a week, as mentioned earlier, every day is associated with a planet. There is again some confusion among Vedic astrologers relating to assigning Ketu co-rulership of the weekdays. My conclusion is that Ketu can be assigned <u>Tuesday</u> and <u>Thursday</u> as its days. It can be seen that this is not arbitrary as Ketu is very closely related to Mars and Jupiter and as discussed earlier it shares the rulership of signs with them.

In my view <u>Ketu is more strongly connected to Thursday</u>. This is because in the sequence of major periods, Ketu's major period is placed between those of Mercury and Venus. Therefore it is not very surprising that it should be connected with a day between Wednesday (Mercury's day) and Friday (Venus's day), which happens to be Thursday.

Within a day, Ketu's energies are seen to be strongest during sunrise and the couple of hours before sunrise. This is why the sunrise time is considered to have strong vibrations. In fact in Vedic culture this time is known as *Brahma Muhurata,* the time of the creator, gods and other divine beings. This is the time when the astral and causal realms are most accessible and thus it is considered the best time for prayer, meditation and other forms of contemplation. In modern Internet parlance this is the time when one can get the best connection!

Ketu like other malefic planets is also strong throughout the night time. It is seen that birth at any of these times often highlights the significance of Ketu in the life of a native.

In my experience I have seen that the results of Ketu like revelations, prophetic dreams, psychic intunements etc. occur mainly during the hours assigned to it. This is a good area of observation for all astrologers.

An important aspect of timing events in Vedic astrology is the assigning of a certain period of time in human life to every planet. This works on the theory that every planet matures at a certain age after which it can fully manifest its results. Rahu is supposed to mature in the 47th year. The period from <u>47 to 54 years</u> is considered the time when Ketu manifests its complete results in a nativity. For convenience's sake this period will be referred to as <u>Ketu-time</u> throughout this work.

It is seen that some natives have a sudden rise, fall or transformation when they reach this age. Even though not drastic in some cases but a change surely takes place in everybody's life in the 47th or 48th year. What exactly will happen depends upon the position of Ketu and the overall inclination of the nativity.

Forty-seven is the age when one is supposed to begin one's spiritual journey. It is interesting to note that 47 is twice of 23 and a half, the age which according to some systems represents the age when one, after completing one's education steps out into the world through establishing relationships. In short this can be said to be a sort of Libra time where the significations of the sign Libra gain precedence. 48th year is the beginning of what can be said to be Scorpio time. The significations of the eighth house and the sign Scorpio, like death, begin to take precedence at this age.

Again nature can never be bound by a set of rules and for some this happens after the age of 69. Sixty-nine as we discussed earlier is the age when Saturn and both the nodes become the most powerful operating influences. It must be kept in mind that for those who have materialistic placements of Saturn, Rahu & Ketu there is no spiritual inclination or transformation even at or after this age.

This time is in a way the revelation time, if one has prepared oneself for it by utilizing the Rahu time (42-47years) for separating oneself from the material world (seventh house activities), and is beginning to open up to other than material realities such as yoga, meditation or other self realization tools.

It is helpful to remember that in Vedic astrology the age from 45-50 is assigned to the fifth house. The fifth house as we know is an auspicious house relating to our spiritual unfoldment, gain of esoteric knowledge and self-realization. The period from 50 to 56 years is assigned to the sixth house that relates to the fact that we have to serve somebody or some cause while we are on earth. It is also beneficial to remember that the period ranging from 42nd to the 56th year is assigned to Mars.

Other important years when Ketu is more active relate to the transit of Ketu. Just like Rahu, Ketu returns to its original position in 18.2/3 years. Therefore the 19th, 38th, 57th, 76th years are also seen as Ketu's years. All these ages are supposed to bring out some churning and subsequent transformation.

Among these the 19th year is the most important, as it is what we can term as the first Ketu-return. This is the year when the reality of the outside world usually hits the sheltered and dreamy adolescent. For some this initiates a spiritual rebirth and for others it is just a passing phase of psychological turmoil. 57th year is an important year in the sense that one gets to experience joy or grief on account of one's male progeny. It is useful to note that Jupiter, which is the natural significator of progeny and their success, rules the time period 57-69 years.

SYMBOLS

The main symbols associated with Ketu are - a Flag fitted to a Pole, a Mace, the *Ouroborous* , the Arrow and the Swastika.

The Flag fitted on to a pole is the most important symbol of Ketu. As mentioned earlier some ancient seers called Ketu by the name *Dhwajah*, meaning the Flag. The flag out here can be seen as an emblem or symbol of divine authority. It represents the connection of Ketu with the divine intelligence. A person strongly influenced by Ketu always feels connected to some higher force, which directs their actions. A flag can thus be seen as a symbol of action without attachment, which leads one to liberation from the cycles of birth and death.

A flag can also be seen to represent increase. Ketu as we will discover later, multiplies the strength of a strong planet by a factor of four when placed in close conjunction with it.

The Mace is Ketu's weapon. It represents its destructive aspect in both lower and higher aspects. It is interesting to note that Ketu's presiding deity as per Vedic astrology, *Ganesha*, also carries a mace in his hand.

The *Ouroborous* as we have discussed earlier, is an ancient symbol representing the cyclic nature of time. It is related to both of the nodes. The symbol ℧ which is widely used these days to represent Ketu, can be seen as the other half of *Ouroborous* discussed earlier in Rahu's symbols' section. It is the lower or southern half of the complete circle of time. As mentioned earlier Ketu is associated with the South of everything. It can also be seen as the tail part of the circle thus representing Ketu, the tail.

Ketu is classified as a *jeeva* (live) planet and is thus connected with the live things. This classification is of use in *Prashna* or Horary Astrology. For example if someone is asking a question when Ketu is placed in the Ascendant of the chart of the moment, than one can conclude that it has to do with some person or some other personal issue involving live things.

The Arrow is another symbol related to Ketu. It is a basically a symbol of aims and desire. Ketu as we know represents the most basic primordial desire, which lead to the formation of the universe. An upward pointing arrow is a symbol of consciousness trying to aim for the highest goal, merging with the absolute source of everything. On a material plane it represents the desire to accomplish things for one's own personal benefit or for the benefit of all. It is interesting to note that the sign Sagittarius is symbolized by an upward pointing arrow. As we have seen earlier Ketu is exalted in Sagittarius and shares a lot of attributes with the 'sign of wisdom'.

As mentioned earlier these symbols are of much use in Palmistry. A flag, an arrow or a mace sign in the hand or the feet or any other part of the body is an indicator of the dominant role Ketu will play in the life of the native involved.

✳ ✳ ✳

4. NAKSHATRAS & NAVAMSHA

As discussed briefly in the last chapter, besides the signs, Vedic Astrology has another way of dividing the zodiac. It divides it into 27 equal parts of 13°20' each. These 27 parts are known as the 27 *Nakshatras*. The term Nakshatra can be interpreted as 'Asterism' or 'Lunar Constellation'. For convenience's sake we will be using either asterism or nakshatra throughout this book.

Each nakshatra corresponds to a star or group of stars lying around the ecliptic. For example the nakshatra known as *Krittika* corresponds to the star cluster *Pleiades*. Since Vedic astrology is based on the Sidereal Zodiac, what one sees in the sky translates directly into the chart of that particular moment. If one sees Moon close to Pleiades in the night sky one can say that Moon is in Krittika. The nakshatras are widely used in Vedic astrology for 'natal' as well as 'electional' interpretations.

Each of the 9 planets, including the nodes and excluding the outer planets (Uranus, Neptune and Pluto), are given rulership of 3 nakshatras. Since we are focussing on the nodes in this book we would just concentrate on the asterisms ruled by the nodes. In numerical order Ketu rules the 1st, 10th and 19th asterisms and Rahu rules the 6th, 15th and 24th asterisms. The nature and functionings of these asterisms gives one added insight into the functioning of the nodes.

KETU'S ASTERISMS

<u>ASHWINI</u> (0° - 13°20' Aries)

It consists of the two bright stars in the constellation of Aries, known in modern astronomy as β and γ Arietes.

Ashwini translates into "the Horsewoman". Its symbol is the Horse's Head. This emphasis on horse signifies constant physical and mental movement as the horse is an ancient symbol for movement and vitality. Its secondary symbol is a horse carriage, which further emphasises its need for movement. Its need for movement furthers a roaming and wandering type of disposition similar to that of a Ketu personality, of which a wandering ascetic is a good example. The materially oriented Ketu personalities who have abundant physical and mental vitality are also represented by this nakshatra. The body part it relates to are the knees, which again emphasize its movement aspect.

It is the first among the nakshatras, representing beginnings of all kinds, and relates to the initiatory impulse inherent in Ketu. As discussed earlier Ketu is the planet of beginnings and endings. One can see that this asterism connects Ketu with horses. It is no wonder then that Ketu is exalted in the sign most closely associated with the horse symbolism, Sagittarius. Since this asterism falls in Aries, a sign ruled by Mars, it highlights the Martian qualities of Ketu mentioned in the previous chapter. This asterism can be seen as a combination of the energies of Ketu and Mars.

Its presiding deities as per Vedic texts are the twins (corresponding to the two stars) known as *Ashvini Kumaras*, which translates into "the sons of the Horsewoman". They are the celestial physicians who roam around in a golden horse carriage attending to the needs of anyone needing help. This association conveys that healing and rejuvenation are one of the most important functions of this asterism. On a day to day level this may manifest as attending to other people's needs.

Ketu is a healing planet in many ways, and this aspect is brought out when it is placed in the sixth house or the sixth sign. This healing may relate to healing of physical or mental dysfunctions or some deep seated soul level healing which is directly related to one's past lives and karma. Among the planets, Ketu represents the power of the past to heal a person in the present. Ketu's power of rejuvenation and regeneration is akin to the Phoenix rising from the ashes. Ketu brings rejuvenation through destruction of old forms which have outlived their usefulness.

Its attributes - masculine, swift, godly, creative, earthy, *sattvic* - highlight the corresponding aspects of Ketu. As far as gender is concerned, it represents the male aspect of Ketu which is clear from its presiding deities being males.

Its swiftness relates to the quickness of Ketu in bestowing good and bad results which was discussed in the earlier chapter. Sometimes however this asterism can be too quick and impatient for its own good and "haste makes waste" axiom applies to the natives in whose charts it plays a prominent role.

It is a lively and happy go lucky nakshatra and represents the optimistic side of Ketu. Ketu has been regarded as the planet of doom and gloom by most astrologers, but this is not really the case. Ketu only brings into the present one's past karmas which are ripe enough to be experienced in the present life. They may be good, bad or neutral. The fact that Ketu is not always the constricting, negating and destructive force it is made out to be is revealed through this asterism. However just like Ketu it can create trouble through spirits, black magic and other dark occult practices in its negative aspect.

Its creativity corresponds to Ketu's primordial creative potential arising from the Will aspect of nature. One must remember that this creative force can sometimes be so strong and overwhelming that it becomes difficult to control or channel. This is when things go wrong with this asterism. Its downfall usually comes through attempting close to impossible feats without proper consideration. However when it succeeds it becomes the pioneer. This asterism has strong faith in magic and the dictum- "anything is possible". These are typical Ketu tendencies.

Its earthy quality relates to Ketu's power to give material

prosperity. It is a nakshatra which is favourable for traders and business people as it is auspicious for gains through travels.

Being a godly and *sattvic* nakshatra, it brings out the benign side of Ketu. Ketu is a very auspicious planet on both worldly and otherworldly planes when functioning through its higher principle. A planet which gives liberation from the cycles of birth and death has to be the most auspicious among planets. As we would discover in the chapter dealing with the esoteric significance of the nodes, Ketu's main deity is Lord Ganesha, who is supposed to be 'auspiciousness incarnate' and is worshipped before starting any important action.

MAGHA (0° - 13°20' Leo)

It is the 10th asterism and consists of a sickle shaped group of stars in the front of the constellation of Leo. *Regulus* (alpha-Leonis) also known as the 'Little King', one of the brightest stars in the night sky, is the principal star of this nakshatra. On a whole it is one of the brightest and biggest asterisms in the night sky.

Magha translates into 'the mighty', 'the great' or 'the bountiful'. Its main symbol is a royal chamber with a throne in it. This symbol is self- explanatory in the sense that this asterism has a lot to do with authority on all planes of existence. The fact that it is one of the brightest and biggest asterisms again points towards prominence, opulence and regality. The body organ it represents is the nose. This goes well with its nature as nose is associated with adjectives like 'high-nosed' etc.

A palanquin is another one of its symbols. A palanquin is different from a horse carriage, which is the symbol of Ashwini, in the sense that it is carried by humans instead of being driven by horses. This again signifies authority and regality. As we have seen in the last chapter, one of Ketu's main symbols is a Flag, which directly relates to authority, eminence, fame etc. This favoured position in the present life is earned due to meritorious past life deeds.

Ketu as we know is the guardian of our past karmas, and it releases the ones that are ripe enough to be experienced in the present life through this nakshatra. Whereever this nakshatra is placed in a chart one will experience the positive effects of one's past karmas. This may manifest as opportunities or favour from those in high positions. These favours are very sudden and based on impulse from those who bestow them.

Leo as we know is the sign of creativity and this nakshatra provides the opportunities for one to be creative. The qualities and attributes of Ketu like deep perception, penetrating insight and independent spirit, which are similar to that of Sun, are exhibited by this Nakshatra. Sun as we know is the royal planet but mostly we don't see Ketu in that light. This asterism brings out the regal side of Ketu. This asterism can be seen as a combination of Sun's and Ketu's energies.

The presiding deities of this nakshatra as per vedic texts are the *Pitris*, a term which translates into "the ancestors". Ancestor worship is a norm in all the surviving ancient cultures and civilizations. The reason for this lies in the simple fact now discovered by modern science that we get our genetic code from our ancestors. Within our genetic code lie our talents and propensities.

In a way we are all indebted to our ancestors for providing us our tools for the present life without asking for anything in return. Ketu as we have discussed earlier, is a genetic planet and represents the paternal grandfather and maternal grandmother in a chart. Our connection with our ancestors has to do alot with our past lives which is again a Ketu domain. To sum it up Magha has a lot to do with the genetic and past heritage aspect of Ketu. It also relates to Ketu's facet responsible for bringing in the wisdom of the ancient ages and civilizations into the present.

Its attributes - feminine, fierce, human, sustaining, watery, *rajasic* (materially active) - highlight the corresponding aspects of Ketu. Just like Ashvini represents the male aspect of Ketu, Magha represents the female aspect of Ketu.

Its fierceness corresponds to the fierce aspect of Ketu which is akin to the fierce aspect of Sun. As discussed earlier Ketu is the most fierce among planets. It can be as fierce as the mid-summer, midafternoon desert Sun. Fierceness as we know is also associated with authority at some level. Authority can either foster magnanimity or produce the merciless tyrants who are blinded by power and authority.

It is a human asterism which brings out the more worldly human side of esoterically oriented Ketu. This is very much a worldly nakshatra which is interested in human affairs. Ketu is known to us as a separative planet which disassociates one from worldly ties, but through this asterism it promotes involvement in mundane affairs for discharging one's worldly duties.

This is an asterism connected to the sustenance and maintenance aspect of nature. Its primary impulse is to maintain established traditions, organizations and civilizations. This is usually the function of those in positions of authority whom this asterism represents. This brings out a hitherto unknown side of Ketu which is usually associated only with creation and dissolution.

In a way ancestor worship is also an act of sustenance where one seeks blessings from the ancestors for the continuance of the family, tribe, nation or humanity as a whole. On a superficial level it can make one too fixed, rigid, unyielding and narrowminded in one's views or caught up in religious and social bigotry

It is a watery nakshatra in the sense that it is like an ocean and represents the expansive watery side of Ketu. Ocean is again symbolic of vastness and prominence inherent in this nakshatra. Water as we know is the secondary element of Ketu. It brings out the emotional side of Ketu which is necessary for qualities like compassion and benevolence, which one needs to have in positions of authority.

The fact that it is a *rajasic* (materially active) nakshatra again points towards its worldly involvement. It brings out the materially active side of Ketu which is very concerned about social status, prominence and discharging of one's worldly duties. This is why its pitfall lies in making one over ambitious in one's material pursuits. However when working through its higher principal, this asterism has a high degree of idealism even when surrounded by worldly attainments.

Ketu as we know is an idealistic planet when functioning in its solar aspect. As a final note it must be said that Ketu is a rebellious planet and consequently this nakshatra is directly related to all types of revolts against authority.

<u>MULA</u> (0° - 13°20' Sagittarius)

It is the 19th asterism and consists of a group of stars in the constellation know as Scorpionis in modern astronomy. They are collectively known as the Scorpion's tail. Among them *Shaula* is the brightest star. This center of our galaxy, the Milky Way, which is supposed to lie around 6° of Sagittarius, lies within this asterism.

Mula translates into 'the root". Its symbol is a tied bunch of roots. Both its meaning and symbol emphasize the word 'root', and this asterism literally relates to the 'root' of everything. The fact that the centre of our galaxy lies in it conveys the same idea. Just like Ketu, this asterism deals with getting to the bottom/core of everything. In the trees and plants roots are usually hidden, which means that this nakshatra deals with all kinds of hidden things, realms, events, motives, propensities etc. Ketu as we know is the planet signifying the root underlying impulses of all thoughts and actions. It is also a planet which gives access and insight into the unseen realms as well as the invisible causes of visible things or events. The tied bunch of roots also symbolizes the restrictive aspect of this asterism.

The term 'root' has another meaning in the word 'rooted'. This nakshatra also relates to something properly rooted. This gives a strong foundation to the actions of this nakshatra. Its symbol also means collecting or tying up what belongs to one. Ketu as we know is the one who stores past karmas and releases the ones ripe enough to be experienced in the present life, so it can help one collect the necessary tools from the past which one requires in fulfilling one's goal in the present life.

Its presiding deity as per Vedic texts is the Goddess of dissolution and destruction known as *Nritti*, a name which translates into 'calamity'. She is supposed to be the daughter of *Adharma* (unrighteousness) and *Himsa* (violence) and the mother of *Mrityu* (death) and *Bhaya* (fear). Some texts also mention Nritti as a destructive demon. In light of the above it is not hard to see that this is not a very pleasant nakshatra. However everything is not doom and gloom with this nakshatra. After all it lies in the luckiest among the signs Sagittarius, which in turn is ruled by the greatest benefic Jupiter.

As suggested by the symbolism of tied roots, it helps one put together in a meaningful way one's talents, which have developed in past lives. Although it may sound bizarre it also promotes non-violence and protects the good. It is also a magical nakshatra, which either confers magical powers or helps those in need in sudden magical ways. Ketu as discussed earlier loses much of its power to give bad results when associated with Jupiter in any way. This asterism can be seen as a combination of Jupiter's and Ketu's energies.

As is the case with the previous two nakshatras, its attributes - neutral, sharp, dreadful, demoniac, destructive, fiery, *tamasic* - highlight the corresponding aspects of Ketu. As far as gender is concerned Mula represents the neutral aspect of Ketu. This is why its presiding deity is sometimes seen as a Goddess and sometimes as a male Demon.

Its sharpness relates to the sharp and often harsh way Ketu functions. This relates more to the destructive aspect of Ketu. Sometimes sharpness is necessary to initiate an important change and wake us up from our sleep. It is an intense nakshatra which initiates spiritual transformation. It is also a philosophical nakshatra which brings out the Jupiterian side of Ketu.

Its dreadful and demoniac nature highlight the negative functioning of Ketu in its lower aspects. It is a powerful asterism which can give dominion and lordship. This can sometimes breed ego, vanity and arrogance which can lead one to do abominable and demoniac actions. The two Titan kings, who are the main characters in the two main Vedic historical texts, *Ravana* and *Kamsa*, are associated with this asterism. They started harassing and killing without discrimination after gaining influence and power. This asterism can give power and influence as it follows the nakshatra known as *Jyeshta* or the Eldest, which signifies the height of material accomplishment. This asterism relates to the state after one has successfully conquered the material realm. Among the body parts it relates to the feet, which emphasizes its capacity to take heavy responsibility, just as the feet take up the load of the body.

Its fieriness relates to the fiery aspect of Ketu. Ketu as we know is a predominantly fiery planet. Through this asterism it gives both good or bad results in a blazing explosive way. Its fieriness makes it favourable for war and other similar activities. It is usually triumphant in all sorts of warfare but a downfall does take place at some point of time.

It is a *tamasic* asterism in the sense that it relates to the dark and passive aspect of nature. Thus it can cause all sorts of confusion, paranoia, fears etc., which fall in the domain of Ketu's significations. It also deals with all types of smoking and intoxication.

Being a destructive asterism it relates to the destructive potential of Ketu. As discussed earlier Ketu's destructiveness is always benign in the sense that it either initiates a new beginning or a spiritual transformation. Mula is the first among the asterisms which symbolize the spiritual journey of the soul. As mentioned above it follows Jyeshta (the 18th Nakshatra), which is the last among the asterisms dealing with material accomplishments. Even the two titan kings mentioned above were finally initiated on a spiritual path after they were defeated in battle by the two incarnations of Vishnu, *Rama* and *Krishna* respectively.

RAHU'S ASTERISMS

ARDRA (6°40 - 20°00' Gemini)

It is the 6th among the nakshatras and consists of only one star, *Betelguese* (alpha-Orionis), which is one of the brightest stars in the night sky. It is one of the stars making up the constellation of Orion.

Ardra translates into 'moist' or 'fresh'. Moist can either refer to the moisture in the air which forms the clouds or the moisture in the eyes in the act of crying. In fact 'a teardrop' is one of the symbols of this Nakshatra. This symbolism associates this nakshatra with all kinds of sorrow. This relates to the troublesome side of Rahu. The fresh symbolism relates to the freshness of green leaves or plants after the rain or the sprouting of new leaves in the spring. This in turn relates to the benevolent side of Rahu when it fulfills one's goals and desires after the trials and upheavals.

Its presiding deity is Rudra, which translates into 'the terrible'. It represents the destructive aspect of *Shiva* (the destroyer among the Vedic trinity). This symbolism relates to Rahu's capacity for creating chaos, disorder, confusion, anarchy, and havoc. Rudra is also seen as the Storm God by some Vedic texts which again points towards a sense of commotion and upheaval. This however can not be taken as a negative indication, as storm is an important phenomenon through which nature finds its release.

Rahu as we know is a planet relating to the future and it releases a native from the decaying past through a series of stormy events. If one does not try to cling to the past one can sail through this phase with ease and be rewarded with a renewal akin to the freshness of the leaves after the rain. For example, one feels disappointed when one loses a job, but this might provide a new opportunity for one to pursue one's favoured vocation and find success there in.

This is the reason why 'a diamond' is the main symbol of this nakshatra. A diamond as we know is formed after been acted upon by extreme heat and pressure for millions of years. In the same way this asterism can produce a glowing personality after they have successfully gone through the stormy tests of Rahu.

This is the most intellectual among the asterisms as it forms a part of the intellectual sign of Gemini. It can be seen as a combination of the energies of Mercury and Rahu, both of which are intellectual planets dealing with the duality of life and nature. Just like a diamond, its intellectualism is usually piercing and multifaceted. Rahu's Mercurial side which was discussed in detail in the previous chapter, is relayed through this nakshatra. Many of the profound thinkers, philosophers and scientists are born with Ardra playing a prominent role in their chart. The body organs it relates to, the eyes and the back and front of the head, highlight its perceptive and analyzing quality. As neurologists are now discovering, most of the brain's controlling mechanisms are located in the front and back of the head.

Its attributes - masculine, sharp, human, destructive, watery, *sattvic* (auspicious) - highlight the corresponding aspects of Rahu. As far as gender is concerned it represents the male aspect of Rahu.

Its sharpness is evident from its ruling deity, the Storm God. It functions in a sudden sharp manner akin to a snake bite. Rahu as we know is a harsh planet. Biting sarcasm and distressful events are associated with this asterism. Even when giving good results it gives them in a sudden sharp manner. Its wateriness is evident both from its symbols and its deity. This shows that there are strong underlying emotions involved within the intellectualism of Rahu and Mercury.

Being a human asterism it relays the worldly aspect of Rahu. Just like Magha this asterism is very involved with humanity and its struggle in the material plane of the planet earth.

The fact that it is destructive as well as *sattvic* (auspicious) at the same time conveys the duality associated with both Rahu and Gemini. This asterism is a part of Orion which is supposed to be strongly connected with the affairs of humanity. It is revered in all the Vedic texts as the gateway from where the souls descend to begin their earthly life. It is thus called the "Giver of Life". It aids in the evolutionary process of humanity through triggering important changes. Some of these changes may appear destructive on an individual or collective level like a violent storm, but they are always auspicious in the sense that they always trigger new growth.

SWATI (10° - 23°20' Libra)

It is the 15th among the nakshatras and is represented by the bright golden star *Arcturus* (alpha-Boötis). This star lies in the constellation known as Boötis which lies between Virgo and Libra.

Swati translates into 'independent' or 'self-going'. These meanings are self explanatory as this asterisms promotes individuality. However this individuality is different from the individuality furthered by Sun's influence as Sun has its maximum debilitation in this asterism. It is not a soul level individuality but a more mental and material individuality based upon some skill or talent developed on these planes.

Its symbol is a young plant shoot blown by the wind. Its presiding deity is Vayu, the God of Wind. The wind symbolism suggests the airy quality of this asterism which promotes restlessness, adaptability, dexterity and a roaming disposition. Rahu as we know has air as its primary element, and its airy qualities are relayed through this asterism. The young plant symbolism suggests delicacy. This is the reason why this asterism strives for strength and independence just like a young plant shoot strives for maturity. It is interesting to note that the root 'Ra' which forms the name 'Rahu' is associated with this asterism.

The body part it relates to is the chest, which emphasizes its connection with the air element and the process of breathing. On an astral level this is related to the flow of *prana* (life force) through the body.

Its attributes - feminine, movable, godly, sustaining, fiery, *rajasic* (materially active) - highlight the corresponding aspects of Rahu. Just as Ardra represents the male aspect of Rahu, Swati represents the female aspect of Rahu. It is directly associated with *Saraswati*, Goddess of music and learning.

Its movable nature is exemplified by its close association with the air element. Its godly nature stems from the fact that this asterism is very conducive to all types of learning. Rahu as we have discussed earlier is the significator of knowledge and this aspect of its nature finds expression through this nakshatra. It is supposed to be a gentle, delicate and mild nakshatra. Falling in the heart of Libra it has a balancing quality. It thus relays the diplomatic pleasing side of Rahu. It can always compromise to achieve its eventual ends. It can be seen as a combined Venus and Rahu energy and relays the Venusian side of Rahu's functioning discussed in the previous chapter. This makes it good in most of the Venusian pursuits like music.

Rahu's Venusian side is usually quite materialistic and this makes this asterism *rajasic* (materially active). It is the best nakshatra for business and other financially profitable activities as it always keeps its own interests above everything else. Many of the world's richest men are born with either Moon or other significant planets placed in this asterism. Working through its lower plane this asterism can be overtly indulgent and function without any regard for morals. Law, sex and money - the three major Libran significations form an integral part of the activities of this asterism.

The fact that it is fiery reveals a hitherto unknown aspect of Rahu which is predominantly an airy and earthy planet. This fieriness relates to the inherent motivation of this asterism, which can range from learning, to acquiring financial gain, to getting worldly prominence. Just like Rahu when functioning in its material mode, it is a cardinal achievement-oriented nakshatra. This is why 'a sword' is also seen as a symbol of this nakshatra to represent its cutting, fiery quality. In a way it can be said that in time this asterism transforms from the delicate young plant shoot into a hard and strong razor sharp sword. Thus those with prominent Swati in their chart are late bloomers and have a stronger second half of their life as compared to the first half.

Its relation to *Saraswati*, the Goddess of music and learning, reveals the higher nature of this asterism which is conducive for all sorts of learning - material, philosophical or spiritual. Just like Rahu when it is functioning through its higher aspect, this nakshatra is eager and open to learning - a rare quality.

SHATABHISHA (6°40' - 20°00' Aquarius)

It is the 24th among the nakshatras and consists of a large group of faint stars in the Constellation of Aquarius. *Sadachbia* (γ- aquarii) is the brightest among these stars. Some sources number these stars as 100 which as we see is a number closely associated with this asterism.

Shatabhisha translates into 'requiring 100 physicians' or simply '100 physicians'. This makes it clear that this asterism has a lot to do with diseases and healing. The diseases which are caused by the planets in this asterism, or begin on the day Moon is transiting this asterism, are always very complicated and hard to cure, as symbolised by the 'requiring 100 physicians' imagery. It is said that only Ashvini, the nakshatra of Ketu can cure the diseases originating through this asterism. The diseases caused by this asterism are usually the severe among the one's listed under Rahu's significations.

Its symbol is an empty circle. It is a deeply philosophical symbol which refers to the essential unity of inside and outside, within and without, microcosm and macrocosm. In its higher aspect this nakshatra relays the most knowledgeable and philosophical side of Rahu. Rahu as we know, being a child of nature, carries within itself the complete knowledge of nature's functionings.

Its main deity is *Varuna*, the God of cosmic and terrestrial waters. The terrestrial waters may refer to anything from lakes, oceans to all kinds of liquid drinks. The important thing to note out here is that this asterism deals with things having a circular sort of boundary, so a river does not come under the influence of this asterism. However all liquid drinks in containers come under its influence. This is why this asterism is said to govern all types of alchoholic beverages. The body part it relates to is the jaw which emphasizes its relation to the acts of eating, drinking and speaking.

In Vedic texts *Varuna* is said to be the God ruling over *Soma*, the favoured intoxicating drink of the celestial realm. Functioning through its lower aspect, it relays the aspect of Rahu, which is responsible for consumption and manufacturing of all types of alchohol, intoxicants and drugs. All the significations of Rahu dealing with poisonous chemicals and substances also fall under the domain of this asterism.

Varuna is also equated with Neptune, which in Western astrology is the planet presiding over cosmic and terrestrial waters. In fact Neptune is named as *Varuna* by the Indian astrologers. Thus this asterism relays the Neptunian side of Rahu, which was discussed in the previous chapter.

Its attributes - neutral, movable, demonic, destructive, etheric, airy, *tamasic* - highlight the corresponding aspects of Rahu. As far as gender is concerned Shatabhisha represents the neutral aspect of Rahu. Even though its deity is sometimes seen as a male God some texts give the rulership of cosmic and terrestrial waters to a Goddess known as *Varuni*. This is similar to the symbolism in the sign Aquarius where either a man or woman can be holding the pot carrying the waters of wisdom.

Its movable and airy aspect is similar to the nature of Rahu and the sign Aquarius. Rahu as we know is the coruler of Aquarius. The etheric aspect of this asterism relates to the subtle electric forces of the etheric or heavenly realm, which the Rahu and the sign Aquarius is seen to represent. It is a deeply mystical asterism which can open one's conciousness to the highest realms. Its empty circle symbolism highlights the truth that all creation arises from nothingness.

It is *tamasic* (representing the dark aspect aspect of nature) in the sense that it leads one to aversion from worldliness and inclines one to isolation and seclusion. It is a meditative and visionary asterism which furthers self-contemplation and leads to enlightenment. However in its negative aspect it can drown one in all kinds of intoxication, hedonism and incline one to practice black magic and other negative occult practices.

The humanitarian, all inclusive, philosophical disposition of this asterism when it is functioning through its higher aspect, is also very in tune with Rahu's disposition in its higher aspect. Rahu as we may recall is the force that attempts to break down all boundaries of race, age, status, nationality and religion to usher in a feeling of oneness of humanity, which in a sense embodies the spirit of Aquarius.

Mula and *Shatabhisha*, the last asterism of Ketu and Rahu respectively are the most separative, ascetic and philosophical among the asterisms. Together they signify the knowledge and enlightenment potential inherent in the nodes.

When a planet is placed in the asterism of a node it reflects the qualities of that particular asterism. It also becomes intimately connected with the node ruling that asterism. For example if Venus is placed in the asterism of Rahu in a nativity its results will be coloured by the position and qualities of Rahu.

Similarly the nodes also become intimately connected with the planets in whose asterisms they are placed. For example if Ketu is placed in an asterism of Sun in a nativity its functioning will become intimately connected with Sun's functioning.

It is useful to remember that Mercury, Venus, Saturn and Rahu revel in Rahu's asterisms, while Sun, Mars, Jupiter and Ketu are more at home in Ketu's asterisms. For example, Saturn a servant planet feels completely at sea in the royal asterism Magha. Similarly Sun cannot shine with full effulgence in the mild asterism of Swati.

NODES IN THE NAVAMSA CHART

Vedic astrology gives prime importance to the *Navamsha* chart which is known as the Ninth Harmonic Chart in the Western system. It is always used along with the *Rasi* (Main) chart for interpretations.

Since the navamsha is based on dividing each sign into 9 equal parts of 3°20' each it correlates well with the concept of the 27 asterisms. Vedic astrology divides each asterism into 4 equal *padas* (parts) of 3°20' each. One *pada* or quarter of an asterism corresponds to 1/9th division (or subdecanate) of a sign.

A sign is assigned to each of these quarters or 3°20' parts. When a planet or an important point like the Ascendant or the Midheaven falls in a particular quarter of an asterism, it is assigned the sign corresponding to that quarter in the Navamsha chart.

A simple way to know which quarter corresponds to which sign is that the sequence starts with Aries, corresponding with the first quarter of (0° to 3°20') of Aries. The second quarter of Aries (3°20' to 6°40') corresponds to Taurus, the third quarter (6°40' to 10°) to Gemini and so on.

When we reach Taurus we just continue from where we left off in the last quarter (26°40' to 30°) of Aries which corresponds to Sagittarius, so the first quarter (0° to 3°20') of Taurus corresponds to Capricorn and so on. When we reach Pisces which corresponds to the third quarter (6°40' to 10) of Taurus we start all over again with Aries, corresponding with the fourth quarter (10°00' to 13°20') of Taurus and so on.

The navamsha sign of the Ascendant degree defines the rising sign or Ascendant of the navamsha chart. For example, if one has the Ascendant at 1° of Aquarius, its corresponding navamsha sign would be Libra and so the navamsha Ascendant would be Libra. The other planets are placed accordingly in their respective signs and thus occupy a particular house in the navamsha chart.

The main function of the navamsha chart is to ascertain the true strength of the planets. The main chart also shows the strength of the planets but the navamsha chart finetunes its indications. If an exalted planet is debilitated (without cancllation of debility) in the navamsha chart, it should be seen as weak and not strong. For example if Sun in Aries in the main chart is in Libra in the Navamsha chart, it can not be considered strong.

A planet which is in the same sign in the main chart and navamsha is said to be *Vargottama* (in good degree). This planet is considered auspicious and is supposed to give strong and good results.

To summarize, we can say that a planet gains strength in the navamsha chart by being placed in its own sign, exaltation sign or the same sign it occupies in the main chart. This applies to Rahu and Ketu as well.

Using the above method and the rulerships, exaltation and debilitation of the nodes discussed in the previous chapter we can find out the strong and weak degree placements for both the nodes.

For example, we know Ketu is exalted in Sagittarius, but it would be considered extremely strong only when it occupies the sign Sagittarius in the navamsha chart as well. This would happen when it is placed in between 26°40' and 30° in Sagittarius.

Another couple of things to keep in mind when seeing the navamsha chart for judging the strength and influence of the nodes in a chart, is their conjunction with important planets and placement in important houses like first and tenth.

The important planets in case of the nodes are the two luminaries, Sun and Moon, and the *Atmakaraka* (soul significator). In Vedic astrology the planet which is occupying the highest degrees (within a sign) is said to be the *Atmakaraka* or the soul signifcator in the chart.

It is a planet which is said to be the King in the chart and it has the final say in all the affairs of one's present life. It is the planet which charts out one's direction in the present incarnation. When a node is associated with the *Atmakaraka* in the main or navamsha chart its overall influence in the chart is boosted.

It must be reiterated that when either of the nodes is placed with a planet in its own or exaltation sign in either the rasi or navamsha chart its power is heightened. A weaker, but still worth noticing condition is the conjunction of a node with the lord of the Ascendant of the navamsha chart.

Let us summarize the key points to look for in a navamsha chart in relation to the nodes:

1. The association of the nodes with the *atmakaraka*.
2. The association of the nodes with the luminaries
3. The association of the nodes with planets in own or exalted signs.
4. The association of the nodes with the lord of the Ascendant of the navamsha chart or the lord of the asterism in which Moon is placed in the main chart.
5. The placement of the nodes in important houses like the first and tenth.
6. The *vargottama* position of the nodes and their placement in own, *moolatrikona* or exaltation sign.

When two or more of the above-mentioned conditions are satisfied the influence of that particular node becomes paramount. For example, if Rahu is placed with an atmakaraka Mercury in the sign of Virgo in the navamsha chart, then its influence is boosted by a factor of three, as it fulfills three of the above mentioned conditions - association with the *atmakaraka*, association with an exalted planet, placement in its own sign. If Mercury is also the Ascendant lord or the lord of the Moon's asterism in the chart under consideration, then Rahu will definitely become a very important planet for that particular nativity.

* * *

5. NUMEROLOGY OF THE NODES

Even though Numerology is not seriously incorporated in interpretation by the majority of modern day astrologers, it is still an integral part of astrology. In modern times numerology has somehow gained an independent status, with the two fields, numerology and astrology lapping only now and then. The signs, the asterisms and the houses are all numbered. The 9th sign Sagittarius having similar qualities and attributes to the 9th house has numerological implications in the sense that they both represent the same energy.

Even the planets are numbered through the weekday system. Starting with Sunday we can number the planets as

1	-	Sunday	-	Sun
2	-	Monday	-	Moon
3	-	Tuesday	-	Mars
4	-	Wednesday	-	Mercury
5	-	Thursday	-	Jupiter
6	-	Friday	-	Venus
7	-	Saturday	-	Saturday

Each planet is intimately associated with its corresponding number i.e. Sun with 1, Moon with 2, Mars with 3 and so on.

We can easily see the underlying astrological ideas behind this numbering. Sun is related to the concept of source or origin which the number 1 represents. Sun is also exalted in the 1st sign (Aries). In Vedic astrology Sun is the natural significator of the 1st house.

Similarly we can establish connections between the other planets and their numbers.

The ancient seers recognized this and made *yantras* (numerological totems) to represent the energies of each planet. Each of these totems had the planet's main number as their base number. For example the totem of Jupiter looks like this -

10	5	12
11	9	7
6	13	8

Jupiter Yantra

We can see that it is based on the number 5. The base number is the smallest number in the square and is always placed on the middle of the top three squares.

One can also see that the total adds up to 27 no matter how we add the numbers - along the rows, along the columns or along the diagonals. The sum total of all the numbers is 81. Hence we can say that the numbers 5, 27 and 81 are intimately connected with the energy of Jupiter.

In the numbering table we can see that Saturn, the last among the weekday planets, has its base number as 7. The ancient Vedic seers ascribed the remaining one digit numbers to Rahu and Ketu. They ascribed 8 to Rahu and 9 to Ketu.

RAHU'S NUMEROLOGICAL SIGNIFICANCE

Let us have a look at Rahu's numerological totem as described in Vedic texts.

13	8	15
14	12	10
9	16	11

Rahu Yantra

We can see that it is based on number 8.
The rows, columns and diagonals add up to 36.
The sum total of all the numbers is 108.

We can derive from its totem that Rahu is related with the numbers 8, 36 and 108.

8 (Eight)

This is the number, which is directly related with the energies of the eighth house and the sign Scorpio. It represents the side of Rahu which most closely relates to the eighth house and sign. As discussed earlier Rahu has a close connection with the sign Scorpio. In fact Scorpio is the *moolatrikona* sign of Rahu. The number 8 represents the two extreme sides of Rahu - the side which creates chaos, upheaval and misery and the side which confers knowledge and prosperity.

In numerology 8 is considered an extreme, eccentric and unfortunate number. It can thus be directly associated with all types of misfortune arising out of Rahu's attributes and significations. When functioning through its lower aspect the symbol of the number 8 is the Scorpion, which is representative of all types of crude, criminal and offensive behaviour and actions.

However the number 8 is not all doom and gloom as in its higher aspect its symbol is an Eagle, which is seen to represent true knowledge and wisdom. This correlates perfectly with Rahu's functioning in its lower and higher aspects.

Since Scorpio is ruled by Mars, 8 usually brings out the Martian aspect of Rahu's functioning to the fore. This is why this is the number associated with revolts, wars and coups of all kind. It also brings out the hidden, secretive and occult side of Rahu which may be negative or positive depending upon the evolutionary level of the soul involved. Since Ketu is the coruler of Scorpio, the number 8 is a meeting point of the energies of Rahu and Ketu. This makes it a very complicated number which can either cause upheavals or bestow supreme enlightenment.

A contemporary figure, *Jim Morrison* (Chart no.12), was born on the 8th of December and his life and work reveal a lot as to the functioning of this number.

36 (Thirty Six)

36 is an important number in the sense it signifies completion. According to Vedic astrology it is the age when Saturn matures i.e. it gives its full results depending upon its position in a chart. In the language of the psychologists, 36 is around the age when the mid-life crisis takes place. Since 36 adds up to 9 which is regarded by numerologists as a fortunate number, the change it brings is supposed to be for the better. It can be seen as the aspect of Rahu which initiates changes in the present for future growth.

108 (One Hundred and Eight)

108 is regarded as the most significant number in Vedic texts. Any Vedic *mantra* attains a cycle of completion if it is recited 108 times. It is considered the most occult among the numbers. It adds up to 9 and signifies completion on all levels. It relates to the highest functioning of Rahu, which as a result of being completely aligned with nature bestows true knowledge and wisdom. The supreme feminine deity presiding over the creation, sustenance and dissolution of the universe is supposed to have 108 main modes of functioning.

The other numbers associated with Rahu are -

6 (Six)

In numerology this number is associated with Venus. However this number is associated with Rahu because of two reasons. Rahu is the ruler of the 6th nakshatra, *Ardra* and co-ruler of the 6th sign, Virgo. Since the 6th nakshatra is part of the sign Gemini, ruled by Mercury, and Virgo is also co-ruled by Mercury, this number primarily brings out the Mercurial side of Rahu.

It can be said to be a combined energy of Rahu, Mercury and Venus. Keeping the nature of these three planets in mind it follows that it is a materially fruitful number and usually bestows material prosperity. It is the number of the 'earth' and relates mainly to the material plane. It is also good for intellectual pursuits if these planets are working through their higher aspect. It can manifest qualities like love and compassion of the highest degree.

The downside of this number is that it brings out the extreme materialistic side of Rahu. Thus it relays all the negative Rahu attributes and significations like sexual deviations, deviousness, greed etc. This number also carries within itself the qualities of the asterism *Ardra* along with the attributes of the sign Virgo. The father of modern psychotherapy, *Sigmund Freud* (Chart no. 3), was born on the 6th of May and his life and work reveal a lot as to the functioning of this number.

<u>11</u> (Eleven)

This number is directly related to the energies of the sign Aquarius as Aquarius is the 11th sign. Since Rahu is the coruler of Aquarius this number is associated with Rahu as well. Uranus is another coruler of this sign and Rahu's Uranian side finds expression through this number. Consequently it deals with all kinds of new technology, group work, new age sciences and philosophies etc. In its lower aspect it can make one concentrate too much on material progress exemplified by present day sciences. In its higher aspect this number relays the humanitarian, all inclusive and pure wisdom aspect of Aquarius.

One of the most original philosophers of the 20th century, *J.Krishnamurthy* (Chart no. 1), was born on the 11th of May and his life, personality and teachings reveal a lot about the functioning of this number. Interestingly Aquarius (the 11th sign) is the sign rising on his Ascendant with Rahu placed there in.

<u>15</u> (Fifteen)

This number is usually associated with the Sun as it is the sum total of the numbers along a row, column or diagonal in the Sun *yantra* given below.

6	1	8
7	5	3
2	9	4

Sun's Yantra

15 represents the complete manifestation of the Solar energy. This number is also associated with Rahu as Rahu is the ruler of the 15th nakshatra, *Swati*. Since the 15th nakshatra is placed in the sign Libra, which is ruled by Venus, this number primarily brings out the Venusian side of Rahu. It can be said to be a combined energy of Rahu, Sun and Venus.

All numbers like 15, 24, 33, 42 etc. whose digits add up to 6 are intimately connected with Rahu. Just like 6, 15 is also a materially fruitful number and usually bestows material prosperity. However the influence of Sun gives it a sense of morals and self righteousness. In many cases the same factor also promotes overriding ambition and megalomania. This effect is akin to Rahu magnifying the Solar energy.

In numerology it is seen as a number which gives mastery in the occult realm. However it is also associated with black magic and other negative occult practices. This is a result of Rahu distorting the Solar energy, and Venus, who is the chief advisor of the demons, supports Rahu. This is a powerful number and can help one accomplish whatever one sets out to. The dictum - 'one should be careful about what one wants as their wanting may materialize' - makes a lot of sense for this number. Working through its higher aspect it is a profound number involved in solving the mystery of life. However in its negative aspect it represents the worst side of Rahu's Solar and Venusian attributes and significations.

This number also carries within itself the qualities of the asterism *Swati* along with the characteristics of the sign Libra. *Napolean* (Chart no. 8), the famous Emperor of France who dreamt of a unified

Europe, was born on the 15th of August and his life and personality reveals a lot about the functioning of this number. *Nietzche* (Chart no. 2), the famous 19th century philosopher, was born on the 15th of October and his life and personality reveals the more philosophical aspect of this number.

17 (Seventeen)

This is the second number in the series of numbers, the sum of whose individual digits adds up to 8. All such numbers are related to Rahu as Rahu has 8 as its base number.

In numerology 17 is known as the Star and is considered a number of luxury, comfort, opulence and extravagance. It can be said to exhibit the Venusian side of Rahu. In its lower aspect it has a tendency to be superficial and to completely immerse itself in the material plane. This often creates a feeling of emptiness and deep sadness in those who are sensitive enough. It usually generates a lot of dissatisfaction if a purely material path is followed. Working through its higher aspect it can generate higher Venusian values like true empathy, kindness, love and compassion. It is seen as an occult number in the sense that it can give astral sensitivity and connection with higher realms.

The life and personality of the famous Hollywood actress, *Elizabeth Taylor*, who was born on the 17th of March, throws a lot of light on the functionings of this number.

18 (Eighteen)

This number is usually associated with Moon as it is the sum total of the numbers along a row, column or diagonal in the Moon's *yantra* given below.

7	2	9
8	6	4
3	10	5

Moon's Yantra

18 represents the complete manifestation of all aspects of the Lunar energy. Since the lunar nodes have a lot to do with the Lunar energy it is intimately connected with both the nodes. A clue lies in fact that the nodes take around 18 months to transit a sign. It is an extreme number in the sense that it can either make one totally materialistic or completely spiritual. We have already seen this quality in both the nodes, especially Rahu. The number '666' which is denoted as the number of the devil in Christian theology adds up to 18. This is nothing but the earthy material side of Rahu manifesting itself on our planet. Six as we discussed earlier is the number esoterically connected with our planet Earth.

It is a highly sensitive and occult number when it is working through its refined mode. *Ramakrishna Paramahansa* (Chart no. 13), an exalted and liberated soul, was born on the 18th of February and his life reveals the spiritual potential inherent in this number.

The other numbers which add up to 8 like 26, 35, 44, 53, 62, 71, 80, 89, 98 etc. are also related to Rahu. They have similar qualities to the number 8.

19 (Nineteen)

As mentioned earlier 19 is the age when Rahu returns to its natal position in a nativity, so this number can be said to be associated with Rahu. In Numerology it is known as the 'Prince of Heaven' and as the name suggests is considered a very fortunate number. It assures success in whatever one tries to pursue - material or spiritual. It is considered as a good omen when it comes in relation to future events. It brings out the fortunate though not necessarily benefic or refined side of Rahu. As we will discover later it is strongly connected to Ketu as well.

24 (Twenty Four)

This number is primarily associated with Mercury as it is the sum total of the numbers along a row, column or diagonal in the Mercury *yantra*.

24 represents the complete manifestation of the Mercurial energy.

This number is also associated with Rahu as Rahu is the ruler of the 24th nakshatra, *Shatabhisha*. The 24th nakshatra is placed in the sign Aquarius, which is coruled by Saturn, Rahu and Uranus, so this number primarily brings out the Mercurial, Saturnine and Uranian side of Rahu.

9	4	11
10	8	6
5	12	7

Mercury Yantra

It can be said to be a combined energy of Mercury, Saturn, Rahu and Uranus. Just like 6 it is also a materially fruitful number and usually bestows material prosperity. In numerology it is considered a fortunate number which signifies gain through the opposite sex. This is because of Rahu and Mercury's combined influence. The influence of Mercury gives it an intellectual bent. It brings out the Mercurial side of Rahu including wit, sarcasm etc. In fact this number can be seen as the 'king of satire'.

This is again a powerful number and can help one accomplish whatever one sets out to. It can give one fame and renown but there is always an inner longing for getting in touch with higher realities. All the indications of *Shatabhisha* discussed in the previous chapter apply to this number. Working through its higher aspect it is a profound number involved in solving the mysteries of life. Working through its negative side it represents the worst side of Rahu's Mercurial and Saturnine aspect.

Queen Victoria (Chart no. 21), the famous Queen of Britain who ruled an empire bigger than anyone in recorded history, was born on the 24th of May and her life and personality reveals a lot about the functioning of this number. *Bob Dylan*, one of the legendary poets and songwriters of the 20th century was also born on the same day and month. His life and works however reveal the more philosophical and intellectual side of this number.

<u>26</u> (Twenty Six)

This number is associated with Rahu as it adds up to '8'. Rahu as we have seen has special connection with the number eight. Just like all numbers whose digits add up to 8, it is usually seen as an unfortunate number by numerologists. However it is a quixiotical number which assures a variety of experiences even if things end up in a mess. The significance of this number can be gauged from the fact that the current international language, English has 26 letters in its alphabet! Rahu as we mentioned earlier is the significator of the English language.

Aldous Huxley, the famous 20th century philosopher, was born on ?6th of July. His life and personality sums up the functioning of this number.

All the other numbers in this series like 35, 44, 53, 62, 71, 80, 98, 107 etc. can be seen as having similar qualities as the numbers 8, 17 and 26.

<u>33</u> (Thirty Three)

This number is primarily associated with Saturn as it is the sum total of the numbers along a row, column or diagonal in the Saturn *yantra* given below.

12	7	14
13	11	9
8	15	10

Saturn Yantra

33 signifies the complete manifestation of Saturnine energy. As mentioned earlier, Rahu is related with all the numbers whose individual digits add up to 6. In numerology 33 is regarded as a significant number as it comes in the series of independent numbers which are multiples of 11 i.e. 22, 33, 44, 55, 66 etc. As discussed earlier 11 is intimately connected with Rahu.

33 relays the Saturnine side of Rahu and can be seen as the combined energy of Rahu and Saturn. If one is ready to let go of the past this is a very fortunate number as it symbolizes new beginnings. It relates to the futuristic side of Rahu. This number functions well on material as well as spiritual planes. It is a highly occult number as it forms a bridge between the material and spiritual realm. It often relays the Uranian side of Rahu which makes this number usually ahead of its time.

It can be seen as a number which combines the energies of the two signs co-ruled by Rahu, Aquarius and Virgo. This makes it a very important number for the upcoming Age of Aquarius. Merging the energies of two signs which share a sixth/eighth positioning from each other is not an easy task, and thus obstacles and difficulties accompany this number in the beginning. The above can also be gauged from the Saturnine aspect of this number. However with persistence success is always assured in the end.

<u>42</u> (Forty Two)

42 is in the series of the numbers whose individual digits add up to 6 and thus relates with Rahu. Its deeper connection with Rahu is revealed by the fact that Rahu matures in the 42nd year. As discussed in the timing aspect of Rahu, the Rahu time lasts from the 42nd to the 46th year.

Numerology ascribes it a similar quality to 24. It can be said to have the characteristics of both 6 and 24.

51, 60 and 66 can be seen as numbers similar to 42. 66 however is a special case as it also falls in the independent number series which as we discussed earlier are multiples of 11. It is a number which carries an energy similar to that of 666. It rules over completion, annihilation and catastrophic events in general. The famous route-66 in the U.S.A which signalled an end of a way of life for a lot of native Indian tribes in that area is a testimony of the energy of this number. It brings out the dark and sometimes mystical side of Rahu. Incidentally the most interesting portion of the route 66 lies in the American southwest, an area under strong influence of Rahu. As discussed earlier Rahu rules the southwest part of everything.

78, 87, 97 and 105 are other numbers before 108 that add up to 6. All these numbers can be said to be having similar properties as the numbers 6 and 15.

KETU'S NUMEROLOGICAL SIGNIFICANCE

Let us take a look at Ketu's yantra and find out the numbers closely related with it.

14	9	16
15	13	11
10	17	12

Ketu Yantra

We can see that it is based on number 9.
The rows, columns and diagonals add up to 39.
The sum total of all the numbers is 117.

So we can derive from its totem that Ketu is related with the numbers 9, 39 and 117.

9 (Nine)

This is the number which is directly related with the energies of the ninth house and the sign Sagittarius. As discussed earlier Ketu has a close connection with the sign Sagittarius. In fact Sagittarius is the exaltation sign of Ketu. The number 9 represents the completion aspect of Ketu. Nine represents completion in the sense that it manifests the full potential of anyone on their particular evolutionary level.

In numerology 9 is associated with Mars and considered a fortunate number except that it promotes wounds, accidents and short life. It can be seen to relay the Martian aspect of Ketu. It is associated with the fortunate side of Ketu on both material and spiritual levels. It usually assures success in the material world by providing expertise in whatever field one selects to pursue. This is a result of repeated past life efforts and Ketu puts them all together and releases them in the present life. It gives an optimistic attitude towards life as the positive karmas from the previous lives bear fruit in the present life. Being representative of the 9th house which symbolizes luck it is not hard to see that it bestows a degree of luck onto those under its influence. It is a known principle in astrology that no planet functions badly in the 9th house or the 9th sign.

Jupiter being the ruler of the 9th sign is intimately connected with this number. It can thus be seen as a sort of combined energy of Jupiter, Mars and Ketu.

When functioning through its lower aspect it represents the horse part of the centaur which is the symbol of the sign Sagittarius. In this aspect it can give the drive to pursue one's goals but the goals may not be wholesome. All the lower and undesirable qualities of Ketu's asterism *Mula* apply in this case. *Mula* as we know assures power and influence but doesn't guarantee its correct use.

When functioning through its higher aspect it gives a balanced personality which tries to act in accordance with the universal mind. It brings out the philosophical Jupiterian side of Ketu in this mode. All the higher qualities of Ketu's asterism *Mula* apply in this case.

John Lennon, the famous member of the group Beatles, was born on the 9th of October and his life, personality and work typifies the functioning and qualities of this number.

<u>39</u> (Thirty Nine)

39 is an important number which relates to the unseen and occult realms. It brings out the mystical side of Ketu. In numerology it relates to the number 30 which is considered a number of mental superiority. Thus this number brings out the Solar side of Ketu which as discussed earlier gives intense concentration, deep perception and penetrative insight. This number can virtually pierce through to the bottom of things in much the same way as the Ketu's asterism *Mula.*

It signifies the end of Saturn's age (36-39). In this respect it signifies completion of a cycle and beginning of a new one. It is a better number than 30 for success on a material plane. *Van Gogh,* the famous painter, was born on 30th of March and his life and work throws light on the philosophical, mystical working of this number.

117 (One Hundred and Seventeen)

117 can be seen as having an energy similar to 108 which as discussed earlier is considered the most occult and mystical among all the numbers in Vedic texts. 108 relates to Rahu and represents an understanding of the 108 secrets of nature's functioning. 117 goes nine steps further and grants liberation from the cycles of birth and death.

The other numbers associated with Ketu are -

1 (One)

In numerology this number is usually associated with Sun. However this number is associated with Ketu because of two reasons. Ketu is the ruler of the 1st nakshatra, *Ashwini* and has its moolatrikona in the 1st sign, Aries. Since the 1st nakshatra is part of the sign Aries, ruled by Mars, this number primarily brings out the Martian side of Ketu.

It can be said to be a combined energy of Ketu, Sun and Mars. Keeping the nature of these three planets in mind it follows that it is the most fiery among the numbers. It relates to the primeval energy which gives birth to all that exists. Just like 39, this number brings out the Solar side of Ketu which as discussed earlier gives intense concentration, deep perception and penetrative insight.

The downside of this number is that it brings out the negative and excessive Martian and Solar side of Ketu. This is a difficult energy to handle as Ketu, Mars and Sun together can produce extreme anger, violence, aggression, combativeness, self centeredness, megalomania etc.

This number also carries within itself the qualities of the asterism *Ashwini* along with the attributes of the sign Aries. *Cheiro*, the famous numerologist, palmist and psychic, was born on the 1st of November and his life and work throws light on the functioning of this number.

8 (Eight)

As discussed earlier eight is directly related with the energies of the eighth house and the sign Scorpio. It is connected with Ketu as Ketu is the co-ruler of the sign Scorpio. It brings out the Plutonian side of Ketu to the fore as Pluto is another co-ruler of the sign Scorpio.

This number can be seen as a combined energy of Rahu, Ketu, Mars, Saturn and Pluto - a truly explosive energy! It is no wonder then that this number is the most difficult to handle and is related with all types of misfortune. As discussed earlier it is a very spiritual number in the sense that it can bestow enlightenment on all levels. It is the energy which wakes us from our sleep and puts us on the path of seeking knowledge and understanding. Because of the nature of its ruling planets it is the most intense among all the numbers and can give good results on both material and spiritual planes if one is ready to dive into the depths of the unknown.

10 (Ten)

This number is associated with Ketu, as Ketu is the ruler of the 10th nakshatra, *Magha*. Since the 10th nakshatra is placed in the sign Leo, which is ruled by Sun, this number primarily brings out the Solar side of Ketu. Also Capricorn is the 10th sign which as we know is ruled by Saturn, so 10 can be said to be the combined energy of Ketu, Sun and Saturn. Since all of these are harsh planets a degree of hardship can be associated with this number.

Just like 1, 10 is a fiery number which wants to be in a prominent position. It is more ambitious than 1 as it relates to the asterism *Magha* which as we discussed in the previous chapter deals with all kinds of authority. In many cases this number promotes overriding ambition and megalomania. This effect is akin to Ketu magnifying the Solar energy.

In numerology it is seen as a fortunate number. In my view this number only gives success after a long struggle. It is very interested in the higher realities as Sun, Saturn and Ketu are all separative and spiritual planets at some level. It is difficult for this number to pursue anything without encountering numerous obstacles. This can be seen from its association with Capricornian energies. In its negative aspect it is associated with black magic and other negative occult practices. This is easy to see when one takes into account the combined energy of Ketu and Saturn working through its lower aspect.

<u>12</u> (Twelve)

This number is directly related to the energies of the sign Pisces as Pisces is the 12th sign. Since Ketu is the co-ruler of Pisces this number is associated with Ketu. Neptune is another co-ruler of this sign and Ketu's Neptunian side finds expression through this number. Consequently it deals with all kinds of mysticism, esoterism, spirituality etc. In its lower aspect it can make one indulge in religious bigotry exemplified by the majority of today's fundamentalist religions. In its higher aspect this number relays the divine, all inclusive and liberating aspect of Pisces.

Numerologists consider it a number of completion. In Astrology this is evident as there are only 12 signs and houses. This number brings out the dissoluting and terminating aspect of Ketu. Just like Ketu, it represents culmination of all things. In view of the fact that it can be hard or soft, weak and strong, forceful yet meek at the same time, it relates to the dualities inherent in Ketu. It can however give good results on a material plane after initial struggle as it has a strong connection with the lucky Jupiterian side of Ketu. Jupiter is the co ruler of Pisces along with Ketu.

One of the most inspiring philosophers of the late 19th century, *Vivekananda* (Chart no.24), was born on the 12th of February and his life, personality and teachings reveal a lot about the functioning of this number.

<u>13</u> (Thirteen)

Thirteen is considered as the most dreaded of numbers by numerologists and occultists alike. It connects with the occult, magical and destructive side of Ketu. It is the first number after 12

NUMEROLOGY OF THE NODES

which as we know is the number signifying completion. In a way it represents a new beginning which follows any type of destruction. It can be seen as the combined energy of Moon, Ketu and Mercury. Most of its negative results arise out of Ketu distorting the mind (Moon) and the intellect (Mercury).

It shouldn't be taken as signifying doom and gloom and can give favourable material as well as spiritual results. Ketu as we know when working through its higher aspect can give deep insight and spiritualize the mind and the intellect. However its energy is very hard to master and usually it creates a lot of upheaval and catharsis in the lives of those primarily under its influence.

<u>16</u> (Sixteen)

The most widely used symbol of this number is 'a tower struck by lightening'. This reveals that this number is directly related to all types of chaos, upheaval and unfortunate events. It has similar functioning to the number 13, the only difference being that 16 has more sorrow attached to it. It relates to the punishing side of Ketu which makes one pay for one's past actions. The misery and destruction bestowed by this number is usually unavoidable. This number can lead one to the depths of depression where one cannot see any light at the end of the tunnel. The only way to deal with its energy is to gracefully accepts one's fate. If this is done this number can reveal many a secret of nature's functionings.

This number can be said to be the combined energy of Jupiter, Venus, Neptune and Ketu. As we know Venus and Jupiter conjunction is related with Rahu, so in a sense this number relates to the nodes and Neptune. As it can relay the dissoluting Neptunian side of Rahu and Ketu it an be seen as the most catastrophic among numbers. However one must remember that all catastrophes are for a purpose. Functioning through its higher aspect this is one of the most mystical among numbers.

<u>18</u> (Eighteen)

This is the second number in the series of numbers, the sum total of whose individual digits adds up to 9. All such numbers are related to Ketu as Ketu has 9 as its base number.

As discussed earlier 18 represents the complete manifestation of all aspects of the Lunar energy. We also discussed its relation with Rahu and the dreaded number '666'. In its '666' aspect 18 brings out the destructive side of Ketu which ultimately destroys all ignorance to connect us with the one underlying truth pervading through the cosmos. It is thus a very spiritual number which can however be distressing on the material plane as it involves dissolution of forms. Moon as we know is directly related to the material world and nurtures forms. In this number its energy reaches a peak and is no longer required. It represents the beginning of the end of involvement in materialistic pursuits.

<u>19</u> (Nineteen)

We have already seen that this number connects with Rahu. It connects with Ketu as Ketu presides over the 19th asterism *Mula*. We also discussed that in Numerology it is considered a very fortunate number. It relates to the Jupiterian side of Ketu which grants success in all pursuits. *Mula* as we know falls in the lucky sign of Sagittarius, which is ruled by Jupiter. The downfall of this number lies in the negative aspects of *Mula*, which were discussed in the previous chapter.

This number combines the energy of Sun, Jupiter, Rahu and Ketu. It is a very fortunate number for giving one some sort of throne and relates to those in high positions. In this sense it relates with the energies of the asterism *Magha* ruled by Ketu. *Indira Gandhi*, the first and only woman Prime Minister of India, was born on 19th of November and her life and personality exemplifies the positive and negative attributes of this number.

<u>20</u> (Twenty)

This is a number of primary importance in Mayan numerology, which associates it with the serpent energy. Thus we can say that this number is related to both the serpent planets, Rahu and Ketu.

It is no wonder then that the 20ᵗʰ century brought about accelerated change in our civilization. The role of the nodes especially Rahu in shaping the 20ᵗʰ century has been discussed in Chapter 14.

It is interesting to note that *Adolph Hitler* (Chart no. 10), one of the most important figures of the 20ᵗʰ century, was born on 20ᵗʰ April. His personality and life reveal a lot as to the strange functionings of this occult number.

27 (Twenty Seven)

This number is primarily associated with Jupiter as it is the sum total of the numbers along a row, column or diagonal in the Jupiter *yantra* described earlier.

27 represents the complete manifestation of the Jupiterian energy. This number is also associated with Ketu as it falls in the series of numbers, the sum total of whose individual digits adds up to 9.

27 can be said to be a combined energy of Mars, Jupiter and Ketu. Just like 9 it is seen in numerology as a very fortunate number. It signifies completion on many levels being a multiple of 3 and 9, which are important completion numbers in the sense that there are nine planets, three main attributes to nature etc. As we have seen there are 27 nakshatras which are able to perfectly divide the 360° zodiac.

In my view this number gives unlimited talent and mastery in one's chosen field. This can be seen from the fact that Jupiter, Mars and Ketu are all friends with each other and can thus work in harmony. It is a very optimistic number as it brings out the Jupiterian side of Ketu. This number signifies the culmination point of talents which have been worked upon in previous lives. This can only happen through the grace of Ketu which is the custodian of past karmas.

The only downfall of this number lies in the fact that it might concentrate its energies on negative things if the above mentioned planets are working through their lower or negative aspect.

Two modern day legends, *Jimi Hendrix* (Chart no. 11) and *Bruce*

Lee (Chart no. 22) were born under the influence of this number. Interestingly both of them were born on 27th of November. Their lives, personalities and works throw light on the potential of this number.

The other numbers whose individual digits add up to 9 i.e. 36, 45, 54, 63, 72, 81, 90 etc. are also related to Ketu. These numbers can be said to have qualities similar to the number 9. 108 also adds up to 9 but it is a special case and will be dealt with later in his section.

<u>28</u> (Twenty Eight)

This number relates to Ketu as it falls in the series of numbers whose digits add up to 1. In numerology this number is described as a number having a lot of potential but not fortunate enough to realize it. Some schools of thought take it to be a number of completion as they think there are 28 and not 27 asterisms. They see 4 times 7 and not 3 times 9 as completion. But 28 does not fit the symmetry of the zodiac as it does not properly divide the 360 degrees. Thus we can see it loses out to 27. This story repeats itself with this number. This can be ascribed to the constricting and restrictive quality of Ketu.

Ketu as we know represents an energy which can stop one from achieving one's destiny by continuously involving them in past life patterns. Ketu is the fear we bring into the present life from past life experiences. This hinders one to take up new evolutionary experiences in the present life. The positive side to this number lies in the fact that it is a peaceful number which seriously adheres to 'live and let live' dictum.

The other numbers whose digits add up to 1 like 37, 46, 55, 64, 73, 82, 91 and 100 are also related to Ketu. Among these 37, 46, 64 and 73 can be seen as having similar qualities to the combination of 10 and 19. 91 is similar to 19 and 100 is similar to 10. 55 is a special case which is discussed separately.

<u>47</u> (Forty Seven)

The connection of this number with Ketu is revealed by the fact that Ketu matures in the 47th year. As discussed in the timing aspect of Ketu, the Ketu time lasts from the 47th to the 54th year.

Numerology ascribes it a similar quality to the numbers 2 and 11. This number relates to all aspects of Ketu's functioning. It can be a lucky or unlucky number depending upon how Ketu is functioning in the chart of the native under the influence of this number.

This number acts as a meeting point for the energies of Rahu and Ketu as in the 47th year the energies of Rahu are receding while the energies of Ketu are gaining strength. In the image drawn on the cover of this book this number relates to the point where Ketu's snake (red,yellow and brown in colour) is swallowing the tail of the snake (blue, green and black in colour) representing Rahu. This is a sensitive point in the sense that future meets the past here to change the present. In this light we can easily see that 47 is a sensitive number which carries within itself the power for profound transformation.

<u>55</u> (Fifty Five)

It is an independent number as it falls in the series of independent numbers which are multiples of 11 i.e. 22, 33, 44, 55, 66 etc. As discussed earlier such numbers are connected with Rahu. The special thing about 55 is that it is the sum total of the numbers from 1 to 10. In many cultures it is seen as the number of perfection.

It is related to Ketu as its digits add up to one. It can be understood as a combined energy of Sun, Rahu and Ketu. We already know that both Rahu time and Ketu time finish by the age of 54, so the 55th year is the culmination point of the energies of the nodes which have been in effect for 12 years. This is the year when we put all our experiences together.

In a more esoteric sense it represents perfection on all levels of existence achieved by the true understanding of the nature of time, which involves merging of the concept of past (Ketu) and future (Rahu) into an eternal present.

<u>108</u> (One Hundred and Eight)

As mentioned earlier it has a strong connection with Rahu. Now we see it is also related to Ketu as it adds up to 9. This goes well with the fact that 108 carries within itself the answer to all the mysteries of the seen and unseen realms. It is the final meeting point of the energies Rahu and Ketu. The completion aspect of this number can be seen from the fact that the interaction of 9 planets with the twelve signs has only 108 (9 times 12) possibilities.

It represents the end of time as time only exists when Rahu (future) and Ketu (past) are separate. When future and past merge there is no tomorrow or yesterday and the manifest universe is dissolved.

6. ESOTERIC & COSMOLOGICAL SIGNIFICANCE

Like all other planets, Rahu and Ketu are representative of cosmic forces in our solar system, which in reality encompass all the celestial and terrestrial realms in our universe. A clue to this fact comes from the Vedic story of the birth of Rahu and Ketu which was delineated in Chapter 1.

The churning of the ocean can be seen as a part of the process of creation. This ocean is in actuality the ocean of celestial waters which pervades the whole cosmos. The churning produced astral/causal plants and animals which can be said to be the originators of their kind on the material plane. Even *Laxmi*, the goddess of prosperity on all planes of existence, was born in this churning. She eventually became the spouse of *Vishnu*, the preserver.

The amrita or the nectar of immortality which came out in the end represents the continuance of life till the universe exists. It also represents the force of renewal and this is the reason why Vishnu didn't want the demons to partake it.

The fact that a demon called *Swarbhanu* was able to deceive the Gods and partake the nectar, shows that a part of the demonic force was destined to become immortal. Both Gods and Demons are equally important for the balanced functioning of nature. In my view, Vishnu's cutting of Swarbahnu's body into two relates to the division of time into past and future. Ketu and Rahu as we know are the planets representing past and future respectively.

In my view there was just an eternal present before this event.

The creator *Brahma* having realized that the separation of time **was** inevitable, bestowed planetary status to Rahu and Ketu. They would represent the division of time till the dissolution of the universe. One legend says that even Vishnu had realized that he was giving the nectar to a demon, but deliberately overlooked it as he knew that this was a necessary step in the scheme of evolution.

This churning process is a metaphor for the churning going on throughout the universe - the rotation of the earth's axis, which leads to the change of Ages; the constant churning going on within all of us, which gives rise to both good and evil, and is representative of the evolutionary process. Since the churning of the ocean in the legend couldn't take place without the involvement of serpent forces, it becomes clear that Rahu and Ketu are involved in all types of churning on all levels of existence.

We can see that the churning of the ocean story repeats itself again and again. Even in the modern times we can experience churning of the ocean through the industrial revolution and the scientific and technological progress. A lot of material goods and luxuries have come out of this churning but not without the deadly poison called pollution.

In the churning story Shiva drinks the poison but we are still not quite sure how we are going to deal with the mess that has been created on our planet. We have already seen how Rahu is directly behind most of the technological and scientific breakthroughs, just like the the churning of the ocean couldn't have taken place without the graciousness of serpent king *Vasuki*. This is why some wise men ascribe the King of the Serpents as Rahu's deity.

At present our civilization is also grappling with the fear that the fruits of scientific and technological advancement shouldn't fall into the wrong hands, which they seem to have done to quite an extent already.

If we trace the lineage of the demon Swarbhanu as described by Vedic scriptures, we would find that he was born of the union of *Viprachitta* or Wise Mind and *Simhika* or Lion Lady. Viprachitta is the son of *Marichi*, a mind born son of Brahma, while Simihika is one of the many daughters of *Dakhsha*, who is also a mind born son of Brahma. The fact that these beings were born when the universe was still in its infancy, again validates our earlier conclusion that the story of the churning of the ocean is staged in the early epoch of creation.

The fact that Swarbhanu was carrying the genes of 'Wise Mind' explains why he was smarter than the rest of the demons. The fact that Rahu's vehicle is a lion is intimately connected with the fact that Swarbhanu's mother is Lion Lady.

Simhika is the sister of many celestial godesses among whom *Parvati*, the wife of *Shiva*, is the foremost. These sisters together represent the various aspects of the feminine energy which sustains our universe. Parvati in turn has many forms to suit different purposes. *Durga* is one of the forms she took to kill a fierce demon called *Mahishasura*.

Goddess Durga is supposed to ride on a lion. Her speciality is that she simultaneously exemplifies both the fierce and benign aspects of the Goddess energy. Some wise men have postulated that she presides over the sign Virgo. This may be due to the fact that she is a Virgin Goddess and is depicted as a little girl in many of her legends.

She is the ruling deity of Rahu. This is clear from the Lion and Virgo connection. Rahu as we know has a lion as his vehicle and is co ruler of the sign Virgo. Durga is supposed to be the destroyer of darkness and ignorance on all planes of existence. Among the deities she is the only one who can nullify the illusory force represented by Rahu.

Many illustrations show Durga carrying the severed head of the demon she slayed. This symbolizes her control over Rahu, who as we know is a demon's head. One of her main legends involves her cutting the head of *Bhairava*, Shiva's mind born son and the Vedic equivalent of *Archangel Gabriel*. His severed head is still worshipped in India, in temples which are nearly always situated in close proximity to temples dedicated to Durga. It is said that Goddess Durga is not pleased until the head is also worshipped. The worshipping of the severed head in a way symbolizes the worship of Rahu.

In my view Ketu's deity is *Lord Ganesha*. This is clear from the legend of the birth of Ganesha. In short the story goes like this -

"Parvati created a mind born son and instructed him to stand as a guard and not to let anyone in while she was bathing. Her husband Shiva, returning home was barred entry by Parvati's son. Shiva had not seen this boy before and did not know who he was, and the boy in turn did not recognize Shiva. Harsh words were exchanged and a battle erupted. Shiva could not defeat this boy and had to retreat. He felt humiliated after being defeated by a mere child and sought the help of Vishnu and other Gods to defeat the child.

In the battle that ensued all of the Gods together were unable to defeat him. Vishnu finally came up with a plan that someone should fight with the boy from the front, while he flew from behind to stealthily take the mace out of the boy's hand. Vishnu's theory was that the boy couldn't be defeated until the mace was taken out of his hand. The plan worked as Shiva was able to cut the boy's head with his trident as soon as Vishnu's vehicle *Garuda* (celestial eagle) snatched the mace.

Since he was Parvati's mind born son she immediately came to know of his death and the whole story flashed before her mind's eye. She became enraged and summoned all the *Shaktis* (feminine forces) of the universe to create havoc on Vishnu, Shiva and the rest of the Gods. The whole creation went completely haywire and all the Gods were scared out of their wits. Vishnu realized that the whole universe would collapse if Parvati was not appeased quickly. This could only be done if the boy was brought back to life.

Vishnu instructed the Gods to descend on earth and bring back the head of the first thing they saw. They saw an elephant and swiftly returned with its head. Vishnu and Shiva attached the elephant's head to the trunk of the boy's body which resurrected him. Finally Parvati's anger subsided and order was restored in the universe. The boy was named 'Ganesha' which translates into 'the leader of all tribes', and was given the boon to be worshipped first before any other Gods."

We can see that Ganesha has a similar birth story to Ketu. He is also similar in the sense that he is a trunk with an elephant's head while Ketu is a trunk with a serpent's head. Ganesha also has a strong connection with Jupiter as some wise men postulate him to be the ruling deity of Jupiter as well. We have already seen that Ketu has a strong connection with Jupiter as it co rules one of his signs Pisces and is exalted in Sagittarius.

Another similarity is that Ganesha represents the beginning of creation as he is the first child of the universe. Among the planets Ketu represents all types of beginnings and endings. Just like Ketu, Ganesha is fat bellied and has a serpent wrapped around his belly showing his connection with the serpent forces.

Lord Ganesha is the presiding deity of the divine science of Astrology. We have already seen how Ketu is intimately connected with the study and practice of Astrology. The fact Ketu's conjunction with Sun and Mercury is considered a boon in an astrologer's chart exemplifies this connection.

The esoteric meaning of Ganesha's birth legend relates to the *Kundalini Shakti* residing in each one of us at the base of our spine. The Kundalini is two and a half coils of serpent energy which contains within it all of our past life experiences and life force. The fact that it is serpent energy shows it connects to the serpent planets Rahu and Ketu.

Kundalini is protected by the first among the seven sacred centres called the *Muladhara Chakra*. Ganesha is the ruler of Muladhara Chakra and is thus responsible for the protection of the Kundalini, which can be seen as the representative of the universal feminine power inside each one of us. This relates to the part in the story where Ganesha is given the task of protecting Parvati.

Rahu can be seen as the significator of the Kundalini as it directly relates to Durga, who as we discussed earlier is nothing but Parvati herself. The awakening of Kundalini and its subsequent journey through the rest of the six centres is necessary for attaining true knowledge and enlightenment.

A detailed discussion on how Kundalini is aroused and the role of the seven sacred centres is beyond the scope of this book. It must be mentioned though that complete enlightenment is supposed to come after it has opened all the thousand petals of the seventh and final centre known as *Sahastrara*.

Ketu is the significator of the final centre. This is why Ketu is seen as the bestower of liberation. The fact that Ketu is the ruler of the first and last sacred centers again emphasizes Ketu's role as the beginning and the end. Rahu on the other hand represents everything in between.

When Rahu or Ketu are strong in a chart, the Kundalini of such natives is sensitive and can get aroused by itself without any conscious effort. This is usually due to the spiritual efforts of past life/lives. Such individuals are as a rule more sensitive to the astral and causal realms. In some cases the individual may not be able to cope with the power generated by the movement of the Kundalini. Maybe this is what happened to *Nietszche* (Chart no. 2).

Moon-Rahu conjunction in the mystical sign of Scorpio in his Ascendant made him sensitive enough to experience the rise of Kundalini but he did not know how to control or harness its energy. *Ramakrishna Paramahansa* (Chart no. 13) on the other hand was able to undergo intense spiritual states represented by his Ketu in Scorpio without losing his sanity in the process. This is because of the overall strength of his chart.

As our civilization will realize in time, the true freedom of any individual lies in their ability to understand and harness the unlimited potential of the Kundalini Shakti. The Kundalini carries the complete code of one's existence including the past, present and future. It is the key to unlocking all the mysteries of the universe. Most of the ancient cultures and civilizations had realized this and conveyed this through the widespread serpent symbolism which we touched upon in Chapter 1. This is also the reason why Rahu and Ketu are said to be custodians of all earthly and transcendental knowledge.

A clue to the cosmological functioning of the nodes comes from their rulership of *Nakshatras* (asterisms). We have already discussed the meanings, attributes and significations of their asterisms in Chapter 4. One thing which we didn't touch upon is the fact that these asterisms relate to the celestial functionings within our surrounding universe. Every ancient culture relates their Gods, myths and symbols to one of these asterisms.

Recent findings have shown that the constellation presently known as *Orion*, or the hunter, was of special interest to the ancient Egyptians. It has been assigned special status in Vedic mythology as well. This constellation houses two asterisms, *Mrigashira* and *Ardra*. Mrigashira is represented by the front three stars which form the bow of the hunter. Ardra as we have discussed earlier is represented by the bright star of *Betelguese* which is situated at the top left part of Orion. We also know that *Ardra* is ruled by Rahu, which connects Rahu with Orion.

According to some Vedic scholars, Betelguese is supposed to be the abode of Shiva. Orion was supposed to come into being when Shiva assumed the form of a hunter and took out one of Brahma's heads with his arrow. This makes sense when one sees that Brahma is the ruling deity of the neighbouring constellation *Rohini*.

Vedic mythology assigns *Rudra*, the fierce form of Shiva as the presiding deity of Ardra. This establishes a relation between Rahu and Shiva, the destroyer among the Trinity. Some Vedic texts have gone to the extent of saying that Rahu resides in the heart of *Neelkantha*, another name for Shiva.

We can see that Rahu and Shiva are relatives, as Shiva is the husband of the sister of the mother of Rahu. His closeness with Shiva is one of the reasons why Rahu co-rules Aquarius, the sign most related to Shiva. They even share the same electric blue complexion, a colour associated with Aquarius.

The significance of Orion lies in the fact that it stands right in the middle of the galactic gateway between Taurus and Gemini. It is said that all the souls incarnating on planet Earth come through this galactic gateway. We can understand this astronomically in the sense that the gateway points away from the centre of our galaxy and can thus be seen as a doorway into our galaxy.

This is why Vedic texts relate Orion with the *Prajapati*, the progenitor of human race. Even ancient Egyptians saw Orion as *Osiris*, the father of all humanity. Orion is also situated very close in the night sky to *Sirius*, the star around which our Sun is supposed to revolve, but a detailed discussion on the importance of Sirius lies beyond the scope of this book.

From the above we can derive that Rahu connects with the foreign influences affecting our galaxy. Thus it has a role beyond the solar system Astrology we are used to in the present times. Orion's sustaining role in an earthly context once again establishes Rahu's role as a sustainer of creation.

If Taurus and Gemini form the first gateway, Scorpio and Sagittarius form the second gateway in the celestial zodiac. This gateway points towards the centre of our galaxy.

As discussed earlier it has been found that the centre of our galaxy can be said to correspond to around six degrees of Sagittarius which as we know falls within the asterism *Mula*. We know that Ketu is the ruler of Mula which relates to the root of everything. It is evident that it relates to the root of our galaxy as the creative source of anything lies at its centre. Even astronomers have now begun to speculate that our galaxy is held together because of a massive black hole in its centre.

The above goes to show that Ketu is directly related with the primordial force which has created our galaxy. We have already seen that Mula's presiding deity is *Nrriti*, the goddess of destruction. She can be seen as the female counterpart of *Rudra*. All types of destruction big or small, takes place through the energy relayed by Mula. Thus Ketu's role as the beginner and the finisher is again established On earthly plane this energy may manifest as earthquakes, wars and other catastrophes, while on subtler planes it involves destruction of old and wornout thought forms, ideas and karmas.

In Vedic mythology most of the main Gods and Goddesses have direct associations with serpent power which can be seen in their depictions. Vishnu's abode is made out of nothing except a serpent.

The hood of the serpent provides an overhang to protect him and the tail of the serpent coils around to form his bed. The serpent separates him from the ocean of celestial waters.

This symbolism means that the serpent force can take one out of the sea of consciousness which encompasses the manifest universe. This is why I think Rahu and Ketu are the only planets which can separate an individual from mass consciousness and put one on an observer rather than participatory status. This also establishes the close relationship of Rahu with Mercury, a planet presided over by Vishnu. Ketu's close relationship with Jupiter, another planet strongly associated with Vishnu can also be derived from the above.

Among other Gods and Goddesses, Shiva has a serpent wrapped around his neck; Ganesha has a serpent wrapped around his belly; and many Goddesses are shown holding serpents in their hands. This just goes to show that all cosmic deities representing different aspects of power and energy have some direct association with serpent power.

Coming back to the birth legend of Rahu and Ketu, we find that there are many associated interesting stories, including one which relates to the appearance of garlic plants on Earth. It is said that when Vishnu cut Swarbhanu's head, drops of blood fell to the Earth. Wherever these drops fell garlic plants grew. This is the reason why orthodox high caste families in India still avoid garlic in their diet. We have already discussed that Rahu is the significator of garlic and other stringent foods like onion.

Another of these stories relates to the naming of Ketu. In earlier times Ketu was the general term used to represent celestial phenomena like passing comets and falling meteors. The birth legend says that after the head was severed from the trunk by Vishnu's discus, the trunk fell to the earth creating a massive catastrophe. This trunk was thus named Ketu as its fall was similar to that of a massive meteor.

Phoenix as we know is an ancient symbol of regeneration. Even in Vedic mythology there is a bird called *Jatayu*, which tried to fly too close to the Sun, just as in the Greek legend of *Icarus*. Ketu as we know is the main planet signifying regeneration and is thus related to all legends of this nature. It has a vulture for its vehicle which connects it with the birds Jatayu, Phoenix etc. The fact that Phoenix rises from its ashes is a typical Ketu imagery.

Vedic mythology divides the universe into fifteen main regions or planes of existence. Earth is the middle region as there are seven regions above Earth and seven regions below. One of these nether regions is said to be populated entirely by snake like beings called *Nagas*. It is not hard to see that this region will fall under the domain of Rahu and Ketu. These Nagas are supposed to have magical powers. There are a lot of legends about them visiting Earth and mating with the human population to aid humanity in its evolutionary process.

If we look at Mayan and Inca legends they talk of *Quetzalcoatl* or serpent men coming from the ocean and giving them knowledge in fields like astrology, architecture etc. There is now a theory gaining ground among serious scholars that these beings arrived from the sinking continent of Atlantis. It is postulated that these beings from Atlantis landed up in lands like India, Egypt and South America. In all the ancient cultures of these lands one can find scriptural evidence of the arrival of these beings which are surprisingly always associated with some kind of serpent imagery.

This leads us to the conclusion that Atlantis was an advanced civilization because its natives had learnt to harness the serpent power encapsulated in the serpent planets Rahu and Ketu. These survivors from Atlantis even carried these serpent symbols through their costume etc. It is now presumed these survivors provided the know how to build the great pyramids, whose building process, despite our technological advancement, still remains a mystery.

The point I am trying to make here is that for a civilization to become truly advanced it has to have a conscious understanding of the serpent forces embodied by Rahu and Ketu. We have already seen how Rahu has been behind much of the technological developments since the Renaissance, but all of this has taken place in an unconscious manner, because the people involved weren't aware of the collective forces that were guiding them. For example *Kekule* wasn't aware that the nodes were responsible for the dream in which the structure of Benzene was revealed to him.

As the energies of the Age of Aquarius grow stronger with each passing day, the knowledge about the deep and mysterious functionings of the nodes and the forces they represent will become clearer to us. Rahu as we know is the coruler of the sign Aquarius and is responsible for most of the technological advancement which astrologers ascribe to the Age of Aquarius.

Humanity is yet to concentrate on the importance of these energies on planes other than material ones. This is probably the reason why internet and not telepathy is the common mode of communication in today's world.

No matter how we pride ourselves on our technological accomplishments, the fact remains that humanity is still in its infancy and is just about beginning to learn its association with other realms of existence. This as we know would require every individual to become conscious of their kundalini and learn how to utilize it for their evolution. For this to happen on a mass scale we require an understanding of Rahu and Ketu, as they truly are the planets signifying all knowledge and wisdom.

* * *

A Demon named Swarbhanu, sees through the trick and disguised as a God, quietly slips over to the row of the Gods

7. ASSOCIATION WITH OTHER PLANETS

Just like other planets Rahu and Ketu form associations with other planets by aspect, conjunction or by being placed in their signs or constellations. We will discuss their placement in different signs in a separate chapter. When a node is placed in the constellation of a particular planet, it gets affected in a similar but diluted way as its conjunction with that planet. In this chapter we would only deal with their conjunctions and trinal aspects with other planets.

As discussed earlier only the trinal and conjunction aspects are important in the case of the nodes, so we will not deal with other aspects like squares, opposition etc. The square aspects are only important in relation to their role in collective phenomenon, which we will discuss in Chapter 14. The opposition aspect doesn't hold much significance in case of the nodes because if one planet is opposing a node it is bound to be conjunct the other node. For example Rahu opposing Sun automatically means that Ketu is conjunct Sun and thus does not need to be dealt separately.

Let's refresh the fact that the aspects are applicable no matter what degrees the planets are occupying in the respective signs and thus no particular orb needs to be defined. However it is helpful to remember that the aspects usually have more significance if they have smaller orbs. A 5° orb usually gives the full results of the aspect or conjunction.

It must be reiterated that the guidelines enunciated below should be applied after careful consideration of the other factors like placement in the signs, asterisms, houses and the overall tone of the chart.

Lets start with Rahu's associations with different planets.

RAHU - SUN

This conjunction gives an opportunity in the present lifetime to seek and establish one's individuality. In its excess this can promote self aggrandizement and in its negative aspect it can promote selfishness and arrogance. The true purpose of this placement however is to further independence of spirit, views and inclinations. It always favours some sort of rebellion but as the axiom goes 'sometimes the rebel may be without a 'cause or clue'.

It gives a fascination for the unusual and bizarre. Such natives usually benefit from strange, atypical pursuits. This is a good combination for gaining professional success in a foreign land or through involvement with foreigners.

This combination often allows one to express one's individuality in the significations of the house it is placed in. This is more likely when this placement takes place in fire signs. This placement usually adds to the materialistic tone of a chart. This is more likely when this placement takes place in earth signs.

This placement gives more balanced results in the air signs except that it doesn't do well in Libra because of Sun's debilitation. Both the positives and negatives of the Solar side of Rahu's functioning are experienced through this conjunction. The trine aspect is similar to the conjunction but has a milder tone to it.

The legendary science fiction writer *H.G. Wells* has this combination in the ninth house giving him a fascination for the unusual. He tried to get some philosophical message across through his writings as Rahu is placed in its own sign Virgo. *Karl Marx,* who birthed the idea of communism in the modern times has this conjunction in Aries.

John Lennon, the famous 20th century musician, has this conjunction in his first house. It gave him the self confidence to be on stage for most of his life. It also gave him an outspoken nature and a predominantly revolutionary mindset. He definitely was the most rebellious among the four Beatles. This combination works in its refined mode as Rahu is placed in its own sign Virgo. The fieriness of Sun and Mars is toned down by being placed in an earth sign Virgo.

RAHU - MOON

This conjunction is of extreme importance as Rahu is closely associated with the Moon. We already know that Rahu is intimately connected with the Universal Mother principle, which in our solar system manifests through Moon. Even though Rahu is said to have an enmity with Moon the major scope of its activity is lunar in a lot of ways. This is because Rahu is born out of the causative force sustaining this Universe, which is supposed to be feminine in its attributes.

In its positive aspect this conjunction vitalizes the lunar energy and as a result strengthens the mind. This conjunction is supposed to generate a powerful *yoga* (combination) which we will discuss in the chapter dealing with the special combinations of the nodes.

It also gives psychic sensibilities and subtle perception to the mind principle. It is very easy for such a native to tap into the unseen realms. This is more likely when this placement takes place in mystical signs like Scorpio, Aquarius and Pisces. Whether one will tap into the higher celestial realms or lower demonic realms depends upon the evolutionary level of the soul involved.

In its negative aspect it furthers the dark side of the lunar nature which as discussed earlier furthers emotional and psychological disturbances, fears and phobias, isolation, lunacy, hallucination, illusion, paranoia and other such distorted mental states.

This combination gives strength to the house it is placed in. If it is placed in the twelfth house it would give prophetic dreams, enhance psychic perception and other twelfth house significations like foreign residence.

Nietzche (Chart no.2), the famous 19th century philosopher, has this conjunction in his ascendant in the sign Scorpio and his life and works reveal the curious functionings of this placement.

RAHU - MARS

This placement assures abundant mental or physical energy. It brings out the Martian side of Rahu to the fore. In the present life the native has the opportunity to express the Martian energy. This may be done consciously or can be purely circumstantial. There is a constant need for activity and movement making this a good placement for worldly accomplishments. Such natives are never short of energy even though there can be a lack of direction. This is a typical go getter combination.

As discussed earlier Rahu can also cause perversion of Martian energy in many a case. Most of the unnecessary violence perpetuated on this planet has its roots in this perversion. In its negative aspect this placement furthers unnecessary anger, aggression and lack of sensitivity. This is more likely to be the case when this conjunction takes place in signs like Aries, Taurus, Leo, Scorpio and Capricorn. In its positive aspect it gives one strength to stand up against injustice. Rahu in trine with Mars gives similar results but the expression is usually more refined.

This combination usually spoils the live significations of a house while promoting the non-live significations. For example if this combination is placed in the fourth house it will help one gain property, give a keen psychological insight, but create troubles for or from the mother and disturbs inner peace.

We have already discussed how it creates criminals like *John Dillinger* or true revolutionaries like *Shivaji*. He single-handedly tried to overthrow the Mogul Empire at the peak of its power in the 17th century. This combination takes place in his eleventh house. This helped him gain support from others and assured success in group activities as eleventh house signifies group activities. Rahu's exaltation in Gemini made him channel his Martian energy for a positive cause. Rahu's presence in Gemini gave him a very shrewd and tactical intellect which didn't mind using any method for attaining victory in battle. His wit and presence of mind in dangerous situations now makes up volumes of literature in Indian folklore.

It also creates deep thinkers like *Aldous Huxley* and *Albert Einstein* (Chart no. 6) with the emphasis being on logic. Reformers like *Abraham Lincoln* are also produced by this combination.

RAHU - MERCURY

This combination usually heightens the intellectual and thinking capacity. Those with this combination in their chart find that for the better part of their lives they are involved in activities with emphasis on communication, thinking or use of the hands. Just like the previous Rahu-Mars combination this gives abundant mental and nervous energy. It boosts Mercurial qualities like wit, versatility, quickness of thought, and communication ability.

It is a fortunate combination in the sense that Mercury is a close friend of Rahu. We have already seen how Rahu shares an intimate relationship with Mercury and functions well in Mercury's signs. It usually boosts the significations of the house in which it takes place. This combination usually gives its best results when it takes place in Gemini ,Virgo or Aquarius.

In its negative aspect this combination can make one misuse one's Mercurial skills for selfish ends or harming others. In some cases the intellect is distorted to an extent that the native doesn't think twice about indulging in criminal actions. It can also get one caught up in the present day information boom which has very little to do with real knowledge. In its higher aspect it can give true knowledge and the ability to look through illusions. It can also connect one's intellect to the unseen realms and as a result give intuitive or psychic perception.

Just like the previous combinations it usually gives success in all things foreign. The trinal relationship usually carries a more refined and subtle energy. The qualities and attributes of Rahu's asterism *Ardra* discussed in Chapter 4. can be applied to this combination.

Edgar Cayce (Chart no. 7) and *Helena Petrovna Blavatsky* (Chart no. 9), two famous seers of the modern times, have this combination in their chart.

We have already discussed the dream episode of the discoverer of the structure of the Benzene, *Kekulé von Stradonitz*, in Chapter 3. Kekule has an exact Rahu-Mercury conjunction in the sign of Virgo, which as we can see is the best placement for this combination as Mercury is exalted and Rahu is in its own sign.

RAHU - JUPITER

Since the prominent theme of Jupiter is expansion and that of Rahu materiality, this placement gives a desire for material acquisitions. It is one of the most materialistic combinations in astrology especially if it happens in an earth sign. It is known as *Guru-Chandala* yoga which we will deal with in the chapter dealing with the special combinations involving the nodes.

In its positive aspect it can give a philosophical and charitable disposition. This usually happens when this conjunction takes place in a water sign or in signs like Sagittarius and Aquarius. In its negative aspect it can make one selfish, vindictive and deceitful. It is however useful to remember that it is a mild placement and is unable to cause any real harm to anyone even if it wishes to. It also gives problems due to over optimism and extravagance. To sum it up it usually bestows a friendly disposition and indulgence in material pursuits.

Another way of looking at this combination is that Jupiter is the planet of law while Rahu is lawlessness incarnate. The merging of these two energies can sometimes create a good balance and at other times cause disaster through over-expansion especially on the material plane.

This combination imparts the same materialistic nature to the significations of the house in which it takes place. For example if it takes place in the fourth house one will have a materially oriented mother. It usually promotes the non-live significations of the house it is placed in. For example if it is placed in fourth house it will make the native experience a certain degree of luck in property matters.

The trinal relationship between Rahu and Jupiter adds to the fortune of a chart. It promotes and gives success in Jupiterian pursuits like teaching, authorship etc.

George Bernard Shaw, the famous 20th century English philosopher, has this combination in the philosophical sign of Pisces which gave him a philosophical disposition and helped him in Jupiterian pursuits like authorship.

Osho' Rajneesh one of the most famous 20th century Gurus has a trinal relationship between Jupiter and Rahu in his chart. It boosts his luck in his primarily Jupiterian vocation but gives him an expansive material nature. His chart is discussed in detail in Chapter Twelve. *Mick Jagger*, the famous singer has this combination in his third house giving him abundant vitality. The spirit of this combination is best communicated through his own words 'I can't get no satisfaction …'.

RAHU - VENUS

This is one of the most indulgent among all the two planet combinations. It brings out the Venusian side of Rahu which as discussed earlier gives a strong urge for comfort and luxury. This again is a primarily materialistic placement which assures success in Venusian pursuits.

In its negative aspect it can give superficiality and a lack of refinement especially when it takes place in earth signs like Taurus and Capricorn. It makes one a slave to one's desires and promotes greed and deceit to gain one's ends. In its higher aspect it gives higher Venusian qualities like diplomacy, compassion and true love. This is more likely when this combination takes place in signs like Aquarius and Pisces.

Just like the previous combination, this combination imparts the same materialistic nature to the significations of the house in which it takes place. For example if it takes place in the fifth house one will have materialistic children or sense of creativity. It promotes the non-live significations of the house it is placed in. For example if it is placed in the tenth house it will make the native lucky in professional matters.

The trinal relationship between Rahu and Venus can be seen as a milder form of the conjunction. The qualities and attributes of the asterism *Swati* discussed in Chapter 4. can be applied to this combination.

Sigmund Freud (Chart no. 3), the father of modern psychotherapy, has this conjunction in his chart. It is no wonder then that he came up with the conclusion that 'sex is the root of everything'.

Jesus Christ has this combination in the mystical sign of Scorpio if his chart is constructed using the findings of Cyril Fagan. He exemplified the higher qualities of this combination.

RAHU - SATURN

This combination heightens the Saturnine energy in a chart which can be for either good or bad. There are two main aspects to this combination - one which can give a depressive, melancholic disposition which makes one wish that it would have been better if one weren't born at all. This is more likely when this placement takes place in water signs like Cancer, Scorpio and Pisces.

In the other aspect it makes one a ruthless, insensitive go getter. In this aspect it makes one more emotionally dry and insensitive to the feelings of others. This conjunction can be a very fundamentalist force and can bring out all the negative Saturnine qualities of Rahu like selfishness, avarice, pessimism, hypocrisy, religious bigotry, which were discussed in Chapter 4. This is more likely when this conjunction takes place in earth signs. This is also the case when it is hardened by an aspect or conjunction with Mars.

It usually gives a deep interest and proficiency in some foreign thing like language, literature, architecture or culture.

This combination functions the best in air signs and can give a highly philosophical and detached attitude when it takes place in

Aquarius. It usually does not function well in fire signs even though it gives neutral results in Sagittarius.

Still, this combination gives obstacles and initial struggle in the house where it is placed. For example if it is placed in the second house there might be anxieties and struggles relating to one's financial situation. The qualities and attributes of the asterism *Shatabhisha* discussed in Chapter 4. can be applied to this combination.

It is seen that if Rahu and Saturn share a harmonious relationship with each other in the charts of dictators, rulers and politicians, the country they preside over experiences good fortune in their period of rule.

Queen Victoria (Chart no. 21), who was the very symbol of the word 'imperialism', has this combination in her eleventh house. This combination gets hardened by the presence of Mars and the debilitation of Jupiter, the dispositor of Rahu and Saturn. One can notice a lot of religious conversions taking place through missionary activity in her time at the throne.

RAHU - URANUS

This is the combination of the eccentric, individualist, maverick, inventor, researcher and the freak in general. This combination brings out the Uranian side of Rahu, discussed in the earlier chapter to the fore. It gives birth to radically different ideas.

In its lower functioning this gives the love of all types of material sciences, gadgets and technology. In the present scenario it gives expertise and gain through computer and internet related professions.

On a higher level it gives a love of understanding the subtle functionings of the Universe. Either way this is a futuristic placement which has a lot of importance in the present times as the energies of the sign Aquarius slowly gain prominence over the energies of the sign Pisces.

Rahu and Uranus are both corulers of Aquarius and as seen earlier both are revolutionary, creative, shocking, individualistic forces. They can be said to be the two main New Age planets. Since they are both collective forces they can make one a vehicle of the collective if the overall chart allows for a prominent personality.

This combination functions the best in air signs, Gemini, Libra and Aquarius. It usually manifests its refined side in Virgo, occult side in Scorpio and expansive side in Pisces. As usual, the trinal positioning gives similar but milder results. The futuristic qualities and attributes of Rahu's asterism *Shatabhisha* discussed in Chapter 5. can be applied to this combination.

Sigmund Freud (Chart no. 3) and *Osho Rajneesh* (Chart no. 20), have this conjunction in the seventh and eleventh houses in their respective charts. It must be noticed that both of them came up with a radical new way of thinking for their times. Major revolutionary thinkers like *J.Krishnamurthy* (Chart no. 1) and *Nietzsche* (Chart no. 2) have a trinal relationship between Rahu and Uranus involving the mystical signs Aquarius and Pisces.

Rupert Murdoch, the present day king of satellite television, cable networks and other media in Asia, has an exact Rahu Uranus conjunction in the expansive sign of Pisces.

RAHU - NEPTUNE

This is the combination of the visionaries, mystics, utopians, idealists, prophets, dreamers, clairvoyants and the like. Such natives always consciously or unconsciously find their lives connected with the Neptunian realm, they might be a rock star or just working in a pharmaceutical company.

In strong charts it assures fame through Neptunian activities like media, cinema, music, astrology, occultism etc. Since both Rahu and Neptune are collective planets this combination dreams big and strives for goals which affect the masses as a whole.

When working through its lower principle this drowns one in illusions and fantasies usually relating to the lower dark sides of existence. It can also make one lose one's self in chasing after mirages or hallucinations, which can either be induced by drugs or other techniques. A lot of modern day entertainment industry falls prey to the negative expression of this combination.

When working through its higher principle this combination produces people who utilize their talents for the collective good. It gives a highly refined sensibility and sensitivity to the higher realms of existence. It can be said to be the most subtle amongst all two planet combinations. Dreams, visions, fantasy and imagination become very important in relation to the significations of the house in which it takes place.

This combination can give a true understanding of the underlying unity of all creation. This is more likely when this combination takes place in mystical signs like Scorpio, Aquarius and Pisces. It can also show refined effects in Virgo where Rahu's energy is refined. As usual the trinal relationship acts in a similar but diluted manner.

John Lennon and *Bruce Lee* (Chart no. 22), two modern day legends in their respective fields have this combination in the sign Virgo. John Lennon's work as a solo artist expressed a primarily Neptunian vision while Bruce Lee's philosophical approach to Martial arts is quite Neptunian in much the same way as Taoism. Bruce Lee even achieved fame through the Neptunian realm of cinema. Both of them acted as mouthpieces for the collective.

RAHU - PLUTO

The keynote of this combination is striving for power in all its varied forms. These forms can include occult, astrology, money, politics, fame etc. In the modern times it has been seen to be more politically inclined. Since the power is rapidly shifting into the hands of the heads of the multinational companies from the hands of the politicians, one can assume that this combination would focus its attention on the main power source of today's world - money.

In its negative aspect it can bring out the worst side of Rahu and Pluto in the form of obsessive power games. This is a combination which stops at nothing to get what it wants. It can be said to be a more dangerous version of Rahu-Mars combination as it magnifies all the negative qualities of that conjunction. It is seen that usually such natives feel intensely dissatisfied after gaining all the power they wanted and suffer a tragic end.

In its positive aspect it can make one search for the deeper meanings of existence. Pluto as we know represents the core of everything and Rahu represents knowledge and so it brings illumination on the deepest level. On an esoteric level this combination gives the courage to battle through all odds in one's pursuit for perfection. In its higher aspect this combination can act as an agent of destruction like *Shiva* (the destroyer among the Vedic trinity), but this destruction would be of long term benefit for all involved. As we have discussed earlier transformation and dissolution go hand in hand.

This combination is again a primarily collective force. It functions best when it takes place in Virgo, Scorpio, Aquarius and Pisces. As usual the trinal relationship acts in a similar but diluted manner. The destructive qualities and attributes of Rahu's asterism *Ardra* discussed in Chapter 4. can be applied to this combination.

Napolean (Chart no. 8), *John.F.Kennedy* (Chart no. 14), *Fidel Castro* are a few among the many prominent ones having this combination. The emphasis on power is clearly seen through these examples. In a way all of the men mentioned are collective sacrifices and act as release valves for collective longings of their respective nations.

Let's now have a look at Ketu's conjunction with other planets:

SUN - KETU

This is one of the most spiritual combinations as Ketu and Sun are both spiritualising influences in their own ways. As discussed earlier Ketu shares a special relationship with Sun in much the same way Rahu does with Moon. Ketu as we know shares qualities like wilfulness, extreme anger, hot temperament, regality, intense concentration, deep perception, penetrating insight etc. with the Sun.

It also resembles Sun in the sense that it is a hot, dry and fiery planet. The cruelty associated with the Sun, which can be felt on a hot summer day in the equatorial region or through the insensitive behaviour of father figures resonates with the cruelty inherent in Ketu.

The dictum -"force which gives life can also take life,"- applies to both Sun and Ketu equally. The solar part of Ketu's nature is highlighted with this combination. It shows that the native has been working on developing the solar part of their nature in their previous life/lives. The degree of perfection achieved depends upon the evolutionary level of the soul in question.

In its negative aspect Ketu can either obstruct, negate, darken or completely dissolve the Sun, which as we know represents our sense of self. However this dissolution aspect is not at all negative in the sense that we can realize our unity with the whole only after this sense of self that separates us from others is dissolved. The problem is that Ketu does not always dissolve the Sun completely but afflicts it partially. This can in some cases manifest as a lack of self-confidence and at other times as self-aggrandizement. We can easily deduce that the former is more likely when it takes place in Libra, and the latter is more likely when it takes place in Leo.

Ketu can distribute Sun's energy in a destructive or a constructive way depending upon which aspect it is functioning through. Since Ketu usually internalises the energy of any planet it is associated with, it can internalise the energy of the Sun giving clear and deep insight. It either leads to clarity or confusion again depending upon the evolutionary level of the soul involved.

This combination usually functions at its best in the signs, Aries, Scorpio, Sagittarius or the asterisms ruled by the Sun or Ketu. As usual the trinal relationship acts in a similar but diluted manner. The qualities and attributes of Ketu's asterism *Magha* discussed in Chapter 4. can be applied to this combination.

Alexander, the famous conqueror, has this combination in the royal sign of Leo in his fifth house. Just for the interest of the reader, both the illustrator and writer of this book have a very close Sun-Ketu conjunction.

MOON - KETU

The keyword for Moon is 'mind' and for Ketu is 'unusual', which means that this combination promotes an unusual mind or way of thinking. This combination in a chart shows that the native has been striving for the perfection of one's lunar nature in one's previous life/lives. The degree of perfection achieved again depends upon the evolutionary level of the soul in question.

This combination adds a psychic touch to the mind of the native involved. A strong psychic connection with mother or a mother figure is seen with this configuration.

Ketu is the most psychic among planets and sometimes its energies are difficult to handle for highly impressionable planets like the Moon. When working through its lower aspect this combination can give rise to all sorts of fears, phobias, idiosyncrasies and other morbid and unnatural mental states.

In many cases this combination gives a strange sense of being pursued or stalked by a curse, spirit, person etc. There is a constant awareness of some sort of danger lurking around which in extreme cases manifests as the phenomenon known as paranoia. Such people usually cannot get over the death of near and dear ones and find themselves haunted by the spirit of the dead.

It is interesting to note that for most of us these fears are usually more pronounced in the childhood stage, which is supposed to be governed by the Moon. It can also give an attachment to the lower dark side of life and an interest in black magic and other such unwholesome occult practices. It can also give a cruel disposition when Ketu completely dissolves Moon's sensitivity. This in extreme cases produces cold blooded maniacs who don't think twice before hurting others.

When strong and working through its higher principle, Ketu can also elevate the mind to a degree that the native has access to the secrets relating to the functionings of the Universe. It can also take the mind beyond the material world thus opening a window of opportunity for liberation.

Ketu governs the spirit world and can thus connect one's mind with that realm. With this combination, some sixth sense faculty is easily noticeable. This combination is usually strong in the signs Aries, Sagittarius and Pisces.

As usual the trine aspect carries the meanings of the conjunction in a milder and less dangerous form. According to some wise men Ketu's position in a trine from any of the luminaries lifts the overall tone of the chart. Ketu is seen to exchange its darkness for light through this trinal relationship.

This combination can be seen to be working through its fierce mode in the charts of *Hitler* (Chart no. 10) and *Chengiz Khan* (Chart no. 15). In its spiritual devotional mode it produced personalities like *Chaitanya* ,*Thyagaraja* and *Ramana Maharishi,* Indian saints who exemplified the *bhakti marga* (devotional path) to enlightenment in their own unique ways.

MARS - KETU

This can be said to be the most fiery and easily combustible among all the two planet combinations. It gives an intensely passionate and highly volatile nature. This te..ds to produce extreme recklessness and impulsiveness if not associated with other planets. This combination shows that the native has been working with the Martian energy in their previous live/lives. They have some Martian talent which has to be utilized for some positive harmonious purpose in the present life. This native experiences extremes of energy levels - they sometimes feel very energetic and sometimes they just feel completely bereft of energy.

Ketu as we know is very similar to Mars and is coruler of Scorpio, a sign ruled by Mars. This combination furthers all significations common to Ketu and Mars – enmity, accidents, violence, domination, arguments, misunderstanding, litigation, anger, energy, will, courage, self-confidence etc.

In its negative aspect this combination furthers characteristics like intolerance, aggression, vengeance, revengefulness, rudeness and impetuosity. When working through its lower principle it can indulge in all sorts of atrocities, tortures and other abnormalities in the physical and mental realms. Ketu on an individual level can pervert the Mars energy and produce psychosis but also cause it to internalize where one fights with the enemy within instead of hurting others.

In its positive aspect it gives a very keen logical insight. The keyword of Mars is 'logic' and that of Ketu is 'intensity'. This combination can give piercing insight and power of intense concentration. Ketu can give the wisdom for the Martian energy to be utilized in a meaningful way for the evolutionary betterment of one's own self and others. This is usually more likely if it takes place in signs like Virgo, Sagittarius, Aquarius & Pisces.

This can be a very intense placement in Aries and Scorpio which can tilt to extremes of benevolence and malevolence. As usual the trinal aspect is a more diluted form of the conjunction. The nature and attributes of the Ketu's asterism *Ashwini* discussed in Chapter 4. can be applied to this combination.

Mark Twain, the famous American author, whose works reveal his keen psychological insight was born with this placement in the sign of Virgo. This takes place in his fifth house and thus sharpens his mind but the energy of Mars and Ketu is refined by the earthy discriminating sign of Virgo.

MERCURY - KETU

Since the keyword for Mercury is 'intellect' and for Ketu is 'unusual' this combination can be said to be the one which gives an unusual intellect or way of thinking. In a nativity it shows that the native has been working with the Mercurial energy in their previous life/lives. They have some Mercurial talent which has to be utilized for some positive harmonious purpose in the present life.

In its negative aspect it can distort the intellect causing confusion on all levels of existence. There is a general scattering of nervous energy and in common parlance the native finds it hard to get it together. In extreme cases it can make one derive pleasure out of unwholesome pursuits and all kinds of nefarious activities.

Ketu's critical nature combined with Mercury's discriminatory power can either produce a genius when these energies are directed inwards or the irritating neighbourhood critic whose energies are scattered outside without attaining a proper understanding.

Ketu is a planet of deep insight, which when combining with Mercury's adaptability and dexterity can give great intellectual and philosophical acumen. This is the reason why it is a considered a boon in the chart of Astrologers. This combination can function well in any sign provided there are other supporting factors like aspect and association of benefics. This combination usually gives a keen insight into the affairs of the house it is placed in. As usual the trinal aspect gives similar but diluted results.

Paul Simon, the famous contemporary poet and musician, has this combination in Scorpio in his fourth house. The presence of Sun and Saturn in the mystical sign Scorpio, adds depth to this combination. His words and music reveal the insightfulness of this placement. In his Mercury and Ketu major periods he turned his attention to the tribal music of Africa and came up with two very soul stirring albums.

JUPITER - KETU

This can be seen as a fortunate combination in the sense that Jupiter is the only planet which can to an extent control the negative functioning of Ketu. It shows good karma from past lives as one has been trying to work in the Jupiterian realm. Such a native has the responsibility of spreading the knowledge and wisdom attained in the present life.

Since the main theme of Jupiter is 'expansion' and that of Ketu 'constriction' one may find that fortune doesn't flow smoothly in the lives of such natives. At some point of their lives they have to undergo some sort of struggle. Success is usually assured if the native has patience and perseverance. In its negative aspect it can sl ow rigidity and dogmatism especially in Jupiterian realms like religion, morality & philosophy. It can promote hypocrisy in these areas.

It can also be a very cruel placement in the cases where Ketu completely negates all Jupiterian energy. Jupiter as we know is our sense of cosmic law and compassion. One can easily guess the results of Ketu completely blocking out this sense of compassion and kindness. This is probably why the ancient seers saw it as a negative combination in a similar vein to Jupiter-Rahu conjunction.

In some cases when Ketu magnifies the Jupiterian energy it can cause downfall through over expansion. This is more likely the case in signs like Sagittarius and Pisces where both Ketu and Jupiter are strong. It also functions strongly in Aries and Scorpio. In such cases the house where this combination takes place becomes the focal point of the whole chart.

This combination usually gives an innate sense of refinement and sensitivity. It is a psychic combination which can give intuition and extra sensory perception. Such natives can surprise people by their ability to do things without any prior experience. It can give a penetrating philosophical insight since Ketu can add penetration to Jupiter's philosophy.

The qualities and attributes of Ketu's asterism *Mula* can be applied to this combination. The trinal aspect in this case is of special importance. If they are in trines it would mean that Jupiter would be aspected with Ketu as Jupiter has a fifth/ninth aspect in Vedic Astrology. This can be seen as one of the fortunate factors that improve the tone of a chart. It makes one especially fortunate as far as male progeny are concerned. We have already discussed in Chapter 3. how Jupiter and Ketu are natural significators of male progeny.

Adolf Hitler (Chart no.10), undoubtedly one of the major figures of 20th century, has this combination in Sagittarius in his third house. We can see the cruelty and over expansion aspects of this combination working through his chart. It can also be noticed that his main talent lay in a third house signification - oratory. *Jawaharlal Nehru* (Chart no. 25), the first prime-minister of independent India and a major international figure of his time, has this conjunction in the same sign in his sixth house. Most of his life was spent in a sixth house affair - fighting the enemy which in his case were the British.

VENUS - KETU

This combination gives the native some eccentricity in Venusian matters like love, companionship, devotion, compassion, occultism etc. It shows that the native has been working out karma in the Venusian realm in the previous life/lives.

As is the case with other planets Ketu can refine Venusian energy or pervert it. This combination can confer artistic talents, which are basically the fruits of past life exertions, in a particular area of art. It can be seen in the charts of prodigies who very early in life start exhibiting their skills, artistic or otherwise. In its negative aspect all the perversions relating to Venusian affairs like love and sex are relayed through this combination. It is generally seen to be unfavourable for marital happiness.

This combination is extreme in the sense that on one hand it has a liking for luxury and comforts in a very Venusian fashion but on the other hand has a tendency to completely shun them. It often manifests these extremes within a single lifetime.

Love is restricted to a few when it is working through its lower aspects and is all-inclusive when it is expressing its highest energies. This combination usually chooses platonic love over other forms of love. This is more likely the case when it takes place in mystical signs like Scorpio, Aquarius and Pisces. It is seen to function well in Aries.

Its love of the collective can be seen as the reason why a lot of present day politicians are born with this combination. Another reason may be that one often receives setbacks in individual matters like love and companionship, enabling one to turn one's attention towards either seeking power or genuinely helping the community.

This combination usually produces some struggle in the house it is placed in as one tries to balance the extremes within the affairs of that particular house. As usual the trine aspect gives similar but diluted results.

Napolean (Chart no. 8), the famous French emperor, has this combination in Gemini in his ninth house. As history tells us he suffered disappointments in both love and marriage. We will learn later how Ketu put an end to his fortune when we discuss his chart in detail in Chapter 12. *Helmut Kohl*, the man behind the unification of Germany, also has this combination in the sign of Aries in his first house.

Turning from politicians onto those in Venusian professions we find that *Christian Dior*, the famous priestess of high fashion, has this conjunction in her fifth house in the inventive and innovative sign of Aquarius.

SATURN - KETU

This can be seen as the toughest of all two planet combinations. It suggests deeply ingrained Saturnine habits and attitudes carried over from past life/lives. This can be a hard thing to deal with in the present life as one always tends to be innately pessimistic about everything from the very beginning.

When Ketu is neutralizing the bad karma from previous lives this combination can be a very limiting, constrictive influence This combination is the master of tragedy and it has no equal as far as manufacturing tragic situations is concerned. It can make one reach the depths of despair through a series of unfortunate events. It can magnify all the negative saturnine effects – depression, melancholy, miserliness, gloominess, selfishness etc. It is quite stuck, stubborn and unyielding when it is working in this mode. This can often lead to fundamentalism in all areas of human affairs. It is very hard for natives born under this combination to embrace the new and get over the old. This is more likely when this placement takes place in signs like Cancer, Leo and Capricorn.

However the lessons learnt under this combination are always for the long-term benefit of the soul involved. It is the case of 'reap as you shall sow' all over again.

In its positive aspect it gives mastery in work involving details and precision. It can also make one deeply philosophical if both these planets are working through their higher aspect. This is more likely when this combination takes place in mystical signs like Scorpio, Aquarius and Pisces. It is useful to remember that in Scorpio it might go either way. Jupiter's aspect on this combination usually has a calming and balancing influence on this combination.

Like Saturn, Ketu is a separative, detaching force and so their combination can lead one to the state of *Vairagya* i.e. disillusionment and detachment from the game of life. This is good in the sense that it can help one grow spiritually but it might also make one neglect one's worldly duties or stop one from fulfilling one's karma in the present life.

This combination usually spoils the significations of the house it takes place in. For example if it takes place in the fourth house one might experience problems relating to mother, property and inner peace. As usual the trine aspect gives similar but diluted results.

Prophet Mohammed, the founder of Islam, has this conjunction in his tenth house in the fixed sign of Scorpio. The dark, fundamentalist and violent religion he came up with gives an idea of the energy of this combination in its negative aspect. The dispositor of the conjunction Mars is debilitated thus making the combination express the negative Scorpionic qualities. His chart, personality and religion brings out the worst aspect of this combination. He also has a Venus-Rahu conjunction in his chart which gave him a twisted mentality as far as rights of women are concerned.

Che Guevera, the famous Cuban revolutionary, has an exactly similar chart with the same Ascendant, Saturn-Ketu and Venus-Rahu combination. The only difference is that in his case Mars is placed in a more idealistic, utopian and all inclusive sign, Pisces. One can however still see some of the negative aspects of this placement functioning through his life

Aldous Huxley, a renowned deep thinker and philosopher of the modern times, has this combination in the discriminatory sign of Virgo in his fifth house. His life and works reveal the positive aspect of this combination which manifested as a true yearning to search for the answers to mysteries of existence. The dispositor of this combination Mercury is nicely placed in conjunction with the Sun. It also is the dispositor of the two benefics Jupiter and Venus making him a much more pleasant personality.

URANUS - KETU

This combination can be seen to be having similar qualities as Rahu-Uranus conjunction except that it is not so much in touch with the current Uranian trends. The Uranian vision it embraces has been ingrained from some past life in an advanced civilization.

This combination also produces eccentrics, individualists, mavericks, researchers and freaks but one can witness a certain degree of conservatism and reliance on the knowledge and wisdom of the past in comparison to those having Rahu-Uranus conjunction. It promotes mediumistic and channelling capacity. It can be said to bring out the spiritual aspect of Uranus relating to awakening of the *Kundalini* and attunement with higher planes of existence.

In its less evolved functioning this can give a scattered and erratic tinge to everything a native does as both Ketu and Uranus promote such qualities. In the present scenario it gives expertise in computer and internet related professions. The flow of fortune through these mediums may not however be as smooth as in the case of Rahu-Uranus conjunction.

Since both Ketu and Uranus are collective planets it gives one a significant part in the collective destiny if the other factors in the chart allow for it. It functions strongly through mystical signs like Scorpio, Aquarius and Pisces. As usual the trine aspect gives similar but diluted results.

Vivekananda (Chart no. 24), one of the most well known preachers of the late 19th and early 20th century, has this placement in his sixth house in Taurus. This gave him an interest in the technological developments of his time but an enmity with Uranian organizations like the Theosophical society. He was a revolutionary in his approach but still conservative by Uranian parameters. His chart is discussed in detail in Chapter 12. *Yogananda*, another famous Indian preacher of the 20th century, has a similar case. He has this conjunction in his third house which helped him spread the Kundalini awakening technique in the West.

Edgar Cayce (Chart no. 7) has this conjunction in the sign of individual consciousness, Leo. He could channel his past life experiences in Atlantis in his present life. His chart is discussed in detail in Chapter 12.

NEPTUNE - KETU

This is one of the most esoteric combinations. It brings out the Neptunian side of Ketu. Ketu as we have seen is related to the outer planet Neptune in the sense that they both represent dissolution on all levels. We also know both Ketu and Neptune are corulers of the sign Pisces.

This combination represents extreme, complex and intense emotional states. In other words it is a psychologist's nightmare. These emotional states are different in their quality than the normal emotions represented by inner planets like Moon and Venus. They can cause severe sense of alienation and estrangement. In its negative aspect it can cause mental derangement by distorting the psyche. It is very easy for this combination to fall prey to drugs, intoxicants and hallucinations. The emotional aspect of this combination is highlighted when it takes place in water signs like Cancer, Scorpio and Pisces.

Just like Rahu-Neptune conjunction, this is the combination of the visionaries, mystics, utopians, idealists, prophets, dreamers, clairvoyants and the like. The only difference being that such gifts are brought over from past life/lives. In case of Rahu-Neptune conjunction they have to be worked on in the present life.

In the same vein as Rahu-Neptune conjunction, when working through its higher principle this combination produces people who utilize their talents for the collective good. It gives a highly refined sensibility and sensitivity to the higher realms of existence. Dreams, visions, fantasy and imagination form an important part of this combination. They are often related to the affairs of the house it is placed in.

Neptune is the planet *Maya* (illusory force of nature) which sustains the drama of life. Ketu is the significator of deepest insight and thus this combination can help one gain access to the secrets of creation. This combination is thus the closest a two planet combination gets to bestowing emancipation. This is more likely when this combination takes place in mystical signs like Scorpio, Aquarius and Pisces or houses like eighth and twelfth. As usual the trinal relationship acts in a similar but diluted manner.

H.G Wells, the famous science fiction writer, has this placement in the sensitive occult sign of Pisces. It takes place in the third house, the house of writing. Through his writings he warned humanity of what the future might be like if all the focus remained concentrated on material science and technology.

PLUTO - KETU

This can be said to be a powerhouse combination as both Ketu and Pluto have 'power' as their underlying theme. As discussed in Chapter 3. Ketu shares a lot of the qualities that are attributed to Pluto in Western astrology. Ketu like Pluto relates with the primordial forces present at the beginning of creation. Ketu and Pluto together encompass the realm covered by the terms enigma and enigmatic. This combination signifies that one has undergone some deep catharsis in a previous life and is thus rewarded by some form of power in the present life.

This combination relates to the depths in every aspect of existence and is more concerned with the underlying forces than the surface superficialities in much the same way as Pluto. As we know Ketu and Pluto are the two planets that lie at the core of everything that exists. This is more likely when this conjunction takes place in signs like Scorpio, Sagittarius, Aquarius and Pisces.

In its negative aspect it relates to the dark, destructive, manipulative side of nature as exemplified by both Ketu and Pluto. It follows that it promotes chaos, disorder on a collective level and idiosyncrasies, unpredictability, paranoia etc. on a personal level. It can make one power hungry and indulge in unnecessary power games. When such natives get into power positions it inflates their ego and they forget that they are just pawns in the great cosmic drama. Ketu and Pluto are both collective planets and together make one a collective sacrifice.

Usually the native with this placement has to witness or be part of some catastrophic event. If this is not the case then they have to face some deep personal loss relating to the house where this conjunction takes place. As usual the trinal relationship acts in a similar but diluted manner.

John.F.Kennedy (Chart no. 14), the famous American president who was assassinated while still in office has this conjunction in Gemini in his tenth house. Ketu as we know is debilitated in Gemini and so had to cut his career short. The presence of Pluto which represents hidden things, cut it short by the manipulations of hidden forces. After 40 years, his assassination is still shrouded in mystery.

Indira Gandhi (Chart no. 23), the first and only woman prime-minister of India has this placement in Gemini in the twelfth house. She was also assassinated while in office. The life and personality of both these individuals reveal a lot relating to this conjunction. Their charts are discussed in detail in Chapter 12.

Thomas Edison (Chart no. 18), the famous inventor and discoverer, has this conjunction in Aries. It takes place in his eleventh house, the house of hopes and ambitions. This combination helped him harness power in a variety of ways including lighting up the world through his invention of the electric bulb. He had an insatiable appetite for improving the quality of life which follows directly from the eleventh house placement of this combination. Keeping in mind the tremendous impact his work had on all of us it can be said that he lived a collective life.

* * *

8. SPECIAL COMBINATIONS

In this chapter we will deal with four special cases of nodal axis placement which have their own unique characteristics.

SHAKTI YOGA (Power Combination)

This is the name given to a special combination formed as a result of placement of Moon and Rahu. This is enunciated in the system developed by Sage *Jaimini*, which forms an integral part of present day Vedic astrology.

According to the Sage, this combination is formed when -
1. Both Rahu and Moon are conjunct in the fifth or ninth house.
2. One of them is placed in the fifth or ninth house and the other aspects* the fifth or ninth house.
3. Both of them aspect* the fifth or ninth house without being placed there.

* The important thing to note is that the 'aspects' are different in *Jamini* system. Here signs aspect other signs according to the table given below.

Sign	Signs Aspected
Aries	Leo, Scorpio, Aquarius
Taurus	Cancer, Libra, Capricorn
Gemini	Virgo, Sagittarius, Pisces
Cancer	Taurus, Scorpio, Aquarius
Leo	Aries, Libra, Capricorn
Virgo	Gemini, Sagittarius, Pisces
Libra	Taurus, Leo, Aquarius
Scorpio	Aries, Cancer, Capricorn
Sagittarius	Gemini, Virgo, Pisces
Capricorn	Taurus, Leo, Scorpio
Aquarius	Aries, Cancer, Libra
Pisces	Gemini, Virgo, Sagittarius

A planet placed in any sign aspects the other signs according to this table. For example if Rahu is placed in Scorpio it would aspect Aries, Cancer and Capricorn.

The fifth and ninth houses should be seen from the Ascendant, Moon sign or Sun Sign. It functions more strongly when it is formed from the strongest among these three. For example if the Sun is stronger than the Moon and Ascendant in a chart, then this combination could be said to be stronger when it is formed by taking the Sun sign as Ascendant in comparison to say, taking the Moon sign as Ascendant.

This combination as the name suggests is supposed to generate tremendous power. The Fifth and Ninth houses as we know represent the merit we carry into the present life from our past lives. This combination basically shows strong potential for the present life as a result of good karma from past life/lives. One should however keep in mind that the power generated by this combination can never exceed what the chart allows for as a whole.

We have already seen the significance of Rahu's association with the Moon in Chapter 7. Rahu is born out of the causative force sustaining this Universe, which is supposed to be feminine in its attributes. Along with Moon it represents the *Shakti*, the feminine power which sustains the manifest Universe.

We have already discussed how Rahu vitalizes the lunar energy and as a result strengthens the mind. It can increase psychic receptivity and also elevate the mind in some cases.

For what purpose would this power be used, depends upon the overall inclination of the chart. However a general rule to keep in mind is that this power is usually used to destroy the significations of the planet placed in the house, fifth or ninth, this combination affects. This is also the case if a planet is conjunct either Rahu or Moon.

As an example, one can have a look at *Adolph Hitler*, whose chart is discussed in detail in Chapter 12. In his case this combination occurs in his ninth house. Rahu is placed in Gemini in the ninth house and is aspected (*Jaimini* aspect) by Moon which is placed in the third house in Sagittarius. Moon in his case is conjunct Jupiter. As a result, all the natural significations of Jupiter like benevolence, compassion, morality etc. were destroyed. This explains his cruelty whilst the power generated by this combination explains the big impact he had on lives of millions of people.

Ramakrishna Paramahansa, one of the most evolved souls to incarnate on earth in modern times, also has this combination in his ninth house. His chart is also discussed in detail in Chapter 12. In his chart this combination again takes place in the ninth house in the sign Libra, as Rahu aspects it from its placement in Taurus and Moon by being placed in Aquarius. In his case the only planet affected by this combination is Saturn which is placed in the ninth house. The power of this combination literally destroyed Saturn, which as we know is the prime agent of sorrow, matter and limitations. Therein lies the difference in the functioning of this combination in his chart as compared to Hitler's chart.

He can be said to be a saint who conquered Saturn. It is important to note that he worshipped *Kali*, the dark Goddess, who is an embodiment of *Shakti*. Thus this combination lives up to its name in his chart.

Even *Albert Einstein*, the famous physicist, has this combination from his Sun sign. Moon is placed in Scorpio, the ninth house from the Sun and is aspected by Rahu which is placed in Capricorn. It can be seen that he discovered the famous mass energy equation which eventually led to the making of the atom bomb. However in his chart the combination doesn't function in a negative manner as he was personally against the use of atomic weapons. The involvement of the sign Scorpio meant that he unearthed a powerful hidden force of nature which ended up being utilized for destructive ends. His chart is discussed in detail in Chapter 12.

GURU CHANDALA YOGA (priest-outcaste combination)

This combination as the name suggests is formed by the conjunction of the *Chandala* (outcaste) planets, Rahu or Ketu with the *Guru* (priest or teacher), Jupiter.

It has been seen as a negative combination by most astrologers for the simple reason that it makes one too materialistic especially in the case of Rahu conjunct Jupiter. The conjunction of Jupiter with Ketu is supposed to produce wicked tendencies even when the native is born in the most pious and godly of families.

This is a lopsided view as in its positive aspect it can give a philosophical and charitable disposition. The positive aspects of this conjunction have already been discussed in Chapter 7. It is true that this combination gives a primarily material nature when it takes place in earth signs and can distort (the nodes) one's sense of wisdom (Jupiter). However this combination can give a generous and highly philosophical nature when placed in signs like Aquarius and Pisces.

ECLIPSES

An 'eclipse' as we know is an observable phenomenon which in astrological terms takes place as a result of relative placement of the Sun, the Moon and the nodes.

The Lunar eclipse takes place on a Full Moon day, when Sun and Moon are conjunct the opposite nodes. The shadow of Earth falls on the Moon.

The Solar eclipse takes place on a New Moon day, when Sun and Moon are conjunct one of the nodes. The dark disc of the New Moon partially or fully covers the Sun.

The full Solar eclipse is a rarity in comparision to full Lunar eclipse as the Moon is just big enough to cover this Sun. The Earth on the other hand is much bigger than the Moon and thus its shadow usually covers the Moon fully. This is also the reason why the Lunar eclipses are usually longer than Solar eclipses.

An eclipse can astrologically affect a person in two ways -

(1) One can be born at the time when an eclipse was taking place. This usually brings with it some life long abnormality relating to the affairs of the house in which it takes place. One must however remember that even though a Lunar eclipse affects two houses, the house in which Moon is placed gets more seriously affected.

The effect of the Solar eclipse is more intense than the Lunar eclipse. The Solar eclipse primarily affects one at the soul level while the Lunar eclipse affects one at the mental level. The eclipses thus bring some distortion into the Solar and Lunar part of one's nature. They usually make one sensitive to unseen realms and other realities but at the same time make one prone to emotional and psychological disturbances, fears and phobias, isolation, lunacy, hallucination, illusion, paranoia and other such states by the negative functioning of the nodes.

They usually bring some problem in the relationship with parents. It is most likely with the the mother in case of a Lunar eclipse and with the father in case of a Solar eclipse. A lot of the times such natives are brought up by surrogate parents or relatives.

In rare cases I have seen the eclipses bestowing extreme good fortune in relation to the affairs of the house they affect. In some cases they bestow a keen psychological, philosophical and spiritual insight.

(2) They affect all of us due to the simple fact that the eclipses, both Solar and Lunar, always take place in a sign thus affecting the affairs of the house in which that particular sign is placed in the natal chart.

The eclipses bring either fortune or misfortune relating to the significations of the house in which they take place. This usually manifests through a sudden event or series of events.

The eclipses have more intense effects if they take place over important natal positions like Ascendant, Midheaven and middle point of houses. As usual, the effects are strongest in case of exact conjunctions but they are significantly noticeable within a 5° orb. In certain cases where they happen in exact conjunction with points like one's Ascendant they can completely change the life of a native involved .

When eclipses take place over natal planetary positions they bring some fortunate or unfortunate event relating to the natural and temporal significations of that planet. If an eclipse takes place over natal Venus one may experience a sudden improvement in Venusian matters like relations with opposite sex, and the affairs of the house in which Venus is placed also improve. In other cases the same transit may signal the complete blocking of Venusian energy leading to frustrations in all the abovementioned matters.

A general rule to remember is that the eclipses which involve Rahu as the central planet can be said to function in a similar way to Rahu, while the eclipses which involve Ketu as the central planet can be said to function in a similar way to Ketu. For example if a Lunar eclipse occurs with transiting Moon conjunct Ketu over a natal planet, then its effects will be similar to Ketu transiting over the natal planet. If a Solar eclipse occurs with Rahu conjunct the Sun and the Moon over a natal point or planet, then its effects will be similar to Rahu transiting over that particular natal point or planet.

Another rule which has been seen to work well is that the effect of the Solar eclipse lasts for the number of years equalling the number of hours it lasts. Thus if a Solar eclipse lasts for 2 hours its results will be experienced within or for a period of 2 years. The duration of a Solar eclipse is the time period between the first contact and the final contact between the Moon and the Sun.

For a Lunar eclipse the effect lasts for the number of months equalling the number of hours it lasts. Therefore if a Lunar eclipse lasts for 4 hours its results would be experienced within or for 4 months. The duration of a Lunar eclipse is the time period between the appearance of the first trace of Earth's shadow on the Moon's surface and the disappearance of the last trace of Earth's shadow on the Moon's surface .

The only exception to the abovementioned rule for determining the extent of duration of an eclipse occurs when in a particular region the Sun or Moon rise after the eclipse has already started. In such cases the rising time of the Sun or the Moon should be taken as the start of the eclipse for that particular region.

Eclipses have been seen as powerful omens by most of the ancient cultures. This is because they not only affect individual lives but like any other major planetary event affect the humanity as a whole. The collective results of the eclipses have been touched upon in Chapter 14.

KALASARPA YOGA (the time-serpent combination)

This combination as the name suggests relates to the time aspect of Rahu and Ketu, the serpent planets. We know that Ketu represents past and Rahu represents future. So together they complete the circle of time which envelops all of us.

This is a very controversial combination as different Vedic scholars have a different view of it. The only point where there is general consensus is that this combination takes place when all the planets are hemmed in between Rahu and Ketu.

The problem starts when the following questions are addressed. Is this combination valid if the planets are hemmed in between Rahu and Ketu (i.e. Rahu lies before Ketu in the nativity) or Ketu and Rahu (i.e. Ketu lies before Rahu in the nativity)? Is this combination valid if the planets are hemmed in the second half (eight to twelfth houses) of the chart or does it only apply for planets primarily hemmed in the first half (first to seventh) of the chart ?

My personal view is based on a method I have come up with to divide the chart into two halves. In this method one should see Rahu-Ketu axis as a line running through the chart. Rahu should be treated as North and Ketu should be treated as South on this axis. Rahu as we know is related to North while Ketu is related to South.

We can now see the chart is divided into two halves. One half, which we can call the "Eastern half", stretches from Rahu to Ketu via the Eastern direction and the other, which we can call the "Western half", stretches from Rahu to Ketu via the Western direction. We can easily decide which is the Eastern direction and which is the Western direction from the North- South axis.

The planets posited in the Eastern half are primarily Solar in nature and functioning while the planets posited in the Western half are more Lunar in their scope of functioning.

One can easily see that if all the planets are placed in only one half, an imbalance is created. As we can see this will make the native involved one-sided. In other words the native will be stuck and lopsided in a conscious or unconscious way. This is why ancient Vedic seers treated this as a special case.

If we go by this theory the *Kalasarpa Yoga* would exist whenever all the planets are hemmed in between Rahu and Ketu. It doesn't matter where and how the planets are placed. The answer to the two questions put up earlier would now be 'Yes'.

It is important to remember when we say 'all the planets' that we are not taking the outer planets into account.

The Yoga would be now of two types. The first type is where all the planets are hemmed within the Eastern half. Such a native will show predominantly Solar qualities like assertiveness, self-assurance, self-reliance etc. but would to quite an extent lack Lunar qualities like gentleness, compassion, fostering etc. Such natives are usually harsh and insensitive like a hot midday Sun.

Joseph Goebbels, the famous propaganda minister and close confidante of Adolph Hitler, has this combination in his chart. All his planets are hemmed in the Eastern half between Ketu in Cancer in second house and Rahu in Capricorn in eighth house. His cruelty and insensitivity during Hitler's reign is well recorded. He was the one who ordered the burning of the books which did not fit in with the Nazi plan.

The important thing to note in this combination is that the affairs of the two houses in which Rahu and Ketu are placed assume prime importance in the native's life. As we can see in Goebbel's case it was all about secrecy (eighth house Rahu) and lying (second house Ketu).

The second type of this combination would occur when all the planets are hemmed within the Western Half. Such a native will show predominantly well developed Lunar nature but would have a poorly developed Solar nature. Such natives are usually too soft, timid, inconstant, moody and changeable in their approach unless the Sun is naturally strong in their charts.

Jawahar Lal Nehru, the first prime-minister of independent India has this combination in his chart. All his planets are hemmed in the Western half between Rahu in Gemini in twelfth house and Ketu in Sagittarius in the sixth house. His life and works reveal a very Lunar personality. He spent his life dealing with enemies (sixth house Ketu) and international affairs (twelfth house Rahu). His chart is dealt with in detail in Chapter 12.

Some scholars seem to have opined that this combination doesn't allow one to rise to a high position in life. As is clear from the examples given above, this is not the case. A native can rise high in life with this combination if the nodes are strong and the other indications in the chart allow for it.

A lot of prominent people have this combination but they usually are not able to do justice to their position because of their imbalanced personalities. This is why the ancient seers saw this as a negative combination.

There is also a certain sort of fatedness attached with this combination in the sense that the free will is at its minimum as far as the general direction in life is concerned. This is why this combination's name conveys the feeling of the serpents encircling one's life force. The native has to function within a certain circular boundary delineated by the nodes. The only way for climbing the evolutionary ladder for such souls is to make a conscious effort to develop the missing side of their personality and fulfil their duty in the present life.

9. PERIODS AND TRANSITS

As discussed earlier, every planet needs a certain window in time to manifest its energies. A planet is only free to influence events at certain times when its energy is dominant. In the 'timing' section in Chapter 3 we discussed the windows in time when the nodes are strongest to relay their energies.

In this chapter we will deal with the two main 'timing' methods - Periods and Transits. We will start with Planetary Periods which as we have discussed earlier is a speciality of Vedic astrology.

Vedic astrology assigns every planet including Rahu and Ketu a major period the values of which range from 6 to 20 years. What planet's major period is operating at birth and what part of its total period is remaining is calculated using the Moon's latitude.

RAHU'S MAJOR PERIOD

Rahu's Major-period lasts for 18 years and is divided into minor-periods according to the following table.

Rahu Major period follows the Mars Major period. The sequence of the major period remains the same as it is in the case of minor Periods. For example if one is born in Sun's Major Period (which would require

Table 2. *Minor Periods within Rahu's Major Period*

Major Period	Minor Period	Time Period (years, months, days)
Rahu	Rahu	2y 8m 12d
	Jupiter	2y 4m 24d
	Saturn	2y 10m 6d
	Mercury	2y 6m 18d
	Ketu	1y 0m 18d
	Venus	3y 0m 0d
	Sun	0y 10m 24d
	Moon	1y 6m 0d
	Mars	1y 0m 18d

one to be born with Moon in one of the three asterisms of the Sun), one will experience Moon Major period after the Sun period, Mars Major period after the Moon period and Rahu Major Period after the Mars period and so on.

Ancient Vedic seers have delineated in detail the results of the minor periods of other Planets within Rahu's Major Period. One can consult *Brihat Parashara Hora Shastra* for these results as delineated by Sage *Parashara*.

Like any other planet Rahu doesn't function in the same way in different nativities and so in my view one cannot apply the same results for every individual. However out here I have outlined some general guidelines of what to expect in Rahu's Major Period -

1. There is usually some sort of transformation at the beginning of the period. It follows the Mars period which is usually an active period in which one is busy in one or the other material pursuit. The Rahu period can be sensed as lethargy sets in and one finds it difficult to concentrate on the things one was concentrating on during the Mars period.

As we can see from the table, Rahu rules both the Major and Minor periods for the first 2 years. Thus Rahu is completely free to display its energies at this time. Old patterns get broken down and one finds oneself in completely new situations. This can be tough for some especially if the new circumstances aren't as cordial as the previous ones. In some cases one loses everything one has at the beginning of this period and has to start all over again. The first six months can be especially hard as one tries to cope with the rapidly changing circumstances.

This period is usually marked by misunderstandings with parents or employers, upheavals of all kinds, rebellious attitudes, social rejection, contact with occult, mystical experiences and extremes of indulgence. The transformation which takes place can take a person on any path, true or illusory, depending upon the rest of the chart. One can usually gauge how the next 18 years of one's life are going to be like through the transformation and experiences which takes place within the first two years of this period.

Overall it can be said to be an adventurous period which makes one explore new territories and helps one step out of one's past life karmic patterns. It is a primarily extroverted and futuristic period full of expectations. It furthers learning as one is ready to embrace the new and the different.

2. Some foreign element usually enters one's life in this period. This may be at a personal or professional level. Everything foreign somehow holds more charm during this period and the native either benefits or suffers losses due to this association depending on the placement of Rahu in the chart. Either way it is a learning process which adds to the experience of the native. The consummation of this foreign element or influence usually takes place in the Saturn Minor period.

3. This period opens up the Pandora's box of deep rooted desires embedded in one's psyche which may be either in keeping with one's true path in life or otherwise, depending upon the overall inclination of the chart. These desires are usually obsessive and insatiable in keeping with the basic nature of Rahu. There is a tendency to indulge in all types of intoxication in this period. It goes without

saying that the relevant among Rahu's attributes discussed in detail in Chapter 3. find expression in this period.

This period has the power to bestow fame, fortune and material prosperity in the present day and age. This will take place within the domain of Rahu's significations enunciated in Chapter 3. It can however cause downfall through over expansion.

The minor periods of Jupiter, Saturn, Mercury and Venus are the most suitable for this to happen. Among them Rahu-Mercury and Rahu-Venus periods are of special importance as Mercury and Venus are both material benefics and close friends of Rahu. This is especially the case when Mercury and Venus are strong and benefic planets in the nativity. The Rahu- Moon period can also give good results if Moon is strong and is in good relationship with Rahu.

4. The relationship of Rahu with minor period planets has to be taken into consideration. If they are placed in houses like 6th , 8th and 12th from the house where Rahu is posited one usually experiences some sort of struggle. One should however remember that these houses can also give good results if the planet posited in them is strong. Similar results follow if the minor period planet is the lord of the 6th, 8th or 12th house from the house in which Rahu is posited.

If they are placed in the 2nd and 7th house from Rahu's house one can usually expect material gains but there is always a danger of sudden accident or death if other factors also points towards the same. Similar results follow if the minor period planet is the lord of the 2nd or 7th house from the house in which Rahu is posited.

5. The position and state of Rahu's dispositor needs to be looked at. Rahu being a shadow planet reflects the results of the lord of the sign it is placed in. If this planet is strongly placed in the chart Rahu will in general give better results. The relationship between Rahu and its dispositor is of extreme importance. If the dispositor is in harmony with Rahu by being placed in trine to Rahu good results

can be expected in this period. If it is placed in difficult houses like 6th, 8th and 12th from Rahu one can expect some sort of struggles and upheavals in this period.

6. Rahu's house placement needs to be looked at. As discussed earlier Rahu is stronger when it is conjunct important points like Ascendant and Midheaven. Like other natural malefics it is also strong in houses like third, sixth and eleventh. Rahu usually gives results depending upon the house it is placed in. Rahu's placement in different houses is discussed in detail in Chapter 12.

7. Rahu's sign placement has to be looked at. As discussed earlier Rahu will give good results when placed in signs like Cancer, Virgo, Scorpio, Sagittarius, Aquarius and Pisces. The results of Rahu's placement in different signs has been dealt with in Chapter Eleven.

8. The asterism in which Rahu is placed is of importance. Rahu will be stronger when placed in its own asterisms or the asterisms of friends like Saturn, Mercury and Venus. Rahu will mirror the results of the lord of the asterism in which it is placed just like it does for its sign dispositor. An important point to remember is that if Rahu is conjunct or aspected by the lord of the asterism it is placed in then it mirrors the asterism dispositor's results more than its sign dipositor.

Rahu will also carry within it the results of the planets which are placed in its asterisms. For example if Venus is placed in Rahu's asterism *Ardra* than Rahu's results are coloured by Venus.

9. Rahu's association by aspect or conjunction with other planets has to be looked at. Rahu gains prominence in a chart if it is

(a) associated with important planets like the Ascendant, fifth, ninth or tenth lords.
(b) associated with the *atmakaraka* (soul significator).
(c) associated with the luminaries (Sun and Moon).

(d) associated with planets in own or exalted signs
(e) associated with the lord of the asterism in which moon is placed in the main chart.
(f) associated with the outer planets (Uranus, Neptune and Pluto)

One can also look at the association of Rahu with other planets in light of their being malefic or benefic. Rahu's association with natural benefics like Jupiter and Venus and temporal benefics for a chart like fifth and ninth lords makes it capable of conferring good results. It follows that its association with natural malefics like Mars and Saturn and temporal malefics for a chart like sixth and eighth lords brings out the negative side of Rahu.

10. Rahu's sign, house placement and association with other planets needs to be looked at in the *Navamsha* chart as well. We have already discussed in detail in Chapter 4. as to what one should look for while gauging the strength of the nodes in the Navamsha chart.

11. Rahu is a natural benefic for Taurus, Gemini, Libra, and Aquarius Ascendants and thus can be said to give better results for nativities with these Ascendants. This is however not to say that it cannot give good results for other Ascendants. If it is strongly placed it can give good results for any Ascendant.

12. In most cases expect some sort of disappointment at the end of the period. This supposed downfall starts with the minor period of Sun who is a natural enemy of Rahu. However if Sun, Moon and Mars are placed in good houses like the trines from Rahu, the bad results are minimised and one can even get good results. This is especially the case when Sun, Moon and Mars are strong and important planets in the nativity.

Since the major period of Jupiter, the greatest benefic, follows the major period of Rahu, its end is not all gloom and doom as purported by some astrologers. If one has been following one's destiny then the transition between these two periods is smooth. If one has wavered from one's true life path then one faces an abrupt ending in the concluding phase of Rahu Major period and has to make a new beginning in Jupiter Major period.

13. It is a long period and one can expect it to give its results slowly. Rahu is in no hurry just like the slow walk of an elephant. There are long periods of inactivity. However events, desirable or undesirable, when they do happen, happen with a quickness similar to a lion pouncing on its prey.

A rule enunciated by some wise men that the first 6 years of Rahu period should be seen as a building period, the middle 6 years as a period for enjoying the fruits of one's efforts and the last 6 years as a folding or completion time can be applied in some cases. The ending phase of this period reveals the worth or worthlessness of what one has been doing in the first two phases of this period. If what one has been doing is meaningful then it gives good results and duration to the purpose. If one has been chasing a mirage than this is the time when one's illusions are shattered.

14. The minor period of Ketu within Rahu's Major Period is a special case and can be said to be a period when free will is at its minimum and the hands of destiny guide one's existence. This is the period of karmic retribution if such a thing is relevant for the native in question. It is no wonder that it is very difficult to predict the results of this period. Usually it is seen that one has to lie low in this period as it is a sort of interlude between two relatively more active and fortunate minor periods of Mercury and Venus.

15. The results of the minor periods of Rahu within the major periods of other planets are to be judged using similar methods as enunciated in the above points. Of prime importance is the strength of Rahu in the chart and its relationship with the major period planet.

KETU'S MAJOR PERIOD

Let's concentrate on Ketu's Major Period. It lasts for 7 years and is divided into minor periods according to the following table.

Table 3. *Minor Periods within Ketu's Major Period*

Major Period	Minor Period	Time Period (years,months,days)
Ketu	Ketu	0y 4m 27d
	Venus	1y 2m 0d
	Sun	0y 4m 6d
	Moon	0y 7m 0d
	Mars	0y 4m 27d
	Rahu	1y 0m 18d
	Jupiter	0y 11m 16d
	Saturn	1y 1m 9d
	Mercury	0y 11m 27d

Ketu Major Period follows the Mercury Major period. One can consult *Brihat Parashara Hora Shastra* for the results of the minor Periods of other planets within Ketu's Major Period as delineated by Sage *Parashara*.

Here are general guidelines of what to expect in Ketu's Major Period -

1. The beginning of this period is usually marked by a sudden end of whatever one was involved in, in the Mercury Major period.

This as we can see from the table is the period when Ketu rules both the major and minor periods. This can be said to be a period completely in control of Ketu. Suddenly one is connected to the well-spring of one's past life experiences. This can be a positive or negative thing depending upon how one utilizes the knowledge and experience gained in past lives. Since Ketu is the planet which is interested in burning up bad karma from previous lives, unpleasant experiences are usually a norm in the beginning of this period. If one overcomes this initial horror of everything going haywire, one gets connected with the talents and faculties developed in past lives. This can often result in one getting sudden inspiration or effortlessly displaying some extraordinary talent.

In some cases one loses everything one has at the beginning of this period and has to start all over again. The first six months can be especially hard as one tries to cope with the rapidly changing circumstances.

One can usually gauge how the next 7 years of one's life are going to be like through the transformation and experiences which take place within the first six months of this period.

Overall it can be said to be a spiritualizing time which makes one review and re-evaluate the way one has been living one's life. It is a primarily introverted and past centric period. It involves sorting out and putting together whatever one has learnt in the past.

2. Some occult element usually enters into one's life in this period. This may be at a personal or professional level. Everything connected with the unseen realms somehow holds more fascination for the native involved during this period. Whether the native will seriously pursue some occult study or path depends upon the overall inclination of the chart.

3. This period is mostly about tying loose ends from the past and is thus not very favourable for any new activity in an unchartered field. It promotes inactivity and internalizes one's energy. It goes without saying that the relevant among Ketu's attributes discussed in detail in Chapter 3. find expression in this period.

This period is not exactly suitable for material gains. However this is possible in rare cases where Ketu is strongly placed in houses like third, sixth and eleventh. The material benefits one acquires in this period are usually a result of native's efforts in past life/lives. In such cases there are chance of getting a quick fortune through hidden treasures, lotteries or utilizing some latent talent.

The minor periods of Mars and Jupiter are the most suitable for this to happen. This will take place within the domain of Ketu's significations enunciated in Chapter 3. This is more likely to be the case when Mars and Jupiter are strong and benefic planets in the nativity and have a good temporal relationship with Ketu. The Ketu-Sun period can also give good results if Sun is strong and is in good relationship with Ketu.

4. The relationship of Ketu with minor period planets has to be taken into consideration. If they are placed in houses like 6th ,8th and 12th from the house where Ketu is posited one usually experiences not so good results. One should however remember that these houses can also give good results if the planet posited in them is strong. Similar results follow if the minor period planet is the lord of the 6th, 8th or 12th house from the house in which Ketu is posited.

If they are placed in the 2nd and 7th house from Ketu's house one can usually expect material gains but there is always a danger of sudden accident or death if other factors also points towards the same. Similar results follow if the minor period planet is the lord of the 2nd or 7th house from the house in which Rahu is posited.

5. The position and state of Ketu's dispositor needs to be looked at. Ketu being a shadow planet reflects the results of the lord of the sign it is placed in. If this planet is strongly placed in the chart Ketu will in general give better results. The relationship between Ketu and its dispositor is of extreme importance. If the dispositor is in harmony with Ketu by being placed in trine to it good results can be expected in Ketu's Major period. If it is placed in difficult houses like 6th, 8th and 12th from Ketu one can expect some sort of struggles and upheavals in Ketu's Major period.

6. Ketu's house placement needs to be looked at. As discussed earlier Ketu is stronger when it is conjunct important points like Ascendant and Midheaven. Like other natural malefics it is also strong in houses like third, sixth and eleventh. Ketu usually gives results depending upon the house it is placed in. Ketu's placement in different houses is discussed in detail in Chapter 12.

7. Ketu's sign placement has be looked at. As discussed earlier Ketu will give good results when placed in signs like Aries, Leo, Scorpio, Sagittarius and Pisces. The results of Ketu's placement in different signs has been dealt with in Chapter 11.

8. The asterism in which Ketu is placed is of importance. Ketu will be strong when placed in its own asterisms or the asterisms of friends like Mars and Jupiter. Ketu will mirror the results of the lord of the asterism in which it is placed just like it does for its sign dispositor. An important point to remember is that if Ketu is conjunct or aspected by the lord of the asterism it is placed in, then it mirrors the asterism dispositor's results more that its sign dipositor.

Ketu will also carry within it the results of the planets which are placed in its asterisms. For example if Jupiter is placed in Ketu's asterism *Magha*, than Ketu's results are coloured by Jupiter.

9. Ketu's association by aspect or conjunction with other planets has to be looked at. Just like Rahu, Ketu gains prominence in a chart if it is -

(a) associated with important planets like the Ascendant, fifth, ninth or tenth lords
(b) associated with the *atmakaraka* (soul significator)
(c) associated with the luminaries (Sun and Moon)
(d) associated with planets in own or exalted signs
(e) associated with the lord of the asterism in which moon is placed in the main chart
(f) associated with the outer planets (Uranus, Neptune and Pluto)

One can also look at the association of Ketu with other planets in light of their being malefic or benefic. Ketu's association with natural benefics like Jupiter and Venus and temporal benefics for a chart like fifth and ninth lords make it capable of conferring good results. It follows that its association with natural malefics like Mars and Saturn and temporal malefics for a chart like sixth and eighth lords brings out the negative side of Ketu.

10.   Ketu's sign, house placement and association with other planets needs to be looked at in the *Navamsha* chart as well. We have already discussed in detail in Chapter 4. as to what one should look for while gauging the strength of the nodes in the Navamsha chart.

11.   Ketu is a natural benefic for Cancer, Scorpio and Pisces Ascendants and thus can be said to give better results for nativities with these Ascendants. This is however not to say that it cannot give good results for other Ascendants. If it is strongly placed it can give good results for any Ascendant.

12.   In most cases the second half of Ketu's period is better than the first half. This can be seen symbolically from the fact that the snake has its poison in its head and not in its tail. From an astrological point of view it is easy to see the reason behind this, as the minor periods of Ketu's friends Mars and Jupiter fall in the second half of its period.

However if other planets like Mercury, Venus, Sun and Saturn share a good temporal relationship with Ketu then the bad results in the first half are minimised and one can even expect good results in some cases.

13.   It is a relatively short major period as compared to Rahu's period. This in a way is a blessing of sorts because of the simple fact that Ketu has a much more intense energy which would be very difficult to tolerate for a period of 18 years.   In many cases it has been seen to be a death inflicting period if other factors point towards the same.   Ketu as we have discussed earlier is a planet of endings and thus facilitates one's exit from the earthly realm.   This period is usually full of some or the other undesirable events.   The events in Ketu's period happen very quickly.   We have already discussed how Ketu imparts its results in the 'motion and mode of functioning' section in Chapter 3.

14.   The minor period of Rahu within Ketu's major period is similar to the minor period of Ketu within Rahu's major period.   It

is a period when free will is at its minimum and one is completely governed by the hands of destiny. This is the period of karmic retribution if such a thing is relevant for the native in question. This is a very difficult period to predict the results of. Usually it is seen as a period where one has to lie low as it forms an interlude between two relatively more active and fortunate minor periods of Mars and Jupiter.

15. The results of the minor periods of Ketu within the major periods of other planets are to be judged using similar methods as enunciated in the above points. Of prime importance is the strength of Ketu in the chart and its relationship with the major period planet.

TRANSITS

As discussed earlier both the nodes have a permanent retrograde motion and so they are always moving backwards through the zodiac i.e. from Taurus to Aries to Pisces and so on. They complete one round of the zodiac in around 18 months. The speed varies from 3' to 11' per solar day.

If we leave out the outer planets, Uranus, Neptune and Pluto, only Jupiter, Saturn, Rahu and Ketu can be categorized as slow moving planets. In all types of astrology the transits of Jupiter and Saturn are given prime importance. However the transits of the nodes are usually neglected. In my experience I have found that the transit of the Nodal Axis has as much significance as the transits of Jupiter and Saturn.

RAHU'S TRANSIT GUIDELINES

Here are the general guidelines for judging the effect of the transit of Rahu through different houses and over natal planetary positions.

1. The transit results of Rahu through different houses should be gauged from both the Ascendant and the Moon sign. In my experience I have found that they should be given equal weightage.

2. Rahu's transit through a house literally brings the spotlight to the affairs of that house. For example if Rahu is transiting through the fifth house the general focus is on creativity. If it is transiting through seventh house the focus is on relationships and so on. It is the area where one tries something new and experiments in unexplored realms. For example if Rahu is transiting the first house one may experiment with their personality and bring about changes in the way one comes across to other people. It is usually fruitful to begin anything new relating to the house Rahu is transiting.

3. It is experienced that one experiences a certain degree of luck in whichever house Rahu is transiting. There are new opportunities and the wind blows one's way if one tries to concentrate on the affairs of that particular house. There is always some gain assured in Rahu's transit through a particular house. For example if it transits through eighth house one can expect some legacy or financial benefit from spouse or others in general. The extent of this gain would depend upon the overall possibilities in a chart.

4. Usually this transit is more beneficial for non-live affairs as compared to live affairs. For example if Rahu is transiting through the fifth house one can expect one's creativity to bring one fame and fortune but it is not exactly the right time to have children. Children born when Rahu is transiting the fifth house usually turn out to be troublesome for the native concerned.

5. In the negative aspect one can expect either confusion or overambitiousness related to the affairs of the house Rahu is transiting. Rahu as we know is capable of putting up a smokescreen and so can cloud one's thinking relating to the affairs of the house it is transiting. For example if Rahu is transiting through the twelfth house one has the tendency to overspend through unnecessary expenditures. There is also an inclination towards extreme indulgence in twelfth house significations like sex and drugs.

6. One can expect sudden results when Rahu just enters a new sign. Strong results are also seen when Rahu touches important points like Ascendant, Midheaven, the cusps and middle points of houses. These can be positive or negative depending upon the over-all inclination of the chart.

7. Rahu's transit over a natal planet bring out the potential of that planet. For example if Rahu transits over natal Mercury in a nativity one can expect the fruition of the results of Mercury for that particular nativity. This as we can see can be both good or bad depending upon how Mercury is functioning in that chart. However Mercury's natural significations like commerce, wit, commu-nication get a boost in the majority of cases.

8. Rahu basically increases or magnifies the natural energy of whichever planet it transits over. If it transits over Mars, the energy level and drive in general gets boosted; if it transits over Jupiter optimism and fortune in general get enhanced and so on.

9. These effects are at their strongest when Rahu is degreecally conjunct the natal planet in its transit. For example if Venus is place at $18°$ of Gemini in a chart then strong results can be expected when Rahu transits exactly over natal Venus i.e. $18°$ of Gemini. These effects can be said to be significantly noticeable within a $5°$ orb.

10. Rahu's transit over natal Rahu is a special case which we can term as Rahu-Return. This as we discussed earlier happens in the 19th, 38th, 57th, 76th, 95th years of everyone's life. This usually brings with it a new direction. Among these the 19th year is the most im-portant as it is what we can term as the first Rahu-Return. This is the year when the adolescent grappling with finding his/her way in the big bad world usually gets a break. Sometimes the direction chosen at this time holds throughout life and in some cases it is just a temporary path meant to be discarded when something better comes along.

11. The time period, when the transiting Rahu makes trines

with natal Sun, Moon, Jupiter, Venus, Mercury and Rahu itself, is seen to bring a certain degree of luck. This luck is usually experienced in relation with the three trine houses involved and the significations of the planet involved. Let's take an example where the natal Jupiter is placed in the second house in Pisces and the Rahu trines it by transiting through Scorpio. In this case the fortune one would experience would relate to the 2nd, 6th and 10th houses and the significations of Jupiter in the nativity. In my experience I have seen that the trines made with natal Jupiter, Sun, Moon and Rahu are more fortunate than the rest. Again these effects can be said to be significantly noticeable with in a 5° orb.

12. The transit of Rahu over the Sun-Mercury-Venus arc has been seen to be a very lucky time period. We know that Sun Mercury and Venus are never more than 48° away from each other in a chart. The Sun-Mercury-Venus arc is the area lying between the farthest two among these three planets. Let's take an example chart where Sun is at 5° in Taurus, Mercury at 27° in Taurus and Venus at 18° in Gemini. In this chart the Sun-Mercury-Venus arc will range from 5° in Taurus to 18° in Gemini. Rahu will enter the Sun-Mercury-Venus arc in its retrograde motion when it touches the 18th degree in Gemini.

KETU'S TRANSIT GUIDELINES

Here are the general guidelines for judging the effect of the transit of Ketu through different houses and over natal planetary positions.

1. The transit results of Ketu through different houses should be gauged from both the Ascendant and the Moon sign. In my experience I have found that they should be given equal weightage.

2. Ketu's transit through a house signals a completion in relation to the affairs of that house. It also usually brings in some restriction or sudden undesirable event relating to the significations of that house. For example if Ketu is transiting through the first house one

has the opportunity to get oneself together as an individual. It is a favourable time to synthesize the various aspects of one's being into a single whole. On the other hand one is likely to face some humiliating situation. This can be positive if one derives some wisdom and understanding from the seemingly negative events.

3. One can expect some unusual experiences in the affairs relating to whichever house Ketu is transiting. For example if Ketu is transiting through the third house, one can find some eccentricity, peculiarity or unconventionality associated with third house activities like writing, singing, instrument playing, dancing etc. This unusual approach can be either scattered or brilliant depending upon the overall tone of the chart.

4. Usually this transit is not beneficial for material affairs but it quickens the spiritual energy. For example if Ketu is transiting through the fourth house one can expect problems in relation to one's living conditions but some inner transformation is likely to take place.

5. In extreme cases one can expect complete negation related to the affairs of the house Ketu is transiting. Ketu as we know is a planet which can completely block off any energy when it is functioning through its karmic retribution mode. For example if Ketu is transiting through seventh house one may lose their partner, may incur losses in personal business and experience a fall in one's social standing. To put it simply, all the significations of seventh house get completely cut off.

6. One can expect sudden results when Ketu just enters a new sign. Strong results are also seen when Ketu touches important points like Ascendant, Midheaven, the cusps and middle points of houses. These can be positive or negative depending upon the overall inclination of the chart.

7. Ketu's transit over a natal planet internalizes the energy of that planet. In some cases some latent talent related to that planet

finds a sudden release. For example if Ketu transits over natal Sun in a nativity one can expect one's sense of self to be sublimated. It is a very intensely introspective period where the spirit of enquiry is aroused. One gets connected with the ocean of one's past life experiences and can draw wisdom from them in choosing the most suitable path for the current life.

8. Ketu can sometimes completely block out the natural energy of whichever planet it transits over. If it transit over Jupiter one finds it difficult to maintain optimism; if it transits over Moon one finds it difficult to deal with one's emotions, mother or mother figure and so on.

9. These effects are at their strongest when Ketu is degreecally conjunct the natal planet in its transit. For example if Mars is placed at 19° of Sagittarius in a chart then strong results can be expected when Ketu transits exactly over natal Mars i.e. 19° of Sagittarius. These effects are significantly noticeable with in a 5° orb.

10. Ketu's transit over natal Ketu is a special case which we can term as Ketu-Return. As expected this happens at the same time as Rahu-Return in the 19th, 38th, 57th, 76th, 95th years of everyone's life. The same results delineated earlier for Rahu-Return apply for this transit.

11. Ketu's transit over natal Rahu is also a special case. It is evident that Rahu will be transiting over Ketu at this point. This first happens in a person's life in the 28th year. This sort of symbolizes a completion of a cycle as represented by the *Ouroboruos* symbol which represents the meeting of the energies of the two nodes. If one has been following one's true path in life this is a period where one experiences contentment at the most inner level. If this is not the case then this is the time when intense upheaval takes place within the psyche of the native involved. It is a point of reflection where one looks back at what one has been doing. If the realization of not following the destined path occurs, one makes a fresh start. It is said to be a fortunate period by some wise men which we can under-

stand from the fact some degree of luck is required for one to make a new start.

12. The time period when the transiting Ketu makes trines with natal Sun, Moon, Jupiter, Venus, Mercury and Ketu itself, is seen to bring some sort of completion. This can at times bring in some positive karma from past lives in the form of sudden good fortune. This luck is usually experienced in relation with the three trine houses involved and the significations of the planet involved. In my experience I have seen that the trines made with natal Jupiter, Mars and Ketu are more fortunate than the rest. Again these effects can be said to be significantly noticeable with in a 5° orb.

TRANSITS OF NODES OVER OUTER PLANETS

The transits of Rahu and Ketu over the outer planets, Uranus, Neptune and Pluto are a special case. They only show noticeable results in charts of collective personalities or those undergoing serious spiritual transformation. They bring the same type of results as those delineated for the association of Rahu and Ketu with the outer planets mentioned in Chapter 7. If Rahu is transiting over Uranus one can expect similar results as Rahu conjunct Uranus, in the backdrop of the house Uranus is placed in the chart under consideration.

As usual exact conjunction brings the strongest results. The effects of the transit are significantly noticeable with in a 5° orb.

OTHER PLANETS TRANSITING OVER NATAL NODAL POSITIONS

When a planet transits over natal Rahu one can expect a new beginning, confusion or rise in fortune in relation to the natural or temporal significations of that planet and the house Rahu is placed in. For example if Venus transits over natal Rahu in the tenth house one can expect an increase in one's income; improvement in one's comforts; beginning of a new relationship or job; excessive indulgence and chasing after desires.

These are usually short term results in case of fast moving planets like Sun, Moon, Mars, Mercury and Venus. Their degree of intensity is also much less as compared to Rahu transiting over the natal positions of these planets. Again, exact conjunction brings the strongest results. The effects of the transit are significantly noticeable with in a 5° orb.

In case of slow moving planets like Jupiter and Saturn the results are more intense and long lasting. This is simply because the slower moving planets take longer to transit over natal Rahu or Ketu.

For planets transiting over Ketu same guidelines apply with the exception of the difference in results. When a planet transits over natal Ketu one can either experience restriction, spiritual awakening or fulfilment of a desire relating to the natural and temporal significations of that planet and the house Ketu is placed in. For example if Saturn transits over natal Ketu in the fourth house one can expect problems in one's living situation; go through an intense churning process with in one's inner psyche as a result of some unwanted condition; feel one step closer to realizing one's true destiny; see materialization of one's innermost desires.

For the outer planets, Uranus, Neptune and Pluto, when transiting over natal Rahu or Ketu, one can apply the same guidelines as enunciated for the transit of Rahu and Ketu over the outer planets. The only difference is that these results would last for a longer period of time as the outer planets have much slower speed of transit than the nodes.

* * *

10. IN SYNASTRY

Judging the compatibility between any two individuals has been one of the major preoccupations of astrologers since the ancient times. Vedic astrology has a whole elaborate system dedicated to judge the compatibility in terms of points between any two individuals getting into a long term agreement like marriage. Western astrology usually relies on mutual aspects between the planets in the charts of the individuals involved as a guideline to make this judgement.

In recent years astrologers from all backgrounds are beginning to realize the importance of the nodes in Synastry. The Lunar Nodes as we know are karmic points in a chart and thus no major relationship in a person's life can take place without their involvement. In relating two charts it is important to look at the conjunction of the natal planets with the natal positions of the nodes in the other chart.

The conjunction applies when they are in the same sign even though strongest results are seen in exact conjunctions. In general a 5° orb gives fairly strong results.

RAHU'S ROLE IN SYNASTRY

The relationships which come about due to Rahu's involvement are usually futuristic in their approach even though they might be carried on from past lives. They are more focused on new growth in the present as opposed to just working out some karma from previous lives.

The general guideline for planetary connections is that when natal Rahu in a person's chart is conjunct a natal planet in another person's chart, the former usually benefits from the latter in matters relating to that planet. The latter in turn contributes to the general happiness of the former and provides beneficial counselling and direction relating to the significations of the planet involved. We will refer to the former as a Rahu person and the latter by the name of the planet involved.

The general guideline for house connections is that when natal Rahu in a person's chart connects with a particular house in another person's chart, the house involved usually carries the focus of their relationship for the latter. They experience a certain degree of luck and confidence relating to that house after entering that relationship. For example if one's partner has Rahu in Aries, a sign which falls in the third house in one's chart, than one experiences luck in all third house matters like writing, publishing, music, group activities etc.

It goes without saying that the relationship gains a lot of significance when natal Rahu in a person's chart connects with important points like the Ascendant and Midheaven in the other person's chart.

Let's take a quick look at what the Rahu's conjunction with other natal planets means in terms of compatibility.

Rahu - Sun

This is a soul level connection. The Rahu person gives the Sun person optimism for the future and in turn receives a sense of self-confidence and material help from the Sun person. If love is involved it is usually deep enough to last a lifetime. This connection usually involves a father figure scene at some level.

Rahu - Moon

This is a primarily mental and emotional connection. The Rahu person receives nurturing from the Moon person and in turn provides mental and emotional support to the Moon person. This is a stable relationship whose only downside is that it may sometimes make both the individuals concerned lose touch with reality. This connection usually involves a mother figure scene at some level.

Rahu - Mars

The Rahu person in this case receives energetic help from the Mars person especially in Martian realms like technology. The Mars person on the other hand gets valuable direction from the Rahu person. This is an okay relationship as long as the Mars person keeps his ego down with the Rahu person. This is a good connection for working in group activities. This connection usually involves a brotherly/sisterly scene at some level.

Rahu - Mercury

This is a communication connection. Both the natives find it easy to relate to each other on an intellectual level simplifying the communication between them. This is usually a good combination for friendship or business partnership but alone does not guarantee lasting marital happiness. This connection usually involves a brotherly scene at some level. This relationship may also involve an uncle and aunt sort of patronizing scene at some level.

Rahu - Jupiter

This connection breeds goodwill and fills both sides with optimism. This combination can work on both levels, material or purely philosophical. Usually Rahu provides the philosophical answers to the Jupiter person and Jupiter person provides material support. This is a very good connection for all types of relationships. This connection usually involves a teacher-taught scene at some level.

Rahu - Venus

In accordance with the nature of the two planets involved, this gives good sexual compatibility and common interests as far as indulgence is concerned. The Venus person wants to share its love in all its forms with the Rahu person who in turn helps them in finding a direction in their lives. This is a good combination for marital type connections, but just like sex it alone does not guarantee marital bliss. Attraction at some level or other is the main theme of this connection.

Rahu - Saturn

This is a serious and grounded connection based upon concrete help from the Saturn person to the Rahu person. The Rahu person in return lightens the Saturnine load on the other person. There is humour involved in this relationship but the background is always serious. It is a good connection for relationships based on philosophy and other serious issues. This connection can sometimes be stifling for both the involved parties. It is thus seen to work better when the two people involved don't live together and communicate from a distance. This connection usually involves patronizing and group activity at some level.

Rahu - Rahu

Both the natives experience a sense of overwhelming similarity in approach to life. Both the natives understand each other's deepest motives which can be both a good thing or a bad thing depending upon the type of relationship. This is a good combination for companionship and friendship as it usually occurs for all those who are born around the same time.

Rahu - Ketu

This is a connection which gives a sense of appreciation of each other's paths in life. There is usually true sympathy for each other's woes which comes about because of the simple reason that the Ketu person is privy to what the Rahu person is about to experience in the present life and vice versa. It is again a good combination for companionship and friendship.

<u>Rahu - Uranus</u>

Since the outer planets are not personal in their scope of functioning, this is a primarily collective connection, which functions well only when both persons are working in tandem for some Uranian collective cause, like Edison and his co-workers working together to invent the light bulb. This is generally good for Uranian fields of activities covered in the Rahu Uranus association in Chapter 7.

<u>Rahu - Neptune</u>

This again is a primarily collective connection which functions well only when both persons are working in tandem for some Neptunian collective cause like making a movie. This gives a good understanding in Neptunian fields of activities covered under the Rahu Neptune association in Chapter 7.

<u>Rahu - Pluto</u>

This is primarily a collective connection which functions well only when both persons are working in tandem for some Plutonian collective cause like constructing a nuclear reactor. This gives a good understanding in Plutonian fields of activities covered under the Rahu Pluto association in Chapter 7.

KETU'S ROLE IN SYNASTRY

The relationships which come about due to Ketu's involvement entail working out residual past life karma. This can be either good or bad depending on what the score is from previous life/lives. Thus unlike Rahu, we can not have any general guidelines for Ketu's role in relationships. However when Ketu is functioning though its benign mode, guidelines similar to those discussed for Rahu's connection with planets as well as houses apply.

It is useful to keep in mind that an involvement of Jupiter or an aspect by Jupiter goes a long way in limiting Ketu's negative functioning in these connections.

Let's take a quick look at what the Ketu's conjunction with other natal planets mean in terms of compatibility.

Ketu - Sun

Just like Rahu-Sun this is a soul level connection. This connection is a spiritualising influence for both the persons involved. It can however create misunderstandings and ego clashes. It involves working out of some soul level or paternal issue carried over from past life/lives.

Ketu - Moon

This is a primarily mental and emotional connection. Both the natives enjoy the philosophical and mystical experiences produced by this connection. However the Moon person may find the Ketu person too preachy and the Ketu person may find the Moon person too inconstant. This connection usually involves working out of some mental or maternal issue carried over from past life/lives.

Ketu - Mars

Both the natives involved enjoy each other's energy in the beginning of this relationship. In time however this relationship usually turns bitter as the Mars person feels stifled. Because of the extremely explosive quality of this connection a lasting relationship is hard to maintain. This is however a good connection for working in group activities. This connection usually involves working out of some physical or sibling issue carried over from past life/lives.

Ketu - Mercury

This connection adds depth to the intellectual aspect of a relationship. If working in its positive aspect this is usually a good combination for pursuing common esoteric goals. The friction arises when the Ketu person starts finding the Mercury person too superficial and changeable while the Mercury person starts finding the Ketu person too rigid and preachy.

Ketu - Jupiter

This connection usually turns out to be fortunate for both parties. The Ketu person usually forms the philosophical backdrop while the Jupiter person takes care of the material side of things. The only stutter in this connection happens when both want to be in the teacher's chair. This connection involves some karmic debt from past lives as a result of which both persons have to help each other in achieving one's destiny in the present life.

Ketu - Venus

This connection usually furthers platonic relationships even though there might be an underlying physical attraction. Again the Ketu person holds the preacher's chair while the Venus person likes to be in the serving position. This is not exactly a favourable connection for marriage as it promotes marital discord. It is usually the Venus person who gets frustrated.

Ketu - Saturn

This cannot be called a favourable connection but becomes inevitable when both the natives involved need some sort of discipline. This is a serious and grounded connection which can in some cases be a very spiritualizing influence. However the atmosphere can get too heavy and pessimistic making it unbearable for both the persons. It is however seen that when in tune this connection gives relationships that last longer than other nodal connections.

Ketu - Rahu

This is the same as Rahu-Ketu because if the natal Rahu is conjunct the natal Ketu in two nativities, it automatically implies that natal Ketu would be conjunct natal Rahu.

Ketu - Ketu

This is the same as Rahu-Rahu because if the natal Rahus are conjunct in two nativities, it automatically implies that the natal Ketus will be conjunct.

Ketu - Uranus

This functions in a similar way to Rahu-Uranus connection. One can however expect a bigger slice of the ancient, unusual, eccentric and unconventional. The natives brought together by this connection would rather research spaceships used by advanced ancient civilizations rather than try to build one in the present.

Ketu - Neptune

This functions in a similar way to Rahu-Neptune connection. It usually brings out more self negating and service oriented energy from both sides. The natives brought together by this connection would rather make documentaries on natural disasters and drug abuse than make stereotype melodramas.

Ketu - Pluto

This functions in a similar way to Rahu-Pluto connection. This is however a more explosive and intense connection. To put it simply it is more of a nuclear explosion than a controlled nuclear reaction in a nuclear reactor.

11. NODAL AXIS IN DIFFERENT SIGNS

Like any other planet the sign placement of Rahu and Ketu determines to quite an extent the way they will behave in a nativity. One can easily determine the way the nodes will function in a particular sign by combining their nature and the nature of the sign. However for the reader's convenience some basic traits of the nodal axis in various signs have been delineated in this chapter.

The nodal axis sign placement throws some light on one's previous incarnation and one's role in the present life. The sign placement has added significance as it also defines the Karmic control planets for any given chart. It is useful to remember that like all other planets the nodes can give good results and work through their higher aspect in all the signs.

The placement of the nodes in the house or a sign produces similar results. For example Rahu's placement in Scorpio, the eighth sign, can be regarded similar to the placement of Rahu in the eighth house. So the reader should combine the results and characteristics of the nodal placement in different houses discussed in the next chapter along with the indications of nodal placement in various signs. For example if in a chart Ketu were posited in Aries, the indications of both Ketu's placement in Aries and Ketu's placement in the first house would apply.

KETU IN ARIES / RAHU IN LIBRA

Ketu's presence in the impulsive sign of the ram signifies that the Martian tendencies and talents come naturally to the native involved. This is due to the fact that the native involved spent his past life in martial pursuits and the focus was on the self. So the significations of the sign Aries - independence, self-expression, initiative, innovativeness, impulsiveness, and combativeness - form the backbone of the native's personality.

Ketu is sort of at home in Aries, as Aries is the beginning of things and so is Ketu. Ketu as we have seen earlier has some qualities similar to that of Mars and so this is a friendly placement for Ketu. This would mean that Ketu wouldn't give too much trouble in this sign in its major or inter periods unless heavily afflicted.

This is however an explosive placement as Ketu is a fiery planet and Aries is a fiery sign. Both Ketu and Aries represent the unconscious primordial forces and the actions of such a native are not always guided by reason or logic. Extreme anger or unusual ideas, tastes, and idiosyncrasies are common with this placement. A high degree of inventiveness is the result when this energy is working constructively.

Rahu is in a friend's sign in Libra as Rahu shares a good relationship with Venus. Its presence in Libra brings out the Venusian side of Rahu's nature, which we have discussed in detail earlier. It is the most diplomatic amongst all placements involving any planet and any sign.

Because of Rahu's Libran impulses, in the present life the native is usually seen trying to develop the significations of the sign Libra - balance, harmony, sociability, justice, relationships, partnership, sublimation of self etc. Thus the present life can be seen as a bit of a rest after the Martian struggles of the past life.

With this placement the native basically learns to achieve a balance between self-sufficiency and dependence upon others. There is a conscious effort to maintain and further relationships that sometimes can be exaggerated making the person to appear as a people pleaser. On the other hand it doesn't take long for such a native to lose their head over trifles.

Such a native usually tries to cover up his strong sense of individuality to appear more friendly and receptive of other's views. In reality what is being sought is the ideal of interdependence where one gets to be what one is and at the same time works in tandem with others for achieving a common goal. The placement usually seeks spirituality through ethical actions and thoughts. Knowledge and action are given importance and thus Gyana (knowledge) Yoga and Karma Yoga are best suited for the natives with this placement.

The karmic past life control planet in this case is Mars and the karmic distribution control planet is Venus. The placement of Mars shows where the native has to pay his dues for past life actions and the placement of Venus shows the area where he receives help for furthering his cause in the present life.

As discussed earlier Aries is the moolatrikona sign for Ketu. It follows that Ketu can bestow favourable material and spiritual results in this sign even though it promotes rash, impulsive actions.

Within Aries, Ketu is stronger when placed in the following degrees;
0° - 3°20', 23°20' - 26°40', 26°40' - 30°. It is strongest at 0° - 3°20'.

Libra is a friendly sign placement for Rahu. Such a Rahu has the capacity to fulfil the material ambitions of the native if there are other favourable supporting influences in the chart.

Within Libra, Rahu is stronger when placed in the following degrees, 0° - 6°40', 13°20' - 16°40' and 26°40' - 30°.

A few famous personalities with this combination are Abraham

Lincoln and Thomas Edison. The chart of Edison (Chart no. 18) whose personality almost typifies this placement, is discussed in detail in the next chapter. His Ketu's placement in Aries in eleventh bestowed on him the gift of ingenuity and innovation. However it was his Rahu's placement in Libra in fifth, which showed that he had to work in partnership with others (his co-workers) to realize his creative potential.

KETU IN TAURUS / RAHU IN SCORPIO

Ketu's presence in the earthy sign of the cow is an indicator of some artistic talent or an exaggerated Venusian tinge in the nature of a native. The native is usually aesthetically oriented and exhibits a heightened sensitivity for refinement in the material realm.

The past life of such a native has usually been a stable one as far as material security is concerned. However in this life the native has to go through a period of uncertainty in this regard, especially in the first half of his/her life. Success material or otherwise comes after a bit of struggle. The 'try twice when you fail once' theory applies to this native as nothing happens for him/her in one go. The second half of life is usually more enjoyable than the first half.

Ketu is supposed to maintain a neutral relationship towards Venus and thus can be said to be in a neutral sign. It cannot give too many material benefits in its major or inter periods. It should be seen as a spiritualising influence, which puts the material world in its correct perspective.

Within Taurus, Ketu is stronger in the following degrees; 6°40' - 16°40'.

The lesson here is not to be too attached to the material world. The evolved kinds with this placement have an innate understanding of how the universe sustains us all and that they 'will always get what they need' on a material plane.

The qualities of the sign Taurus - earthy, fixed, obstinate, stable, acquiring, refining, accumulating, idealism in love, beauty, relationships etc. - form the backbone of such a native's nature.

Because of Rahu's presence in the mysterious sign of the eagle, the native has to confront the scorpionic realm - death, destruction, regeneration, renewal, depth, intensity, passion, obsession, sexuality, profundity, and the continuing battle between light and dark.

Rahu is supposed to be neutral towards Mars and so this is a neutral sign placement for Rahu. As discussed earlier Scorpio is one of Rahu's favourite signs besides being its moolatrikona sign. It revels in the scorpionic realm because of its basic attributes. This is an extreme sort of placement as Rahu can magnify and bring out the usually hidden scorpionic energies to the surface.

Within Scorpio, Rahu is stronger when placed in the following degrees; 6°40' - 10°, 13°20' - 20°, 26°40' - 30°. It is strongest at 6°40' - 10°.

This can be quite an uncontrollable energy if the rest of the chart is not well equipped to handle it. It is one of the most intense placements of a planet in a sign as Rahu is placed in Ketu's sign symbolizing completeness. Only an evolved soul can utilize the destructive and regenerative powers of Scorpio in a constructive manner in the outer world. It is a Rudra (destructive, chaotic) energy, which brings about renewal through destruction of old forms.

A lot of reformers, revolutionaries, soldiers, social workers, spies, detectives, researchers in every field, astrologers, philosophers, occultists and other people involved in bizarre vocations are born with this placement. Any vocation which involves an element of danger suits this placement.

Balancing of the extremes represented by the second and eighth house in a natal chart, which this placement requires one to do, is not an easy thing. This can be said to be one of the more difficult sign placements of the nodal axis to handle. Here the positioning of Venus highlights the latent talents, and the position of Mars signifies the area where the drive and opportunities lie in the present incarnation.

It can be said to be one of the prime revolutionary impulses in the modern times. If working on a base level this placement can bring out the worst of the negative Martian qualities discussed in the earlier chapter. This placement pursues spirituality through every possible path - knowledge, devotion and right action. It is however very interested in the occult paths like tantra, which translates into 'weaving' and entails using all the personal attributes (good or bad) for attaining perfect wisdom & understanding. In a way this placement is interested in all the short cuts to evolution, Jyotish or Astrology being one of them.

Venus becomes the karmic suction control planet while Mars is the karmic distribution control planet for this placement. The positioning of Venus highlights the latent talents and the house placement of Mars signifies the area where the drive and opportunities lie in the present incarnation.

Swami Vivekananda's (Chart no. 24) life, typifies the struggle and eventual rewards associated with this placement. His twelfth house placement of Rahu in Scorpio initiated him through a series of transformational experiences, which a lot of the times involved extreme austerities and self-negation. The same Rahu however gave him success and reputation in a foreign land (America), so that he could share with the world at large what he learnt and experienced.

KETU IN GEMINI / RAHU IN SAGITTARIUS

The presence of Ketu in the sign of the twins makes the native pursue the mercurial realm. The native is usually very keen on gathering information. This information may be in diverse fields ınd so he might not have the chance to delve deep into anything. nformation overdose in this information age cannot be ruled out or this placement.

Most of the 'jack of all trade' types belong to this combination. The native is also given to spend a lot of time with siblings and his ımmediate neighbourhood. Here we have an ideal community)erson who sometimes goes out of his way to help others. When his is taken to the extreme it can mean that the native has very little ime left for personal pursuits.

Humour is one of the strong points of this placement. Communication is the forte of such natives - a big help in these media entric times.

Ketu shares a neutral relationship with Mercury and thus it an be seen as a neutral sign placement for Ketu. One shouldn't xpect too many material gains from a Ketu major or inter)eriod. In fact its periods cause of lot of abrupt changes in a ıative's life when it is placed in Gemini. A philosophical and ontented attitude needs to be maintained, as this can be a very estless period.

The presence of Rahu in the optimistic Sagittarius brings the ninth ıouse affairs - religion, philosophy, psychology, ethics, code, ıniversal law and functionings etc. - into the centre stage of the ıative's life. The native has to learn to look at the bigger picture, as here is a tendency to get lost in small details. Respect for other's ●oints of view and openness needs to be cultivated.

Such natives are usually able to develop their own philosophy of fe, but care needs to be taken so that it is not forcefully forced down ther's throats. A great number of intellectuals, philosophers, media ●ersons and researchers have this nodal axis placement.

To sum it up this is a wonderful combination for learning, sharing ınd communicating in as pleasant a way as possible on our planet.

If a balance is established between the two opposing tendencies of physics and metaphysics, this is one of the most fortunate combinations to be born under.

This placement usually strives for spirituality through knowledge and right action. It has an intellectual curiosity about occult paths but usually keeps a distance from them. In some cases when the placement involves devotional houses like fourth, fifth, eighth and twelfth it furthers devotion to a cause or deity as a way of attaining salvation.

Jupiter and Mercury are the karmic control planets - Jupiter's house placement defines the new area of growth while Mercury's house placement defines the latent talents.

As discussed earlier Gemini is the debilitation sign of Ketu. Thus one cannot expect it to bestow material prosperity. Some sort of struggle is involved in the material significations of the house Ketu is placed in. It is important to note that the debilitation of Ketu is not good for progeny. When placed in the fifth it usually denies male progeny.

Within Gemini, Ketu is stronger in the following degrees; 3°20' - 10°; 16°40' - 23°20'.

Sagittarius is the debilitation sign for Rahu and thus it is not very conducive for material prosperity, unless there are other overriding factors influencing it. Rahu, however, is at its most peaceful in this Jupiterian sign. Rahu, as mentioned earlier, is quite at ease in Jupiter's signs. It usually furthers the luck of the live signification of the house it is placed in. For example Rahu in the fourth house in Sagittarius will further the luck and longevity of the mother and give a strong bond with the mother or maternal figures.

Within Sagittarius, Rahu is stronger when placed in the following degrees: 6°40' - 10°; 16°40' - 20°; 23°20' - 30°.

Napoleon Bonaparte (Chart no. 8), whose chart is discussed in the next chapter is a good example for this communicative placement of the nodal axis. Since this placement fell in his $3^{rd}/9^{th}$ house axis, communication becomes a key element in his life. Various instances from his life showed that his oratorical skills saved the day for him. He was very much a man concerned with action and knowledge.

KETU IN CANCER / RAHU IN CAPRICORN

Ketu's presence in the sign of the cat is an indicator of a developed feeling nature due to repeated past life experiences. The sense of home and family is quite important in such a native's life. Here in lies a natural nurturing capacity and a desire to be placed in situations where they can be of help to others within their immediate family and social circle.

There is a strong attachment to the home, family, motherland and the native feels reluctant to venture out of their protective Cancerian shell. They can appear very laid back and calm on an outer level but can be highly strung on an inner level, and can react very quickly to situations. The second half of life is much better than the first half.

Ketu in Cancer always gives some deprivation of happiness in regards to all Cancerian affairs such as home, relationship with the mother, root emotional needs, happiness in early childhood, property matters. Natives usually find difficulty in pursuing professions related to agriculture, dairy farming, nursing, driving vehicles, restaurant business and all other such occupations requiring a Cancerian touch.

They are the cats of the zodiac and their behaviour pattern greatly mimics those of cats. For example, they can be as lazy and self indulgent as they want to be if the outer conditions support them.

Rahu in Capricorn, on the other hand, wants to step out of the immediate environment and achieve some concrete goals. It is a career-oriented energy, which is similar to the placement of Rahu in the 10th house. We can already see that a balancing of energies is required, if the native as described by Ketu in Cancer has to achieve Capricornian goals which Rahu sets.

There's a constant struggle between family life and the career in such a native's life. Giving enough time and emotional attention to the family is very important to them. They are secretive about their feelings and thus may appear shy, reserved or even suspicious.

One can expect them to be doing well on a career level if the family life is also doing well. They are the easygoing types in the outer world if everything is all right at home, otherwise they can be the worst kind of people to deal with. Any strain in the home life is definitely going to show in the career. They have a tightly knit small circle of friends and do not socialize on a wide scale. Rahu in Capricorn can be very industrious on the outer career level if they sort themselves out on an internal emotional level.

Many mass leaders, politicians, organizers, executors, managers, people working in big organizations have this placement. Natives with this placement take a long time to step out of their shell and thus are only able to find their societal role in the latter half of their lives. Success never comes easily to them, as Capricorn is a slow sign.

Patience and perseverance are the two key qualities which have to be kept operating throughout their lives, because there is always a tendency to crawl back into their shells if things are not working out on a career or worldly level.

This placement produces the greatest achievers, those who have done what they set out to do against all the odds. It also produces the recluses, hermits, retiring types who have withdrawn themselves completely from the outer world. In some cases the native is able to live both types of lives within the present life.

Cancer is the sign representing the original state of the universe before full fledged material creation took place. This state is akin to a calm ocean without any ripples or waves. Creation only takes place after the divine spark impinges on this ocean and disturbs its equilibrium. Therefore Ketu's placement in Cancer has the capacity to take an individual to that timeless and motionless state within his own self. It can stop the churning process within an individual, which leads to true peace and contentment.

Ketu finds itself in an enemy's sign in Cancer. As stated earlier, it considers Moon as its worst enemy and so one cannot expect it to bestow material prosperity with this placement, unless there are other very powerful overriding factors. It can however give a penetrating insight into human psychology.

Within Cancer, Ketu functions strongly in the following degrees: 0° - 3°20' ; 13°20' - 20° and 26°40' - 30°.

Rahu is in a friendly sign in Capricorn and is thus capable of bestowing material success to the native with this placement. It must be kept in mind that since Capricorn is a slow sign, the progress or rise is usually slow but lasting.

Within Capricorn, Rahu is stronger in the following degrees: 3°20' - 6°40' ; 16°40' - 20° and 26°40' - 30°.

Moon and Saturn are the Karmic control planets for this placement. The positioning of Moon highlights the latent talents, and the house placement of Saturn signifies the area where the drive and opportunities lie in the present incarnation.

Albert Einstein's (Chart no. 6) life, typifies the struggle and eventual rewards associated with this placement. His family life (2nd house Ketu placement) suffered because of his intense dedication to his research (8th house Rahu placement). The position of Saturn, the sign dispositor of Rahu, in tenth, allowed him to have a serious impact on world affairs.

KETU IN LEO / RAHU IN AQUARIUS

The presence of Ketu in the sign of the Lion gives a well-developed solar nature as a result of past lives. This automatically implies that the native is usually very conscious of their individuality. There is a certain degree of pride and self-absorption seen with this placement. The native is very dignified. A lot of their actions are fuelled by a need for respect and authority. They are the kinds who never like to commit acts that are wrong or criminal for the fear of tarnishing their reputation and self-image.

Their self-image is for the most part guided by how others perceive them. They are not exactly the kind who appreciate being the butt of jokes or who can act the clown even for a day. They are authoritative individuals who like to have the final say on things and like to be taken seriously. A lot of righteous snobs belong to this category.

There's a lot of creativity in such individuals if they are bringing positive karma from past lives. The evolved types among this category radiate a great deal of warmth and light to inspire and nurture those around them. The light they carry is not the false light of the ego but the outer radiance of inner knowledge and wisdom.

This is one of the most explosive placements as Ketu is an extremely fiery planet and Leo is one of the fieriest signs. A lot of explosive sort of personalities are born under this placement. Uncontrollable anger, ambition or behaviour is usually the result.

Such people have strong likes and dislikes and an almost exaggerated sense of right and wrong. They like to make their own set of rules relating to how things should be and tend to follow it to the letter. This again can be a good thing or a bad thing depending on the evolutionary stage of the native in question.

Rahu feels completely at home in Aquarius as it is occupying its own sign. It's the ideal placement for all the eccentric, inventive and bizarre side of Rahu to find expression. Rahu functions in a Uranian sort of way in the electric sign.

Within Aquarius Rahu is stronger in the following degrees: 3°20' - 6°40'; 16°40' - 20° and 26°40' - 30°.

Rahu in Aquarius has a revolutionary but idealistic view of things. It is however an ideal placement for any sort of group activity. This placement helps the native to overcome his sense of ego or pride to be able to work with others. It usually gives some degree of detachment and asceticism from worldly matters. Rahu is not able to function on a purely material plane in this sign, so outer worldly success is hard to come by. In my view it is one of the most philosophical placements of a planet in a sign. Every Rahu in Aquarius person is a sort of philosopher of one kind or another.

For the present times it is a futuristic energy, which is always open to new ideas. On a material plane this might manifest as ease in accepting and incorporating new technology. On a spiritual plane it shows readiness to venture into subjects like Astrology, and other such so called occult sciences that relate to establishing an understanding of the functioning of our universe.

This is a very difficult placement of the nodal axis in the sense that its energies are very hard for a native to balance. There is a high degree of self-centeredness and self-indulgence associated with Ketu's placement in Leo, while Rahu in Aquarius is asking the native to work in a group as an equal. Such natives have to work hard to tone down their ego in order to relate with others. If they are able to do that this placement assures a very fulfilling life, full of opportunities and possibilities. Humility is a keyword for bringing out the potential of this placement.

Ketu finds itself in an enemy sign in Leo, but as mentioned earlier, Ketu is less inimical towards Sun as compared to Moon. In certain cases, when it is under a benefic aspect from Jupiter, or Sun is placed with or aspected by Jupiter, it can bestow all types of prosperity.

Within Leo, Ketu is stronger when placed in the following degrees: 0° - 3°20' ; 13°20' - 16°40' and 23°20' - 30°.

Sun and Saturn are the Karmic control planets for this placement. The positioning of Sun highlights the latent talents, and the position of Saturn signifies the area where the drive and opportunities lie in the present incarnation. Sun becomes the karmic suction control planet while Saturn is the karmic distribution control planet for this placement.

J.Krishnamurthy's (Chart no. 1) life and teachings, whose chart is discussed in detail in the earlier chapter, brings out the essence of this placement. His teachings emphasized individuality above everything else, which as we know is a Ketu in Leo expression. The fact that he was chosen as the messiah for the coming age of Aquarius, highlights his Rahu placement in Aquarius in the Ascendant. One cannot but notice the underlying Aquarian imprint in the majority of his writings.

KETU IN VIRGO / RAHU IN PISCES

Ketu in the sign of the virgin gives a clear understanding of all the affairs which are the domain of the 6th house - health, hygiene, healing, purity, attention to detail, discrimination, discipline, routine, service, structure, order, organization and a need for perfection.

Such a native has learnt the Virgo lessons in his previous life and as a result has the ability to put the material world in order in the present life. The danger here is that they might carry their need for purity and perfection to an extreme.

This placement can thus produce hypochondriacs, people who have an excessive need for cleanliness or an over critical nature, the kinds who can lose themselves in details. Virgo as we know doesn't have a sense of balance but it does have a sense of limits. It is important for these natives to use their sense of limits in all Virgoan activities.

Ketu represents the past and thus the Virgoan realm is something they need to get over rather than indulge in again in the present life. It is however their duty to set an example for others so they can understand the wisdom encapsulated in the esoteric sign of the maiden.

Virgo is the sign most related to the feminine principle or shakti (primordial feminine power) in most cultures. It carries the seed for any sort of enlightenment anyone is looking to achieve. We are all aware that for anything to happen on a physical, mental or spiritual plane some sort of order or structure is necessary. Such natives usually hold the key to this sense of order if they can get in touch with their Rahu in Pisces energies.

Rahu in Pisces as we would expect stands in exact opposition to Ketu in Virgo energies. Pisces is a sign which relates to the following keywords - all inclusive, scattered, diffusive, chaotic, illusionary, dreamy, unlimiting, fluid, creative, intuitive, mystical, inspiring, compassionate, utopian. Rahu's placement in this sign means that the native has to develop the above-mentioned sides of their nature in the present life. They have to make a conscious effort to get out of the Virgoan realm to take a plunge in the waters of Pisces.

This placement of the nodal axis requires the native to establish a balance between these seemingly conflicting energies. However difficult it might sound this balance can be achieved. For example, a musician learns to play an instrument through the order and structure imbibed in the sign of Virgo, but finally he must express himself through the fluid creativity imbibed in the sign of Pisces.

A lot of medical workers, healers, artists, mediums, psychics, people dealing with atomic energy, people working in charity and health organizations, people in the film industry and those in the pharmaceutical industry fall under this placement.

Mercury becomes the karmic suction control planet while Jupiter is the karmic distribution control planet for this placement. The positioning of Mercury highlights the latent talents, and the house placement of Jupiter signifies the area where the drive and opportunities lie in the present incarnation.

Ketu shares a neutral relationship with Mercury and can thus be said to be in a neutral sign in Virgo. One shouldn't expect too much material gain in Ketu's sub and major periods with this placement. However Ketu can be a spiritualizing influence by putting the material world in its correct perspective.

Within Virgo, Ketu is stronger when placed in the following degrees; 6°40' - 13°20' and 26°40' - 30°.

Rahu shares a neutral relationship with Jupiter and Pisces is thus a neutral placement for Rahu. However Rahu functions well in Jupiterian signs, so one can expect good results on a material plane in Rahu's sub and major periods if there are other supporting factors in the chart.

Within Pisces, Rahu is stronger when placed in the following degrees; 6°40' - 10°00', 13°20' - 20°00' and 23°20' - 30°.

Rahu never does too much harm when it is placed in the Sign of the Fishes. When heavily afflicted it can however cause trouble relating to the live issues indicated by the house this placement falls in.

Pisces as we know is co-ruled by Ketu and Rahu's presence in Ketu's sign allows for a sort of completion, which is symbolised by the Ouroborous symbolism (the snake biting its own tail). There is an opportunity to tie in the loose karmic ends from previous lives and develop an understanding of the paths to liberation. If Rahu brings out the negative side of Pisces then this placement produces most of the religious fundamentalists.

Queen Victoria (Chart no. 21), gained a vast empire due to the placement of Rahu in Pisces in the 11th house. Rahu in Pisces is an expansive energy, but in her chart it only functioned on a material plane because of its association with Mars and Saturn. Ketu in Virgo in the 5th house however had its say in the way it shaped the puritanical Virgoan psyche of her era.

On the other hand Osho's chart (Chart no. 20), highlights the more philosophical side of this placement. He was able to get over the Ketu in Virgo puritanical side. but the expansive nature of Rahu was very evident in the way he lived his life.

KETU IN LIBRA / RAHU IN ARIES

Ketu in the sign of the scales usually gives a balanced personality. The significations of Libra - sociability, diplomacy, harmony, grooming, judgement, business, commerce, and relationships - are naturally inbuilt in natives with this placement.

Libra as we know is the most material among the signs. Such natives usually have had a past life in which they had to completely immerse themselves in worldly affairs. Through this past life experience they have an innate understanding of the three main significations of the sign Libra in the present times - law, sex and money. Such natives also have an understanding of the social hierarchy on all its operating levels.

Due to the compromising attitude carried over from the past life, they have an urge to please everyone all the time. They have a lot of tact and diplomacy, but sometimes take it to such an extreme that no conclusion can be reached about anything. An active social life has a lot of importance for them. Ketu as we know likes to carry the past life patterns in the present life as well. Such natives feel at home with Libran activities but the present life has a different script for them.

This is related to the positioning of Rahu in Aries, which wants these natives to plunge themselves into the domain of the sign Aries - self-awareness, initiative, independence, courage, innovation, leadership, decision making, pioneering, primordial, wilfulness, impulsiveness, quickness.

Libra is a sign that denotes balance and fairness on all levels of existence. Its spiritual potential lies in establishing right relationships on all levels between man and man, man and nature etc. It is also the sign representing the dissolution of the ego, or the sense of self. However such natives have to guard against completely losing their sense of self, which makes them directionless instead of leading them to liberation.

The beauty of this sign lies in the ability to see things from other's point of view, which is essential for gaining experience and knowledge. Again the catch is that one has to have sufficient self-awareness in order to synthesize this learning. The key to this self-awareness lies in the positioning of Rahu in Aries.

The native has to learn to consciously develop the Arian qualities mentioned earlier. It means that the native must learn to stand alone instead of relying on a social circle. One has to start listening to one's own higher self instead of relying purely on what others have to say.

They have to learn to trust their own judgement and act upon it without getting approval from everyone around them. Rahu in Aries energy is all about learning to take a stand, which is very foreign to Libran sensibility. Such natives are usually very concerned about their social image, and doing one's own thing does not always guarantee an approving social circle.

Aries is a childlike sign, which is not bothered at all by what others think and is not interested in keeping up an image. It relates to the basic primordial urge, which led to the creation of the universe. It is thus a creative sign without any boundaries. Libra as we know is a sign full of boundaries, as balance cannot be maintained without a sense of limits.

The task facing such natives is akin to balancing the first and seventh house energies in a chart, which involves establishing harmony between the self and others. They have to use their inbuilt sense of balance to attain a delicate balance between the signs Aries and Libra. This is no easy task but these natives are the best equipped to achieve this. They have to make sure that Rahu in Aries doesn't give rise to too much selfishness and that Ketu in Libra doesn't give rise to too much superficiality.

Ketu in a Venusian sign usually denotes some sort of artistic talent carried over from past lives. In the present life this artistic talent has to be blended with the freedom, innovation and pioneering spirit inherent in Aries. Venus becomes the karmic suction control planet while Mars is the karmic distribution control planet for this placement. The positioning of Venus highlights the latent talents and the position of Mars signifies the area where the drive and opportunities lie in the present incarnation.

This placement of the nodal axis is helpful in producing psychologists, lawyers, sexual therapists, artists, pioneers, explorers, models, actors, media people and consultants in every field. The professions involving direct use of the personality are generally favoured by this placement.

Ketu has an inimical relationship with Venus and can be said to be in enemy camp in the sign of Libra, and thus cannot be expected to give good results on the material plane.

Within Libra Ketu can be expected to give better results in the following degrees - 0° to 10°00' and 16°40' to 23°20'. Even in these degrees it is better for expanding spiritual awareness rather than giving material prosperity. The only exception would be a strong material placement for Venus in the chart.

Rahu has a neutral relationship with Mars and thus Aries is a neutral sign placement for Rahu. It can thus give good material results if placed in the following degrees - 0°00' to 3°20' , 6°40' to 10°00' and 16°40' to 20°00'. It gives better spiritual results when placed in 16°40' to 20 °00' and 23°20' to 26°40'.

The noted psychologist Sigmund Freud (Chart no. 3), is a good example of this nodal placement. Interestingly he has Ketu placed in first house and Rahu in the seventh, which intensifies the first-seventh balancing issues related with this placement. It is no wonder then that he spent his life trying to get to the core of human relationships.

Paramahansa Yogananda, one of the most celebrated spiritual teachers in the west, has this nodal axis placement in the third/ninth house axis in his chart. He used the love principle perfected over several lives in his interactions, shown by Ketu in Libra in the third house, the house of communication. Rahu in Aries in the ninth helped him sow the seeds of a new idea in a foreign land.

KETU IN SCORPIO / RAHU IN TAURUS

Ketu in the sign of the eagle heightens the role of the Scorpionic realm in one's life. It represents a past life which was spent confronting scorpionic issues like - death, regeneration, shared resources, loss, separation, perversity, dark side of nature, chronic diseases, accidents, longevity, sexuality, transformation, mystery, occultism, metaphysics, profound thinking, research, exploration, overseas travel, strange adventures and events.

It is clear from the above significations that the past life of the native has been full of churning. It is no surprise that the main concern of most of the natives with this placement in the present life is stability - mental, material or spiritual.

This placement often produces hardcore materialists at one end of the spectrum and hardcore spiritualists at the other. It is difficult to find balanced personalities with this placement. Those who completely align themselves with the material and earthy energies of Rahu's placement in Taurus represent the former, while those who utilize the knowledge gained in their past life in order to further expand their consciousness make up the latter types.

Rahu in Taurus prompts the native to take an interest in the Taurean realm - physicality, senses, perception, refinement, luxury, tastes, expression, speech, resources, desires, personal earnings, ownership, property, security, stability, social prestige, logic, common sense and rationality.

As we can see if the native completely follows Rahu's dictates he/she will end up a staunch materialist. However when Rahu is working through its higher principle it produces enlightened materialism, which shows itself as reverence for all nature. Such natives are capable of seeing the divinity inherent in matter.

Ketu in Scorpio gives them an interest in the realm of the occult and supernatural, but it is seen that they won't wholeheartedly venture into these areas until there are other supporting factors in the chart. Those who do fully embrace the other side often end up solving the puzzle of existence.

Ketu is a friend of Mars and thus Scorpio is a friendly sign placement for Ketu. Ketu as we know shares corulership with Scorpio along with Mars and thus is in its own sign in Scorpio. It is a very intense placement, which if utilized properly can lead to transformation on a very deep level. The secrets and the mysteries of nature's functionings are very easily revealed. However this happens only when the dark side of nature is confronted in one of its myriad forms - death, dark deities etc. Ketu when functioning through its lower aspect gives a highly suspicious nature as the native concerned is always looking for the underlying motives behind all thoughts and actions.

Within Scorpio Ketu gives better results in the following degrees - 13°20' to 20°00' and 20°00' to 23°20'.

Rahu is in a friendly sign when placed in Taurus. However Taurus brings out the earthy and materialistic side of Rahu to the fore. This is the most materialistic placement among all the planetary placements in different signs. It is important to note that Rahu can function through its higher principle and give one a correct understanding of the purpose of the material world and the wisdom to correctly handle material resources.

Within Taurus Rahu gives better material results in the following degrees - 23°20' to 30°00'. It gives better spiritual results when placed between 3°20' to 6°40' and 13°20' to 16°40'.

Mars becomes the karmic suction control planet while Venus is the karmic distribution control planet for this placement. The positioning of Mars highlights the latent talents and the house placement of Venus signifies the area where the drive and opportunities lie in the present incarnation.

Ramakrishna Paramahansa (Chart no. 13), epitomises the spiritual potential of this placement. In his case both the dispositors of the nodes are exalted refining the energies. He lived a very materially secure life, not because he was materially well off, but because he had little or no material desires. Rahu in his case functions on a philosophical, spiritual plane as it is placed in Aquarius in Navamsha.

The famous mass murderer Theodore Bundy also has the same nodal axis sign placement. In has case both the nodes are placed in the worst degrees within their respective signs. This means that Rahu is placed in Cancer along with twisted Mercury while Ketu is placed in Capricorn with the malefic Mars in the Navamsha chart. Even in the main chart the dispositors of both the nodes are in material signs.

KETU IN SAGITTARIUS / RAHU IN GEMINI

Ketu in the sign of the centaur represents a fruitful past life lived in the Sagittarian domain - long journeys, philosophy, inner life, foreign influences, ethical disposition, optimism, faith, luck, freedom, higher mind, initiation, self realization.

It is understandable that one having gone through a good life would have an optimistic and carefree attitude in the present life. This in fact does hold true for most of the natives with this placement. It gives a zest for life. When Ketu, the most separative, contracting and detaching among planets is working in an optimistic mode there is not much to worry about.

The only catch here is that in some cases the optimism might turn into over confidence or over expansiveness, which usually leads to one's downfall. Natives with this placement are born to spread love, joy, and freedom in the world. They carry within themselves the Sagittarian message of respect for all life, earthly and beyond. It is their function to lift the spirits of fellow human beings and give hope to the hopeless.

This is a very philosophical placement and when Ketu is working through its higher principle such natives can possess the most all inclusive philosophy or spiritual insight. However when Ketu is functioning through its lower aspect the only thing such natives tend to care about is material expansion.

Ketu needs some sort of communication ability to relay its Sagittarian experiences and learnings. This is provided by Rahu's placement in Gemini. Communication ability is not exactly their forte and is something which they have to work on in their present life. Life always puts them into situations where they have to communicate whether they like it or not. It is seen that their communication ability increases with age.

Besides communication they have to work on other Gemini

attributes - companionship, mental and physical co-ordination, adaptability, swiftness, flexibility, duality, intellectual prowess, oratory, scientific rational thinking and writing ability.

Just as the opposite placement of the nodal axis (Ketu in Gemini/ Rahu in Sagittarius), needs to use its communication ability and other Gemini attributes to imbibe the higher learnings represented by Sagittarius, this placement needs to spread Sagittarian wisdom through communication and other Gemini attributes.

Just like the opposite placement of the nodal axis, this placement calls for a balance between third house and ninth house affairs. A delicate balance between materialism and spiritualism, logic and faith, common sense and higher sense etc. needs to be established. This is the main area of struggle for the natives with this placement. It is useful to remember that accomplishment exists only where struggle lies.

This placement produces writers, spiritualists, philosophers, teachers, religious leaders, dictators, compulsive gamblers, politicians, stockbrokers, speculators, risk takers, explorers, philanthropists, athletes, and sports persons in general. It is seen that natives with this placement can find happiness in everything they do and are thus found working in a wide variety of fields.

Ketu as we have seen earlier is exalted in Sagittarius and gives its best results when placed in the following degrees: 0° 00' to 3°20 and 23°20' to 30°00'.

When Ketu is working through its higher principle this becomes one of the most philosophical placements. Its downfall as mentioned earlier lies in over expansiveness and egotism.

Rahu is also exalted in Gemini and gives its best results in the following degree placements - 3°20' to 6°40', 13°20' to 16° 40', and 26°40' to 30°00'.

When working through its higher principle such a Rahu functions in sync with the universal mind and works for the benefit of all. Its methods are still not orthodox and it does not usually stick to ethics or rules. When working through its lower principle it becomes more selfish and can utilise its deceptive power to lie, cheat, betray etc. It can be the most dangerous placement if the overall inclination of the chart is tilted towards base/lower aspects of nature.

Jupiter becomes the karmic suction control planet while Mercury is the karmic distribution control planet for this placement. The positioning of Jupiter highlights the latent talents, and the house placement of Mercury signifies the area where the drive and opportunities lie in the present incarnation.

Adolph Hitler (Chart no. 10) has this placement in his third/ ninth house axis. It is no secret that he used his oratorical ability (Rahu in Gemini, Ketu in Sagittarius in third house along with Jupiter) to further his own over expansive imperialistic visions (Rahu in 9th and Ketu in Sagittarius). It is also a known fact that he used every form of manipulation and deceit to achieve his ends and never stood by any of the treaties he himself signed. This is very typical of the functioning of Rahu in Gemini.

Krishna (Chart no. 4), the eighth incarnation of Vishnu in the present round of Ages, according to Vedic texts has the same placement. He also used Rahu's manipulative potential in Gemini to bring about a world war. However in his case it was not for self-aggrandizement or any personal imperialistic visions. He did it to reduce the military power of the kings who were becoming corrupt and tyrannical. In accordance with the divine law he saw to it that good prevailed over evil in the end.

KETU IN CAPRICORN / RAHU IN CANCER

Ketu in the sign of material perfection represents a past life spent primarily in pursuit of worldly affairs. The Capricornian realm -

karma, vocation, organization, aspiration, pragmatism, perseverance, perfection, practical realization, concrete relationships and recognition - occupied centre stage.

Such natives show a high degree of practicality and are willing to take up responsibility from an early age. They have a cautious approach to things and do not like to do anything in haste. Their overall outlook on life however can be said to be a little pessimistic. They are also slow in absorbing new ideas and can be said to be on the conservative side. They usually have a hard outer personality and there is a tendency to conceal their inner emotions.

However when the native in consideration is an evolved enough soul, then this placement gives a perfect understanding of the cosmic laws. Such natives have the ability to assign everything its rightful place. They understand the material world for what it is and perform their karma with complete non-attachment. They don't shy away from their earthly duties and at the same time are open to experiences relating to the other realms.

In not so evolved souls this placement can produce staunch materialists who don't believe in any reality except the material reality. They have a lot of material ambition and a driving need to be at the centre stage of things.

However Rahu's placement in Cancer gives them a different calling for the present life. It directs them towards the Cancerian realm - home life, family, maternal relationships, nurturing, property, aesthetics, psychic receptivity, intuition, emotions, refinement, and peace of mind at an inward psychological level.

This means that the native has to find the peace within themselves rather than the outside world. They have to learn to respect their emotions and develop the softer side of their nature. It is seen that in the latter half of their lives such natives become very caring, sympathetic and receptive to realms besides the material.

The native experiences heartbreak if he or she persists on making a big impression in the tenth house issues like career etc. Even when pursuing tenth house goals they are only successful if they function from a caring and humanitarian perspective.

The transformation, which such natives are required to undergo in their present lives, is akin to stone turning into water. This obviously doesn't happen easily and a lot of sacrifice is required. In a way this can be said to be the toughest sign placement of the nodal axis as it usually involves a life full of struggles both inner and outer. These struggles do sometimes produce true humanitarians and at other times psychological wrecks. Since both Cancer and Capricorn are conservative signs at some level, this placement of the nodal axis usually makes such natives very suspicious, untrusting and skeptical.

Ketu can be said to be in an enemy's sign in Capricorn. Usually it does not give any prosperity unless Saturn has a very strong material placement in the chart. It's best degrees are - 6°40' to 13°20'.

Cancer is an enemy's sign placement for Rahu. However Rahu in Cancer in some ways is similar to Ketu in Leo and can give good results. As mentioned earlier Sage Parasara lists Cancer as one of the better sign placements for Rahu. It is stronger when placed in the following degrees - 0°00' to 3°20', 6°40' to 10°00' and 23° 20' to 26° 40'.

Saturn is the karmic suction control planet and Moon is the karmic distribution control planet for this placement. The positioning of Saturn highlights the latent talents and the house placement of Moon signifies the area where the drive and opportunities lie in the present incarnation.

M.K Gandhi (Chart no. 16), who was one of the front-runners in India's struggle for independence, has this placement in his 4th /10th house axis. Even though he was a humanitarian, he still epitomised the ultra conservative tendency of this placement. As is common with this placement he became a mass leader by highlighting the soft Cancerian image. The Karmic distribution control planet in the 10th house was mainly responsible for his worldly status.

Jim Morrison (Chart no. 12), also has this placement, but epitomised the other all-inclusive side of this placement. He wasn't a conservative by any stretch of the imagination and rebelled against the false and self-serving Capricornian society of the modern times.

KETU IN AQUARIUS / RAHU IN LEO

Ketu in the humanistic sign of the water bearer reveals a past life dedicated to humanitarian and philanthropic activities. All the significations of Aquarius - knowledge, aspirations, philanthropy, idealism, philosophy, wisdom, friendship, sharing, group relationships, humanitarianism - come naturally to natives with this placement.

Such natives are usually shy and self effacing in their childhood and for some this extends to their adult years. They are the kinds who never say no and are always ready to lend a helping hand. Most of them appear as being impractical to others but this is not generally the case. As they grow the spotlight gradually shifts to themselves and they become more self absorbed. This is the doing of Rahu's placement in Leo.

Rahu wants them to be a light unto themselves by developing their sense of self and respecting their creativity. It wants them to explore the domain of the sign Leo - creativity, self-consciousness, love of the self and others, acting, confidence, leadership, pride etc.

The karma of this placement is to relay the Aquarian wisdom and knowledge gained in the past life through the creative energies of Leo. The danger here is that the native as they grow older become more and more self absorbed and lose their ability to be of use to others. This placement requires a delicate balance between the sense of self and concern for others. A healthy sense of self is required for anyone to have a positive effect on one's surroundings, but at the same time an exaggerated sense of self can jeopardize the noblest of intentions.

It is seen that such natives go through two major transformations. In the first one they slowly build up their self worth by fighting off their innate self effacing nature. In the second transformation they are required to sublimate their sense of self to regain their humanitarian all-inclusive perspective.

A lot of evolved souls are born with this placement, as it allows for the unhindered dissemination of positive qualities like love, joy, wisdom and knowledge. They have the capacity to simultaneously inspire confidence and instill compassion in others.

Leo and Aquarius are both individualistic signs. Their function is to create individuals out of the majority steeped in mass consciousness. This process is in an accelerated state in the present times as the energies of the Age of Aquarius are getting stronger, and replacing the energies of the Piscean Age, which was in operation for the last two thousand years. No meaningful group or humanistic activity is possible without the individualization process. This placement is the perfect channel for quickening this process on our planet.

If the nodal axis is working through its lower plane this placement will produce rebels without a cause or a clue. Eccentricity is a word which typifies this placement, but whether it will be used positively or negatively depends upon the overall inclination of the horoscope.

This placement favours artists, spiritual guides, philosophers, revolutionaries, social workers, philanthropists, astrologers, people involved in new age activities like Light Networkers, internet related professions and those dealing with electricity and advanced technology. To sum it up this placement is common among those involved in all kinds of unusual professions.

Since Ketu shares a neutral relationship with Saturn, Aquarius is a neutral sign placement for Ketu. It is useful to note that Ketu is in a sign co-ruled by Rahu and thus can be said to be in a friendly sign. As discussed earlier, a sort of completion is associated with Ketu and Rahu placed in each other's signs. Ketu is thus capable of bestowing good material and spiritual results if there are other supporting factors in the chart.

Within Aquarius Ketu is stronger in the following degrees: 3°20' to 10°00' and 13°20' to 23°20'.

Leo is an enemy sign placement for Rahu. As discussed earlier, Rahu is more inimical towards Sun as compared to the Moon, and thus cannot be expected to give good material results unless there are other powerful overriding factors. In experience it is seen that such a Rahu when placed in important houses like the 5th, 9th and 10th provides one or two opportunities for Bhagyodaya (rise of fortune).

Within Leo Rahu is stronger in the following degrees: 6°40' to 10°00', 16 °40' to 20°00' and 23°20' to 30°00'.

Saturn becomes the karmic suction control planet and Sun the karmic distribution control planet for this placement. The positioning of Saturn highlights the latent talents, and the house placement of Sun signifies the area where the drive and opportunities lie in the present incarnation.

Jimi Hendrix (Chart no. 11) and Helena Petrovna Blavatsky (Chart no. 9), are two notable personalities born with this placement. They are both very new age type of personalities who fought off their initial shyness and self effacing nature to emerge as supremely confident individuals. Both have this placement in their third /ninth house axis. The only difference is that Blavatsky expressed herself through writing, while Hendrix expressed himself through electric guitar, both of which are third house significations. In case of HPB the karmic distribution control planet Sun is in the second house, boosting her capacity for retaining esoteric knowledge, while in case of Hendrix it is in the 12th house giving him success in a foreign land.

KETU IN PISCES / RAHU IN VIRGO

Ketu in the mystical sign of the fishes points towards a past life spent in luxury or isolation pursuing spiritual and occult realms. It shows a past life which was either full of material pleasures or full of spiritual experiences. The attributes of the sign Pisces - all inclusive, scattered, diffusive, chaotic, illusionary, dreamy, unlimiting, fluid, creative, intuitive, mystical, inspiring, compassionate, utopian - are strongly imprinted on the consciousness of the native.

Pisces as we know is a dual sign dealing with extremes. In the same way the behaviour of such a native can touch all types of extremes. This placement can produce the all-encompassing, tolerant and compassionate types as well as the bigoted, narrow-minded and confused types of individuals. This depends upon whether Ketu will relay the higher or lower aspects of Pisces, which in turn depends upon the evolutionary level of the individual.

This placement gives the ability to see the bigger picture, but the positioning of Rahu in the sign of details, Virgo, is asking such natives to not lose sight of the small things. In the present life such natives have to confront the Virgoan realm - health, hygiene, healing, purity, attention to detail, discrimination, discipline, routine, service, structure, order, perfection, organization etc.

One can imagine that this transformation can be quite painful for some of these natives, as it is akin to a poet made to do mundane clerical work. This struggle is basically related to the balancing of 6th and 12th house issues. Since both these houses are difficult houses this becomes a very challenging placement. Those who can find a correct balance between the Virgoan and Piscean energies emerge as saviour figures for their self and their surroundings.

This placement provides numerous opportunities for self growth and material success in the life of the native, but there is always some sort of struggle involved. One shouldn't expect a smooth, uneventful life when having this placement. This is a placement where a lot of churning takes place within an individual and their surroundings.

The present life is full of experiences, of both a material and spiritual nature. It is seen that following the middle path in everything is the key to attaining enlightenment and liberation symbolised by Ketu's positioning in Pisces. They have to find a delicate balance between intellectualism and emotionalism, materiality and spirituality, worldly duties and heavenly aspirations, human laws and universal laws, morality and personal freedom. In a way it can be seen as a fortunate placement, as Ketu in Pisces takes care of the spiritual side of life, while Rahu in Virgo takes care of the material side of life.

This placement favours artists, intellectuals, philosophers, politicians, media people, people working in common everyday jobs, and experts in their respective fields.

As discussed earlier, Ketu is in its own sign in Pisces and so can bestow all types of prosperity if there are other supporting factors. When Ketu is working through its lower principle it can lead to religious bigotry which is one of the main ailments that plagues humanity in the present.

Within Pisces Ketu is strong in the following degrees: 13°20' to 20°00' and 26°40' to 30°00'.

Rahu is also in its own sign in Virgo and can give very good material results, along with the ability to rise above competitors and enemies if Mercury is strong in the chart. This is one of the most intellectual placements of a planet in a sign. However, when working through its lower principle, Rahu can be a trickster for furthering selfish ends or harming others.

Within Virgo Rahu is strong in the following degrees: 3°20' to 6°40', 16°40' to 20°00' and 26°40' to 30°00'.

Jupiter becomes the karmic suction control planet and Mercury is the karmic distribution control planet for this placement. Jupiter's house positioning highlights the talents, while Mercury's house positioning highlights the area where opportunities lie in the present life.

The martial art legend Bruce Lee (Chart no. 22), was born with this placement. Since Rahu is placed in the 6th and Ketu in the 12th house, the significations of this placement became doubly effective. This helped lessen the confusion usually associated with this placement and brought clarity to his life purpose. Rahu made him famous through his 6th house martial art mastery and his ability to defeat his opponents, but his intense spiritual and philosophical side represented by Ketu in the 12th eluded the public eye. Jupiter's placement in the 1st house meant that his talents lay within his physical body, while Mercury in seventh gave him opportunity to reach out to a wider audience through the cinematic realm.

Bob Dylan, the legendary singer songwriter, has this placement in his second/eighth house. His Rahu in Virgo in the second house (house of poetry) helps him give a concise and relevant voice to the surreal and scattered Piscean vision of the eighth house Ketu in Pisces.

* * *

12. NODAL AXIS IN DIFFERENT HOUSES

This is the chapter where the emphasis is on putting it all together as we take a look at the charts of some famous personalities to illustrate the workings of the nodal axis.

Since the houses also have different axii comprising of opposing houses like the first and seventh and so on, we have divided this chapter into six sections each dealing with the presence of the nodal axis in a particular house axis. This method of division helps because there are a lot of commonalities between the opposite placements of Rahu/Ketu axis within a certain house axis. For example, the placement of Ketu in third house and Rahu in the ninth house shares a lot of common results with the placement of Rahu in the third house and Ketu in the ninth house.

It is seen that the nodal axis placement in houses is very similar to the nodal axis placement in signs. For example, Rahu in third house and Ketu in ninth house placement is akin to Rahu in Gemini and Ketu in Sagittarius placement. Thus while applying the general attributes of the house placements of the nodal axis, it would be helpful to include the attributes of the corresponding sign placements of the nodal axis mentioned in the previous chapter.

IN THE FIRST/ SEVENTH HOUSE AXIS

RAHU IN THE FIRST / KETU IN THE SEVENTH

This combination is supposed to be fortunate in the sense that it allows one to successfully project one's personality onto the outside world. This is due to the presence of Rahu in the first house, which according to both Vedic and Western astrologers, is as good a placement for Rahu as in the ninth or tenth houses.

Rahu in the Ascendant highlights the first house significations – self-assertion, early childhood, personality, physical appearance and vitality, body constitution, health, nature, individuality, self-esteem, ethical and moral disposition, career, fame, recognition, and honour - in the life of a native.

If Rahu is placed exactly conjunct or very close to the Ascendant degrees, then it gives an out of the ordinary physical appearance and personality. The person is usually on the taller side and has a peculiar sort of lordliness attached to his manners, which of course is not always very pleasing to others. A heightened sense of self, which can often turn into a false sense of pride and vanity, is noticed in the natives with this placement. It can drive them to act mindlessly on many an occasion.

If Rahu is working through its higher principle in this position it often provides a very keen insight and a capacity for constant self-introspection. This is the reason why this combination produces so many philosophers and saints. These men having the true understanding of the workings of the cosmic forces don't like to be addressed by either of the titles as they are beyond every title.

Rahu here can also provide deep insights into mass psychology and the future trends. Again whether the native will use this knowledge for personal gains or the general good depends upon the overall inclination of the chart.

There are no preferred vocations relating to this placement as these natives are found uniformly in all walks of life, even though such placement figures prominently in the charts of scientists, inventors, explorers and adventurers. The only thing they usually care for is independence in whatever they are doing.

Rahu in the first provides good physical stamina and vitality that might be overextended in taking up explorations in extreme conditions, or make the native indulge in so-called adventure sports.

Loneliness is something the natives with this placement are very used to. Their sense of individuality does not depend on social intercourse and so they have capacity to be all to themselves for long periods of time.

The seventh house Ketu hinders the formation of any lasting relationship. Thus it is not supposed to be a good combination for a happy married life unless there are other overriding positive factors. Lifelong bachelors are a norm with this placement.

Relationships with such a native can only last if they are given adequate space to exist as an individual. This is not to say that the native does not have any knowledge of social conduct. In fact such natives are very sweet and humble in their social conduct unless the nodal axis is badly afflicted.

They always stand by the way they think and feel and are very frank and outspoken about it. This habit of course does not help win them many friends excepting those with enough understanding to gauge their real intent. Public speaking comes naturally to such natives even though they may seem shy off stage.

This placement requires balance between the first and seventh house significations. The native has to take the spotlight off one's own self in order to understand and accommodate others.

Such natives are usually caught up in the dilemma that why should one scatter one's energies outside when the whole universe

exists with in the Self. This often causes them to completely ex-
clude the world outside from their attention, though the more
evolved souls do not make this mistake through the understanding that self- realization has no meaning, unless it is shared with
and includes the world outside as well.

The first chart with this combination belongs to a man described
by George Bernard Shaw as the most beautiful human being he
had ever met. He was also hailed as one of the most original thinkers
of the 20th century.

Chart no 1.   **J. Krishnamurthy**

11-05-1895   00:56 A.M.L.M.T.   12°N12' 79°E07'

Rashi (MainChart)

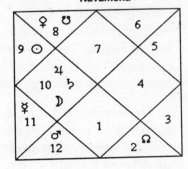

Natal Positions	
Ascendant	02°00' Aq
Sun	27°27' Ar
Moon	20°05' Sc
Mars	04°44' Ge
Mercury	10°57' Ta
Jupiter	05°20' Ge
Saturn	11°50' Li
Rahu	09°18' Aq
Ketu	09°18' Le
Uranus	25°22' Li
Neptune	22°3' Ta
Pluto	19°30' Ta

Planetary Periods

Planet	Begins At
Mercury	11-05-1895
Ketu	19-01-1908
Venus	19-01-1928
Sun	19-01-1935
Moon	19-01-1941
Mars	19-01-1951
Rahu	19-01-1958
Jupiter	19-01-1976

Navamsha

Even on the first look, one can see the immense strength in this chart arising from two exalted planets and an exchange between Mercury and Venus, the fourth and fifth lords. Obviously this exchange involving two *yogakarakas* for Aquarius Ascendant is in itself a powerful *Rajayoga* giving an extraordinary intellect and good communication abilities.

The main events in his life are intimately connected with the nodal axis placement. The presence of Rahu in the Ascendant boosts the inherent philosophical nature of the sign Aquarius. The fact that the sign dispositor of Rahu, Saturn, is exalted in the most benefic of houses, the ninth house, means that Rahu acts through his higher principle. Rahu is placed in the asterism of *Shatabhisa* which gives it a capacity for embracing loneliness and carrying out profound self-introspection.

Incidentally both of his karmic control planets are exalted, as Sun the dispositor of Ketu is placed in the sign of Aries in the third house. This is a very fortunate combination for any chart signifying good karmas carried over from previous lives, and usually denotes an incarnation where one can achieve whatever one sets out to.

This position of Sun and Saturn had its problems too, which manifested in the long legal battle between his father and his mentor Annie Besant over his custody. Sun representing his father is placed in direct opposition to Saturn, the planet indicating his mentor, due to its position in the ninth house.

Since Saturn is the lord of the twelfth house, it was a foreigner who adopted him. It was no normal person who had adopted him, as Annie Besant was the head of the Theosophical society at that time. This is indicated by the strength of his ninth house whose lord Venus is placed in the other trine.

He was taken out of India when he was only 14 years of age. Ketu major period was in operation at that time. Ketu in the seventh usually denotes foreign travel and since his nodal axis is unafflicted it could give its result without any obstructions.

In his Venus major period he was projected and trained by *Annie Besant* to be the New World teacher. Venus is very strong, being placed in the fifth as the lord of ninth and is also involved in an exchange. She had a vision of Krishnamurthy becoming the messiah for the coming age of Aquarius and so she established a new order known as the 'Order of the Star', and made him the head of that order. It can be seen that his karmic distribution control planet Saturn was doing everything for him.

Since Ketu was the initiator of this relationship it was quite clear it was not going to last. He disbanded the 'Order of the star and broke all his relationships with the Theosophical society in his Ketu sub major period in (1929-1930).

His Sun major period (1933-1939), made him establish his own identity as an individual and set up a new foundation known as Krishnamurthy Writings Inc. in Ojai, California. It is well known that the death of his younger brother Nitya sparked off this disillusionment with his mentor, which is to be expected since Sun, is placed in the third house, ruling over younger coborns.

This is a classic example of struggle taking place within the two karmic control planets. Sun, being the karmic inlet control planet, made him go inward and discard the fame and power that Saturn had planned for him. Later in his life the energies of Sun and Saturn seem to merge to produce a beautiful philosophy of life.

His life and works also demonstrate how this nodal axis placement needs to be balanced to achieve harmony between the self and others.

Ketu in the seventh made him stay a bachelor for life. His Rahu time brought him before the public again as he began to give talks in Europe and the U.S. Starting in his Ketu time (1947) he made frequent trips to India to share his thoughts with his countrymen. Ketu as we see is placed stronger than Rahu as it is placed in its own sign Scorpio in Navamsa. Its placement in eighth in Navamsa made him go into the very depths of the meaning of human life.

The next chart belongs to a brilliant thinker, intellectual and philosopher of the 19th century.

Chart no 2.   Nietzsche

15-10-1844   10:00 A.M.L.M.T.   51°N15' 12°E08'

Rashi (Main Chart)

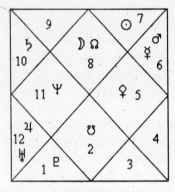

Natal Positions

Ascendant	05°25' Sc
Sun	00°25' Li
Moon	17°14' Sc
Mars	06°13' Vi
Mercury	12°26' Vi
Jupiter	04°27' Pi
Venus	14°39' Le
Saturn	09°00' Cp
Rahu	15°18' Sc
Ketu	15°18' Ta
Uranus	12°15' Pi
Neptune	29°10' Aq
Pluto	03°17' Ar

Navamsha

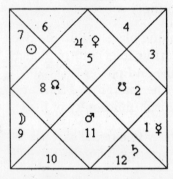

Planetary Periods

Planet	Begins At
Mercury	15-10-1844
Ketu	20-01-1861
Venus	20-01-1868
Sun	20-01-1888

The fifth house, the house of intellect and subtle thinking is exceptionally strong in this chart. Jupiter is placed in the fifth in the all-encompassing and intuitive sign of Pisces along with the inspirational Uranus. A rational and earthy touch is added to this combination by the aspect of Mars and Mercury, both placed in the sign governing ordered thinking, Virgo.

The real source of his quest for understanding the rea

meaning of existence, comes from his Moon-Rahu conjunction in the Ascendant. The research-oriented sign of Scorpio rises in the Ascendant. Starting from Aries, Scorpio is the first sign where the search for the unknown begins. This Moon-Rahu combination heightens and intensifies his Scorpio personality.

The aspect of Jupiter adds a benefic quality to this combination and makes his life and work free from the negative side of Scorpio energy. As discussed earlier, the aspect of Jupiter on any of the nodes refines the energy of that particular node, so that it may work through its higher aspect.

His life and work bordering on genius and insanity is a classic example for the Moon-Rahu conjunction. Since Moon is the ninth house lord, the significations of the ninth house like philosophy are boosted. It would however not be correct to assume that he went insane just because of this conjunction.

Moon in fact has its debility cancelled by being placed in a quadrant and thus functions like an exalted planet. This exaltation effect is more internalized endowing Nietzsche with a profound mind.

The real cause of his insanity lies with the weak twelfth house Sun placed in its debilitation sign Libra. Saturn's tenth house aspect further weakens the Sun almost dissolving his ego and sense of self. It is no wonder then that his mental health started to deteriorate in the Sun major period before he was finally pronounced insane in the same major period. This placement of the Sun was good in a sense that it gave him a reclusive nature very conducive for deep contemplation.

Ketu in the seventh house as usual did not allow for any lasting relationship in his life. The fact that all his work and writing took place in the major period of Venus, which is the karmic inlet control planet being the dispositor of Ketu shows that his wisdom originated from his past life experiences.

This knowledge gained in past lives was given expression in this incarnation by the tenth house Venus. The sign exchange between Sun and Venus accounts for his stress on the theory stating that the interplay of two opposing tendencies, Apollonian and Dionysian, forms the basis of existence. He obviously sided with the Dionysian worldview because of the strong Scorpio and Venus influence in his chart.

The Moon-Rahu combination in Scorpio, the sign governing the *kundalini shakti* (serpent energy) made his *kundalini* (serpent energy lying at the base of the spine) rise on its own allowing him to have many mystical experiences involving the astral and causal realms. Since this combination is a very strong and psychic force it required a strong Sun to handle it properly. It does not come as a surprise that his Rahu-time was in operation when he finally went insane at the age of 44.

It can also be seen that Rahu is very strong from his Navamsa chart as it is placed in its favourite sign of Scorpio. When a planet is placed in the same sign in the rasi and navamsa it is supposed to gain power. It is also placed in the fourth house representing the internal psyche.

Ketu in the First / Rahu in the Seventh

The peculiar thing about this placement of the nodal axis is that usually the native is pronounced worldly wise even when they are functioning on an otherworldly plane.

This is due to the presence of Rahu in the seventh house, which takes good care of one's social standing and reputation in the period signified by the seventh house, which usually ranges from 24 - 42 years, unless there are other overriding negative indications in the chart.

In fact all of the significations of the seventh house – balance, partnership, love, passion, soul-mate, long term relationships sociability, sublimation of self, harmony, justice, known enemies, personal enterprise, public image – get highlighted.

The seventh house basically represents the time in life when one establishes oneself in the world and creates a family and with it a sense of permanence. Its time starts when one, after having firmly established one's own sense of self, seeks relationships in the outside world.

The presence of Rahu in the seventh aids one in forming these relationships, which in the end are nothing but another way of understanding one's own self.

If the other factors in the chart support it, then the spouse is usually more mature than the native and the *Bhagyodaya* (rise of fortune) takes place after marriage. If Rahu is working through its lower principle than the motive behind the formation of these relationships is subject to question. Also a sense of balance is not maintained causing misunderstandings, break ups and even abuse at various levels.

Such natives with an afflicted nodal axis in this position usually carry out the mindless exploitation of sexuality in today's media. A sense of balance in terms of sexuality is absent resulting in the darker sides to take over.

The natives with this position of Rahu enjoy vocations involving relating to and handling people like counsellors, psychologists, management experts, project coordinators etc. Such natives usually start something of their own as they would rather be a boss of some small private set up rather than work under someone in a bigger set up.

Ketu rising in the Ascendant usually adds some psychic dimension to the personality and gives a self-effacing nature. Whether the native will use this psychic force consciously or unconsciously for the better or the worse depends upon the overall inclination of the chart. As always any association or aspect with Jupiter solves ninety percent of the problems that can arise with this placement.

Natives with this placement are usually short in height and have an out of the ordinary appearance if Ketu is placed very close to the Ascendant. With this placement it becomes necessary for the Ascendant lord to be placed in a strong position so that the native is not too under confident in regards to personality and appearance. A certain kind of exaggerated self-consciousness is seen in a native with this placement of the nodal axis.

Ketu in the first house is also supposed to give low appetite and peculiar tastes in food. Ketu in this position can internalize one's energies and thus allow the native abundant opportunity to develop along spiritual lines. It is generally seen that the spiritual transformation takes place in the latter years usually from the onset of Ketu-time.

What was discussed in the opposite placement of the nodal axis regarding the balancing of the first and seventh house energies holds true for this placement as well. The only difference being that here the native has to guard against completely depending on relationships to derive his/her sense of self.

The first chart with this placement belongs to one of the founding fathers of the development of psychoanalysis and psychotherapy in the modern era.

The interesting thing about this chart is that it so clearly defines the individual it belongs to, that somehow one cannot help but believe in a cosmic mind overseeing proceedings and astrology being its handwriting.

The seventh house is exceptionally strong in this chart as it houses an exalted Sun, the Ascendant lord Venus and Rahu along with the outer planets Pluto and Uranus. The seventh lord Mars also aspects the seventh house by its eighth house aspect, so naturally the passion of Freud was to get to the core of human relationships.

The presence of Rahu along with Sun magnifies the intensity of the already powerful Sun but in an externalized way. This intensity is used to illuminate only the outer energies of Venus and the seventh house. Predictably the final result he got from his research was that sex was the underlying principle of all relationships.

It is quite clear that this theory is far from the truth, but was to be expected from his chart because he could not get beyond the illusory power of *maya* represented by Rahu. This is a classic case of Mars –Venus influence on Rahu where sexuality assumes prime importance in a native's life. Here Mars and Venus are also the karmic control planets being the dispositors of Rahu and Ketu respectively, and so their affect is more pronounced and has its roots in his past lives.

Though he went wrong in his seventh house analysis, he was the first to bring out into the open the concept of a collective consciousness as well as a collective unconscious. As discussed earlier the collective realm is primarily the domain of the nodes and the outer planets.

In his case, the outer planets Pluto and Uranus are in conjunction with Rahu. Thus Rahu in his chart becomes a sort of mediator that relays the outer planet energies to the inner planets like Sun and Venus, who give expression to those energies in prevalent sociological terms.

Freud was very intrigued by human biology, which again is a Pluto signification. This can also be seen from his sixth house placement of Jupiter in Pisces. He tried to be as scientific in his studies as possible in a characteristically Uranian way. Of course the placement of Saturn in the ninth house meant that he kept on denying the spirit and concentrated on the material side of life.

Ketu in the Ascendant gave him a penetrating insight into the functionings of his own as well as other's minds. It also served to balance the outgoing nature of his seventh house planets by giving

Chart no 3.   **Sigmund Freud**

06-05-1856   6.30 P.M.L.M.T.   49°N38' 18°E09'

Rashi (Main Chart)

Navamsha

Natal Positions

Ascendant	13°20'Li
Sun	24°28'Ar
Moon	22°48'Ta
Mars	11°30'Vi
Mercury	05°56'Ar
Jupiter	07°47'Pi
Venus	04°20'Ar
Saturn	05°52'Ge
Rahu	01°37'Ar
Ketu	01°37'Li
Uranus	29°04'Ar
Neptune	27°51'Aq
Pluto	14°22'Ar

Planetary Periods

Planet	Begins At
Moon	06-05-1856
Mars	25-09-1856
Rahu	26-09-1863
Jupiter	25-09-1881
Saturn	25-09-1897
Mercury	26-09-1916

him the ability for mental seclusion necessary for any original thinking to take place.

Ketu's position in his chart is highlighted due to the fact that his Mercury, Venus and Rahu are placed in Ketu's asterism, *Ashvini*. As discussed earlier, Ashvini is related to healing and therapy which can basically sum up his entire life. Jupiter's position in the sixth house in its own sign of Pisces, the sign of mental sensitivity and undoing, adds to this energy in his chart and this is where modern psychotherapy was born.

Considering the nature of his chart, it is needless to add that he had many relationships and he learned through the difficulties encountered in them. The presence of twelfth lord Mercury along with the tenth lord Moon in the eighth house helped him turn his research into the collective basis of humanity as his vocation.

The karmic distribution control planet Mars is placed in the twelfth house in the puritanical sign of Virgo. His field of activity involved uncovering the superficial layers of the Victorian age society and morality. When we discuss the chart of Queen Victoria we will get to see why Victorian society was a Virgoan society.

Since Mars is involved this was done sometimes in an offensive way. We can see that Rahu is placed along with Mars in Aries in his Navamsha chart. Rahu is relaying martian energies and is revolutionizing the martian energy in the process. As mentioned before, the nodes get strong when placed with an exalted or own sign planet. The vargottama positioning of Rahu makes it the strongest among his seventh house planets. We can see that Rahu is also placed along with the Atmakaraka Sun in the Rasi Chart adding to its prominent riole in his chart.

It is amusing to see that Freud was also just a mouthpiece of the collective he was studying, in the sense that he acted out nature's opposing force in a society which suppressed sexuality by tipping to the other extreme and stating 'sexuality is everything". Of course the Rahu-Pluto combination was mainly responsible for this voice.

In my view the time had come for humanity to acknowledge the primordial forces of nature underlying the thin outer veil of civilization. Freud and others who followed, just served their part in the cosmic plan. *Carl Gustav Jung* in particular, who incidentally was his disciple, corrected a lot of flaws in his works by presenting a more unified and evenly balanced view of reality. Freud's fifth house Neptune manifested as his student as he had totally neglected the Neptunian realm in his own work.

The next chart belongs to the eighth incarnation of Vishnu in the present round of ages.

Chart no. 4   Krishna

Rashi (Main Chart)

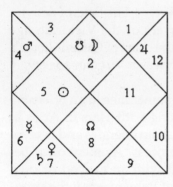

Since no accurate date is available for his birth, this chart is compiled from historical Vedic scriptures relating to his life and works. Information available is something like this — a midnight birth in the dark half of the lunar month; the constellation rising at the time of birth; scattered remarks on his planets. Being an incarnation most of the planets are either exalted or placed in their own signs.

Rahu is placed in its favourite sign Scorpio in the seventh house. It is supposed to work through its highest principles, as this chart belongs to a divine incarnation. Still it is seen that Krishna had no problem in using all the tricks like lying and deceit to achieve his ends. This exemplifies the devious and manipulative side of Rahu in Scorpio. He was also the main architect behind the great World War known as the *Mahabharata*, which, through the immense destruction it brought about, signalled the ending of an Age and the beginning of another. He used his Rahu in Scorpio power to overcome his open enemies (represented by seventh house).

He is the most symbolic figure of the Taurean Age (4000-2000 B.C), which can be easily seen by the accentuated Taurean influence in his chart symbolized by Ascendant, Ketu and Moon in Taurus. He started his life as a cowherd. Most of his personality traits (beauty, charm) and activities, have a distinct Taurean imprint.

He was a revolutionary of his time, in the sense that he

questioned the orthodoxy in every sphere of life like religion, courtship etc. There are a lot of beautiful stories in the legends that show how he faced even the wrath of Gods like *Indra* (King of the Gods), for persuading his people to stop worshipping the Gods they had been worshipping for generations.

The Karmic control planets are Mars and Venus. Mars is the main planet for his incarnation as it is the dispositor of Rahu. It is placed in the third which gave him excellence in all third house matters like communication and proficiency in battle. The debility of Mars is cancelled by the exaltation of Moon in the Ascendant. All his work and achievements stem from his ability to outwit others through the use of his intelligence. Venus in the sixth shows his involvement with enemies throughout his life. Since sixth house represents maternal uncle, his first enemy turned out to be his mother's younger brother. The fact that Ketu in Taurus unaspected by Jupiter doesn't augur well for male progeny, all his male offspring died an early death within his own lifetime.

Rahu's positioning in the philosophical and illuminating sign of Scorpio, aspected by Jupiter in the mystical sign of Pisces, made him come up with his brilliant view of the meaning of human life and its connection with the universe, encapsulated in the famous book now known as *'Gita'*. Rahu in Scorpio can give deep and penetrating insight into the hidden mysteries of life and death.

It was during his Ketu major period that he orated the verses, which now comprise the *'Gita'*, to *Arjuna*. Rahu's dispositor Mars (signifying younger friends/partners), is in the third house (house of brotherly associations), indicating that he would pass his wisdom to his younger friend and disciple Arjuna. Krishna and Arjuna shared a special and intimate relationship and worked as a team throughout their lives. This is obvious from the fact that his seventh lord is in the third house and is aspected by the eleventh lord. Jupiter in eleventh gave him an elder brother that fits the Jupiter in Pisces bill.

Mars, the planet signifying his latent talent, is placed in third house giving him an invincible and courageous personality. There are a lot of stories, which exemplify his courage in battlefield and his strategic prowess in tough situations. Mars aspected by Jupiter boosts this effect.

He had to witness the destruction of his entire family because of the nodal placement in the first/seventh house axis. This was the result of a curse, which was a direct result of his manipulations for winning the war. The first house Ketu made him pay for his seventh house Rahu actions.

There is an interesting story about his own death, which relates to his previous incarnation as Rama. Rama had killed the monkey king Bali from behind his back. Bali reincarnated as a hunter whose arrow mistakenly hit Krishna instead of the deer he was aiming at. Ketu's dispositor Venus is in the sixth, the house of enemies. This highlights his first house Ketu's tendency to give death as a result of some past life enmity. It also highlights the fact that no one is spared from Ketu's power of karmic retribution.

IN THE SECOND / EIGHTH HOUSE AXIS

Rahu in the Second / Ketu in the Eighth

This is considered a good placement for wise management of resources, material or spiritual, available at one's command unless the nodal axis is afflicted. If that is the case the native is sure to go through a period of deprivation that usually follows a period of plenty.

Due to the presence of Rahu in the second house, the second house significations – face, physicality, senses, perception, refinement, tastes, expression, speech, early childhood, reading books, resources, desires, personal earnings, ownership, property, social prestige, mathematical ability, rationality - get highlighted. All in all it can be considered to be a good combination for material well-being, but the problem which often arises, is that the desires never seem to end.

Though this happens with most of us, the natives with this placement suffer more because they are always more intense about getting exactly what they want. This native has to deal with the illusory force of *maya* in the realm of the second house, which in Vedic astrology is considered as one of the two houses governed by *maya* itself. Satisfaction or the lack of it becomes the keynote for the natives with this placement.

In physical terms, the second house Rahu usually gives an attractive personality, especially to the female natives if there are other favourable supporting factors. It usually imparts an unorthodox sort of beauty and a captivating quality to the native's face. Maturity reflects on such a native's face from an early age.

Though such natives are engaged in a wide variety of livelihoods, this placement of the nodal axis has a tendency to favour mathematicians, linguists, astrologers, economists, financiers, bankers, explorers, researchers, singers and musicians. Rahu in the second can also be said to favour the capitalistic mindset unless aspected by Saturn. If badly afflicted it can make a native lose his sense of proportion and earn through indulging in trickery, deceit, bribe, blackmail or theft.

If a survey were to be carried out, a lot of pushers and drug dealers would be found having this placement. The money earned through such devious means is usually spent on various indulgences. Such a native seems to acquire a taste for smoking, alcohol or any other form of intoxication quite quickly.

The association of Jupiter in any way with the nodal axis is again one of the best relieving factors for curbing unwanted tendencies. It should be considered a very sensitive placement for Rahu as a lot of the present day evils arise from this combination. In its higher aspect this combination gives a love of truth and a charitable disposition.

The presence of Ketu in the eighth house is good for carrying out deep research in any chosen field. If working through its higher principle it relieves the native of the fear of death in every sphere.

Experiencing the beauty of death and understanding its power of renewal is important for such a native.

When it is more materially oriented and strong, it promises legacies and other's resources. The change in fortune is usually sudden and comes late in life. If weak it only gives an expectation but does not fulfil the desire.

It is not considered a favourable position for Ketu as far as the fate of male progeny is concerned. If afflicted, it is also supposed to give diseases of the generative organs and the native is advised to guard against contracting sexually transmitted diseases.

This position of the nodal axis calls for balance between the second house and eighth house affairs. There is a need to maintain one's calm in the worldly game of loss and gain. If the native gets carried away by either of the two, then this nodal axis placement can be quite unforgiving.

A balance between practicality of the earthy second house and emotional eighth house is also sought. In fact this is the most difficult thing to achieve, as the signification of these houses are as dissimilar to the common man as life and death.

The following chart with this placement belongs to an acclaimed Vedic astrologer of the 20th century.

The combination of the lords of the fifth, ninth and tenth houses in the seventh house constitutes a formidable *Rajyoga* in this chart but it does not exactly specify his vocation as an astrologer. This is where the nodal axis with its genetic influence comes into picture.

Since Rahu is the genetic transmitter from the paternal grandfather, it is the main planet of interest in this chart, as his grandfather *B.Suryanarain Rao* was a noted astrologer who had written many important books on astrology. Rahu is placed in Pisces, a sign ruled by Jupiter and receives a fifth house aspect from Jupiter, the planet supposed to represent the teacher in Vedic astrology. It was under his tutelage that he learnt astrology. It comes as no surprise that his contact with his grandfather lasted only in the Rahu major period as B.S. Rao died at the beginning of his Jupiter major period. It can be seen that Rahu is prominently placed in the Ascendant in the Navamsha chart along with Sun. As discussed earlier conjunction with a luminary enhances the status of the nodes.

Chart no. 5   B.V. Raman

08-08-1912   07:35 P.M. L.M.T.   13°N04' 80°E17'

Rashi (Main Chart)

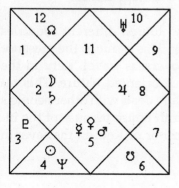

Natal Positions

Ascendant	11°33'Aq
Sun	22°59'Ca
Moon	23°38'Ta
Mars	21°21'Le
Mercury	13°58'Le
Jupiter	12°56'Sc
Venus	02°15'Le
Saturn	10°09'Ta
Rahu	22°47'Pi
Ketu	22°47'Vi
Uranus	08°27'Cp
Neptune	01°41'Ca
Pluto	07°48'Ge

Navamsha

Planetary Periods

Planet	Begins At
Mars	08-08-1912
Rahu	11-06-1919
Jupiter	11-06-1937
Saturn	11-06-1953
Mercury	10-06-1972
Ketu	10-06-1989
Venus	10-06-1996

It is interesting to note that his grandfather also had Rahu placed along with Jupiter in the sign of Pisces. He also inherited the mantle of being the editor of 'The Astrological Magazine' from his grandfather. This is due to the fact that his karmic distribution control planet Jupiter, which in his case is relaying energy directly from his grandfather, is placed in the tenth house of vocation. This meant that his ancestral inheritance of astrology became his vocation.

Rahu in the second also gives him a capacity to look into the future mass trends in advance, which made him successfully predict events like the outbreak of the Second World War. Uranus in the twelfth house helps this process by acting like an antenna that picks up future political and social happenings much before they happen.

Mars aspects Rahu by its eighth house aspect, which in his case is not always good for making verbal predictions, but it aids in enhancing his writing capabilities. Thus it comes as no surprise that B.V.Raman has become a legend in his own lifetime mainly through his written works.

The fact that Ketu in the eighth is not good for male progeny is highlighted in his chart. This can be seen by the fact that his Ketu-time was in operation (1963) when his only son *Surya Prakash* died at a young age. Since Ketu in the eighth house does not affect female progeny his daughter *Gayatri Devi Vasudev* is still alive and is also keeping the family tradition of astrology alive.

He got recognition in the West and toured different countries as soon as he entered Ketu-time (1959). This is due to the presence of Ketu in the eighth, the house of overseas travel. Ketu in the eighth also gives him a deep research oriented nature. This research involves astrology, which basically deals with other people's lives, an area represented by the seventh house because of the involvement of Mercury, the sign dispositor of Ketu in the seventh house *Rajayoga*.

Ketu in the Second / Rahu in the Eighth

This combination is said to confer long life as per the dictums of Vedic astrology. This generally holds true unless there are other overriding negative factors in the chart.

The presence of Ketu in the second house is not considered good for maintaining a smooth financial situation throughout life. If Ketu is placed in the sign of Sagittarius or Pisces then a steady livelihood is promised. Even with such a placement the native has to suffer substantial losses at least once in life.

This position of Ketu gives strange peculiarities in the way the native handles money. A touch of miserliness in small spending and a carefree attitude towards bigger spending is noticed. Gambling is one of the major downfalls of this placement. This is the worst nodal axis positioning for luck in speculation, but at the same time this placement fuels the desire to gamble. In extreme cases such a native is inclined to gamble on almost everything including one's life. A lot of natives who squander ancestral property are born with this placement.

This position of Ketu is said to give a wandering nature but the travels of such a native are generally pleasurable. Many renowned traveller of past as well as present have this placement of the nodal axis. Since such a native is not very inclined to follow the orthodox religious rituals he should strive to develop some personal philosophy of life.

Ketu in the second also causes some bitterness in family life, which requires cultivation of patience on the native's part. Some astrologers say that such a native is usually under the control of one's life partner, which in my view holds true in the majority of cases at some point of time in life.

Ketu in the second is also supposed to add a sarcastic tone to the voice and the native as a result can prove to be a bitter critic. In some cases the native has a tendency to use foul language. As always an aspect of Jupiter on Ketu sorts out most of the bad effects of this placement.

The presence of Rahu in the eighth promises legacies, and finances are often acquired through the partner. The extent of these gains depends upon the strength of Rahu and the eighth lord. At some point of time in the native's life he is forced to learn the humility of accepting resources from others.

Rahu in the eighth house boosts all the eighth house significations - legacies, shared resources, loss, separation, perversity, dark side of nature, chronic diseases, accidents, death, longevity, sexuality, regeneration, transformation, mystery, occultism, metaphysics, profound thinking, research, exploration, overseas travel, strange adventures and events.

Scientists, researchers, explorers, adventurers, insurance agents, bankers, spies, detectives, writers of mystery stories, occultists and all types of vocations that require dealing with old things are favoured by this placement of Rahu.

If Rahu is working through the lower principle, it can make the native commit some bad deeds in much the same way as explained for the placement of Rahu in the second house. It is one of the most dangerous placements, as the dark side of the eighth house is a very destructive force. There is a thin line dividing the balanced use and excessive use of eighth house energies.

There is a need to establish a balance between the second house and eighth house affairs in much the same way as discussed earlier for the opposite nodal axis placement. Here the only difference is that the native is prone to either totally neglect second house affairs or handle them in their own peculiar manner.

Control of speech is one of the key things that this placement demands of a native. The native is usually better off communicating through the written word, as he is prone to be misunderstood otherwise.

As mentioned earlier one's greatest potential lies where one's Ketu is positioned in the chart. Such a native has an ability to maintain that fine balance of not wanting more in material terms than is actually required in a particular incarnation. Optimism is another key virtue which needs to be cultivated as Ketu in the second can make one overtly pessimistic

The first example chart with this placement belongs to Albert Einstein, one of the most recognized genius' of the 20th century.

The strong *Rajyoga* formed by the conjunction of first, fifth and ninth house lords in the tenth house puts this chart beyond the realm of the ordinary. As if this was not enough, the ninth and tenth house lords are involved in an exchange of signs and houses. This makes the chart very strong and the person owning this chart was bound to become a renowned worldwide figure.

Since he was a scientist by vocation, what we are really interested in is his research capability. This is where the nodes come into picture as Rahu is placed in the eighth house along with an exalted Mars. We have already discussed that Rahu in the eighth gives research ability, and we are well aware of the fact that the nodes get very powerful when they are placed with an exalted planet. Rahu and Mars strengthen each other making his eighth house really strong. The presence of Mars in the eighth house also shows his mathematical acumen, which played a major role in his discoveries even though he never really enjoyed the mathematical part.

He is the man who stated that any discovery is 99% perspiration and 1% inspiration. This statement is so much in tune with his Mars/Rahu placement. In his case, Mars represents the perspiration and Rahu governs the inspiration. Rahu gains importance in his chart as the Ascendant is placed in *Ardra,* an asterism ruled by Rahu. As discussed earlier, *Ardra* is the most intellectual among the asterisms and favours all types of thinking. This is why all Einstein used to say in form of advice was "Think".

Rahu as we know is the giver of intuition and sudden inspiration. It can birth a new idea in someone's head in a flash; an event, which is not deliberate and thus cannot be made to happen at will. This idea is usually so revolutionary that it just cannot be birthed or sometimes even understood by Mercurial reasoning, Martian rationality or Saturnine common sense.

This is indeed what happened when he put forward his Special Theory of Relativity in 1905. He was undergoing his Venus-time (25-28y) in that period and Venus major period was also in operation. Venus is quite strong in his chart, as it is exalted in the tenth house being the lord of fifth house, the house of creative intelligence.

It is quite interesting to note that he did not receive the Nobel Prize until 1921when he entered his Rahu-time, and that too for a different work (photoelectric effect), even though the theory of relativity, which in a way changed the course of modern physics remains his most appreciated work till date.

His famous mass-energy conversion principle eventually resulted in the making and subsequent use of an atomic bomb. This immense potential of energy for humanity he unearthed, was again due to his eighth house Rahu. He confessed in his autobiography that he was given the theory of relativity in a dream.

He was against the destructive use of his discovery because of his humanitarian nature, exemplified by his ninth house Jupiter, placed in the humanistic sign of Aquarius. It is also placed in the asterism *Shatabhisha*, which as discussed earlier, promotes seclusion and contemplation necessary for gaining piercing insights into the functionings of nature.

Chart no 6.   **Albert Einstein**

14-03-1879   11.30 A.M. L.M.T   48°N30' 10°E00'

Rashi (Main Chart)

```
        4              2
        ☊          ℙ
  5 ψ         3            ♅ 1
                      ♄
        6          ♀ 12
                   ☉ ☿
  7
                      ♃
        9          ☊ ♂  11
        8   ☽    10
```

Navamsha

```
   12           10
   ☊            ☽
 1      ♂ ♀         9
            11
 2          ♃ 8
                    ♄ ☿
 3       5          7
     ☉          ☊
     4          6
```

Natal Positions

Ascendant	15°21'Ge
Sun	01°19'Pi
Moon	22°38'Sc
Mars	21°09'Cp
Mercury	04°44'Pi
Jupiter	12°56'Aq
Venus	24°48'Pi
Saturn	11°50'Pi
Rahu	09°18'Cp
Ketu	09°18'Ca
Uranus	09°04'Le
Neptune	15°35'Ar
Pluto	03°39'Ta

Planetary Periods

Planet	Begins At
Mercury	14-03-1879
Ketu	11-03-1889
Venus	10-03-1896
Sun	11-03-1916
Moon	12-03-1922
Mars	11-03-1932
Rahu	12-03-1939

The presence of Saturn, the karmic control planet, being the dispositor of Rahu in the tenth house, made him a legend within his lifetime. This was the main factor behind the worldwide implications of his work.

As expected, Ketu's presence in the second house meant that he had quite a disturbed and unhappy family life. Since his Ketu was working through its higher principle, he lived an ascetic sort of life and was not at all interested in material possessions beyond his bare necessities. Ketu is placed in the eighth house in the Navamsha chart thus aiding his research abilities.

The sign dispositor of Ketu, Moon, is having its debility can-celled due to the exaltation of Mars, and thus endows him with a deep and profound research oriented mind. Moon is in fact re-sponsible for his mathematical acumen being the lord of second house (mathematics).

It was the major period of Rahu that saved him from the Holo-caust and made him reside in the U.S. until the end of his life. This just goes to show the ability of the eighth house Rahu to confer longevity.

The presence of Uranus in the third house (house of physics) helped him revolutionize physics. He took physics to the begin-ning of metaphysics. Before his death he was working on the Uni-fied Field Theory, which would encompass all the forces and ener-gies operating in nature - a very Uranian vision!

The next chart belongs to one of the most celebrated psychics and seers of the 20th century.

Chart no. 7   Edgar Cayce

18-03-1877   03.00 P.M. L.M.T   36°N50' 87°W30'

Rasi (Main Chart)

```
      ☊  ♅
       5              3
  6         4
                  ℙ  2
       7        ☽ 1
                Ψ
  8        10        ☉
                        12
    ♃ ♂       ☊ ☿
     9        ♄ 11 ♀
```

Natal Positions

Ascendant	18°10'Ca
Sun	06°12'Pi
Moon	19°36'Ar
Mars	19°03'Sg
Mercury	19°30'Aq
Jupiter	09°54'Sg
Venus	23°32'Aq
Saturn	20°41'Aq
Rahu	18°33'Aq
Ketu	18°33'Le
Uranus	00°06'Ca
Neptune	11°23'Ar
Pluto	02°15'Ta

Navamsa

Planetary Periods

Planet	Begins At
Venus	18-03-1877
Sun	24-10-1887
Moon	24-10-1893
Mars	24-10-1903
Rahu	25-10-1910
Jupiter	25-10-1928
Saturn	25-10-1944

The first thing one notices in this chart is the heavily tenanted eighth house. This indicates that he could access hidden realms and dimensions. However a lot of charts have a heavily tenanted eighth house without any connection to the esoteric realms. The planets in such cases are usually working on an exoteric level bringing in legacies and so forth. To understand what makes his eighth house function in an esoteric manner, we have to concentrate on Rahu's placement there.

Rahu is placed in its own sign Aquarius and thus brings out the mystical side of this air sign, that has little to do with earthly matters. The fact that Rahu is conjunct the co-ruler of Aquarius, Saturn, helps stabilize the energy of Rahu and makes it function on a higher plane. Rahu as we mentioned earlier works well in association with an exalted or own house planet.

Rahu is very closely conjunct Mercury, the twelfth lord posited in the eighth house. Mercury carries all the twelfth house energies as no planet is posited in the twelfth house. His eighth and twelfth houses, the houses of psychic perception and sleep are intimately connected. It was no surprise that all his channelling took place in a sleeping state. He became famous as 'the sleeping prophet'.

Mercury's close conjunction with Rahu gives him the opportunity to realize his potential within his present lifetime. As mentioned earlier, it is one's duty to relay the energies of the planet posited in close conjunction to the nodes. Rahu and Mercury are also placed in the asterism of *Shatabhisha,* which as discussed earlier, is a mystical asterism dealing with diseases and healing.

His Sun in the ninth house in Pisces shows his conservative Christian upbringing. His Ascendant lord Moon in the tenth house in Aries gives him a commoner's attitude to life. Everyone knew him as a simple, uneducated man when he was not in his channelling state. Since Moon, his Ascendant lord, governing his sense of Self has no relation with his eighth house energies, he could never understand how the channelling was taking place. In other words his conscious mind represented by Moon had no connection with his unconscious (eighth house) mind.

This is the reason why he couldn't come out with his talents and abilities when the major periods of the Sun and Moon were in operation, even though he was aware of them from a very young age. Moon made him take up ordinary jobs after he quit school early.

He had a strange disorder in his 22nd year, which nobody could diagnose. It resulted in a complete loss of speech. His Ketu in the second house (house of speech) can be seen in action here. Since Sun is the dispositor of Ketu the event happened in his 22nd year, the year of Sun's maturity as per Vedic astrology. As we know Ketu's dispositor is the planet signifying latent potential. The Sun being placed in the auspicious ninth house (house of fate) helped open up his destiny. He cured himself through his own channelling process and this is when he started taking his gift seriously.

It wasn't until he was 24 that he started to heal others on a regular basis. This is due to the onset of his Mars major period. Mars, the tenth lord is placed in the sixth house (house of healing) in one of its favoured fire signs Sagittarius. Jupiter, the sixth and ninth lord joins Mars causing a *Rajayoga* (kingly combination). It was his destiny and *dharma* (life purpose) to heal others through his eighth house ability.

Jupiter-Mars conjunction in the auspicious sign of Sagittarius meant that he would become famous within his lifetime for his healing work (sixth house signification). Jupiter ensured that his healing was much more refined as compared to the surgical and poisonous Western healing methods prevalent in his time.

A second look at his eighth house reveals that Rahu is placed with its bosom friends Saturn, Mercury and Venus. It can thus function without obstruction, and all these planets support each other in a friendly sign. Another interesting thing to note is that all these planets are all placed within an orb of 5 degrees. This means that their energies are completely in tune.

It wasn't until his Rahu major period started, that he came up with futuristic prophecies and began covering topics such as astrology, reincarnation, ancient civilizations like Egypt, India and Atlantis. All these areas are intimately connected with the sign Aquarius.

The lord of the fourth house, Venus, is placed in the eighth house conjunct Mercury, the twelfth lord and Saturn, the eighth lord making him a time traveller. Fourth house represents past, eighth house relates to the cycles of time while twelfth house relates to the future.

Rahu being very strong in Aquarius could channel the combined energies of Mercury, Venus and Saturn. Rahu is the most important planet in his chart as it connected these planets with the astral realm and *Akashic* records (the universal library for all the past, present and future events).

Ketu in the second meant that he was never in a comfortable situation as far as finances were concerned. He would get strange illnesses and pains if he tried to earn money through his channelling. Also his healing planets Mars and Jupiter have no connection with the 2nd and 11th lords (lords signifying gain of wealth).

A strong and active Ketu is required to recollect one's past lives. In his case we get a clue to Ketu's strength from the Navamsha chart, where it is placed in the tenth house along with Moon and Mars. As discussed earlier the nodes get prominence by being placed along with the luminaries.

Another interesting thing, which tells us how much his healing was connected with the nodal axis, is the fact that he had his head towards the south and his feet towards the north whenever he lay down to channel. Ketu represents the south while Rahu represents the north. In his chart Ketu is placed in the first half of the chart (signifying head), and so his energies harmonized better when he lay down with his head in the direction ruled by Ketu. If Rahu and Ketu would have been the other way round, he would have been better off channelling with his head towards the north and feet towards south.

Saturn is the karmic distribution control planet along with Rahu, and so his life was fully focused on the eighth house affairs. He died in his Saturn major period, as Saturn is a strong *maraka* (death inflicting planet) for Cancer ascendant. Being the eighth lord in eighth it gave him the ability to accurately predict the time and day of his death.

The presence of Neptune along with Moon intensified his astral sensitivity, and gave him fame as this combination takes place in the tenth house. The conjunction of Uranus with Ketu gives a clue to a past life in Atlantis, a very advanced Uranian civilization, which he desribes in vivid details in his readings.

IN THE THIRD / NINTH HOUSE AXIS

RAHU IN THE THIRD / KETU IN THE NINTH

Both Vedic and Western astrologers consider this positioning of the nodes auspicious. In my view this is due to the fact that the third house is an *Upachaya* (3rd, 6th, 10th, 11th houses) house and thus favours the position of a supposed natural malefic Rahu therein.

Also Ketu does well in the ninth house even though it is a trine because of Ketu's natural affinity with the sign Sagittarius. Sagittarius being the ninth sign is similar to the ninth house in a numerological sense as well as in its significations. The native is supposed to have the best of both worlds with this combination; Rahu provides the material success while Ketu takes care of the inner life.

This is true to an extent but this combination has its downside as well. Rahu does provide a courageous disposition but often causes misunderstandings with the younger siblings.

As is the case with natural malefics the live things represented by the third house – younger brothers and sisters, companions-suffer, while the non live things represented by the third house like mental and physical energy, passions, prowess, leadership ability, oratory, scientific rational thinking, writing ability etc. are boosted. In some cases strong assistance from younger brothers and sisters are seen in helping one get ahead in life or vice versa.

Short journeys are seen to bring luck to a native with this combination though they are unpleasant sometimes. Longer journeys to distant countries do not turn out to be suited for a native with this combination unless Ketu is in a very strong position by being in a friendly sign and being posited along with a *yogakaraka* (the most auspicious planet) or an exalted planet.

A peculiar thing with this placement is that it can motivate a person to hold either a gun or a pen with consummate ease. What a native will finally choose among the two depends upon the overall inclination of the chart. It seems that it was one such person, who having chosen the latter option, coined the phrase " the pen is mightier than the sword ".

Writers, orators, painters, sculptors instrumentalists, soldiers, athletes (especially representing those sports which require skill and strength of the arms), generals, revolutionaries, political and spiritual leaders are the sort of people produced by this combination. The physical or mental ability provided by Rahu in the third house can be utilized in a positive creative way if the other placements in the chart provide for an integrated personality.

In my experience I have found that this placement produces quite a number of atheists who swear by science and scientific thought. This is because they are overemphasizing the third house attributes and philosophy and in the process completely blocking out the ninth house energy. This is quite natural, as the place where Rahu is positioned in the chart calls for attention in the present incarnation. Late in life such people also swing to the opposite pole and completely denounce everything material.

This placement of the nodal axis is all about striking a balance between the third house and the ninth house attributes – physics and religion, aggression and compassion, the drive and the path, matter and spirit. Only the evolved souls are able to strike this difficult and subtle balance and it is through their lives only the beauty, dexterity, gentleness and genius of this placement finds expression.

In most cases with this placement, the first half of life is more fruitful than the second half. If a native with this combination acquires fame and fortune in his youth, more often than not he loses it in his forties.

Forty-seven is an important age for this native as this is the time when a new episode begins in their life. For those who have had a relatively uneventful existence until this age, this time generally provides some opportunity to make one's mark on the world. As I mentioned before Ketu should be quite strong for such an event to happen.

Such a Ketu tries to bring into light the ninth house attributes like religion and fortune, if they have been lying dormant. For those who have spent their lives pursuing material ambitions and have been successful to an extent, the Ketu time (47-54 years) proves to be a miserable experience, especially if they are not willing to change their course in life.

The first example chart I would like to use for elucidating this placement of the nodal axis is of a man who chose the path of the 'sword', and in doing so became a great general and emperor of his time.

This chart is self-explanatory when one tries to understand why its owner rose to the heights of political and military power despite his birth in an ordinary family. The mutual reception and exchange of houses between Saturn and Moon, the fourth and the tenth lords respectively; the conjunction of Saturn and Mercury, the fifth and ninth lords respectively in the tenth house; the presence of the two fiery, royal and military planets, Sun and Mars, in the kingly sign of Leo in the house of easy gains, the eleventh house; the presence of Ascendant lord Venus in the ninth house of fortune; all these factors clearly demonstrate that a ruler of men is born.

The point I wish to raise is whether he could have demonstrated the military acumen that he did without the presence of Rahu in the third house in the sign of Sagittarius? My answer to this question is a simple 'no'.

It is not a mere coincidence that it was the major period of Rahu that propelled him to power. His fall only started in Jupiter major period, which began in 1804. He proclaimed himself emperor – this is due to the fact that Jupiter, the lord of third and sixth houses, the houses of power and ambition, is situated in the Ascendant providing a false sense of personal vanity.

Chart no.8   **Napoleon Bonaparte**

15-08-1769   11:30 A.M. L.M.T.   41°55'N 08°40'E

Rasi (Main Chart)

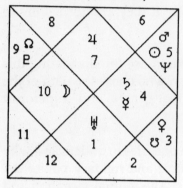

Natal Positions

Ascendant	10°46'Li
Sun	02°05'Le
Moon	07°31'Cp
Mars	21°23' Le
Mercury	15°29'Ca
Jupiter	24°48'Li
Venus	16°22'Ge
Saturn	04°44'Ca
Rahu	00°09'Sg
Ketu	00°09'Ge
Uranus	21°10' Ar
Neptune	18°02' Le
Pluto	25°40'Sg

Navamsa

Planetary Periods

Planet	Begins At
Sun	15-08-1769
Moon	29-06-1770
Mars	28-10-1780
Rahu	29-10-1787
Jupiter	29-10-1805
Saturn	29-10-1821

Rahu gains prominence in his chart in a variety of ways. It is the ruler of the asterism *Swati* in which his Ascendant is placed. The materially ambitious side of *Swati* is reflected in his personality. Rahu is also the ruler of the asterism *Ardra,* which houses his Ascendant lord Venus. Rahu is placed in conjunction with an exalted Sun in his *Navamsha* chart. This increases the strength of Rahu and imparts unlimited ambition to his Sun.

This is another case of a node getting prominence by being conjunct with a luminary. In this case the effect is pronounced as the luminary is exalted. Sun's ambitiousness is also increased by being placed in the royal asterism *Magha.* Rahu's ambitiousness and cruelty is fuelled by its placement in *Mula*. His chart brings out the authoritarian aspect of these two asterisms ruled by Ketu.

It is interesting to note that he played the role of a revolutionary throughout the Rahu major period, only to become the establishment in the Jupiter major period. This throws a light on how differently these two planets function even when related to similar houses. It is a testimony to the revolutionary nature of Rahu and the predominantly pro-establishment feel of Jupiter.

The presence of Pluto along with Rahu in the third house, as I mentioned before, brings about a strongly authoritarian nature with its roots in the subconscious part of the personality. It represents an incarnation that has a big role in shaping the destiny of nations and humanity in the historical era it has taken birth in. Napoleon could be said to be directly responsible for the wars he waged in his dictatorial pursuits, and the loss of human life and misery that resulted from these pursuits.

Napoleon's power and influence started to decline in his forties, as is usually the case with natives with such a placement of the nodal axis. It is interesting to note that the biggest setback he faced was when he tried to conquer Russia. As mentioned earlier ninth house Ketu is not very helpful in long travels made in foreign lands, and his attack on Russia was the longest campaign he ever undertook in terms of the distances involved.

Ketu's conjunction with the Ascendant lord Venus also affects his appearance and gives him a short, chubby build with a receding hairline, which is so characteristic of Ketu. He would have had a taller, more attractive appearance had Venus been posited alone in Gemini in the ninth house.

Besides the negative influence of the Jupiter major period, Ketu's conjunction with the Ascendant lord was the main factor behind the humiliation of defeat, loss of power and exile he faced in Ketu time (47-54 years), before he finally died at the age of 52. This chart clearly exemplifies the power of reversal, which Ketu possesses, which in my view is greater than that of any other planet. Ketu is also placed in the tenth in his Navamsha chart signifying a fall from position at some point. Ketu has the final say in the affairs of his life, as Rahu his main planet is placed in the asterism of Mula, which is ruled by Ketu.

The next chart with the same placement belongs to some one who chose the 'pen' instead of the 'sword' and ended up being the founder of the Theosophical movement.

Helena Petrovna Blavatsky, or 'HPB' as she was popularly known, was a writer, linguist, clairvoyant and a seeker of the knowledge of the mystery of life.

Chart no. 9   H.P. Blavatsky

12/08/1831   02:17 A.M. L.M.T.   48°27'N 35°01'E

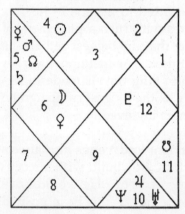

Rasi (Main Chart)

Natal Positions	
Ascendan	19°59'Ge
Sun	26°57'Ca
Moon	17°39'Vi
Mars	11°19'Le
Mercury	17°42'Le
Jupiter	26°10'Cp
Venus	22°09'Vi
Saturn	11°19'Le
Rahu	00°23'Le
Ketu	00°23'Aq
Uranus	21°03'Cp
Neptune	01°18'Cp
Pluto	21°12'Pi

Navamsa

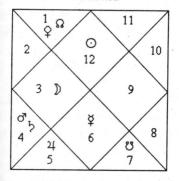

Planetary Periods

Planet	Begins At
Moon	12-08-1831
Mars	11-11-1835
Rahu	10-11-1842
Jupiter	10-11-1860
Saturn	10-11-1876
Mercury	11-11-1895
Ketu	11-11-1912

Her authorship qualities emanate from a strong third house, which houses Rahu, Mercury, Saturn and Mars in the creative sign of Leo. It is a known fact in astrology that the house, which the Ascendant lord occupies, which in this case is the third, gets special attention in the life of a native. Also Gemini as an Ascendant is always considered suitable for intellectual pursuits. Her Ascendant is placed in the asterism of *Ardra,* and this brings out the thinking, intellectual side of Gemini to the fore. As is the case with *Ardra,* she faced a lot of upheaval in her life till she finally was able to fulfill her destiny.

It is correct to assume that Venus in the fourth with its debility cancelled, gave her access to astral and other more subtle realms, but the important factor which gave an esoteric bent to her writings, was the placement of Rahu in the third house along with the Ascendant lord and the ninth lord. Otherwise she would have been a regular writer dealing with human psychology.

The word 'esoteric' came into prominence only after her writings had introduced to the West the ageless wisdom of the East, as well as the lost traditions of Egypt and Greece. All the new developments like the new-age movement, esoteric astrology and other institutions dealing with the occult and metaphysics in the West do a owe a lot to the movement she initiated.

Another facet of her personality was her mediumship ability, which is often expected when either of the nodes is in conjunction with the Ascendant lord. The presence of Sun, the Karmic distribution control planet being the dispositor of Rahu, in the second house, gave her excellent powers of communication.

Most of her writing took place in her travels, which again proves a point I made earlier about this placement of the nodal axis, that travelling enhances luck and the latent powers of such natives.

She was a widely travelled lady for her time; absorbing and disseminating information, learning new languages wherever she went, before finally establishing the Theosophical Movement in 1875. As one can notice this takes place in her Rahu time (42-47 years). Also it was the Rahu Major period that started in 1841, which sparked her interest in the esoteric realm of existence. It is quite a simple case of Rahu gaining strength through its association with the major planets in the chart. Rahu is also associated with Venus in the navamsa chart.

In her case Ketu time (47-54 years) brought about a decline in her health and made her entirely incapacitated. This is due to its direct opposition with the Ascendant lord Mercury. It did not bring about a decrease in her influence as it did in the case of Napoleon. Ketu gains strength from the fact that her Mars and Saturn are exactly conjunct (a rare happening), in the royal asterism of *Magha,* which as we know is ruled by Ketu. The energies of *Magha* helped make her an authority figure and even gave her a throne (symbol of *Magha*), as the head of the Theosophical society.

Saturn aspects its own sign Aquarius and the Ketu posited therein. This aspect strengthens Ketu and since the Saturn Major period (1875-1891) was operating at this time in her life, the movement initiated by her gained momentum. Ketu's placement in the eighth house in Navamsa is an indicator of her intense involvement with the occult sciences in this period.

Due to her third house (house of associations) Rahu, she was ble to attract brilliant minds like Annie Besant, Alice Bailey and .W. Leadbeater, who played a major part in making Theosophy mainstream force throughout Europe and America.

The presence of Uranus and Neptune in the eighth house helps une into the collective urges of humanity, and bring into light a nystical (Neptune) but ordered (Uranus) vision of the Universe.

KETU IN THIRD / RAHU IN NINTH

This positioning of the nodes is also considered auspicious but ɔ a lesser extent. This is because of the inherent bias against the presence of Rahu in Sagittarius, which can be taken to be similar ɔ the ninth house and Ketu in Gemini, which corresponds to the hird house.

In my view Ketu, because of its fiery nature, functions well in he third house as do the other fiery planets Sun and Mars. Also ahu's presence in the ninth is usually beneficial as it provides the ative many opportunities for *Bhagyodaya* (rise of fortune). The atives with this combination usually meet their destiny either in foreign land or through foreigners.

The native with this placement usually believes in religious sym- olism though not strictly in the orthodox sense. Since the place- ent of Rahu in a particular house shows the area where work eeds to be done in the present incarnation, the native is seen to ɔncentrate on the ninth house affairs – long journeys, philoso- hy, inner life, foreign influences, ethical disposition, higher mind, iitiation, self realization.

It must not be misunderstood that such a native will always ɔllow organized religion. He might develop a personal philoso- hy, which is usually for the better unless there are other negative idications in the chart.

Ketu in the third shows some sort of skill related to the third house like writing, painting and other types of skills involving the hands etc., as Ketu is the storehouse of whatever we have learnt in our past lives. As is usually the case with Ketu it requires some good conjunction or aspect to bring out this talent into the open.

Ketu is more dangerous than Rahu for the live things related to the third house like younger siblings. Another important point associated with this combination, which can be attributed to Ketu's position in the first half of the horoscope, is an unhappy first half of life. Barring exceptions, the childhood time especially is not worth remembering. Ketu when badly placed in third house is akin to a dog roaming around the street and thus gives lot of unnecessary and fruitless travels and wandering.

Whether a person rises from the childhood scars as a saviour or a revengeful maniac, depends upon the overall strength and inclination of the chart. It is usually seen that the aspect or conjunction of Jupiter or the dispositor of Ketu, helps achieve an ordered outlet for the suppressed energy. Ketu's harmonious relationship with Jupiter and its dispositor is the key to its good functioning in a horoscope.

This placement of the nodal axis is similar to Rahu in the third and Ketu in the ninth placement, in the sense that it is all about striking a balance between the third house and the ninth house attributes – physics and religion, aggression and compassion, the drive and the path, matter and spirit. Only the evolved souls are able to strike this difficult and subtle balance, and it is through their lives only the beauty, dexterity, gentleness and genius of this placement finds expression.

The first example chart for this combination is of a man whose name generated and continues to generate more terror than any other name did in the 20th century.

Even from a first look at this chart it becomes clear why its owner rose to the heights of power like he did. The idealistic and political sign of Libra is rising in the Ascendant; the *yogakaraka* Saturn is placed in the tenth house; the Ascendant lord and the ninth lord combine in the seventh house, the house of power and conquest, along with the lord of the seventh and an exalted Sun; Sun is also very near its maximum degree of exaltation.

All these factors have the makings of a great General. We have already discussed in Chapter 8. how *Shakti Yoga,* a very powerful combination involving Rahu and Moon operates in his chart and accounts for his power and actions.

The domination of the fiery planets Sun and Mars in the seventh house also points towards the in built ruthlessness of the person involved. However it was in oratory, which is a third house affair, where lay the true talent of this man. Moon, Jupiter and Ketu conjoin in Sagittarius, the sign occupying third house in his chart.

Chart no. 10   **Adolph Hitler**

20-04-1889   6:30 A.M. L.M.T.   21°44'N 69°33'E

Rasi (Main Chart)

Natal Positions

Ascendant	03°42'Li
Sun	08°30'Ar
Moon	14°14'Sg
Mars	24°04' Ar
Mercury	03°21'Ar
Jupiter	16°06'Sg
Venus	24°23'Ar
Saturn	21°07'Ca
Rahu	23°45'Ge
Ketu	23°45'Sg
Uranus	27°03' Ar
Neptune	08°26' Ta
Pluto	13°37'Ta

Navamsa

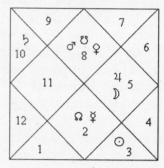

Planetary Periods

Planet	Begins At
Sun	20-04-1889
Moon	29-06-1770
Mars	28-10-1780
Rahu	29-10-1787
Jupiter	29-10-1805
Saturn	29-10-1821

As I mentioned earlier, Ketu becomes really powerful when it is in conjunction with a planet in its own house. Its presence with Jupiter in its own sign has boosted the strength of Jupiter four times as per Vedic astrology. We also know that Ketu has a natural affinity for the sign Sagittarius.

It was this Ketu, which provided the hypnotic touch behind a backdrop of Sagittarian fieriness and Jupiterian self-righteousness and enthusiasm, which mesmerized the masses. The presence of the tenth lord Moon along with this combination allowed him to make this talent his vocation.

His unhappy childhood and a youth spent in struggle are all very typical of this placement of the nodal axis. The bitterness and hatred he harboured against the Jews had its seeds in his childhood, and in astrological terms, Ketu is the planet, which was responsible for sowing these seeds.

Ketu is placed in the Ascendant along with *Atmakaraka* Venus and *Amatyakaraka* Mars in its own sign Scorpio in the *Navamsha* chart. Ketu thus gains immense power in his chart as it influences Mars and Venus, the two key planets in his chart in more ways than one. Mars is the final dispositor of the chart. Venus is the Ascendant lord. Hitler could not pursue his artistic (Venusian) ambitions and as a result turned his attention to Martian pursuits (soldier, politician). In the end Venus being in the sign of Mars in both Rasi and Navamsa also favoured a military way of life.

Ketu boosts the destructive tendencies of Mars and the sign Scorpio in the *Navamsha* chart. Ketu when working on its lower principle has a great penchant for revenge. In my view there is no other planet as serious about revenge as Ketu, and there are no extremes that it cannot force a person to go to in order to get even. This is where the destructive aspect of Ketu comes out and the rest as we know is history. Ketu gains more power in his chart as Sun and Mercury are posited in its asterism *Ashvini*, which as we know stands for aiming for near impossible goals - which is exactly what he did!

Though Ketu provided the talent, it was Rahu in the ninth house in his favoured sign of Gemini, which provided him the luck to achieve his ambitions. It was in the Major period of Rahu (1928-1945) that he rose to power. Rahu is associated with Mercury in Navamsha chart in the material sign Taurus.

Since he was born in Austria, Germany could be said to be a foreign land for him and interestingly it was in his Rahu time (42-47y) that he rose to power and was able to enjoy it. The period from 1931 to 1936 was the period when he was seen as a peacemaker and the man who rebuilt Germany. Even historians say that had he died or fell from power in 1936, he would have been hailed as a very positive personality in times to come.

This clearly shows the marked difference between the functionings of Rahu and that of Ketu in his chart, as he made a sudden shift to being a warmonger as soon as his Ketu time (47-54y) began in 1936. He started the 2nd World War and brought about the Holocaust all within the Ketu time. It is interesting to note that he put the 2nd World War into motion just around the time Ketu transited over his natal Sun and other seventh house planets.

Again this brings home the point I made earlier about Ketu being the planet associated with mass catastrophes. In my view, all these events were destined for humanity due the path it had

chosen, and Hitler was just a pawn in the game of nature. It would
be unwise to put all the blame on one individual for such collective
happenings. It was a case of karmic retribution for everyone involved.

The next chart belongs to a musician, messenger, and prophet
all rolled into one.

Jimi Hendrix burst into fame as a guitar genius at the age of 25
(1967), and died before he turned 28 (1970). Within this short
span of time he revolutionized not only electric guitar playing but
also shattered all the existing definitions of the word 'music'. Using electricity he took music into another dimension – an act that
has not been duplicated since his death though many have tried.

Now, guitar being a stringed instrument, guitar playing is a
third house affair. In his chart Ketu is the only planet in the third
house, which is occupied by the mystical Aquarius. Saturn aspects this Ketu posited in Aquarius by its 10th house aspect. This
strengthens Ketu, as is the case in the chart of 'HPB', and this Ketu
in turn allows Hendrix to relay the energies emanating from the
sign of Aquarius through his music.

Chart no. 11   Jimi Hendrix

27-11-1942   10:15 A.M. L.M.T.   47°36'N 122°19'W

Rasi (Main Chart)

Natal Positions

Ascendant	15°40'Sg
Sun	11°49'Sc
Moon	05°31'Ca
Mars	24°30' Li
Mercury	09°57'Sc
Jupiter	01°47'Ca
Venus	14°35'Sc
Saturn	16°19'Ta
Rahu	06°16'Le
Ketu	06°16'Aq
Uranus	09°42' Ta
Neptune	08°39' Vi
Pluto	14°27'Ca

Navamsa

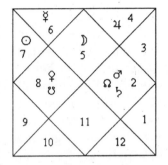

Planetary Periods

Planet	Begins At
Saturn	27-11-1942
Mercury	15-10-1958

His music and words carry prophetic images symbolizing the dawning of the Age of Aquarius in the very near future. It is now widely known that Aquarius is the sign ruling over electricity, which puts his use of electricity in reproducing cosmic sounds in musical form, into perspective.

In my view, this Ketu is responsible for the otherworldly feel in his music, though there are other factors in his chart, which aided him in relaying his message to the world. Ketu is also posited along with Venus in its own sign Scorpio in the *Navamsha* chart. Thus it is able to relay its energy through music (Venus). Ketu is also placed in the 23rd *Nakshatra* known as *Dhanishta,* which is supposed to be the most musical and rhythmical among the 27 asterisms. Its symbol is a drum or a flute, and involves becoming a hollow instrument by dissolving one's ego so that the divinity can express itself through music.

Jupiter is conjunct Moon in Cancer in the mystical eighth house; Jupiter is close to its maximum degree of exaltation; Sun, Mercury and Venus are posited in the twelfth house, the house of psychic receptivity, in the mystical sign of Scorpio; the mystical planet Neptune is posited close to the Midheaven; the revolutionary Uranus, the ruler of electricity is conjunct the third lord Saturn.

His chart reaffirms the fact that Ketu is the significator of the knowledge we bring into this life from our previous incarnations in this and the other worlds.

He had an unhappy and lonely childhood, which as I said before is a sort of a norm with this combination. In his childhood he got to spend a lot of time with his part *Cherokee* (a Native American Indian tribe) paternal grandmother, Nora, who is represented by the Ketu in his chart. He treasured the time spent with her as she instilled in him his native Indian heritage by telling him old Indian stories. In his own words, she was the one who helped bring about the sense of Self in him in those early lonesome years. This exemplifies the power of Ketu to connect one to one's genetic and racial roots and the purpose of one's incarnation.

His success came in a foreign land (England) with the help and involvement of foreigners. This is his Rahu in action in the ninth house. Sun, the Karmic distribution control planet, being the dispositor of Rahu, is placed in the foreign (twelfth) house assuring him success in a foreign land. Rahu aids him in his vocation as it is placed in the tenth in the *Navamsha* chart along with Mars and Saturn. As we know Mars and Saturn in angles help one achieve one's aims in life.

The fact that his Rahu is placed in Leo, the sign ruling stage performance, made him work against his inherent shyness and take to stage. This again just goes to show that the sign and house associated with Rahu are the areas that require effort in the present incarnation. Rahu is placed in the asterism *Magha*, which as we discussed earlier relates to utilization of talents acquired in the past lives to gain recognition and prominence in the present life. By the time he was in his Rahu inter period in his Mercury major period, he was virtually sitting on a throne by being regarded as the king among guitarists.

Interestingly his most creative phase was when Rahu was transiting Aries (1967), which happens to be his fifth house, the house of creativity. This is why I am of the opinion that fellow astrologers should pay attention to the transit results of the nodes, especially Rahu. It is a great help in ascertaining which area of the chart will receive attention at a certain point of time in the native's life.

The next chart belongs to a remarkable poet, singer, shaman and prophet of the 20ᵗʰ century.

This chart has been chosen, because in my view any discussion on the significance of the Lunar Nodes would be incomplete without an analysis of this contemporary figure. His life perfectly embodied what the nodes are all about. He was a revolutionary not in the physical but more mental sense of the word. He produced poetry and music in the same years as Jimi Hendrix, during the times of musicopolitical social revolution of the late sixties and died at the same age (28y).

'Jim', has the mystical and prophetic sign of Scorpio rising in the Ascendant. When he was just four years old a strange incident took place which he later recalled as the most important event of his life - he, his parents and his grandparents were driving through the desert in New Mexico, USA when they came across a fresh accident scene. The accident involved Native American Indians whose bodies and blood was scattered all over.

According to his account, he could see the souls of some of those dead Indians just hanging around and a few of them jumped straight into his soul. In his own words," *Indians scattered on the dawn's highway bleeding, ghosts crowd the young child's fragile egg-shell mind"*.

Jim Morrison - Chart no.12

8-12-1943   5:45 A.M. L.M.T.   25°46'N 80°12'W

Rasi (Main Chart)

Natal Positions	
Ascendant	15°40'Sc
Sun	11°49'Sc
Moon	05°31'Ar
Mars	24°30' Ta
Mercury	09°57'Sg
Jupiter	01°47'Le
Venus	14°35'Li
Saturn	16°19'Ge
Rahu	06°16'Ca
Ketu	06°16'Cp
Uranus	09°42' Ta
Neptune	08°39' Vi
Pluto	14°27'Ca

Navamsa

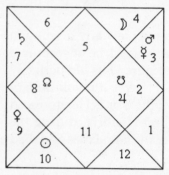

Planetary Periods

Planet	Begins At
Ketu	08-12-1943
Venus	26-12-1943
Sun	26-12-1963
Moon	26-12-1969

Now this incident in astrological terms is surely the result of the presence of Ketu in his third house, the house of travel and childhood (till around 5 years). The fact that his grandparents (representing his nodes) were present when this incident took place, leaves no doubt as to what forces were behind it. Since his Ketu is placed in the earthy, concrete sign of Capricorn, the journey was taking place by road and the incident had a permanent effect on his psyche. In many individuals with this placement, some sort of psychic and otherworldly encounter takes place in the early childhood that may or may not have lasting effects.

In his case, he voiced the sentiments of the Native American Indians through his songs. In my view, there was no bitterer critic of the American State, the way it was formed, the way it was run and the way it was heading, than Jim Morrison. It is interesting to note that his Mercury, Moon and Jupiter are in Ketu's asterisms *Mula*, *Ashvini* and *Magha* respectively. As discussed earlier Ketu's asterisms, especially Magha and Mula are all for revolt against authority. This is a unique combination, and these three asterisms complimented each other to help him gain prominence. Magha always likes to bestow thrones, and he was regarded as the king of rebellion and psychedelia in America in his time.

When he got famous he proclaimed that his parents were dead – a statement very typical of the nodes, who like to block out the father (Sun) and the mother (Moon) planets, which in a sense meant that he was a free individual having cut himself off from his roots.

Also he was rebelling against the very establishment, which his parents were a part of; his father was a Rear Admiral in US Navy signified by his tenth lord Sun in the watery sign of Scorpio. This position of Sun was also responsible for providing him with a towering outer personality.

The sign dispositor of Ketu, Saturn, is placed in the eighth house intensifying the basic psychic quality of the chart. This also caters for the fixation he had on death. He was always trying to overcome the fear of death (Saturn) by going to the extremes. In light of that it is no wonder his actions seemed suicidal to most.

In this quest he also gained cosmic knowledge and wisdom springing from the Universal consciousness. He was known to make repeated trips to the desert (another Ketu signification) in order to meditate. This exemplifies why Ketu is considered the key to liberation from the cycle of time. In his own words –*"cancel my subscription to the resurrection"*.

Most of his planets are placed in the asterisms ruled by the nodes, boosting the significance of the nodes. Especially the main planets signifying his vocation Moon, Mercury and Jupiter are placed in Ketu's nakshatras. This makes Ketu the most important planet in his chart.

Ketu's co-rulership of Scorpio and Rahu's corulership of Aquarius can be seen functioning through his chart. His inner personality governed by the Ascendant was very much influenced by Ketu; it revealed itself as he proclaimed himself the *Lizard King*. A lot of his songs are full of reptilian imageries (especially snakes).

His clothing (mostly leather) and public image (shaman) governed by the fourth house, clearly shows the influence of Rahu. The Aquarian part of his nature which was so very important for making an impression on the masses in those days, was also brought out by Rahu since he has no planets in Aquarius.

The aspect of Jupiter on the sign Aquarius added a benefic quality to his actions. His second house, the house of poetry and singing combines influences received from Mars, Saturn and Jupiter by aspect.

Interestingly his Mercury and Saturn are placed in exactly similar positions as the chart of Nostradamus (discussed later), providing a prophetic touch to his writings.

His singing quite often turned into oratory (third house) and that's when the nodal axis took over the proceedings; to hear his songs is like listening to the nodes!

Nodes are the forces, which as I said before, represent the cycle of time and thus can provide insight into the past as well as future.

Mercury in the second aspected by Jupiter is a good combination for writing poetry. The presence of second lord Jupiter in the tenth helped turn his interest in poetry into his vocation. Ketu's presence with Jupiter in the tenth house in the *Navamsha* chart reveals how his vocationinvolved preaching (Jupiter), the concept of karmic retribution and liberation (Ketu). Ketu's presence in Taurus shows his intimate soul level connection with the earth cultures like Native American Indians.

The presence of Mars as the dispositor of the Sun, Moon and Ascendant in the seventh house shows his excessive Martian tendencies causing trouble in his relationships. Venus in the twelfth in its own sign is responsible for his Dionysian tendencies.

Public recognition came in his 24th year, which is governed by Moon according to Vedic astrology. Moon, the ninth lord, is also the karmic distribution control planet being the dispositor of Rahu.

The placement of Pluto along with Rahu, Uranus along with Mars and Neptune along with Saturn allowed him to become a vehicle for the collective. Since Rahu is placed in the mystical sign

Scorpio in the Navamsha chart, it is no surprise that most of his poetry dealt with the imminent collapse of the present civilization and the concept of gaining freedom through embracing fear.

IN THE FOURTH / TENTH HOUSE AXIS

RAHU IN THE FOURTH / KETU IN THE TENTH

The first thing that can be said about this placement is that everything is fine, as long as the native is not over ambitious as far as one's vocation is concerned. Contentment is the keyword for the natives with this combination.

The presence of Rahu in the fourth ensures that the fourth house affairs like mother, home life, family, property, aesthetics, basic emotions, refinement, and peace of mind at an inward psychological level, take a front seat.

A strong attachment to the mother or a mother figure is seen with this placement very similar to the effects of Rahu conjoining with Moon.

Usually some help from mother or mother's side in getting ahead in life is also seen. The father figure is usually absent as either he is lost in a young age or ignored if present.

Such natives usually do not like to choose vocations that involve a lot of travelling. They very much prefer to have a permanent home in a particular village, town or city where they spend the best part of their lives. They usually prefer smaller towns to bigger cities.

The people connected with the fourth house vocations like property dealers, agriculturists, dairy farmers, transporters, professional drivers, child psychologists, children's story writers, interior decorators, architects, construction engineers etc. are favoured by this placement of Rahu.

At least a couple of changes in profession are very common with this placement. The presence of Ketu in the tenth house hinders what is now commonly known as job satisfaction. As I said before with this placement, it becomes the native's duty to inculcate the emotional aspect of life instead of concentrating too much on the practical aspects of life.

Practicality is something, which the native already has as shown by the presence of Ketu in an earthy house, which is very similar in characteristics to the sign of Capricorn. A sudden fall is imminent if the native gets over ambitious with regards to the tenth house significations.

This life's lesson usually involves learning to strike a balance between emotions (water) and practicality (earth). Any attempts to suppress the active subconscious can make their lives dull and sad.

The first chart with this placement belongs to a man who was a living embodiment of what godliness means.

Ramakrishna Paramahansa became famous worldwide through the mission established in his name by his foremost disciple *Vivekananda*. It is interesting to note that he spent all his life in a small town in what is now West Bengal. He never travelled farther than Calcutta that was just a few miles away. This is very much in keeping with the facts I mentioned earlier regarding this placement.

Chart no. 13   **Ramakrishna Paramahansa**

18-02-1836   5:30 A.M. L.M T.   22°55'N 87°58'E

Rasi (Main Chart)

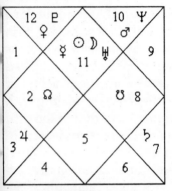

Natal Positions

Ascendan	08°07'Aq
Sun	06°53'Aq
Moon	22°11'Aq
Mars	22°15' Cp
Mercury	15°07'Aq
Jupiter	14°24'Ge
Venus	09°05'Pi
Saturn	13°34'Li
Rahu	03°52'Ta
Ketu	03°53'Sc
Uranus	09°08' Aq
Neptune	12°43' Cp
Pluto	23°49'Pi

Navamsa

Planetary Periods

Planet	Begins At
Jupiter	18-02-1836
Saturn	01-07-1849
Mercury	01-07-1868
Ketu	01-07-1885

The power inherent in this chart is self evident with three exalted planets. The Sun and the Moon are placed in the Ascendant
in the mystical and philosophical sign of Aquarius making him a
triple Aquarius. Uranus, the coruler of Aquarius, is also placed in
the Ascendant. If anyone wishes to understand what Aquarius is
all about they should take a look at the life of this remarkable man.

He was a great devotee of the Divine Mother in her most terrible and fierce form *Kali*. In my view this devotion sprung from,
besides other factors, by the presence of Rahu in the sign of Taurus, a feminine sign governing the Mother Goddess principle.

We have already discussed in Chapter 8. how *Shakti Yoga*, a very powerful combination involving Rahu and Moon operates in his chart and accounts for his power and actions.

Rahu's strong influence in this chart can be seen from the fact that his Ascendant, Sun, Mercury, Jupiter and Ascendant lord Saturn are all placed in the asterisms of Rahu. Ascendant, Sun and Mercury are placed in the asterism of *Shatabhisha*, which as discussed earlier, is the most mystical, philosophical and detached among the asterisms. His personality perfectly embodied the higher aspects of Shatabhisha discussed in the earlier chapter dealing with the asterisms of the nodes. Jupiter's placement in *Ardra* in the fifth house, gave him a thinking disciple whose chart is discussed in detail later in this chapter. Ardra as we know is the most intellectual among the asterisms. Saturn finds its maximum exaltation in *Swati* and gave him the capacity to be precise with his judgements and a maintain a balanced view on religion and philosophy.

Rahu is also the *Atmakaraka* (soul significator) in his chart and thus assumes even greater significance. It is strongly placed in *Navamsa* chart in its own sign Aquarius along with Jupiter, Mercury and Saturn. Thus Rahu also establishes contact with the key sign governing his *Avatar* (incarnation). This placement also takes away the worldliness usually associated with Rahu's placement in Taurus.

In the *Jaimini* system of Vedic Astrology where the chosen deity is seen from the sign in which *Atmakaraka* is placed, it is no wonder he chose the dark aspect of Mother Nature as his route to enlightenment, as Aquarius is a dark sign presided over by Shiva and his consort Kali.

Ketu in the tenth house in its own sign Scorpio kept him away from worldly ambitions. The fact that both the karmic control planets Mars and Venus are exalted in his chart, helped refine the energy of the nodal axis. The nodal axis in his chart was working at a level much higher than the worldly plane of existence, and thus helped him transcend the material realm and attain Self-Realization through the process of devotion and surrender.

The presence of Mars, the karmic distribution control planet in the twelfth house, the house of liberation, shows a life devoted to austerity and self-negation. Everyone who is born needs a reason to die and in his case Ketu provided the reason in the form of throat cancer. The presence of sixth and eighth lords, Moon and Mercury respectively, in the Ascendant also points to some serious health disorder.

Interestingly his Ketu major period and Ketu-time started together in 1883. This is about the time his disease started. Ketu, which represents stored up karma from previous incarnations, did not spare even a man of his spiritual stature, the severe pain that accompanies a disease like cancer.

He did not use his yogic powers to cure the disease even when his well wishers wanted him to. He remained calm and contented in face of pain and death just like a soul on brink of liberation should be.

The next chart with the same placement belongs to a man whose assassination has captured the fascination of the media and public alike for the last four decades.

This man was the President of the U.S.A. for only two short years. On the first look it seems quite extraordinary that he became the President of a superpower in the first place. His chart on first look shows no indication as to why its owner should wield such authority. There is no relation between the ninth and tenth houses; there are no exalted planets; the Ascendant lord is posited in the eighth house.

Chart no. 14   J.F.Kennedy

29-5-1917   2:51 P.M. L.M.T.   43°22'N 71°08'W

Rasi (Main Chart)

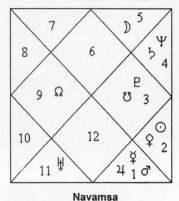

Natal Positions

Ascendant	25°20'Vi
Sun	15°07'Ta
Moon	24°26'Le
Mars	25°43' Ar
Mercury	27°42'Ar
Jupiter	00°19'Ar
Venus	24°01'Ta
Saturn	04°26'Ca
Rahu	19°46'Sg
Ketu	19°46'Ge
Uranus	01°14' Aq
Neptune	09°57' Ca
Pluto	11°20'Ge

Navamsa

Planetary Periods

Planet	Begins At
Venus	29-05-1917
Sun	28-09-1920
Moon	28-09-1926
Mars	28-09-1936
Rahu	28-09-1943
Jupiter	28-09-1961

Without the involvement of the nodal axis we cannot really understand the power of this chart. Jupiter and Mercury are the karmic control planets being the dispositors of Rahu and Ketu respectively. Their conjunction in the eighth house, the house of legacy, along with the eighth lord Mars is where the strength of this chart lies.

I use the word legacy because JFK was in a way groomed by his father from his early childhood to become what he finally did become. Mercury as we can see is the tenth lord as well signifying his father. In my view he merely acted out his father's ambitions.

He became the president at the age of 44 (1961), which as we know falls in Rahu-time. Interestingly again it was the Rahu major period which was in operation at that time. Rahu gave such good results because it was reflecting the results of its dispositor Jupiter, which was one of the planets in his powerful eighth house combination. Rahu gains strength on account of its placemnet in its own sign Virgo in the navamsha chart.

As I have mentioned before, this placement of the nodal axis works well in the first half of life due to Rahu being in the first half of the chart. His chart should be an eye opener to all those who believe Rahu cannot function well in Sagittarius because of its supposed debilitation. According to Sage *Parashara*, Sagittarius is one of the four signs in which Rahu functions best.

Since Ketu is in the tenth house, one thing was certain, he could not have completed his 5-year presidential term. Now the key to the way this term was going to be cut short again lies with his eighth house karmic control planets. Their association with Mars, which presides over weapons, in the fiery and impulsive sign of Aries meant that it was his destiny that his term had to end quickly with his assassination.

The point to note is that this happened as soon as he got into the 47th year i.e. the beginning of Ketu-time. This shows Ketu was very much involved in this final episode of his life, which again highlights the power of Ketu to bring in past life influences into the present life. Ketu is also strongly placed in its own sign Pisces in the eighth house, house of endings and intrigue, in the navamsha chart. This among other factors accounts for the complex forces at work behind his assassination and the intrigue generated by it.

According to Vedic astrology Mercury in eighth is good for fame. This dictum also is proved right in this case, but he had to pay the price for it with his life, as Mercury is the sign-dispositor of Ketu.

Ketu is also conjunct with Pluto, which again points towards the sinister secret forces at work that carried out his assassination. Pluto's conjunction also accounts for the psychological impact this event had on the American public and the world at large.

KETU IN FOURTH / RAHU IN TENTH

This placement of the nodal axis is known to subject the native to various extremes throughout his life. It is very clear from the positioning of Ketu in the fourth house that the first half of life is usually full of unpleasant or psychic experiences. Since the fourth house especially relates to the childhood time (3-14 y), it is this period that is usually the most difficult and often leaves some scars on the native's psychological make up.

As we know fourth house is a very sensitive house, as it relates to the emotional body, which is created during the childhood years. Mishandling on part of the parents, peers or other elders in these early years results in psychological disorders which tend to show influence in the later years.

Those natives with a strong Ketu come out of these experiences even stronger and those with a weak overall chart succumb to the outside influences. When strong, such a Ketu gives a very keen insight into the functionings of the subconscious within the Self and others as well. A piercing and penetrating intellect is the result.

Psychic powers are heightened with the presence of a strong Ketu in the fourth house, but a strong personality is required to harness these powers for the benefit of all. The fourth house is directly related with the universal mother principle, and the presence of Ketu there can connect one to the wellsprings of wisdom and the core forces of creation.

Relationship with parents is usually not very smooth with this combination, and there is strong connection with one of the grandparents. Though one may receive financial and other sort of help from them, there are always misunderstandings. A strong psychic contact with the mother is seen with this placement, but the relationship might not be pleasant because of the extremes involved. This is the combination that experiences the so-called generation gap to its fullest degree especially in the present day and age. The sooner such a native is separated from their parent's influence, the better it is for both.

This is a wonderful combination for getting out in the world and making one's mark. It gives the ability to head big organizations or undertakings. In fact both Vedic and Western astrologers agree that this is the best placement for Rahu. It is a very fortunate combination if Rahu is also associating with other vital centers of the nativity. The closer Rahu is placed to the Midheaven the more its power to help the native. The tenth house Rahu favours these natives in the second half of their lives. Rahu in this position usually gives a strong sense of purpose and destiny.

Ketu in a moksha house gives an innate understanding of the primeval forces which create and sustain the manifest universe. In younger souls it gives an emotional and hypersensitive disposition. The challenge here is to check the excessive emotionalism and take a more practical approach in achieving one's goals in life. Again a balance has to be established between the water and earth elements. An analogy such natives should remember is that 'earth needs to be watered just enough to raise the crops - more water leads to flooding and less water drought'.

Besides its major period, Rahu brings about positive changes in the life of these natives at the ages of 19, 38 and 42. This combination often requires sacrificing private life at the expense of public life. The native should guard against not totally neglecting the fourth house affairs or else there is very little inner peace and contentment even after all the fame and glory.

The tenth house Rahu gives leadership qualities, which can either be used for personal aggrandizement or for the benefit of one's circle of influence. The tenth house significations - *karma,*

vocation, organization, aspiration, pragmatism, practical realization, concrete relationships, recognition- get highlighted with this
placement of the nodal axis.

The presence of Ketu in fourth usually gives a strong attachment and knowledge of one's roots. The key here is to utilize the
wisdom inherent in one's roots through the tenth house Rahu i.e.
in an all-inclusive humanitarian manner.

The first chart with this placement belongs to a widely feared
and enigmatic man, who can be rated among the top five con-
querors in recorded history.

Chart no. 15   **Chengiz Khan**

16-8-1186   1.30 A.M. L.M.T.   37°00'N 65°00'E

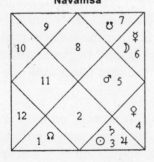

Rasi (Main Chart)

Navamsa

Natal Positions

Ascendant	16°06'Ca
Sun	16°42'Vi
Moon	29°32'Vi
Mars	29°26'Vi
Mercury	27°35'Vi
Jupiter	17°28'Vi
Venus	21°22'Vi
Saturn	19°20'Vi
Rahu	02°12'Ar
Ketu	02°12'Li
Uranus	12°24' Ta
Neptune	01°53' Aq
Pluto	07°32'Ca

Planetary Periods

Planet	Begins At
Mars	16-09-1186
Rahu	11-06-1190
Jupiter	11-06-1208
Saturn	11-06-1224
Mercury	11-06-1243

One can straightaway see that this chart is something special as seven planets have gathered together in the third house, in the sign Virgo. However this doesn't quite explain the fact that he ended up conquering almost half of Asia after being born as the son of a small-time Mongol chieftain.

Once again we have to turn our attention to the nodal axis. The presence of Ketu in the fourth house shows a mediocre childhood. In fact his father was not present at the time of his birth and died when he was thirteen years old. This happened in his Mercury minor period within Rahu major period. As we know the presence of the nodal axis in the fourth/tenth house axis usually separates one from one's parents. Mercury is the killer planet for his father being the lord of second from tenth and placed sixth from tenth house.

Ketu in fourth also suggests some strange circumstances surrounding his birth. He is said to have been born with a clenched fist holding a coagulated blood clot. This was nature's omen for the bloodshed he was going to cause.

Rahu in the tenth shows ambition and luck in one's chosen vocation. His vocation as a warrior is not hard to see from the placement of all the trinal and quadrant lords in the third house, the house of competition, courage, aggression and warfare. The dispositor of Rahu, Mars is strongly placed in the third house. Mars has a strong placement in the tenth house in the royal sign of Leo in the Navamsha chart. This assures him a kingly status. It should be noted that Mars is placed in the sixth house with respect to Rahu which indicates that he had to overcome a lot of enemies and opposition to achieve his ends. This fact is validated by historical records of his life. Rahu is aspected only by Mars and so the Martian realm defines his main vocation in life.

We can see that Rahu gains strength by being Vargottama (placed in the same sign in Rasi and Navamsha chart). Its placement in the sixth house in the Navamsha chart again indicates constant involvement with enemies and obstacles. His legendary fierce and cruel nature is brought out by the double positioning of Rahu in the insensitive and ruthless sign, Aries. It was in the major period of Rahu that his conquests began.

It was at the age of 43, which as we know falls within Rahu-time, that he finally settled down after the endless warfare he had indulged in since the age of 15. He also assumed the title of Emperor and the name *Chengiz Khan* at this time. We can again see his tenth house Rahu at work. He is said to be a very shrewd and manipulative person in keeping with Rahu's basic nature. However he is also said to be very just in his dealings, which is usually the case with a seven planet combination.

One interesting thing to note in his chart is that both the karmic control planets, Venus and Mars, are conjunct together in the third house. This made him very singleminded in his approach to life. Unlike most people, he had no confusion about what he wanted to do.

His chart is a wonderful example for understanding the workings of the *Kalasarpa Yoga*, which we discussed in Chapter 8. It gave him a one sided personality and the inability to see both sides of the coin. This is what in fact made him relentless and ruthless. As a result of this yoga and the presence of seven planets in the third house, he came to believe that everything could be won by the sword.

However he realized otherwise when he couldn't win the love of his life using this mindset. Some historians say that he became more philosophically oriented in his latter years, especially after he entered his Ketu time (47th - 54th year). Ketu in the fourth, a spiritual house, can make one go inside to search for the deeper meanings of life. May be he came to regret the bloodshed he had caused, but his overall chart suggests otherwise. Pluto in the Ascendant affirms that he was a collective personality, born to bring large scale destruction of life and a change in political situation.

The following two charts belong to two men who both worked in their own ways to secure independence for India.

Chart no. 16   M.K. Gandhi

02-10-1869   8:30 A.M. L.M.T.   21N37 69E49

Rasi (Main Chart)

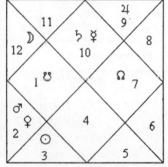

Natal Positions	
Ascendant	10°53'Li
Sun	16°55'Vi
Moon	28°13'Ca
Mars	26°22' Li
Mercury	11°45'Li
Jupiter	28°10'Ar
Venus	24°25'Li
Saturn	20°16'Sc
Rahu	12°09'Ca
Ketu	12°09'Cp
Uranus	29°47' Ge
Neptune	26°13' Pi
Pluto	27°15'Ar

Navamsa

Planetary Periods	
Planet	Begins At
Mercury	02-10-1869
Ketu	02-01-1872
Venus	02-01-1879
Sun	02-01-1899
Moon	03-01-1905
Mars	02-01-1915
Rahu	02-01-1922
Jupiter	02-01-1940

Since they both have this placement of the nodal axis, they played the role of the revolutionary, the role of fighting against an oppressive regime. Both had a childhood with some very formative influences as one can expect with Ketu in the fourth house. Both dumped their esteemed professional careers to join the freedom movement which meant their lives were full of extremes, which is so very characteristic of a tenth house Rahu.

Both started their life's work in a foreign land highlighting the fact that Rahu brings foreign influence to the house it is located in. Both worked around the same period of time in history, which meant that they had ample opportunity to interact with each other. Both were leaders in their own right and got public recognition for whatever they did.

Chart no. 17   **S.C.Bose**

23-1-1897   12:00 P.M. L.M.T.   20°38'N 85°44'E

Rasi (Main Chart)

Natal Positions

Ascendant	26°24'Ar
Sun	11°09'Cp
Moon	07°25'Vi
Mars	19°25'Ta
Mercury	09°36'Cp
Jupiter	16°28'Le
Venus	26°18'Aq
Saturn	06°38'Sc
Rahu	23°32'Cp
Ketu	23°32'Ca
Uranus	05°53' Sc
Neptune	25°17' Ta
Pluto	20°39'Ta

Navamsa

Planetary Periods

Planet	Begins At
Sun	23-01-1897
Moon	17-03-1898
Mars	18-03-1908
Rahu	18-03-1915
Jupiter	28-03-1933

However this is where the similarity ends. The methods they used to achieve the same end were poles apart. In fact Bose went as far as resigning from the Congress party, the party that was the spearhead of the freedom movement, because of his differences of opinion with Gandhi. He organized a military force known as the INA from scratch and tried to drive out the British, weakened by the 2nd world war, by force.

Gandhi on the other hand, as we all know, was using supposedly peaceful means like the non-cooperation movement to force the British into leaving. There are obvious indications in their charts to show a preponderance of Martian instinct in Bose as compared to Gandhi. The real factor that makes them so different is the planet associated with Rahu in the tenth house. In Bose's chart Sun and Mercury are conjunct Rahu in the sign Capricorn aspected by Saturn.

The conjunction of Sun with Rahu adds a fiery, *kshatriya* (military) touch to his vocation, as Sun is basically a *kshatriya* planet as per Vedic astrology. Also Mercury being the lord of third and sixth houses, both houses of power and military acumen, makes his Rahu more attacking in its approach to achieve its ends. This just goes to prove what I mentioned before that the nodes partake the nature of the planets they are in conjunction with.

In his case Rahu is also in the constellation *Dhanishtha*, ruled by Mars, again making it even more martial in its approach. Also the sign dispositor of Rahu, the karmic distribution control planet Saturn is placed in a Martian sign aspected by Mars.

It is also interesting to note that he came into public prominence in the major period of Rahu. His most politically and militarily active period started with the advent of the 2nd world war in his Rahu-time (42-47y). Rahu's power to give him good results in the tenth house affairs is enhanced by its placement in the tenth house in the navamsha chart along with the two *karakas* (significators) for the tenth house affairs, Jupiter and Saturn.

His supposed death took place in mysterious circumstances as soon as his Ketu-time started. Ketu in the fourth suggest a termination of his tenth house activity but does not exactly show death.

The presence of Saturn in the eighth house in the *Rasi* chart is also indicative of a long life. It is still not known whether he actually died in the plane crash he was supposed to have died in.

In Gandhi's chart Moon is the planet in conjunction with Rahu in the sign of Cancer. Moon is by nature a gentle and peace loving planet and it transmits these qualities on to Rahu. Also Cancer is a sign ruled by Moon having similar characteristics as its ruler, and thus amplifies the peace loving quality in his Rahu.

Rahu has no connection whatsoever with the military planets, Sun and Mars, in his chart. Rahu is placed in a constellation ruled by Saturn, which is placed in the second house. Saturn in the second house often gives a separative and ascetic nature. Rahu also imbibes this ascetic tendency from Saturn and makes that a part of his public image.

Interestingly there is an inherent respect for these qualities, especially their outward expressions, in the Indian mindset since the advent of Buddhism. This made him more popular and respected than Bose as finally the Man and the Nation had become one.

Gandhi was basically a mouthpiece for the collective urge of India as a nation, at that point of time in history. This can be seen in his Rahu Uranus association. Uranus acts as an antenna, which catches the future political and social trends and transmits them to Rahu, which uses its tenth house arena to translate them into mass movements.

It is no wonder that his political rise also took place in the major period of Rahu. This clearly demonstrates the power of a tenth house Rahu to propel a person into public prominence. Rahu's placement in the tenth house in the navamsha chart boosts the tenth house potential of Rahu in the Rasi chart. Its placement in Libra, the sign of balance, indicates the nature of his political efforts. The fact that his Ascendant is placed in *Swati*, Rahu's mild and balanced asterism, which is deeply involved in worldiness, indicates that the mild, balanced and diplomatic aspect of Rahu got relayed through his personality.

IN THE FIFTH / ELEVENTH HOUSE AXIS

RAHU IN THE FIFTH / KETU IN THE ELEVENTH

This is a combination that can produce the best and worst type of human beings, as the fifth and eleventh houses deal directly

Chart no. 18   **Thomas. A. Edison**

11-02-1847   12:45 P.M. L.M.T.   45°27N 9°10E

Rasi (Main Chart)

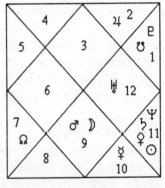

Natal Positions

Ascendant	27°26'Ge
Sun	00°32'Aq
Moon	07°04'Sg
Mars	09°00' Sg
Mercury	26°39'Aq
Jupiter	15°03'Ta
Venus	14°16'Aq
Saturn	10°12'Aq
Rahu	00°18'Li
Ketu	00°18'Ar
Uranus	20°06'Pi
Neptune	05°45'Aq
Pluto	04°21'Ar

Navamsa

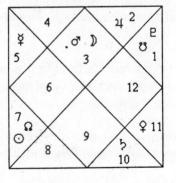

Planetary Periods

Planet	Begins At
Ketu	11-02-1847
Venus	27-05-1850
Sun	27-05-1870
Moon	26-05-1876
Mars	26-05-1886
Rahu	26-05-1993
Jupiter	27-05-1911

with one's mental make up and interaction with others. This is due to the abundant mental energy which is available with this combination, that can be used for either good or ill.

Rahu in the fifth house provides this mental energy along with highlighting the fifth house affairs – intellect, creativity, self-consciousness, past life merits and demerits, children, love of the self and others, acting, confidence, education, publications, *mantra*, the chosen deity etc.

This is also the house governing mass media and cinema. This is the reason why most actors and other people associated with movie and stage productions have this combination. In my view photography is one art, which can be said to completely originate from this placement of the nodal axis. I have come across the charts of many accomplished photographers, both professional and amateur and found that 90% of them had this combination.

Under malefic influences, Rahu in the fifth can cause megalomania and produce dictators if Sun or Mars are also involved. When talking about dictators I am not only referring to the dictators that torment whole nations but the self styled dictators in every home and workplace.

It can also produce crooks, swindlers, thieves and thugs if Mercury is afflicted or involved in this combination. It is thus a very sensitive place for Rahu where one needs to channel one's creative energies and intellect for benefit of the group or sphere of one's influence. In other words ideally this energy needs to be channelled through the eleventh house.

There is usually a break in formal education in the life of a native with this placement. Such natives do better in vocation-oriented education as opposed to classical education.

The eleventh house Ketu when working through its higher principle allows this channelling to happen with ease. When afflicted it can block the eleventh house, which means that the native has few friends and usually is not involved in any humanitarian or social endeavor. A self-centered life is the result.

A balancing act between the fifth and eleventh house is required. The self-consciousness has to sublimate and become part of the group consciousness, and form a part of the greater collective human consciousness, before finally merging with the greater universal consciousness.

The fifth house is dominated by the fire element, being similar to the sign Leo, and eleventh house by the air element, being similar to the sign Aquarius. As we all know fire cannot burn without air and air has no warmth without fire. The fire that is produced in the fifth house should be dissipated through the eleventh house air so it reaches those who require it. This is the challenge for a native with this placement in the present incarnation.

Ketu in the eleventh is often seen to cause some misunderstandings with the elder brethren and is not considered favourable for them in majority of the cases. Some anxiety on part of children, their birth and development, is also seen. If having children the native usually makes a concerned parent.

The first example chart belongs to a man who literally lighted the world and was responsible for inventing most of the contraptions that defined the life style of the 20th century, which we take for granted these days.

Gemini an intellectual and inventive ascendant rises in his chart with the Ascendant lord Mercury placed in the eighth house of research in the sign of material manifestation, Capricorn. This indicates a life dedicated to research that has definite utility in day-to-day life. It is the presence of Rahu in the fifth that gives him the creative energy to carry out that research. His chart exemplifies the intuitive capabilities of Rahu placed in the fifth house.

The sign dispositor of Rahu, the karmic distribution control planet Venus, is placed in the ninth house along with the lord of the eighth house Saturn in the sign governing electricity, Aquarius. This combination of fifth and eighth lords, which is so important for any researcher, in the electric sign of Aquarius, shows the realm in which his inventions took place. Venus and Saturn are also placed in Rahu's asterism *Shatabhisha*, which as discussed earlier, gives a capacity for seclusion and contemplation so very necessary for the birth of ideas.

This strong placement of Venus boosts up his Rahu, and thus it is no wonder that most of his over 1000 inventions, including the famous electric bulb, took place in his Rahu time (1899-1904) and Rahu major period which started in 1904. In his case Rahu gains strength by being *Vargottama* . It is placed in Libra in both the *Rasi* and *Navamsha* chart.

As per Vedic astrology, Rahu is supposed to be the ruler of artificial lighting as it tries to imitate the Sun, and so it comes as no surprise that someone with Rahu in the fifth house of creativity invented the electric bulb. Rahu is also placed in the fifth house in Navamsha chart thus doubling its fifth house creative potential.

Most of the facilities which we now enjoy, in the supposed beginning of the Age of Aquarius are thanks to the Aquarian instincts of Edison. The presence of Uranus, the planet governing the electric realm in the tenth house, besides providing sparks of inspiration in his research helped turn his hobby into his vocation

It was his Ketu in the eleventh house that kept open the channel for his inventions to reach and benefit humanity, though there were occasional frustrations in this regard as is usually the case with Ketu. Just like Rahu, Ketu also gains strength by being Vargottama. It is also placed in the eleventh house in the navamsha chart doubling its eleventh house benefits. Ketu is also placed in its own asterism *Ashvini*, which as we know promotes new beginings.

It also gave him the ability to work in a group. If it weren't for the combined effort of his co-workers, a lot of his inventions would never have seen the light of day. The sign dispositor of Ketu, Mars placed in the seventh house, the house of relationships, along with Moon gives him a hardworking but sociable nature. Moon and Mars are both placed in ketu's asterism *Mula*, which as we know wants to go to the root of everything. This quality definitely helped him in his inventions and discoveries.

One interesting thing to note in his chart is that both the nodes are placed in the first degree of their respective signs. This is an indicator of the creative potential inherent in the first degree of any sign. Many astrologers think that a planet becomes incapable of giving significant results when placed in the first degree of a sign. In my view such planets are full of ingenuity and inventiveness, even though one cannot expect them to give strong results relating to one's well being and general prosperity.

The presence of his Neptune in conjunction with Venus, Saturn and Sun was the reason for his interest in the development of the motion picture. Neptune governs the cinematic realm, being the planet of fantasy and illusion. It is no surprise that he made the first motion picture and the first movie camera, which again involves Rahu in his chart. As mentioned earlier, Rahu in the fifth invariably gives an interest in photography.

The next chart belongs to a 15th century prophet and seer who became more famous than any other prophet in the 20th century.

This is a chart where all the energies are concentrated in the eighth house, the house of prophecy and divination. Interestingly the eighth sign Scorpio also rises on the Ascendant.

This chart can be understood very well through the karmic control planets. The sign dispositor of Rahu, the karmic distribution control planet Jupiter, is present in the eighth house along with the Ascendant lord Mars and fourth lord Saturn. This means his self (Ascendant lord) used his house (fourth lord) as a place where he put his mind and intellect (fifth lord) to the pursuit of predicting future events (eighth house).

The presence of Jupiter highlighted almost all the significations of the eighth house throughout his life. He saw death from very close quarters when the bubonic plague swept Europe. In fact he gained a big reputation as a doctor who could cure this then fatal disease. This is due to the presence of sixth lord Mars in the eighth house. He also had to suffer when his own wife and children succumbed to the disease. This was mainly due the placement of Jupiter and the nodal axis.

Chart No.19   Nostradamus

14-12-1503   6:00 A.M. L.M.T.   48°50'N 02°20'E

Rasi (Main Chart)

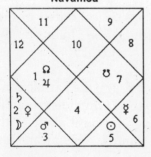

Natal Positions

Ascendant	21°35'Sc
Sun	14°26'Sg
Moon	26°03'Li
Mars	29°30'Ge
Mercury	17°36'Sg
Jupiter	22°05'Ge
Venus	15°25'Cp
Saturn	24°02'Ge
Rahu	11°45'Pi
Ketu	11°45'Vi
Uranus	20°06'Aq
Neptune	05°45'Sg
Pluto	04°21'Li

Navamsa

Planetary Periods

Planet	Begins At
Jupiter	14-12-1503
Saturn	06-09-1512
Mercury	07-09-1531
Ketu	06-09-1548
Venus	07-09-1555
Sun	07-09-1575

Mercury, the sign dispositor of Ketu, is placed in the second house, the house important for making verbal predictions, aspecting the eighth house. It is having an exchange of signs and houses with Jupiter further strengthening the second and eighth houses, so both the karmic control planets are acting in the second/eighth house axis making prophecy his karma in this incarnation.

The presence of the tenth lord Sun along with Mercury, the inlet karmic control planet shows that his vocation in present life has connections to his past lives and that his work would be appreciated within his lifetime, but more so after his death, as Mercury is the eighth lord as well. The reason for the current popularity also lies in his heavily tenanted eighth house, the house of fame after death.

His education took place under the tutelage of both his grandfather symbolized by Rahu (paternal grandfather) and Ketu (maternal grandfather). Only the placement of the nodal axis in the fifth/eleventh house (houses of education and learning) can give this result. In other placements usually only one of the grandfathers does influence one's life.

It comes as no surprise that the subjects he was taught were those related to the second/eighth house axis like classical literature, history and astrology. This shows how the nodes governed the pattern of his destiny since his childhood.

Rahu major period was in operation during this learning period. It was in Rahu time (around 1547) that he started to fully realize the potential of his prophetic powers and started writing down his predictions. In the navamsha chart Rahu is placed in the tenth house, representing one's true vocation in life.

His first almanac of prophecies was published in the year 1550 (beginning of his Ketu time), after a long thought process involving whether he should publish his findings or not. This hesitancy is very characteristic of this placement of the nodal axis.

Rahu enabled the writing and the research (fifth house affair), and Ketu made possible the publishing for the benefit of all humanity (eleventh house affair). His famous work "The Centuries" was all compiled during his Ketu time (1554-1557). In the navamsha chart Ketu is placed along with Jupiter (planet of teaching, publication etc.) in one of its favourite signs Aries.

Uranus in the fourth made him turn his house into a magical and alchemical laboratory. His eighth house planets also gave him the knowledge about the time of his own death. His curse which prophesized the death of whosoever disturbs his tomb also came true.

KETU IN FIFTH / RAHU IN ELEVENTH

This combination again is the one that takes the natives to extremes. The analogy of the phoenix rising from the ashes usually does hold true for a native with this placement.

As often is the case with Ketu in the first half of the chart, the first half of life is not very enjoyable. There are usually breaks in the native's formal education. The presence of Ketu in the fifth gives an attitude that doesn't think much of formal education even though the native may go through it under the garb of social obligation. A break in formal education is usually the norm with this placement of the nodal axis.

When Ketu is strong in this position it does give the native a penetrating and piercing intellect. As is Ketu's disposition the learning is usually internalized. I have noticed that the native with this placement of Ketu usually pursues some form of mysticism, which might be either in an accepted or a purely personal way.

The native usually chooses platonic love over other forms of love if the Ascendant lord conjoins with Ketu in this position. There is some sort of frustration and disappointment encountered with love in the adolescent years that makes the native harbour a negative feeling towards love in general.

This position of Ketu is not considered auspicious for having and raising progeny unless the fifth house is very strong and receiving benefic aspects, especially that of Jupiter. In charts of females this placement of Ketu denotes difficult childbirth.

Both Vedic and Western astrologers consider the placement of Rahu in the eleventh house auspicious. It is supposed to fulfil most of the native's desires within this lifetime. Though this is true in one sense, in my experience I have seen that this doesn't always happen and even if it does it happens late in native's life (usually in the forties).

There is no denying the fact that this placement of Rahu makes the native ambitious, but whether these ambitions would be fulfilled depends upon the overall strength of the chart. There is a distinct degree of frustration noticeable in such natives if their aims are not achieved.

The eleventh house affairs – goals, aspirations, elder brethren, sources of gain, philanthropy, idealism, friends, sharing, group relationships, humanitarianism, realization of objectives – get highlighted with this positioning.

Among these, what the native will pursue and what they will choose to ignore depends upon the influences on Rahu and overall inclination of the chart. Elder brethren if they exist are a source of gain for the native and vice versa, provided the other indications in the chart allow for it.

According to Vedic astrology, Rahu in the eleventh is a great bestower of material gains, but it is seen that this has to be supported by other indications in the chart.

A balance between the fifth and eleventh house indications is sought by this placement of nodal axis. It is the native's karma to understand and work out the opposites like self-consciousness and group-consciousness, acquisition of resources and sharing of resources, personal ambition and the humanitarian perspective.

Friendship is the keynote of the lives of these natives and any unnecessary selfishness needs to be avoided. It might turn out to the native's disadvantage, as those who can help him realize his destiny, might choose to part ways with him if he tries to act in a selfish manner.

It is seen that if the native with this placement acquires a fortune by devious means, then it is usually spent away very quickly through undesirable expenditures.

The first chart with this placement belongs to one of the wealthiest *Gurus* (preacher) the 20th century has known.

'*Osho*,' as he was popularly known, has a chart, which even on the first look has an exceptional touch to it. The presence of five planets in the eighth house of mystery, secret knowledge, profundity of thought, foreign travels, controversy and other's resources, signifies a personality focused in these domains.

Jupiter and Mercury are the two significators of wealth for Taurus ascendant. Incidentally in his chart they become the karmic control planets as well.

Chart no. 20   **"Osho" Rajneesh**

11-12-1931 5:13 P.M. L.M.T. 13°05'N 80°17'E

Rasi (Main Chart)

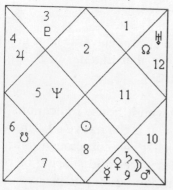

Natal Positions

Ascendant	16°14'Ta
Sun	26°17'Sg
Moon	28°45'Sg
Mars	22°47' Sg
Mercury	08°52'Sg
Jupiter	09°03'Ca
Venus	06°50'Sg
Saturn	23°14'Sg
Rahu	01°38'Pi
Ketu	01°38'Vi
Uranus	22°57'Pi
Neptune	15°05'Le
Pluto	29°20'Ge

Navamsa

Planetary Periods

Planet	Begins At
Jupiter	11-12-1936
Saturn	07-06-1942
Mercury	07-06-1961
Ketu	07-06-1978
Venus	06-06-1985

Jupiter, being the dispositor of Rahu, is the karmic distribution control planet and is placed in the third house of oratory in its exaltation sign Cancer. This placement shows that his talent lay in his hypnotic delivery of speech, the hypnotic touch being provided by the influence of Rahu, as Rahu aspects the third house by its fifth house aspect.

Exalted Jupiter provides the icing on the cake and makes him an excellent storyteller. Here Jupiter is also aspecting Rahu in its own sign by its ninth house aspect. This merging of energies of Rahu and Jupiter make his gain's house very strong. It is no surprise that it was in his Rahu major period and his Rahu time (1973 onwards) that his rise took place from virtual scratch.

Interestingly, this position of Rahu and Jupiter with the same Ascendant is found in the supposed chart (source: *Bhrigu Nadi*) of the richest *Puranic* character of the heavenly realm, *Kubera*.

The presence of Ketu in the fifth provides him with a piercing insight into human affairs, especially those covered by the sign Virgo. The presence of its sign dispositor Mercury in the eighth house in the philosophical, lucky and optimistic sign of Sagittarius along with his Ascendant lord Venus, third lord Moon, ninth and tenth lord Saturn, seventh and twelfth lord Mars, produces an excellent *Rajayoga*. Mercury is also placed in *Mula*, an asterism ruled by Ketu. Mula, as we know, can bestow a high degree of philosophical insight.

It aids him in inventing his own philosophy of life and acquisition of wealth from his disciples. Jupiter is the dispositor of all these eighth house planets and is also having an exchange with Moon. This lends even more power to his chart, which in his case is manifesting through his Rahu.

His *Bhagyodaya* took place in a foreign land, which again shows the eighth house at work. A loaded eighth house also shows his exploration of the sexual realm (its collective aspect), which caused much controversy. He was always a controversial figure both in India and the U.S.A., which again is a strong eighth house trait.

He was driven out of U.S.A in his Ketu time because of his over expansive nature and activities. Here we can see the principle of Ketu working against Rahu within one's chart. Ketu's position in the sixth in the navamsha chart in one of its least favoured signs Libra, is also indicative of difficulties arising through enemies. The fact that his Ascendant lord Venus is placed in Mula, shows that he would definitely have a setback after a rapid rise. Mula as we discussed in an earlier chapter, can give authority and dominion, but there is always some upheaval and eventual loss of authority associated with it.

His chart is also a testimony to the fact that Rahu indeed is the significator of the foreign element within a chart, as most of the people in his group (an eleventh house indication) were foreigners. Rahu's placement in the twelfth house in the navamsha chart along with Saturn (signifying the foreign element) has similar indications. Rahu is also in conjunction with Uranus giving certain newness, energizing power and a revolutionary nature to his teachings.

The next chart belongs to a Queen (Chart No. 21) who got to rule over an Empire larger than anyone in recorded history of the current age.

On the first look it doesn't look like a chart belonging to someone who ruled an empire larger than anyone in recorded history since 3000 BC. This is a chart where without taking the nodes and *Jaimini Sutras* into account, one cannot gauge its strength.

The main planets, Ascendant lord Venus and the second and fifth lord Mercury are posited in the twelfth house, not a very encouraging sign!

There are no exalted planets except Moon in the Ascendant. Moon, as the third lord is not a planet of much consequence for natives with Taurus Ascendant. Jupiter is debilitated in Capricorn in the ninth house. In other words things don't seem too bright.

Now we come to her eleventh house Rahu, that is placed exactly in the same way as the Rahu in Osho's chart. In this case it derives its strength by being conjunct with the *yogakaraka* (ninth and tenth lord) Saturn, and Mars, the lord of the imperialistic seventh house.

Rahu is also *vargottama* (occupying the same sign in *Rasi* and *Navamsha* charts), which further increases its power. Its placement in twelfth house (foreign affairs) in the navamsha chart gives her power. Rahu's sign dispositor in the rasi chart, Jupiter, though debilitated, is involved in a sign exchange with Saturn that not only cancels its debility, but also lends strength to all the houses ruled by Saturn and Jupiter. In this case these are the eighth, ninth, tenth and eleventh houses, which are the houses very much responsible for the worldly position of a native.

It was thus no wonder that it was is in her Rahu time the consolidation of her famous Empire, where Sun never did set, took place. Talking about her Sun one finds it is exalted in the navamsha chart, giving her the status of a Monarch.

Rahu is also conjunct Pluto, which shows that her personal fate was entangled with the destiny of the masses of her vast empire. She was a sort of representative of the collective movement known as British Imperialism.

The sign dispositor of her Ketu, Mercury, though seemingly weak by its twelfth house placement, gains strength on the basis of a

Chart no. 21   Queen Victoria

24-05-1819   4:04 A.M. L.M.T.   51°30'N 00°10'W

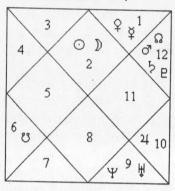

Rasi (Main Chart)

Navamsa

Natal Positions

Ascendant	10°41'Ta
Sun	10°46'Ta
Moon	12°15'Ta
Mars	26°19' Pi
Mercury	17°35'Ar
Jupiter	26°01'Cp
Venus	05°14'Ar
Saturn	07°18'Pi
Rahu	26°53'Pi
Ketu	26°53'Vi
Uranus	02°04'Sg
Neptune	06°32'Sg
Pluto	08°24'Pi

Planetary Periods

Planet	Begins At
Moon	24-05-1819
Mars	10-09-1827
Rahu	10-09-1834
Jupiter	09-09-1852
Saturn	09-09-1868
Mercury	10-09-1887
Ketu	10-09-1904

rule in aforementioned *Jaimini Sutras*. It states that the lord of the *Varnada Lagna* (a type of secondary ascendant), if placed in the eleventh house from it bestows great wealth and splendour. In this case Gemini is the Varnada Lagna and its lord Mercury is placed in the eleventh from it in the sign of Aries. Accordingly Britain saw its best period financially in her Mercury major period.

Victorian morality is a term that came into being because of her excessively puritanical nature, derived from the presence of Ketu in the fifth house in the puritanical sign of Virgo. The excess part comes from the placement of Ketu in the navamsha along with her *Atmakaraka* (soul significator) Mars in the sign of Virgo. Her Ascendant lord Venus is placed in Ketu's asterism *Ashvini* adding to Ketu's influence. At the same time the initiatory impulse of Ashwini made her eager and supportive of new conquests.

This emphasizes that if either of the nodes is placed with Atmakaraka in the rasi or navamsa chart, the sign in which this combination takes place governs the inherent nature of the native. Such a placement also enhances the significance of the nodal axis in such a native's chart.

IN THE SIXTH / TWELFTH HOUSE AXIS

RAHU IN SIXTH / KETU IN TWELFTH

This is considered a fortunate combination by Vedic astrology as Rahu being a malefic is supposed to function well in the sixth house, as it is an *Upachaya* house, and Ketu is supposed to do good in the twelfth because of its natural affinity with the twelfth sign Pisces, which has similar significations as the twelfth house. This analysis is correct to an extent, but in my view when it comes to giving hard times, this is the toughest nodal axis placement.

The placement of Rahu in the sixth means that the sixth house significations – work, service, health, enmity, distillation and discrimination, dietary and personal habits, accidents, diseases, discipline and austerity, opposition, litigation, power, helpers, medicine, healing – get highlighted.

Thus it is clear that the sixth house has a lot of indications, which most people would be just too happy to avoid. The natives with this placement have to come to terms with most of them in good measure.

Sixth house is the house governing the adolescence stage in the life of a person. This is a very sensitive period where such a Rahu makes the native more capable of realizing one's goal in life. Such natives show an immaculate sense of method and order in their lives even in their adolescent years, provided there are other supporting indications in the chart.

On the other hand such a Rahu if afflicted, can cause the native to indulge in mindless actions harmful to both themselves and their surroundings, which they might come to regret later in life.

This is a good combination for producing physicians, healers and all people involved with all types of therapeutic vocations. This position of Rahu is also said to involve the native in dealings with foreigners and usually the native benefits through them. In present times this combination represents people involved in foreign services, tourism, import-export business, shipping etc. This position of Rahu also shows a capacity for hard work. A dint of fearlessness is also noticed in the natives with this placement.

The presence of Ketu in the twelfth usually gives some sort of psychic experiences through either dreams or visions. This position of Ketu is considered quite good for spiritual pursuits, but I have noticed that this only happens when Ketu is working through its higher principle. Mostly the native has some understanding of the divine forces that make up our universe, though the interpretation is usually personal.

This position of Ketu usually brings about some unpleasant experiences – imprisonment, isolation, accidents - in the native's life, but this is usually for the good, as the native is getting rid of their past life bad Karma. Any sort of isolation for such natives is very important in the sense that it can bring out latent qualities, which have been developed over past lives. After this realization follows the hard work attributed to the sixth house Rahu.

A peculiar thing that happens with natives with this placement is that no matter how hard they try to stay free from enmity, it always seems to follow them. Dealing with enemies is a part and parcel of destiny of such a native, so forgiveness is one of the important qualities that such natives need to develop.

This is also the reason why this combination produces politicians in the present day and age, as dealing with behind the scene manoeuvres comes naturally to these natives. Though this position helps one prevail over one's enemies the majority of times, the downfall or some times even death by the machinations of the enemy is also seen.

This positioning of the nodes usually gives a strong constitution, but afflictions to the nodal axis can cause some serious diseases and strange disorders that are often hard to diagnose. Sudden death without any apparent illness is often seen with this placement if there are other contributing factors in the chart.

Outer worldly recognition and success if it is deserved usually comes to such a native after a long struggle. The natives with this positioning, are, to use a present day terminology, 'very career conscious'. There is always a danger of misuse of power with this placement due to the headstrong nature of these natives. If this is the case then it is generally seen that the twelfth house Ketu usually evens things out by bringing about a downfall.

This combination again calls for a balance between the practicality of the earthy sixth house, and the emotions of the watery twelfth house. The native has to guard against the rigidity, which results from excess of order and discipline in one's life. They also have to make sure that they don't lose themselves in extreme indulgence, which comes through a complete lack of discipline.

In financial terms the native is expected neither to be a miser and nor a spendthrift. This position of the nodal axis prompts the native to take up either extreme asceticism or extreme indulgence as a means of attaining liberation from the cycle of birth and death. Some natives with this placement do prefer to take up the middle path whenever the wisdom dawns on them.

The first chart with this combination belongs to a man who, besides being a martial arts legend of the 20th century, was a brilliant thinker and philosopher as well.

Even today the public image that *Bruce Lee* has is of a brilliant fighter who practiced Kung Fu and popularized martial arts through his movies. The fact is he had much more to offer, and it is a pity that the philosophical side of his personality is often ignored.

Since the accurate birth time is not available, I have taken up a time, which gives him an Aries Ascendant because this is the only Ascendant that matches with his physical and mental traits.

Chart no. 22   **Bruce Lee**

27-11-1940   03:20.P.M.L.M.T.   37°N46' 122°W25'

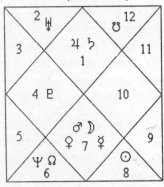

Rasi (Main Chart)

Navamsa

Natal Positions

Ascendant	14°54'Ar
Sun	12°33'Sc
Moon	23°23'Li
Mars	11°44'Li
Mercury	22°32'Li
Jupiter	14°28'Ar
Venus	08°44'Li
Saturn	16°26'Ar
Rahu	14°56'Vi
Ketu	14°56'Pi
Uranus	00°57'Ta
Neptune	04°24'Vi
Pluto	11°34'Ca

Planetary Periods

Planet	Begins At
Jupiter	27-11-1940
Saturn	04-11-1952
Mercury	04-11-1971

The conjunction of Jupiter and Saturn, the ninth and tenth lords respectively in the Ascendant, forms a powerful *Rajayoga* (auspicious combination), which manifests through his body (first house signification).

The presence of Rahu in sixth was the reason behind the hard work he put in his adolescence years to learn the various disciplines of martial arts. His Rahu also brought him into contact with foreigners. In fact his wife was American, as the sign dispositor of Rahu, Mercury is placed in the seventh house, the house of partnership and marriage. Most of his students and disciples were also Americans, and his worldwide fame came only when he made movies under the Hollywood banner.

Both his karmic control planets, Mercury and Jupiter are related to his first house showing that his field of action would be his body. The Ascendant lord Mars also aspects the Ascendant from the seventh house where it is posited along with Moon, Venus and Mercury further heightening the martial nature of the sign Aries. Every planet excepting the Sun is influencing his Ascendant making it very strong. The presence of Mercury along with Mars allows his Rahu energy to blend with his personal energy.

The presence of Neptune, the planet presiding over the cinematic realm, along with Rahu, made him interested in reaching out to as many people as possible through this medium. It is no wonder his movies always had a dragon element in their titles - "Enter the Dragon", "The Way of the Dragon" and "Return of the Dragon". The connection between the nodes and 'dragon' is quite well known as discussed earlier, and so it is no mystery where the magic factor was coming into his art, which no one else has since been able to recapture.

Rahu's influence on his career can also be gauged from its tenth house positioning in the *Navamsha* chart. It is placed along with exalted *Atmakaraka* Moon. As discussed earlier, the nodes become strong when placed with the luminaries, an exalted planet or the

atmakaraka. In this case all three of the above conditions are satisfied in the house of worldly influence. It is thus no wonder that no
martial artist has been able to gain similar worldwide recognition.

Rahu's influence can also be gauged from the fact that his
atmakaraka Moon along with Mercury is placed in *Swati*, an
asterism ruled by Rahu. Swati, as we know, is a materially benefical
asterism which tries to gain strength in time. This is very
characteristic of his practising of martial arts to gain strength. Swati
also helped him gain through the Venusian world of cinema.

A lot of people have practiced martial arts especially in China
since ancient times, but Bruce Lee was a revolutionary in the sense
that he refused to be restricted by any traditional framework, and
went on to establish his very own method known as *Jeet Kune Do*
(JKD). This revolt against authority, so very characteristic of Rahu,
earned him a lot of enemies in the martial arts establishment. As
mentioned before, enemies are something that a native with such
a placement has to deal with.

Even though Bruce Lee came out on top of his opponents all
the time, he did suffer from the machinations of his enemies. He
received severe injuries during an attack from behind by his
detractors in a fight especially arranged by them. To the surprise
of all the doctors who said he would not be able to practice his art
again, he regained his normal fitness within a year. This can be
attributed to the healing powers of Rahu in the sixth house.

The presence of Ketu in the mystical sign of Pisces gave him a
deep insight into the mystery of life and the functionings of the
cosmic intelligence. Ketu relays its influence to his self (Ascendant)
through its sign dispositor Jupiter. Its placement in its own sign
Scorpio in the navamsha chart in the fourth house, a mystical house
representing psychic sensitivity, deepens Ketu's mystical
functioning.

It was in a period of forced isolation recovering from his multiple injuries, he was able to finish his book, which besides covering various aspects of JKD, carried a fair bit of his own philosophy on life as well. This is probably why Ketu is considered a liberating influence in the twelfth house because even though it gives unpleasant times, it helps a native to turn his energies inward and bring forth the wisdom from deep inside.

His death took place suddenly at the young age of 33 in mysterious circumstances. This was due to the fact that he was running the Mercury age and Mercury is in the *maraka* (death inflicting) house being a malefic lord (lord of 3rd and 6th house). He was also running the Mercury major period.

A lot of theories propounded that his detractors had poisoned him but the truth is yet to be revealed. Mercury the sixth lord is in Swati, a serpent asterism related to poisons, in conjunction with eighth lord Mars!

The Moon is quite dark because of its proximity to the Sun. Mercury- Moon combination in Venus's sign in seventh shows a feminine influence surrounding his death. He died in the house of a female friend (Moon is the lord of the fourth). There is a definite connection between third, sixth, seventh and eighth houses in relation to Mercury. Further Saturn and Mars mutually aspect each other in first/seventh axis. It implies that his death was not entirely due to natural causes.

The next chart belongs to the first and only woman Prime Minister of independent India.

This is an unusual chart in the sense that it has three house and sign exchanges, which involve six of her planets. Even one such exchange is capable of propelling a native into political power if the native chooses to take up politics as a vocation. Therefore this is an extremely strong chart, but it was not all smooth sailing mainly because of the nodal axis placement.

Her political career started under the tutelage of her father who was occupying the Prime Minister's post at that time. This happened mainly in her Rahu time when her Jupiter major period was in operation.

Jupiter is the karmic distribution control planet being the dispositor of Rahu, and is involved in an exchange with Venus. Thus it is strong enough to propel her into the top political position in the country, which she eventually did attain with a stroke of luck in the same major period in Ketu time (1965). This elucidates the importance of the karmic distribution control planet in

Chart no. 23   **Indira Gandhi**

19-11-1917   11:11 P.M.L.M.T.   25°N27' 81°E51'

Rasi (Main Chart)

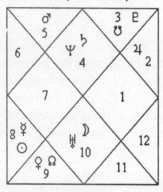

Navamsa

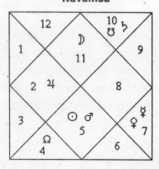

Natal Positions

Ascendant	21°35'Ca
Sun	14°26'Sc
Moon	26°03'Cp
Mars	01°38'Le
Mercury	17°36'Sc
Jupiter	22°05'Ta
Venus	15°25'Sg
Saturn	24°02'Ca
Rahu	11°45'Sg
Ketu	11°45'Ge
Uranus	27°29'Cp
Neptune	14°20'Ca
Pluto	13°15'Ge

Planetary Periods

Planet	Begins At
Sun	19-11-1917
Moon	08-11-1919
Mars	07-11-1929
Rahu	07-11-1936
Jupiter	07-11-1954
Saturn	07-11-1970

defining the worldly position of the native. Here the thing to note is that Jupiter has no connection with the tenth house, the house of political power.

Ketu gains the power to bestow tenth house results, as the tenth lord Mars is placed in its asterism *Magha*, which as we know is the main nakshatra dealing with authority, and in her case she literally got the throne (symbol of *Magha*) of India.

It was under her leadership that India was sucked into a war with archenemy Pakistan in the ending of her Ketu time (1971). It goes without saying that with her nodal axis placement she showed a lot of courage in the tough times and came out victorious.

Interestingly, this was the victory that made some people compare her to Goddess *Durga* (the fierce form of *Parvati*, consort of *Shiva*), who, as mentioned before, is the main deity represented by Rahu. Though this was not done with any conscious astrological sense, it is clear that her victory did originate from the sixth house Rahu. Rahu is placed in the asterism of *Mula*, which as discussed earlier, makes one lucky and confident in battle and other harsh endeavours.

This also goes to show this placement is a good one in the house of political leaders whose destiny is intimately related to the destiny of their nation. In the *Navamsha* chart Rahu is again placed in the sixth house reinforcing her sixth house strength.

She became all-powerful and in total control after this war, and couldn't help succumbing to the misuse of power, which as mentioned, is so often the case with this combination. This misuse of power involved one of her sons, as Mercury, the sign dispositor of her Ketu, is placed in the fifth house.

She declared a state of Emergency in the country (1975), which made her a sort of a monarch within a democracy. This placement of nodal axis is too autocratic to respect things like democracy especially in a nation like India.

Since twelfth house Ketu makes one pay the price within this lifetime, she fell from power after she lost in a general election she had ordered herself. This was followed by a period of humiliation in which she was even taken prisoner on the behest of her political rivals. In the navamsha chart Ketu is placed in the twelfth house, signifying loss and imprisonment along with the hard taskmaster Saturn. Ketu is also placed in the nakshatra of *Ardra*, which as we know always causes some upheaval of some sort.

In her chart Ketu and Rahu have an asterism exchange as they are placed in each other's asterisms. This usually indicates a strong hand of destiny overseeing one's present life leaving little room for free will or choice.

Her chart again proves the point that one's enemies do cause trouble for such a native at least once at some point of time in their lives. This reversal also sparked an interest in pursuing the spiritual path that made her meet and take advice from all noted teachers of her time including the likes of J. Krishnamurthy. Ketu's intention of changing one's approach to life through such reversals is clearly seen.

The fighting spirit of this placement in times of adversity held sway, and she bounced back to power in the 1980 general elections. She continued with her relentless political manoeuvring after coming to power, which continued to produce new enemies for her. It was at the hands of one such enemy that she was finally assassinated in 1984.

Ketu's close conjunction with Pluto shows a tragic end. She in fact was a sort of collective sacrifice in the same sense as 'JFK', but because of her stronger overall chart, stayed in power for around 17 years.

KETU IN THE SIXTH / RAHU IN THE TWELFTH

This is the placement, which is usually seen more often than others to oscillate between opposites with a thin line separating them, such as insanity and genius, paranoia and self-discovery. It becomes a very difficult combination to handle and usually has a strange sort of fatedness attached to it.

Rahu in twelfth as usual highlights the twelfth house significations - receptivity, negation, seclusion, destiny, past lives, karma, escapism, excessive indulgence, luxury, losses, expenses, charity, foreign affairs, limitation, imprisonment, connectivity with subtle planes, fantasy, paranoia, subconscious mind, dreams, visions, sorrow, renunciation, liberation.

When one takes a look at the nature of the twelfth house and takes into account the fact that it would be the main field of activity in a native's life, one can understand why this is such a sensitive placement for the nodal axis. Even a very evolved soul has difficulty handling this combination.

It can give a taste for all kinds of intoxicants and smoking is really addictive for such natives. There is always the desire to completely immerse the ego in the sea of illusions resulting from excessive indulgence. Usually a strong Ascendant is the key to minimizing the bad effects of this placement.

It is also a very useful placement, in the sense that it can often give the native the taste of the supernatural and allow him to look far beyond the material realm of existence. It can also give the knowledge of the ocean of *Maya* in which the divine play of life is played.

In my view, half the problem is solved if the native can keep away from all types of drugs and alcohol. It is also important that the native doesn't blindly follow religious orders or any other type of institutions.

Such natives have a tendency to end up as doctors, nurses, healers, mediums, preachers, counsellors, lawyers, social workers, politicians, detectives and law enforcers. Rahu in the twelfth also gives some foreign connection relating to the significations of its dispositor or the planets associated with it.

Ketu in the sixth is supposed to be a very powerful force and according to Vedic astrology, it gives worldly riches and power. Only thing I want to add here is that there are better chances of this dictum holding true if Jupiter is associated with Ketu by aspect or conjunction.

Sixth house Ketu has a tendency of making the native expect too much out of those working under him. Such natives also are not very good at taking orders and generally get frustrated in regular nine to five jobs. An independent enterprise is better for their mental well-being.

Such natives should avoid making too much of sixth house affairs like diseases, servants, enemies etc. as there is a tendency to unnecessarily dwell upon these issues. Most of the strange diseases and disorders can be seen to be a result of this combination.

Such natives usually have no dearth of enemies either of their own making or those conferred by providence. The way such natives deal with their enemies differs on the basis of overall inclination of the chart, but diplomacy at least in this sphere is not their strong point.

Sixth house Ketu has definite ideas about work ethics, purity and morality and there is a tendency to pass judgements and impose one's ideas on others. The strong will power that such natives possess helps them achieve their desired goals sooner or later. One thing such natives must guard against is overextending their energies.

The need for striking a balance between the sixth house and twelfth house affairs, which we have discussed in the previous section dealing with the opposite placement of the nodal-axis, holds true for this combination as well.

The first chart with this placement belongs to a philosopher, patriot and preacher who introduced to the West the timeless doctrine of *Vedanta*.

The strength of this chart is obvious from the Saturn-Mercury exchange. This exchange is taking place between the second (speech) and tenth (vocation) houses, relating and strengthening both the houses. This is the reason why most of his admirers were swayed as much by the eloquence and sweetness of his speech as they were by the content of his talks.

Sun in the Ascendant adds nobleness to the figure and also denotes an ethical and upright disposition. It is needless to add that Sun also adds a sense of self-esteem to the personality since it is posited in one of its favoured fire signs. In the *Navamsha* chart Sun is again placed in Sagittarius in the Ascendant doubling the above qualities.

The spiritual key to this chart lies with the positioning of the nodal axis. The presence of Rahu in the twelfth in the mystical sign of Scorpio, was responsible for his spiritual training under the tutelage of *Ramakrishna Paramahansa*, whose chart we have discussed earlier.

Chart no. 24   **Swami Vivekananda**

12-01-1863   06:33.A.M.L.M.T.   22°N40' 88°E30'

Rasi (Main Chart)

Natal Positions	
Ascendant	27°24'Sg
Sun	29°25'Cp
Moon	17°28'Vi
Mars	06°19'Ar
Mercury	11°46'Cp
Jupiter	04°01'Li
Venus	07°06'Cp
Saturn	13°27'Vi
Rahu	22°14'Sc
Ketu	22°14'Ta
Uranus	25°41'Ta
Neptune	09°14'Pi
Pluto	19°12'Ar

Navamsa

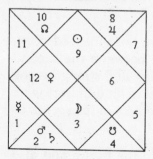

Planetary Periods

Planet	Begins At
Moon	12-01-1863
Mars	05-06-1867
Rahu	05-06-1874
Jupiter	05-06-1892

It is not surprising that his Rahu major period was running when he first came into contact with his teacher. All of his association with him took place in this major period only. It is interesting to note that Ramakrishna's chart (Chart no. 13) has the nodal axis in exactly the opposite signs i.e. Rahu in Taurus and Ketu in Scorpio. This brings home the point about attraction between natives of opposite house or sign placements of the nodal axis. It is also interesting to note that his Ascendant with Sun in Sagittarius in the *Rasi* Chart is the same as Ramakrishna's Ascendant in the navamsha chart. He was in a way the soul expression of his teacher.

His name used to be *Narendra* at that time, which places his Moon in Scorpio along with Rahu, even though his natal Moon is in Virgo. This is quite significant as it shows how names affect one's destiny through the different positioning of the Moon.

He resisted initially but finally became a great devotee of the dark divine Goddess *Kali* on the behest of his teacher. The presence of Rahu in the dark mystical sign of Scorpio was responsible for his choosing a terrible form of the divine as his deity.

Saturn aspects Rahu from the puritanical sign of Virgo enhancing the ascetic tendencies of Rahu. It also brings about a sense of order to his spiritual discipline. Rahu made him neglect his home and worldly responsibilities in quest for knowledge and enlightenment before he finally renounced the material world to become a *Sanyasi* (monk).

All these events took place in his Rahu major period (11-29y). In this period of his life one can see the twelfth house indications – deprivation, neglect of the body, poverty, meditation, other worldly experiences, self realization – at work. In the navamsha chart Rahu is placed alone in the slow testing sign Capricorn giving him hard times on the worldly plane.

The sign dispositor of Rahu, Mars, is placed in the fifth house in its own sign Aries giving him a piercing intellect and good writing abilities. It is interesting to note that his Mars is placed in Ketu's asterism *Ashvini* whose propensities colour most of his life's works. Fifth house is the house of patriotic feelings and he tried his best to heal his own country steeped in *tamoguna* (retarding aspect of nature). Ashvini as we know is a nakshatra which has a liking for action.

Jupiter's aspect on Mars further strengthens it besides adding a benefic quality to it. The good placement of Mars is what makes his Rahu work so well. This is the reason why this twelfth house Rahu could bring him recognition in a foreign land in the Mar's times (28-32 y).

Here again we see an example of the karmic distribution control planet helping the native manifest in the outside world what is inside of him. The Martian touch so dominates his writing and teaching that he went to the extent of saying that liberation can be attained on a football field. Of course these words were meant to awaken his sleepy nation steeped in *tamoguna* (inert principle of nature).

Mars also accounts for his patriotic nature being placed in the fifth, the house governing patriotic feelings. Pluto's conjunction with Mars brings out the prophetic element in his writings. For example, he says that the Chinese are going to present the biggest threat to the West in times to come, which is exactly what is happening today.

Jupiter major period was in operation at the time of his famous Chicago address, which is usually quite favourable for preaching and establishing institutions. He, as is well known, went on to establish *Ramakrishna* mission to spread the teachings of his teacher (Jupiter) in the same major period.

Ketu in the sixth made him face a lot of opposition and criticism from his detractors. It also provided him with the inner strength to respond with dignity. He very seldom in his life lacked courage in his actions. Ketu's placement in the mystical eighth house in the navamsha chart gave him a piercing insight into matters concerning liberation (Ketu) from the cycle of earthly life .

As expected from his sixth hosue Ketu, there was an excessively puritanical touch in his approach to life, but he possessed a broad enough intellect to be flexible enough to respond favourably to the lessons he was taught by divine forces, whenever his actions smelt of narrow-mindedness. The famous incident when he rebuked a dancing woman as a creature unworthy of his time, only to apologize later brings home this point.

He was always beset with diseases despite his strong outward constitution due to the sixth house Ketu, which in his chart is not aspected by Jupiter. Some of these diseases were a direct result of overwork, which is a sixth house indication.

The presence of Uranus with Ketu shows his fascination with the modern advances in technology in his time. His almost utopian vision of India modernizing itself, without losing any of her ancient wisdom has not been realized as yet. This placement of Uranus also accounts for his enmity with Uranian institutions like the Theosophical society.

Rahu in the twelfth is the force behind the meaningful dreams that he had, which he has dealt with in detail in his biographical accounts. These dreams often revealed the truth relating to areas that his conscious mind could not access.

His prophecy that he would not live to be forty came out to be true. This was also made possible by the developed psychic powers of the twelfth house Rahu. He even had the premonition of the exact day and time of his departure from the material world. Rahu

Chart no. 25   **Jawahar Lal Nehru**

14-11-1889   11:21.P.M.L.M.T.   25°N28' 81°52'

Rasi (Main Chart)

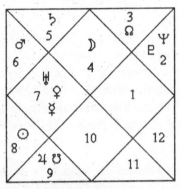

Natal Positions

Ascendant	26°29'Ca
Sun	00°16'Sc
Moon	18°01'Ca
Mars	09°59'Vi
Mercury	17°09'Li
Jupiter	15°18'Sg
Venus	07°22'Li
Saturn	10°47'Le
Rahu	12°33'Ge
Ketu	12°33'Sg
Uranus	01°47'Li
Neptune	11°01'Ta
Pluto	15°10'Ta

Navamsa

Planetary Periods

Planet	Begins At
Mercury	14-11-1889
Ketu	21-02-1905
Venus	22-02-1912
Sun	21-02-1932
Moon	21-02-1938
Mars	21-02-1948
Rahu	21-02-1955

in Scorpio. the sign of death, is the key behind this intuitive insight.

The next chart belongs to the first Prime Minister of independent India.

On the first look, all his chart reveals is the presence of three planets in their own signs. He was born in one of the most wealthiest and famous Indian families of his time. As we know fortunate birth is a ninth house signification. Since there is no planet in the ninth house we have to take a look at the ninth lord.

The ninth lord in his chart is Jupiter, which is placed in its own sign Sagittarius along with Ketu in the sixth house. It is this combination wherein lies the key to this chart. One will notice that the same combination takes place in the chart of *Adolf Hitler* in the third house.

As mentioned earlier, Ketu if posited with a planet in its own or exaltation sign, increases the power of that planet by a factor of four. Thus Jupiter gains considerable power, which reflects in the houses he owns in the chart. This means his ninth house becomes very strong, which is indeed the case considering his aristocratic background. The point to note is that his sixth house, the house of enemies also becomes very strong.

In his case Jupiter in the sixth represents the British, who initially were friends with his family, but later turned out be his main enemies. His life was a constant struggle against the British rule in India, ever since he came back from London after completing his education. Due to the strong sixth house Ketu, he showed immense courage in taking on the mighty British and eventually did win the battle, as the British had to leave India.

He was a celebrated jailbird in the sense that he spent around 16 years in total in prison. This can be seen from the presence of Rahu in twelfth in its exaltation sign of Gemini, enhancing the twelfth house effects. Most of his Rahu-time (1931-1936) and Ketu-time (1936-1943) was spent in prison. It once again goes to prove how this placement of the nodal axis keeps a native involved with his enemies. The nodal axis is again in the sixth-twelfth house axis in the *Navamsha* chart supplementing the sixth-twelfth house effects of the nodal axis in the *Rasi* chart.

It is also interesting to note that most of his writing took place within the prison. This is due to the presence of Mercury, the sign dispositor of Rahu in the fourth house.

The aspect of Saturn ruling the eighth house, the house ruling historical studies, on Mercury, made him rewrite the history of India in his much acclaimed work "The Discovery of India".

Since Mercury is the karmic distribution control planet, any planet associated with it gains power to affect his workings in the outside world. In his case Uranus is the planet that made him a staunch supporter of industrialization of India. In his reign at the top post of the country this was indeed carried out to an extent, but the aspect of Saturn on this combination made him wear a socialistic mask. However, Venus the other planet in conjunction with Mercury, in its own sign Libra, gave him a flair for capitalistic living and good clothes. He started the trend of wearing a rose (Venusian element) on half jackets.

His Rahu major period that started in 1953 made him concentrate more on international affairs, which is what one would expect from a twelfth house Rahu. He was the driving force behind the formation of international organizations like the Commonwealth of Nations. This again elucidates the diplomatic and international perspective of Rahu as a planet. Rahu is placed in the twelfth in the navamsha chart as well.

This diplomacy failed when Ketu struck from the sixth house in the form of Chinese invasion in 1962. He could not recover from this setback and his health deteriorated, which again is so very characteristic of this nodal axis placing. Ketu is placed in the sixth in the unforgiving sign of Capricorn along with two harsh planets Saturn and Sun in the navamsha chart. This means Ketu would keep on producing one enemy after the other despite the best diplomatic effforts by Rahu. Ketu is also strong by being placed in its own asterism *Mula*, which as we know is the asterism which promotes chaos and upheaval.

As mentioned earlier, natives with this placement of the nodal axis, usually cannot mentally adjust to failures in the sixth and twelfth house affairs. Despite deteriorating health he continued to overwork leading to his death from a heart attack in 1964, which in astrological terms meant that he could not survive the Rahu major period.

* * *

13. IN GENETICS AND REINCARNATION

Rahu and Ketu are the two main generational planets. The key to this statement lies in the fact mentioned earlier that Rahu is the significator of paternal grandfather and maternal grandmother, while Ketu is the significator of maternal grandmother and paternal grandfather. Together they are the significators of both paternal and maternal grandparents and thus represent the genetic heritage of an individual. Even modern day genetics has now come to the conclusion that it is the genes of the grandparents which are more important than the genes of the parents.

This is based on the evidence that in a change from one generation to the next the dominant genes become recessive and vice versa. If a particular gene was dominant in the grandparents it would become recessive in their children (parents) and would again become dominant in their grandchildren.

As understood by modern genetics, genes define the character traits of an individual. With this information it is just a case of putting two and two together to realize that Rahu and Ketu define our character traits to a greater extent than the Sun (father planet) and Moon (mother planet).

To give an example, we would take the case of the relationship between *B. V Raman* and his paternal grandfather *B.Surinarayana Rao*. We have already touched upon it when we discussed his chart in Chapter 12.

Chart no 26.   **B.Suryinarayana Rao**

12-02-1895   12:21 P.M.L.M.T.   42°N00' 71°E00'

Rasi (Main Chart)

3 ♄	♇ ♅ 1 ☊	
4	2	♂ 12 ♃ ♀
5	☉ 11 ♆	
6 ☋ ☽	8	☿ 10
7	9	

Natal Positions

Ascendant	18°14'Ta
Sun	01°42'Aq
Moon	09°24'Vi
Mars	00°33'Pi
Mercury	10°34'Vi
Jupiter	16°52'Pi
Venus	17°26'Ge
Saturn	15°49'Ge
Rahu	16°41'Pi
Ketu	16°41'Vi
Uranus	29°33'Ar
Neptune	26°59'Ta
Pluto	13°41'Ar

On comparing their charts it can be seen that Rahu is the main connecting planet between their charts. Rahu is in Pisces in both charts. B.Suryanarain Rao was a noted astrologer who had written many important books on astrology. He can be said to be the one who revived Vedic Astrology in modern times.

In his grandson's chart (chart no. 4), Rahu is placed in a sign ruled by Jupiter and receives a fifth house aspect from Jupiter, the planet supposed to represent the teacher in Vedic astrology. This clearly indicates that his grandson learnt astrology under his tutelage. It must be mentioned at this point that Sage *Parashara* is of the opinion that Jupiter also signifies paternal grandfather while Ketu signifies the rest of the three grandparents.

If we apply the synastry guidelines we will come to the same conclusion. His Jupiter, Venus and Mars are conjunct the natal Rahu of his grandson which make him very fortunate for his grandson. It is because of these connections that he was able to transmit the knowledge gained through these eleventh house planets to his grandson.

It comes as no surprise that his contact with his grandson lasted only in his grandson's Rahu major period. He died at the beginning of B.V. Raman's Jupiter major period.

His grandson also inherited the mantle of being the editor of 'The Astrological Magazine' from him. This is due to the fact that in his grandson's chart, the karmic distribution control planet Jupiter, which is relaying Rahu's (grandfather's) energy, is placed in the tenth house of vocation.

If a comprehensive study is done one would find that the nodal axis in people's charts relates to the important natal positions like the Sun and Moon in the charts of their grandparents rather than one's parents. For example if one's seventh house lord is conjunct Ketu one would find their spouse very similar in nature to the paternal grandmother.

As we know it is usually the grandparents who give everyone a sense of one's genetic heritage through telling stories and such. We have already encountered this in the case of *Jimi Hendrix*, whose chart was discussed in Chapter 12. History is full of such evidence of grandparents being directly or indirectly instrumental in the lives of many a famous personality.

It is seen that in a chart if a node is closely conjunct the Sun or the Moon, then the grandparent related with that node usually has a strong influence in the life of the native. It is a fatherly influence if Sun is involved and motherly influence if Moon is involved. For example if the Sun is conjunct Ketu in a chart, either one of the paternal grandmother or maternal grandfather would act as a sort of father figure. In some cases the natives are brought up by one of the grandparents represented by the node in question. Similar results are seen if a node is conjunct either the fourth house or its lord or tenth house or its lord. It goes without saying that the connection with fourth house denotes a motherly influence while the connection with tenth house denotes a fatherly influence.

Another thing which adds weight to the genetic theory is that barring exceptions the children of very successful and outgoing parents are usually introverted and restricted in their achievements and vice versa.

If we take the tenth house as that representing the father (seventh from fourth), we will find that the first house being fourth from tenth represents the paternal grandmother. Similarly we find that being tenth from fourth, the first house also represents maternal grandfather. We know that first house represents our sense of self and personality. This again hints towards the fact that the grandparents are closer to our real personality as represented by the Ascendant. This also shows that in a way they affect our personality more than our parents.

It is important to note that there is an essential difference between Rahu and Ketu in relation to genetics. Ketu is all for maintaining genetic purity while Rahu furthers genetic mixing.

It can be easily seen that the so-called primitive civilizations, who as we discussed earlier are more influenced by Ketu, are very conscious of maintaining genetic purity. For example the Native American Indian tribes would not even allow interbreeding among the tribes and in some cases even clans within the tribes. The words 'grandfather' and 'grandmother' have sacred meanings for these tribes. They represent the wisdom figures which the child is supposed to learn from. In some of these tribes the chief or the shaman is called 'grandfather'.

Ketu also influences more past oriented cultures like India where the majority of marriages are still arranged according to a caste system, the primary underlying motive of which is to preserve racial or genetic purity. Even today the countries like Iceland which can be said to be relatively cut off from the mainstream are able to maintain genetic purity to quite an extent. The whole Icelandic population can trace its roots to a single couple!

Personalities with a strong Ketu influence carry within themselves a vision of racial purity just like *Hitler* carried within him a vision of the supremacy of the Aryan race. In fact all the atrocities of the *Nazi*'s before and during the second world war

358

were carried out in the name of protecting and promoting racial purity.

According to Vedic mythology all of humanity has descended from the 'Seven Sages' represented by the seven main stars of the constellation of Great Bear. These seven sages are in turn the mind-born sons of *Brahma*, the creator. Ketu can allow us to trace a common ancestry if we look deep enough into Ketu's domain - past.

Rahu on the other hand represents the so-called advanced civilizations, which always promote genetic mixing. Today America is the hotbed for interbreeding among different races and cultures. At an earlier point in time the land now known as India housed the most advanced civilization. This is why the present day Indians are a mixed race and cannot be categorized in any of the main racial types. Similarly the average American will soon be uncategorizable.

Rahu wants to create as much diversity as possible. The whole creation process is based upon the simple dictum of 'creating many out of one'. As the universe becomes older, more and more diversity is created. Rahu can thus be seen as furthering the expansion of the universe in the realms of time, space and diversity. Interbreeding can not be seen as bad as it usually produces more tolerant and all inclusive individuals. However an apparent dichotomy arises as Sage *Parashara* assigns the genetically mixed persons to Ketu. Rahu is just seen as a foreign or outcaste person. It is interesting to note that Rahu's energy, which promotes interbreeding among foreign elements, produces Ketu personalities!

Since the recent advances in genetics, man has started playing the role of nature, and artificial genetic mixing in plants and animals has become the norm. The day is not far when such methods would be applied to humans as well to enhance some characteristics and, of course, to repress some as well. In fact some say that this process is already underway in some countries. Rahu can be said to be directly responsible for all types of genetic experimentation including cloning, which is going on today. Nature however has a finely tuned equilibrium and these artificial genetic experiments have already started revealing their negative effects.

From the above it is easy to see that extremes of both **Rahu** and **Ketu** have their negative points. Once again we come to realize that a balance needs to be established between the two nodes. The perfect blending of the past and the future creates an eternal and fulfilling present.

Linked closely with the topic of genetics is that of reincarnation. In all ancient cultures reincarnation was an accepted reality, while today it is a topic of debate. This as we will find is because of yet another tussle between Rahu and Ketu.

Genetics can tell us that we behave a certain way because we inherit certain genes by being born in a particular family. However it cannot tell us why we are born in that particular family and not in any other? The Western civilization overlooks all such questions and lays supreme emphasis on the 'one life' concept. The reason behind this lies in the strong influence of Rahu and Saturn over the Western civilization.

Rahu is the force which wants to ignore the past and concentrate on the future. According to Vedic scriptures the memory of past life/lives is stored in a memory bank which is kept hidden from the consciousness of the incarnating soul. The present life is considered just a visible link in a long chain of links, while the rest are hidden in the ocean of consciousness. This is for the purpose that one's work in the present life is not disturbed by the past. Working on a similar principle, Rahu tries to block out the past so that one can freely delve into new experiences.

Saturn comes into the picture when it limits the situation further by denying the possibilty of a life after the present one. Saturn as we know works through the principle of negation and thus negates the presence of a life before and life after. Saturn as we know rules the western direction and consequently it is the Western world that has quickly lapped up this line of thinking.

Rahu represents the energy which can allow one to see the

future. Ketu represents the energy which allows one to the see the past. Any of the above event establishes reincarnation as a reality. Since Ketu is more concerned about establishing reincarnation as real, it is usually through people recalling their past lives that reality of reincarnation is established. This is also the reason why the all the surviving ancient cultures have no difficulty in accepting reincarnation as reality.

A lot of cases of people who have been able to tap into their past life and reveal information which they couldn't have known in their present life, have been witnessed all over the world. To give a few examples - little kids can start speaking in languages completely foreign to them, people can tell exact location of a hidden treasure or recall minute details about their last family. Nature allows for these exceptions so that the modern man wakes up to the true reality of the cosmos.

In some cases like that of the famous psychic *Edgar Cayce*, the ability to see both the past and the future is present. His chart has already been discussed in detail in Chapter 12. He was a firm advocate of reincarnation in the Western world, where modern science completely denounces it. The present day science is based only on the study of matter and thus cannot understand astral processes like reincarnation. This is also the reason why there is so much doubt relating to divine sciences like astrology.

Finally it all comes down to the core of astrology itself. Astrology only exists if reincarnation exists and both of them exist only if other realities besides material, like astral and causal, are accepted. Astrology sees the present chart of an individual as a map of his present life based upon their karma in the previous lives. The fact that there are previous lives has to be taken as true, otherwise it is impossible to explain how the legendary musician *Mozart* could write whole symphonies at the age of four without ever having a past life in which he learned music !

Ketu as we can see is the main planet involved here. Ketu symbolizes the talents we have honed in our past lives and in some cases like that of *Mozart* gives fruitition in the present life. In some cases it gives problems because of the negative tendencies and habits acquired through thousands of lives. Such tendencies and life patterns are so deeply ingrained in the psyche of the individual involved that they can only be dealt with when conscious changes are brought about on an astral and causal level.

Modern day psychologists don't obviously believe in reincarnation and try to cure such patients by a process known as 'desensitization'. This is however a near impossible task as the combined effect of thousands of lives is far stronger than what any psychotherapy can do in the present life. Even if some desensitization does occur, it blocks not only the negative impulses but all the impulses leaving the native completely clueless as to their path in the present life.

The mystery of reincarnation can be understood better through the Vedic classification of karmas. There are said to be four types of karmas - *Sanchita, Prarabdha, Kriyamana* and *Agama. Sanchita* is the sum total of all our karmas in all our previous lives. Of course, in most cases, one can't experience all the stored karma in one life. *Prarabdha* is the small ripe part of the stored karma which we are ready to experience in the present life. *Kriyamana* is the karma we create in the present life by using our free will. *Agama* is the karma we create by visualizing and making plans for the future. It is the karma created by us in defining our future path.

It is easy to see that Ketu presides over *Sanchita* and *Prarabdha* karma. Ketu stores all our past lives karmas and decides the part of it which is suitable for experiencing in the present life. Rahu being the planet of free will and future presides over *Kriyamana* and *Agama* karma. Rahu helps us make conscious choices in our present life and also helps us outline our future course.

Ketu can be seen as a planet which represents old souls who have more or less experienced the whole spectrum of life represented by the twelve signs and nine planets. This is why one can see that old and more mature souls have Ketu playing a prominent role in their charts. It is usually conjunct important points and planets. Rahu on the other hand is more prominent in the charts of young souls who have a lot left to experience. This however does not mean that Rahu can not be strong in the charts of old souls and vice versa. A musician may have a strong Ketu channeling the music he learnt in his past life but that does not necessarily make him an evolved soul. In the same way Rahu's strength in a chart which is important for fulfilling one's karma in the present incarnation does not indicate a young soul.

Ketu is the most difficult to handle among the planets, as one needs to draw from the past to be able to follow one's true path in life, but not get caught up in it by dwelling on it. Oftentimes we can get caught up in past life patterns and in the process forget our karma in the present life. This is why the so called new-age fads like 'pastlife regression' are dangerous in the sense that they can stagnate one's evolutionary process if one gets caught up in the immensely complex past life experiences. The past life patterns are always very alluring as we can derive a sense of security from them. It is the same as travelling on a road we have travelled many times. Ketu also accounts for our behaviour in the present life, based upon past fears and successes. For example one would try one's best to keep relationships going or avoid them completely if one experienced a painful break-up in the previous life. Similarly one would have a happy go lucky attitude about money if one has had a financially secure previous life.

Rahu on the other hand is a road we haven't travelled as yet and so it always presents a challenge. If one overcomes one's initial hesitation Rahu provides one with all the luck required to travel the unknown path. Ketu provides the wisdom which has come from travelling other paths. In this way Rahu and Ketu complement each other as we evolve through our numerous incarnations.

* * *

14. RELEVANCE IN THE PRESENT DAY AND AGE

The nodes, as we have seen, are collective planets in the same vein as the outer planets, Uranus, Neptune and Pluto. In fact the nodes play the lead role in the rise and fall of civilizations. The imagery of the two serpents having each other's tail in their mouth suggest that Rahu and Ketu are astrological significators of the cyclical nature of space, time and evolution.

Rahu is the force which makes a civilization overstretch itself while Ketu is the force which triggers a collapse. Rahu, the planet of illusion, always creates a general mindset in a technologically advanced civilization, that scientific progress is an infinite one way street and evolution is an endless process.

Unfortunately our present civilization has been caught up in that illusion ever since the arrival of 'Darwin's theory of evolution'. Darwin himself was not as rigid about his theory as the scientific community has been in the last century. The fact that Rahu has been the major planetary force behind the rapid scientific and technological development of the last two hundred years is not very hard to see.

As discussed earlier Rahu is the planet which governs sudden inspiration and ideas which have been the key to scientific development over the last two centuries. It always helps out when the scientific community gets stuck at a point. For example, when the scientific community could not work out the structure of Benzene, Rahu revealed the secret to a German chemist *Kekule* in a dream which had snakes following each other's tails in a circle. We have already discussed in Chapter 3. how this discovery ushered in a complete revolution in organic chemistry, which in turn is directly responsible for advances in plastics, pharmaceuticals and other chemical products, which make us feel more advanced than the so-called primitive civilizations.

Albert Einstein had the idea 'Theory of Relativity' come to him in a daydream while travelling in a train. *Thomas Edison*, the man who is responsible for most of the inventions and discoveries which make us consider ourselves modern and advanced, had Rahu placed in the fifth house, the house of thoughts and creativity. It is no secret then, which planetary force was influencing his mental processes. Hundreds of such examples of scientists and inventors being influenced by Rahu can be found.

Rahu has worked in tandem with other planets to bring about the major changes of the last two centuries. Rahu along with Venus is behind the automobile explosion of the 20th century. Along with Mercury it is responsible for the communication media revolution. Along with Neptune it is responsible for the motion picture and the spread of all types of synthetic drugs and chemicals. Along with Uranus it is responsible for the electronic, satellite and internet revolution. We have already talked about the most important among these topics under Rahu's significations in Chapter 3.

Through all these changes Rahu has brought about the concept of the global village. It has made everything foreign very accessible to everyone. In a way humanity is breaking geographical and national boundaries to realize this unity. Like always, there is a downside to what Rahu has been doing. Since earth is a planet of finite resources, restraint is the key to humanity's survival on this planet. Rahu creates an illusion that the resources are infinite, which is the way most of the so- called economists are thinking. The fact that the amount of 'money' floating around in the world today would need ten planets like earth to cater for the resources they are supposed to represent, just puts this point into perspective.

If Rahu stands for expansion, Ketu represents the breaking point after which the cycle starts again. As discussed in Chapter 1., the serpent symbolism showing the cyclical nature of time is rampant in all ancient civilizations. The concept of '*Pralaya*' or 'dissolution' after a World Age is common to most of these cultures. Ketu along with Pluto represents the cosmic forces responsible for this periodic dissolution. Ketu is the planet which makes a civilization pay for its excesses.

Let us now turn our attention to the major events of the 20th century to see how the nodes were involved.

The First World War could be said to be triggered on June 28th, 1914, when the Duke of Austria was murdered. The chart is drawn for midday on 28th of June. The Ascendant doesn't matter as we are only interested in relative positions of planets.

Chart no 27.   **First World War**

28-06-1914   12:00 P.M.L.M.T.   52°N32' 13°E25'

Rasi (MainChart)

Natal Positions

Ascendant	10°11' Vi
Sun	13°13'Ge
Moon	12°43' Le
Mars	08°40' Le
Mercury	05°33' Ca
Jupiter	29°08' Cp
Venus	17°11' Cp
Saturn	01°08' Ge
Rahu	16°17' Aq
Ketu	16°17' Le
Uranus	18°28' Cp
Neptune	04°25' Ca
Pluto	08°56' Ge

We can see how Ketu is conjunct Mars in the fiery sign of Leo and is aspected by Saturn. Ketu and Mars conjunction in a fiery sign is an explosive combination which is given duration by Saturn. Pluto, the planet of mass catastrophes, is relaying its collective destructive energy to this combination through its conjunction with Saturn.

The Second World War can be said to have officially begun on 3rd September 1939 when Britain and France declared war on Germany.

Chart no 28.   Second World War

03-09-1939   12:00 P.M.L.M.T.   52°N32' 13°E25'

Rasi (Main Chart)

Natal Positions

Ascendant	25°36'Li
Sun	17°01' Le
Moon	07°03' Ar
Mars	01°43'Cp
Mercury	00°42'Le
Jupiter	13°46'Pi
Venus	16°22'Le
Saturn	11°50'Ar
Rahu	09°18'Li
Ketu	09°18'Ar
Uranus	25°22'Vi
Neptune	22°3' Le
Pluto	19°30'Ca

We can see that Saturn and Ketu are exactly conjunct in the fiery sign of Aries. Mars aspects this conjunction from its strong position in Capricorn. Pluto is again relaying its energy through its opposition with Mars.

We can derive from the above two examples that for a major collective catastrophe to be triggered Mars, Saturn and Pluto should be combining their energies with Ketu. Ketu should preferably be in Scorpio or a fire sign and unaspected by Jupiter.

We can also see that Rahu is virtually absent from the field of action in both the cases. This is why some wise men regard Rahu as a peacemaker and a diplomat while Ketu is considered a war-monger. Ketu is more connected to catastrophes than Rahu.

We have already seen while discussing Hitler's chart how Ketu was transiting the imperialistic seventh house planets around the beginning of the second world war.

We know that the second world war was more disastrous in terms of both property and life than the first one. This goes to show that Saturn-Ketu conjunction is more dangerous than Mars-Ketu conjunction. Mars-Ketu gives sudden but short conflagrations while Saturn-Ketu gives rise to long term conflicts.

The second world war ended with the use of atomic bombs on the Japanese cities of Hiroshima and Nagasaki. We have made a chart for the dropping of the atomic bomb at Hiroshima at the exact time of the bombing.

Chart no 29.   Atomic Bomb dropped at Hiroshima

06-08-1945   09:45 A.M.L.M.T.   34°N30' 132°E30'

Rasi (MainChart)

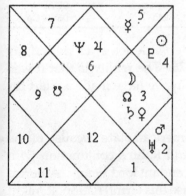

Natal Positions

Ascendant	13°33'Vi
Sun	20°06'Ca
Moon	25°45'Ge
Mars	16°10'Ta
Mercury	11°42'Le
Jupiter	03°14'Vi
Venus	08°41'Ge
Saturn	25°14'Ge
Rahu	14°13'Ge
Ketu	14°13'Sg
Uranus	23°27'Ta
Neptune	11°14' Le
Pluto	17°09'Ca

As we can see, both Mars and Saturn are aspecting an exalted Ketu. *Ardra*, the destructive asterism ruled by Rahu, gains a lot of strength in this chart as it is placed at the Midheaven and is occupied by Rahu itself along with its friend Venus. Both the nodes are strong due to their exaltation.

We already know that Pluto is the main significator of atomic energy and weapons, but the connection of Pluto with Ketu is not clear from these charts. To look deeper into why America decided to use an atomic bomb on Japan, we have to look at the American birth chart, which we can take as the American Independence Chart.

Chart no 30.   **United States of America**

02-08-1776   01:00 A.M.L.M.T.   38°N55' 77°W04'

Rasi (MainChart)

Natal Positions

Ascendant	24°37'Ta
Sun	19°39'Ca
Moon	20°50'Aq
Mars	19°39'Ge
Mercury	00°29'Ca
Jupiter	21°24'Ge
Venus	17°13'Ge
Saturn	25°39'Vi
Rahu	15°21'Ca
Ketu	15°21'Cp
Uranus	19°38'Ta
Neptune	02°20'Vi
Pluto	08°24'Cp

It is a fallacy that American Independence was signed, as commonly believed, on 4th of July, 1776. The reality is that it was signed on 2nd August, 1776. This is why we have made a chart for 1.00 am on the 2nd of August.

This chart fits in better with the American state because of the Jupiter-Mars conjunction in Gemini and Rahu's conjunction with important planets like the Sun and Ascendant lord Venus. America is primarily a 'Rahucentric' (if we can use this term!) nation. It might involve digressing from our discussion a little bit, but I should make it clear that all technologically advanced so-called First World countries are more closely related to Rahu as compared with Ketu. This is especially true of new cultures like the American, which is not even 250 years old. This can be seen from the attitudes prevalent in these cultures and nations. On the other hand all the surving ancient cultures are closer to Ketu's energy.

We can see that Pluto is conjunct the natal Ketu in the materially active cardinal sign of Capricorn in the American chart. It shows that America would not hesitate in using atomic weapons against its adversaries. On 6th August 1945, Pluto created tension by directly opposing this combination from its transit through Cancer.

It can be seen that Pluto was transiting at around 18 degrees in Cancer, while Rahu and Ketu lie at around 15 degrees of Cancer and Capricorn respectively. The conjunction and opposition with the two nodes is within the 5 degree orb of maximum influence. Third house as we know is an impulsive house which signifies attack, and Pluto's presence there over important natal planets like the Sun, the Ascendant lord Venus and the nodal axis made the decision to drop the bomb fructify.

Ketu was transiting through the eighth house of the American chart. Eighth house as we know is the most destructive among the houses. It is thus clear that Ketu and Pluto together caused the dropping of the first atomic bomb in the modern times.

Even the chart of *Hirohito*, the Emperor of Japan at that time reveals this atomic bombing and the direct involvement of Ketu and Pluto.

We can see that his Ketu is placed in the sixth house along with Pluto. Sixth house as we can see represents enemies. Ketu and Pluto together make it clear that his country would go through some collective catastrophe because of the enemy. It is interesting to note that the sign in his sixth house is Taurus, the rising sign in the American chart !

At the time of the bombing, Pluto is transiting his eighth house while Ketu is transiting over his first house. This obviously points to some collective disaster that would fall on his kingdom.

Chart no 31.   **Emperor Hirohito**

29-04-1901   10:10 P.M.L.M.T.   35°N42' 139°E46'

Rasi (MainChart)

	10		♅ 8 ☊
11	♃ ♄ 9		7
12 ☿		☽ 6	
⊙ 1 ♀	♆ 3		♂ 5
♇ ☋ 2		4	

Natal Positions

Ascendant	03°41'Sg
Sun	16°01'Ca
Moon	00°11'Vi
Mars	04°02'Le
Mercury	29°55'Pi
Jupiter	20°34'Sg
Venus	15°37'Ar
Saturn	23°54'Sg
Rahu	00°09'Sc
Ketu	00°09'Ta
Uranus	23°49'Sc
Neptune	00°42'Ge
Pluto	23°48'Ta

As the ancients have known for a long time, eclipses also affect collective human affairs. Let's take a look at the most recent total solar eclipse which interestingly took place on June 21, the summer solstice!

The chart is made for the moment Moon's disc touches the Sun. In judging the collective results of an eclipse, the most important factor is the nature of the signs Rahu and Ketu are transiting. The sign in which the eclipse takes place is of primary importance.

This eclipse as we can see takes place in the 6th degree of the sign Gemini. It will affect all Geminian areas like communication, discrimination, intellectual waves, collective trends and attitudes. Since it takes place in the ninth house it will further higher awareness and make people come out of their mass and individual shells to bring about a positive change in the world. Since Rahu is the main node involved in the eclipse, it carries a futuristic and expansive energy. It lasts for around 5 hours and so its effects can be said to last 5 years.

Chart no 32.   Solar Eclipse on Summer Solstice 2001

21-06-2001   15:05 A.M.L.M.T.   28°N22' 79°E27'

Rasi (MainChart)

8 ♂ ♇		6	
9 ☋	7		5
10 ♆			4
♅ 11 12	♀ 1	♄ ☌ ☉ 3 ♃ 2 ☿	☽ ☊

Natal Positions

Ascendant	13°36'Li
Sun	06°13'Ge
Moon	04°50'Ge
Mars	26°24'Sc
Mercury	29°03'Pi
Jupiter	01°14'Ge
Venus	20°59'Ar
Saturn	14°07'Ta
Rahu	12°44'Ge
Ketu	12°44'Sg
Uranus	00°58'Cp
Neptune	14°23'Cp
Pluto	19°16'Sc

The presence of Jupiter along with the eclipse lends a benefic touch to it.

Ketu's positioning in Sagittarius shows a change in the mental processes of humanity as a whole. The Lunar eclipse on July 5th, 2001 in the sign Sagittarius, follows this Solar eclipse, and has Ketu as the main planet. A Solar eclipse will take place in the sign of Sagittarius on 14th December, 2001. Sagittarius is a sign of exploration and a lover of truth. The treasures from the past are now in a process of being unearthed and the findings from various ancient cultures are being synthesized.

Ketu has been over the years, slowly triggering a silent revolution of sorts. This relates to the unravelling of the mysteries of the ancient civilizations. New findings are showing that the ancient civilizations like the Mayans, Egyptians and Vedic were much advanced than has been understood in our times.

With each new finding it is becoming clear that 'astrology', along with its cousin 'astronomy', is the only common link between all ancient civilizations and the key to all their knowledge. A lot of the answers are thus likely be found in the home of the real astrology,

India. Vedic mythology carries within itself the most comprehensive knowledge on all things just like it does for Rahu and Ketu. Just like *Alice Bailey* said, "India hides the light".

One must keep in mind that the past is not always bad and the future is not always good. Rahu and Ketu together prove that time and reality are cyclical and not linear as our civilization would like to believe. This eclipse will give momentum to this line of study until the message of the ancients is heard loud and clear.

Vishnu, coming back to his original form, cuts off the head of Swarbhanu

15. PROPITIATION

As is the case with all other planets, the communication lines with Rahu and Ketu are open if one wants to establish contact. There might be different reasons as to why one would want to establish contact - it might be due to suffering, a thirst for material gains, a desire to gain knowledge or just a sincere recognition of these universal forces. The propitiation of any planet never goes empty, as *Brahma*, the creator, has laid down the following code for all planets to follow - " If anyone asks you for a favour, you have to reciprocate by fulfilling their wish". Vedic astrology as we know sees planets as celestial beings. This personal approach makes propitiating them akin to getting a person to act in one's favour. There are different ways to approach *Messrs*. Rahu and Ketu. First we will look into the ways to propitiate Rahu.

PROPITIATING RAHU

1. Deity

As discussed earlier Rahu's presiding deity is Goddess *Durga*. Propitiating her is the best way to get Rahu on your side. She can be propitiated by the regular repetition of the following *mantra* (sound totem) -

" Om Shree Durgaye Namah"

This should be repeated 108 times every Wednesday, Friday or Saturday. Sage *Parashara* gives the figure of 18,000 for the repetition of Rahu's mantras. My view is that, taking into consideration the nature of the times we live in, all mantras prescribed for Rahu should be repeated 108 times in one sitting unless otherwise indicated. It is good to face the South Western direction while reciting these mantras. It is also advisable to have an image of Goddess Durga in front of you.

This remedial measure does not have any negative side effects and is especially helpful when one is facing difficulties in life due to Rahu's adverse functioning. It also connects one to the higher forces aiding one's evolutionary process.

As is clear from the birth story of *Ganesha* delineated in Chapter 6., Ganesha has to be remembered before approaching any other deity, so it is important to say - "Om Shree Ganeshaye Namah" - once before you start reciting Durga's mantra. This rule will apply for all the mantras prescribed in this chapter.

2. **Mantra**

The main mantra for Rahu is - "Om Rahave Namah"

The alternative smaller mantra is - "Om Ram". "Ram" is pronounced as "Rahm" out here.

The tantric mantra for Rahu is -

"Om Bhraam Bhreem Bhrom Sah Rahave Namah"

The full Vedic mantra is -

"Om Bhraam Bhreem Bhraum Sah Om Bhoorbhava Svaha Om Kyanishchitra Abhoov Dooti Sadavriddha Sabha Kayasha Chisth-Yavrita. Om Svaha Bhuvah Bhah Om Sah Bhraum Bhreem Bhraam Om Rahave Namah"

The Puranic mantra for Rahu is -

"Om Shrardhkarya Mahavirya Chandra Aditya Vimardanam,
Simhikaya Bhrasambhut Tam Rahu Prun Mamyaham."

Those who have difficulty pronouncing these longer mantras should stick to the smaller mantras. Shiva's root mantra - "Om Hoom" is also helpful for curbing the negative effects of Rahu. Even Durga's root mantra - "Om Dhoom" can be used.

The regular use of any of these mantras is the best way to get Rahu on your side. They have no negative side effects and will always relieve one's suffering and aid in one's evolutionary process.

3. Yantra

We have already seen Rahu's *Yantra* (numerological totem), in Chapter 5. One should draw this yantra on a piece of paper and keep it with them in their purse, pocket or under the pillow. Alternatively one can inscribe it on a square piece of silver which can be worn around the neck as a pendant or kept on an altar. The dimensions of the piece of silver can be either 1.08 cm square or 1.08 inches square.

It is advisable to start using the yantra from a Wednesday, Friday or Saturday, when the Moon is waxing. It is better to choose a day among the days mentioned, whose corresponding planet is most closely related to Rahu in the chart. Moon occupying one of the asterisms of Rahu on the day of wearing is another factor which improves the auspiciousness. It should also be empowered by reciting Rahu's mantra 108 times.

4. Gems

We have already seen that Rahu is most closely related to *Gomed* or Hessonite Quartz. One can use a clear piece of this gem weighing at least 5 carats. It should preferably be set in *Panchdhatu*, a special mixture of 5 metals, which was discussed in Chapter 3. Alternatively one can use silver, copper or bronze. The other gems which can be worn for Rahu are Brown Agate and Brown Tourmaline.

The ring is worn on the middle finger. It should first be put on a Wednesday, when the Moon is waxing. It can also be worn on a Friday or Saturday. It is better to choose a day among the days mentioned, whose corresponding planet is most closely related to Rahu in the chart. Moon occupying one of the asterisms of Rahu on the day of wearing is another factor which improves the auspiciousness.

One must remember that a gemstone for Rahu should only be worn after careful consideration. It should only be worn if Rahu is a *yogakaraka*, a very strong benefic force in the chart. This is usually only possible in the case of Taurus, Gemini, Libra and Aquarius Ascendants. Even then one should test the stone by keeping it under the pillow and sleeping on it for a couple of nights. If one gets good dreams then only should one consider wearing the stone.

Gemstones increase the energy of the planet for better or worse, so wearing them is a sort of a gamble. If a gem is worn for Rahu one will see an increase in its good effects but one will also see an increase in its negative effects. This is why it is dangerous to wear its gemstone to cure its adverse results.

5. Herbs, Foods, Scents and Oils

Herbs such as Eucalyptus, Sage, Basil and Calamus can be used for controlling the negative energy of Rahu. Amongst them Basil is the best herb. It has been extolled in Vedic scriptures as the Queen of all herbs.

For increasing the energy of Rahu, one can use Rahu plants like garlic and onions. In fact taking any of the foods which were delineated as Rahu significations in Chapter 3. increases Rahu's energy.

Donating these foods helps reduce the ill effects of Rahu in one's life. Rahu as we know is most closely associated with Black Gram. Feeding this to ants, birds and other animals is a simple way of propitiating Rahu.

Among the oils, Rahu is most connected to Mustard and Linseed Oils. The use of these oils through personal use as in massage or cooking, or donating them to charity is another way of propitiating Rahu.

The use of fragrances belonging to the flowers that fall under Rahu's significations as mentioned in Chapter 3. increases Rahu's energy. Strong aromas like Camphor, Frankincense and Wintergreen are also helpful for balancing Rahu's energy. Sandalwood has been seen to be the best fragrance to calm down Rahu's disturbing energy. This is probably the reason why in India, there is a custom of putting sandalwood paste on the forehead every morning after a bath.

6. Symbols

Rahu's symbols which are mentioned in Chapter 3. can be used for propitiating Rahu, in the same way as Rahu's Yantra. The method of utilising these symbols is exactly the same as for Rahu's Yantra. The only exception to this rule is the sword, which as we discussed earlier is a symbol of Rahu. Donating a sword is one way of warding off the negative effects of Rahu.

7. Colours & Clothing

We have already seen the colours associated with Rahu in Chapter 3. The use of these colours in one's clothes and surroundings helps increase the energy of Rahu. Wearing clothes and fabrics which fall under Rahu's domain is another way of boosting Rahu's energy. Donating Rahu clothes and things having Rahu colours helps ward off the negative effects of Rahu.

For example, blue and black are colours associated with Rahu, and blankets as we know are special Rahu significations. Donating blue or black blankets in charity is a good way of propitiating Rahu.

8. The 'Red Book' Remedial Measures

As mentioned earlier, *Lal Kitab* or the Red Book is an obscure astrological treatise which has special insights into the functioning of Rahu and Ketu. It also contains many remedial measures for different placements of Rahu and Ketu in the chart. Below are some general remedies for Rahu which seem to work quite well in my experience.

a) Drop one blue flower in flowing water for 42 days.
b) Donate blue or black blankets to a religious place or institution.
c) Drop one kilogram of lead, divided into 8 parts, in a river, or any other source of flowing water.
d) If one is a smoker, one should if possible, smoke through a silver pipe or silver cigarette holder.
e) Offer cigarettes to smokers.
f) Do something positive for your maternal grandmother or paternal grandfather.

It must be noted that all these remedies are not for increasing Rahu's energy but for warding off its negative effects. Given below are the different remedial measures suggested for the different house placements of Rahu -

a) If Rahu is in the 1st house, donate articles related to the Sun like wheat, copper, ruby, red cloth, red flowers, musk, saffron and brown cow.
b) If Rahu is in the 2nd house, solid piece of silver or gold should be kept by the native. Keeping saffron and yellow articles will also be helpful.
c) If Rahu is in the 3rd house, keeping a piece of ivory will be beneficial.
d) If Rahu is in the 4th house, drinking water in a silver glass will be helpful.

e) If Rahu is in the 5th house, the native should marry twice with their spouse. The alternative is to keep an elephant made of silver.

f) If Rahu is in the 6th house, keeping a small round ball of lead will be helpful. Keeping a black dog as a pet will also be helpful.

g) If Rahu is in the 7th house, one should try not to marry before 21 years of age.

h) If Rahu is in the 8th house, 8 old coins should be thrown in running water for 42 days.

i) If Rahu is in the 9th house, one should try to live in a joint family and avoid entering into litigations with their own blood.

j) If Rahu is in the 10th house, one should avoid miserliness and narrowmindedness. It is always helpful not to be bare headed.

k) If Rahu is in the 11th house, one should wear gold and donate to cleaners, sweepers and domestic workers.

l) If Rahu is in the 12th house, one should have their meals in the kitchen itself, where they are prepared.

9. Miscellaneous

When Rahu is giving problems, one should avoid living in big cities, using high technology gadgets, trying to copy mass trends etc. One should not jump into new experiences, keep aspirations to a minimum and concentrate on the present rather than the future.

A retreat into the country or the wilderness usually goes a long way in balancing Rahu's negative energy. All types of intoxication which can cloud one's thinking should be avoided. Anything to do with the media, television, cinema should be avoided. One should also avoid modern forms of yoga, psychotherapy and visualization processes. Sticking to a vegetarian diet, wherever possible, is also a good way of reducing Rahu's illusory effect.

PROPITIATING KETU

1. Deity

As discussed earlier, Ketu's presiding deity is Lord *Ganesha*. Propitiating him is the best way to get Rahu on your side. He can be propitiated by the repetition of the following mantra -

" Om Shree Ganeshaya Namah"

This should be repeated 108 times and be done regularly every Thursday or Tuesday. Sage *Parashara* gives the figure of 17,000 for the repetition of Ketu's mantras. Again for the reason mentioned in Rahu's section, mantras for Ketu should be repeated 108 times in one sitting unless otherwise indicated. It is good to face the South Western direction while reciting these mantras. It is also advisable to have an image of Lord Ganesha in front of you.

This remedial measure is the best among all the ones we would deal with, in the sense that it does not have any negative side effects and is especially helpful when one is facing difficulties in life due to Ketu's adverse functioning. It also connects one to the higher forces aiding one's evolutionary process.

2. Mantra

The main mantra for Ketu is - "Om Namah Ketave"

The alternative smaller mantra is "Om Ket". These mantras should be recited 117 times in one go.

The tantric mantra for Ketu is -

"Om Praam Preem Prom Sah Ketave Namah"

The full Vedic mantra is -

"Om Praam Preem Praum Sah Om Bhoorbhava Svaha Om Ketum
    Krinavanketave Peshomaryaa Peshase. Samush Dwibhar
Jayathah. Om Svaha Bhuvah Bhoo, Om Sah Praum Preem Praam
                    Ketave Namah"

The Puranic mantra for Ketu is -

"Om Palasha Pushpa Sankasham Taraka Grahamastakam,
    Roudram Raudratmakam Ghoram Tam Ketum Prun
                    Mamyaham."

Shiva's root mantra - "Om Hoom" is also helpful for curbing the
negative effects of Ketu. Regular recitation of Shiva's full mantra -
"Om Namah Shivaye" usually takes care of the negative effects of
both Rahu and Ketu.

The regular use of any of these mantras is the best way to get
Ketu on your side. They have no negative side effects and will always
relieve one's suffering and aid in one's evolutionary process.

3. Yantra

We have already seen Ketu's *Yantra* or numerological totem in
Chapter 5. One should draw this yantra on a piece of paper and
keep it with them in their purse, pocket or under the pillow.
Alternatively one can inscribe it on a square piece of silver which
can be worn around the neck as a pendant or kept on an altar. The
dimensions of the piece of silver can be either 1.17 cm square or 1.17
inches square.

It is however advisable to start using the yantra from Tuesday or
Thursday when the Moon is waxing. It is better to choose a day
among the days mentioned, whose corresponding planet is most
closely related to Ketu in the chart. Moon occupying one of the
asterisms of Ketu on the day of wearing is another factor which

enhances the auspiciousness. It should also be empowered by reciting Ketu's mantra 117 times.

4. Gems

We have already seen that Ketu is most closely related to *Cat's Eye* or Chrysoberyl. One can use a clear piece of this gem weighing at least 5 carats. It should preferably be set in *Ashtadhatu*, a special mixture of 8 metals which was discussed in Chapter 3. Alternatively one can use silver or bronze. The other gems which can be worn for Ketu are Turquoise, Lapis Lazuli and Tiger's Eye.

The ring is worn on the little finger. It should first be put on a Thursday, when the Moon is waxing. It can also be worn on a Tuesday. It is better to choose a day among the days mentioned, whose corresponding planet is most closely related to Ketu in the chart. Moon occupying one of the asterisms of Ketu on the day of wearing is another factor which enhances the auspiciousness.

One must remember that a gemstone for Ketu should only be worn after careful consideration. It should only be worn if Ketu is a *yogakaraka*, a very strong benefic force in the chart. This as we know is only possible in case of Cancer, Scorpio and Pisces Ascendants. Even then one should test the stone by keeping it under the pillow and sleeping on it for a couple of nights. If one gets good dreams then only should one consider wearing the stone.

Gemstones increase the energy of the planet for better or worse, so wearing them is a sort of a gamble. If a gem is worn for Ketu one will see an increase in its good effects but one will also see an increase in its negative effects. This is why it is dangerous to wear its gemstone to cure its adverse results.

5. Herbs, Foods, Scents and Oils

Herbs such as Bayberry, Sage, Juniper, Basil and Calamus can be used for increasing the positive qualities of Ketu. Once again Basil is the best herb.

For increasing the energy of Ketu one can use Ketu foods like wild ginger, saffron and groundnuts. In fact taking any of the foods which were delineated as Ketu significations in Chapter 3. increases Ketu's energy. Donating these foods helps reduce the ill effects of Ketu in one's life. Ketu as we know is most closely associated with Horse Gram. Feeding Horse Gram to birds and other animals is a way of propitiating Ketu.

Among the oils Ketu is most connected to Castor and Sesame oils. Aromatic oils like Camphor and Cedar are also good for controlling the energy of Ketu. The use of these oils through personal use as in massage or cooking, or donating them to charity is another way of propitiating Ketu.

The use of fragrances belonging to the flowers that fall under Ketu's significations as mentioned in Chapter 3. increases Ketu's energy. Cooling aromas like skullcap and passion flower can be used controlling the negative energy of a strong Ketu. Sandalwood is again the best fragrance for calming Ketu's irritable energy.

6. Symbols

Ketu's symbols which are mentioned in Chapter 3. can be used or propitiating Ketu, in the same way as Ketu's Yantra. The method f utilising these symbols is exactly the same as for Ketu's Yantra.

7. Colours & Clothing

We have already seen the colours associated with Ketu in Chapter . The use of these colours in one's clothes and surroundings helps increase the energy of Ketu. Wearing clothes and fabrics which fall under Ketu's domain is another way of boosting Ketu's energy. Donating Ketu clothes and things having Ketu colours helps ward ff the negative effects of Ketu.

For example, earthy colours associated with Ketu, and striped clothes, as we know are special Ketu significations. Donating earth coloured striped sheets in charity is a good way of propitiating Ketu.

8. The 'Red Book' Remedial Measures

Given below are some general remedies mentioned for Ketu in the Lal Kitab.

a) Drop one earth coloured flower in flowing water, preferably a sewer, for 47 days.
b) Donate striped blankets to a religious place or institution.
c) Get your ears or nose pierced.
d) Feed street dogs regularly for 47 days.
e) Put a dry coconut in flowing water for a couple of days.
f) Do something positive for your paternal grandmother or maternal grandfather.

Given below are the different remedial measures suggested for the different house placements of Ketu -

a) If Ketu is in the 1st house, one should donate articles relating to Saturn - blue sapphire, iron, black cow, black dog and black horse.
b) If Ketu is in the 2nd house, tilak made preferably of sandalwood, should be applied on forehead. The tilak can be a triangle, trident or any of Ketu's symbols.
c) If Ketu is in the 3rd house, one should try to wear gold and throw yellow flowers in running water. To apply tilak of saffron on the forehead will also be beneficial.
d) If Ketu is in the 4th house, donating yellow items or gold to a temple will be helpful.
e) If Ketu is in the 5th house, one should donate articles related to Mars - red coral, copper, wheat, red cloth, red flower and red sandalwood.
f) If Ketu is in the 6th house, one should wear a gold ring on the left hand.
g) If Ketu is in the 7th house, one should be open in

communication. Otherwise one will suffer from diseases.

h) If Ketu is in the 8th house, donation of a black and white blanket to a temple is helpful. To avoid its malefic effects on children one should donate gold and have a tilak of saffron.

i) If Ketu is in the 9th house, wearing a gold chain around the neck is beneficial.

j) If Ketu is in the 10th house, the native should have control over his character. Excusing his siblings for envious attitudes will make the native more prosperous.

k) If Ketu is in the 11th house, radish should be donated in a temple in the morning.

l) If Ketu is in the 12th house, keeping a dog is beneficial. To avoid financial difficulties the native should suck their thumb after dipping it in milk.

9. Miscellaneous

When Ketu is giving problems, one should avoid living in big cities, using high technology gadgets, trying to copy mass trends etc. One should stop brooding over past, go for a change of situation and concentrate on the present rather than the past.

A retreat into the country or the wilderness usually goes a long way in balancing Ketu's negative energy. All types of intoxication which can cloud one's thinking should be avoided. One should also avoid excesses of any kind. Meditation on death is one of the ways to tap into the spiritual side of Ketu. A general introspective outlook is good but a sense of balance must be maintained as one can get too caught up in oneself. One should guard against being too closeminded, pessimistic and hypocritical.

There are special and elaborate remedial measures suggested by sage *Parashara* for those who are born when the Ascendant or Moon is placed in the first two quarters of Ketu's asterisms, *Ashvini*, *Magha* and *Mula*. One can look them up in "Brihat Parashara Hora Shastra". Sage Parashara also delineates the remedial measures for those born on eclipses.

There are millions of ways in which one can propitiate Rahu and Ketu. Everyone can make up one's own way of getting in touch with their energies through connecting with their significations. For example, dealing with and feeding animals which fall under their domain is a way of propitiating them. This is why feeding milk to snakes on a particular day every year is still an alive tradition in many parts of India. One can appease both the nodes through making offerings to snakes, which as we know symbolize both Rahu and Ketu. The same applies to helping out those among us who are under their strong positive or adverse influence. Meditating on the images of Rahu and Ketu provided through the illustrations in this book is another way of establishing a rapport with them. When we come to think of it, even reading this book is also a way of propitiating them !

Lord Brahma granting Planetary Status to Rahu and Ketu

AFTERWORD

Life is a continuous thread, which stretches from the beginning of time to the end of creation. Among the planets, only the lunar nodes represent this life thread. Rahu and Ketu, along with the Sun and the Moon, chart the course the soul has chosen for the present life. The other planets are just the indicators of how the journey will be undertaken.

I have had a multitude of fascinating and extraordinary experiences while writing this book. It is a tribute to the curious functionings of the nodes, that this book should be written when both of them occupy their respective exaltation signs!

Prash Trivedi
March 2002

OSFA ORION SCHOOL & FOUNDATION FOR ASTROLOGY

OSFA is dedicated to enhancing public awareness about Vedic Astrology (Indian Astrology) and its related fields through lecturing, research, writings, media, readings and courses. Its founders Prash Trivedi and his wife Vela have recently appeared on BBC radio and London Television to further the cause of Vedic Astrology in the Western world.

OSFA accepts donations. It also welcomes lecture opportunities, event collaborations and organized reading sessions. Those wanting to help, associate or contribute can write directly to us at astrology@karmablueprint.com

OSFA is open to all who would like to further the cause of Astrology and welcomes other Astrologers to join its team.

OSFA is an open forum for all those who want to share their thoughts on Astrology and other Esoteric subjects. You can send us your Piece or Article via Email

For more information about OSFA please visit -

Website: www.osfa.org.uk

Online Course: www.osfa.org.uk/onlinecourse.htm

Consultations & Readings: www.osfa.org.uk/consult.htm

BIBLIOGRAPHY

Sage Parashara. *Brihat Parashara Hora Sastra: Volume I.*

Sage Parashara. *Brihat Parashara Hora Sastra: Volume II.*

Sage Jaimini. *Jaimini Sutram.* Translation by P.S. Shastri.

Varahamihira. *Brihat Jataka.* Translation by V.S. Shastri, Sadhana Press 1981, Bangalore, India.

Mantreswara. *Phaladeepika.* Translation by V.S. Shastri, Yugantara Press 1961, Bangalore, India.

Pt. Girdhari Lal. *Lal Kitab.* No official English Publication till date.

Nodal Sign Transits
for the next 19 years

SIGN	RAHU's TRANSIT *
Aquarius	Nov 2006 to May 2008
Capricorn	May 2008 to Nov 2009
Sagittarius	Nov 2009 to May 2011
Scorpio	May 2011 to Jan 2013
Libra	Jan 2013 to Jul 2014
Virgo	Jul 2014 to Jan 2016
Leo	Jan 2016 to Sep 2017
Cancer	Sep 2017 to Mar 2019
Gemini	Mar 2019 to Sep 2020
Taurus	Sep 2020 to Apr 2022
Aries	Apr 2022 to Oct 2023
Pisces	Oct 2023 to May 2025
Aquarius	May 2025 to Dec 2026

* Ketu will always be in the seventh sign from Rahu

Rahu is given a special lordship of a period equivalent to "8 months" by Sage Parashara. This special time period allotment can be used to ascertain whether a certain event has been triggered by Rahu or not. For example, if one begins a travel or job which lasts for around 8 months, one can infer that Rahu was behind that travel. One can also understand this time period in the sense that Rahu acts in 8 month spurts.

Ketu is given a special lordship of a period equivalent to "3 months" by Sage Parashara. In the same way this special time period allotment can be used to ascertain whether a certain event has been triggered by Ketu or not. If one begins a travel or job which lasts for around 3 months, one can infer that Ketu was behind that travel. One can also understand this time period in the sense that Ketu acts in 3 month spurts.

It is useful to remember that Rahu is a dhatu (metal) planet. This means that it relates to the mineral kingdom in general. This fact is of use in horary astrology where questions are answered on the basis of the chart at the time of query. If Rahu is rising in the Ascendant in the chart at the moment of query, the astrologer can infer that the question is about money or other material resources.

Ketu is a jeeva (live) planet, which means that it relates to the biologically live things such as people, animals or plants. If Ketu is rising in the Ascendant of the query chart, the astrologer can infer that the query relates to either personal, health or some live thing of importance to the querent.

* * * * *

Real Galactic Home of Rahu & Ketu

There has been a lot of debate amongst astrologers as to what signs (or the region of the zodiac) are the real domain of Rahu and Ketu (the lunar nodes). An unlikely source from Central/South America helps us solve this mystery. The Barasan People of Northwestern Amazonia recognize a polarity between Pleiades (Krittika) and Scorpio (the Anuradha part). They consider Pleiades to be the serpent's tail and Scorpio to be the serpent's mouth. The Quichemaya People refer to Scorpio as a doorway to the underworld and Pleiades to be the snake's rattle. These traditions make it clear that the serpent's tail should be identified with Pleadies and the serpent's mouth should be identified with the constellation of Scorpio.

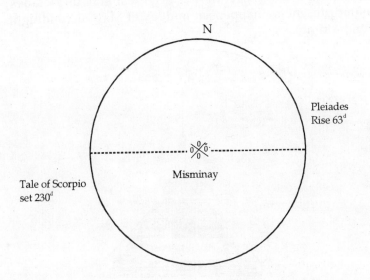

The Milkyway (our galaxy) can be seen as the Great Serpent which unites these points. From this we can easily derive that Ketu (the serpent's tail) would find its home in Pleiades (Krittika) and Rahu (the serpent's head) would finds its home in Scorpio (Anuradha). The fact that the galactic center is very near the constellation of Scorpio and there is a visible dark rift in this region of the sky makes it the perfect abode for serpent's head both literally and symbolically.

As far as the exact degrees are concerned I would place Ketu's abode as 5-10 degrees of Taurus and Rahu's abode to be 5-10 degrees of Scorpio. These degrees are calculated using the exact position of the seven stars of Pleiades within the constellation Taurus as a marker. This conclusion should be taken as an update on the discussions regarding Rahu & Ketu's sign rulership in my Book on these Serpent Planets.

It is interesting to note that the Mayan pyramid at ChichenItza was made especially to mark the Sun's exact zenith conjunction with the serpent's tale (Alcyone the brightest star in Pleiades) which in our present era happens at midday of May 20 (midnight; May 21 India time).

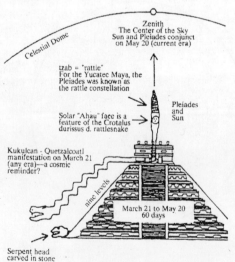

Zenith
The Center of the Sky
Sun and Pleiades conjunct
on May 20 (current era)

Celestial Dome

tzab = "rattle"
For the Yucatec Maya, the
Pleiades was known as
the rattle constellation

Solar "Ahau" face is a
feature of the Crotalus
durissus d. rattlesnake

Pleiades
and
Sun

Kukulcan - Quetzalcoatl
manifestation on March 21
(any era)—a cosmic
reminder?

nine levels

March 21 to May 20
60 days

Serpent head
carved in stone

The GIST

In the 'churning of the celestial ocean' tale, mentioned earlier in the book, it was the asuras who are holdin the mouth of the serpent Vasuki, while their coputerparts Suras (also known as Devas) are holding the tail. This makes Rahu more connected with the Asuras (A-Su-Ra = Not so Good Phire) while Ketu would be more connected with the Devas (Su-Ra = Good Phire). In fact in puranic tales, Rahu, the mouth of the serpent, is seen as the advisor of the asuras. So what excatly makes Rahu an Asura ? It is its quest for happiness, bliss & immortality without bowing down to Narayana, the supersoul & originator of the multiverse. If one notices today's world clearly one would find that many beings are trying to discover happiness in various ways without surrendering to the divine in its various forms/aspects. All of these ways are eventually leading to frustration because eternal happiness/bliss cannot be found without surrendering to the embodiement of perfection itself. This is Rahu's predicament. Rahu doesn't want to relinquish its self to the divine superself while at the same time atttain the serene, blissful,eternal state of Narayana.

Funny how the term sur-render has Sura as its begining root. Sura's (devas) gain happinees as they are ready to align with the divine plan. This brings continous joy & a painless existence. In todays world this can be seen as aligning with nature & allowing one's self to be controlled by the wishes of the divine.

Keeping the above in mind one would find there are only 2 types of beings on the planet, now known as earth, regardless of race, creed & gender. And the reader would now know which these 2types are !

Aeioum Namoh Narayane !